GW00570328

Statistics in Britain
1865—1930

to my Mother and Father

Statistics in Britain

1865 – 1930

The Social Construction of Scientific Knowledge

. . . .
. . . . .
. .
.

Donald A. MacKenzie

for the Edinburgh University Press

1981

.

© Donald A. MacKenzie 1981
Edinburgh University Press
22 George Square, Edinburgh

ISBN 0 85224 369 3

Printed in Great Britain by
Redwood Burn Limited
Trowbridge & Esher

Contents

. . . . .
  . . .
    .

Acknowledgements

. . . . .
. . .
.

Many individuals and organisations provided invaluable assistance
in the writing of this book and in the research on which it was based.
The Carnegie Trust for the Universities of Scotland and the Social
Science Research Council provided financial support. The Librari-
ans of University College London, St John's College Cambridge,
and the American Philosophical Society allowed me to consult un-
published papers in their care, as did the Secretaries of the Eugenics
Society and Royal Statistical Society, and several individuals: Dr
Alan Cock, Professor C. D. Darlington, Messrs David and Richard
Garnett, Mr George B. Greenwood, Dr Roy MacLeod and the late
Professor Egon Pearson.

Some of the chapters of this book draw on material already published in the following articles: 'Eugenics in Britain' and 'Statistical
Theory and Social Interests: a Case-Study', both in *Social Studies of
Science* (SAGE Publications Ltd, London and Beverly Hills) *6*
(1976) 499–532 and *8* (1978) 35–83; 'Arthur Black: a Forgotten
Pioneer of Mathematical Statistics', *Biometrika 64* (1977) 613–6;
'Karl Pearson and the Professional Middle Class', *Annals of Science
36*, (1979) 125–43; 'Sociobiologies in Competition: the Biometrician-Mendelian Debate', in Charles Webster (ed.) *Biology, Medicine and Society 1840–1940* (Cambridge: University Press, 1981). I
am grateful to the holders of the copyright in these articles for
permission to make use of the material here.

Preparation of this book has left me with intellectual debts. These
are too many to acknowledge in full, but I should like to offer
particular thanks to Garland Allen, David Bloor, Geoff Cohen,
Ruth Schwartz Cowan, David Edge, Lyndsay Farrall, Jon Harwood, Jon Hodge, Dan Kevles, Bernard Norton, Egon Pearson,
Helen Rugen, Steve Shapin, Oscar Sheynin, Gary Werskey and,

vii

above all, Barry Barnes. I know they do not all agree with what I have said, but discussion with them has helped sharpen my ideas even where we differ, and whatever is good in what follows owes much to them.

It is too often forgotten that it is not only authors whose work goes into the making of books, and I should like to thank everyone involved in the production of this one, and all those friends who have given me support, comfort and encouragement over the eight years in which this book has been in the making.

1

Introduction

. . . . .
. . .
.

Traditional images of science are under attack. The notion of a continuous process of discovery steadily accumulating neutral, objective knowledge has been seriously questioned, and the idea of an unambiguous divide between 'science' and 'ideology' no longer seems as secure as it did ten years ago. That there is an 'internal logic' of scientific development unaffected by its social context appears increasingly doubtful. Questions that were closed in reaction to the Nazis' 'Aryan physics' and to the Stalinists' 'proletarian biology' have been reopened.

This questioning of the taken-for-granted is a healthy development. Yet we are unlikely to get very far with our questions if we ask only in the abstract. We must look at particular sciences and examine their relations to their social context to find concrete answers to these puzzles. This book is an attempt to do this for one science, statistical theory as it developed in Britain in the last third of the nineteenth and first quarter of the twentieth century, though I shall also make excursions into the closely related histories of genetics and evolutionary biology.

There are advantages and disadvantages in the focus on statistics. One advantage is that the 'science and society' debate has so far dealt largely with sciences such as psychology and biology. To take as the example a mathematical discipline – indeed that discipline most frequently employed to 'harden' the 'soft' sciences – is perhaps to move the debate a step further. A major disadvantage, however, is that the mathematical nature of statistical theory renders it relatively inaccessible to many people. I have been acutely aware of this in writing this book, and have tried to keep firmly in mind the needs of those with little or no statistical training. This book would be a failure were it to be readable only by 'experts'. One of its aims, after all, is to provide an insight for the non-expert into one of the most potent sources of expertise: the sophisticated mathematical treatment of numerical data.

With this in view, I have banished most of the mathematics into the appendixes and provided a glossary (appendix 8) of the technical terms used most often in the text. What remains can all be read, I hope, by those who know arithmetic and some school algebra. In addition, I have tried to arrange the material so that the parts containing technical material (chiefly chapters 3, 6, 7 and 8, although 6 deals with biology rather than statistics) are separate from the non- technical sections. It would thus be possible to grasp much of the argument by reading the remaining sections first, and postponing the more technical sections for later reading.

To facilitate this, a survey of the historical developments to be discussed and of the argument of this book will be provided at the end of this chapter. But first of all it is perhaps worth while to discuss some of the general issues raised by this study.

Science and its Social Context

No one doubts that there must be *some* relationship between science and the social context in which it develops. Disagreement centres on the nature of this relationship and, broadly speaking, two distinct views can be identified. The first is the older and more influential, whereby society can indeed affect science, but in a strictly limited way. The extent of social support for science influences the pace of scientific advance, and the direction in which this support is channelled may lead to one scientific discipline growing more quickly than another. The social context can affect the *content* of scientific advance, as well as its pace, but only in a negative way. As the examples of Nazi Germany and Stalinist Russia show, over-strong social influences can cause bad science. They can divert scientific advance from its proper path. As Joseph Ben-David puts it, 'ideological bias' can lead science into 'blind alleys', but good science is determined in its content by 'the conceptual state of science and by individual creativity – and these follow their own laws, accepting neither command nor bribe' (Ben-David 1971, 11–12).[1]

Thus, in discussing the emergence of modern statistics, Ben-David points to various social and institutional factors affecting the development of the discipline in Britain and the United States. He attributes the rapid growth of statistics in the United States to the responsiveness of American universities to practical needs. Britain's universities were not responsive in this way, but there was a 'functional equivalent' in the 'semiformal and informal networks and circles comprising the academic elite and outstanding researchers and intellectuals outside the academic field' (*ibid.*, 151). The fact that Britain had, by comparison with the United States, 'a far more developed scientific tradition at the time and a less abstract school of mathematics' (150) is taken by Ben-David to explain the fact that theoretical advance was much faster in Britain than across the Atlantic. The 'eugenics movement' (discussed below) is seen as giving rise to 'interest in biostatistics' (151). So in Ben-David's work the structure of social institutions, in particular of universities, and the existence of social movements, such as the eugenics movement, are taken as explaining the rate of advance of statistics. These factors could hinder or promote work in the field and perhaps condition the quality of work done. They are, however, not taken by Ben-David as explaining the content of the theoretical advances.

The second viewpoint sees social factors as playing a much greater role than the first viewpoint admits. The content of 'good' science as well as 'bad' can potentially be affected by its social context. The growth of scientific knowledge cannot be understood entirely in terms of 'its own laws'. Science should not be bound off *a priori* as an intellectual activity to be studied in isolation. Both the social organisation of science itself and that of society at large can affect scientific thought and activity.

One (weak) version of this point of view would be that the production of new ideas in science is socially influenced, but that these ideas are then judged according to general, objective criteria. So social influence on the content of science would be short-lived. Society might be the source of innovation, but in the long run scientific judgement would be 'objective', only worthwhile ideas surviving. It is possible, however, to put forward a stronger version in which not only the production of new ideas but also the process by which these are accepted or rejected can be affected by social factors. Scientific judgement would then be essentially social – and this would be true of *all* judgements, not only 'wrong' or 'biased' ones.

T. S. Kuhn's classic *The Structure of Scientific Revolutions* (1970, first published in 1962) can be read as a statement of this second view in its strong version. In Kuhn's work the society that influences scientific judgement is typically taken to be the community of practising scientists in a particular specialty. This community defines acceptable and non-acceptable ways of doing science. Certainly, it is impossible to imagine a valid sociology of scientific knowledge that did not fully take into account this community, its structure and values. But there seem to be no overwhelming grounds why *only* social factors internal to the community of scientists must necessarily be at work. If the basic point of the social nature of scientific judgement is taken, then it seems reasonable to search society at large, as well as the scientific community, for determinants of it. Among those who have done so are Bob Young (1969), for evolutionary biology in the nineteenth century, and Paul Forman (1971), for physics in Weimar Germany. Both claim to have found thoroughgoing links between scientific thought and society and culture, although their conclusions, especially those of Forman, have not been universally accepted. Attempts have been made by Barnes (1974), Bloor (1976) and, from a different perspective, the editorial collective of the *Radical Science Journal*,[2] to explore this general position and its implications.

One issue, then, that is explored below is the relationship between science and the structures of the scientific community and society at large. But there is another problem to be faced, which I have so far evaded by vague talk of social 'factors': how is it possible to relate society and its structure to the beliefs of particular people?

Beliefs and Society

Here again, two approaches can usefully be contrasted.[3] The first can be labelled the 'individualist-empiricist' approach. Its primary aim is to discover, by empirical methods, regularities in the relationship between the beliefs of individuals and their social positions. Typically, this approach relies on surveying large numbers of people and determining their 'attitudes' by means of questionnaires or interviews. Their responses are then related to such factors as their social class, gender, religion and ethnic group.

Undoubtedly, such an approach can yield interesting information. But there are major problems in relating responses to questionnaires – or, in general, people's professed beliefs – to what people 'really' believe. And even if a perfect instrument for discovering 'real' belief were available, all that would be produced would be a *description* of associations between social position and belief. *Explaining* those associations would remain a further task, and it is not clear that this can be done within the confines of this approach.

4

Further, it is for purely practical reasons extremely difficult to apply this kind of approach to the past, especially where the beliefs in question are of a relatively esoteric nature. For example, we know very little about the distribution among social groups of beliefs about evolution in Britain around 1900 (a subject discussed below in chapter 6). Certainly, it would be impossible to make decisive statements about this without much painstaking work in social history.

In any case, there are good reasons to doubt the theoretical usefulness of this approach. In practice the relationship between belief and social position is often found to be an extremely 'messy' one. Frequently groups or large sections of them seem to hold beliefs that are quite inappropriate to their situations. Members of one group identify themselves with another group, even if the interests of the two groups appear opposed. As socialists and feminists can testify, members of subordinate groups are, in many cases, loyal to systems of belief that justify their subordination. Beliefs seemingly appropriate for one group are often developed by members of other groups: Marx and Engels were not manual workers. So the quest for patterns of association between social position and belief does not seem likely to produce information with immediate and clear-cut implications, and few guidelines have been provided by exponents of this approach to help us assess the complex patterns we are likely to uncover.

The second approach has its origins in the work of Georg Lukács (1971, first published in 1923), and has more recently been employed by, for example, Lucien Goldmann (1964). It faces up directly to the problems referred to in the last paragraph, by seeking theoretically plausible relationships between belief and social position while accepting that these relationships may in actuality be hidden or only partially manifest. First of all, we have to identify social positions whose occupants may reasonably be held to have similar interests and experiences. We then argue that these interests and experiences constrain the set of beliefs 'appropriate' to occupants of these positions. 'Appropriate' beliefs will be ones justifying a group's privileges, advocating an advance in its situation, furthering its coherence or the interests of its members and reflecting the salient features of the typical experiences of its members. It is not that the nature of an appropriate 'group consciousness' can be deduced *a priori* from the position of the group within the social structure, for the pre-existing states of belief and the ideologies of other groups obviously affect the beliefs appropriate to the group.[4] Nor is there any reason why only one set of beliefs should be appropriate to a group; indeed, conflicting beliefs may arise, reflecting, for example, different aspects of its experience, or tensions between the short-term and long-term interests of its members. These provisos aside, it should be possible to identify 'tendencies' of thought that express the influence of the social situation of the group. These need not be manifest in the thought of all of the group's members, nor even in that of a majority of them. Nor need they be restricted in their manifestation to the members of the group: outsiders who identify with the group may well manifest them, often, indeed, in heightened form.

An analogy from the sociology of politics may clarify the status of this kind of explanation. To say that political party P expresses the interests of group G is not to imply that all members, or even most members, of G vote for P. It is rather to assert that P's policies, if put into effect, would enhance the wealth, status, power, security and so on of G. One might then anticipate that members of G would be more likely to support party P than would members of other groups. However, this sort of empirical fact would be at most only evidence for the hypothesis, which is itself structural rather than statistical.

It is this second approach to the sociology of knowledge that I shall employ here. I believe it to be both more practicable in this kind of study and theoretically more fruitful. Nevertheless, its use implies two reservations about the material that follows. The sociology of knowledge arguments that will be found below are not susceptible to easy empirical proof. They must remain tentative hypotheses. At most I can hope only to have shown that they are hypotheses that are fruitful for the understanding of the episodes I am discussing. Secondly, because the arguments relating belief and social position do not imply any automatic correspondence of the two, I am in no sense claiming that the thought and behaviour of the individual statisticians discussed below was socially *determined*. Psychological make-up, accident and other similar factors were undoubtedly operative in each individual case. I am not denying to these statisticians their 'free will'; but I am arguing that this free will worked in a given social context and on occasion worked in a way that manifested systematic relationships between systems of belief and social structures.

Survey

What is statistical theory? There would be little point in trying to provide a rigorous definition, but it might be useful to indicate roughly how I am using the term. My aim is to distinguish the subject-matter of this study from, on the one hand, the activity of gathering quantitative information typically engaged in by official bodies and social scientists and, on the other, the mathematical theory of probability. Statistical theory I take to mean the construction of a theoretical framework for the analysis of numerical data. Statistical theory provides tools that can be used to analyse, for example, the information gathered by government statistical agencies. Normally, it employs concepts drawn from the mathematical theory of probability in constructing these tools. Nevertheless, it is itself not simply gathering data nor simply the abstract study of mathematical probabilities.

The theory of correlation – which we shall return to many times below – provides an instance of what I mean. Broadly speaking, this is a study of the association of two (or more) series of numbers: for example, the heights and weights of a set of people. In studying correlation, statistical theorists mathematically examined typical patterns formed by series of numbers such as this. From these mathematical studies, they deduced methods of expressing the degree of correlation, of relatedness, of these series. Not all tall people are heavy, and short people light, but we know that height and weight are to some degree related; a coefficient of correlation measures the degree of this relatedness. Clearly, developing the theory of correlation in this sense is not the same as simply measuring people's heights and weights, nor is it purely a mathematical study of patterns of numbers.

The gathering of quantitative information by state agencies and private bodies and individuals was well established in Britain by the beginning of the period discussed here. The early Victorian period had seen a 'statistical movement', which, although relatively short-lived, gave birth to a tradition of empirical social research and contributed much to the development of official statistical agencies.[5] This movement was, however, by no means committed to sophisticated mathematical methods. The term 'statistics' had, originally, no such connotation. The 1797 edition of the *Encyclopaedia Britannica* defined the term as a 'word lately introduced to express a view or survey of any kingdom, county, or parish' (Cullen 1975,

10–11). It was only very gradually that 'statistics' came to refer exclusively to quantitative studies. 'The contents of the *Journal of the Royal Statistical Society* would suggest that it was not until the present century that "statistics" came to mean solely numbers and the methods of analysing numbers' (*ibid.*, 11). The early Victorian statistical movement should thus be seen not as the forerunner of the modern discipline of statistics, but, Cullen argues, as a group of social reformers producing and utilising 'facts' to advance their programmes:

> The statisticians wanted to contribute more than voluntary and legislative action in the fields of public health and education: they were also free traders, supporters of the new poor law (if not framers and administrators of it), opposed to trade unions and working class radicals, suspicious of factory acts.
>
> (*ibid.*, 147)[6]

So the 'statistical movement' left behind it no tradition of statistical theory, in the sense described above: the gathering of quantitative information remained largely divorced from developments in the mathematical theory of probability. The latter was an old and respectable area of study. While many of its examples may have seemed trivial – most were drawn from dice-tossing and other games of chance – it had given birth to a formidable body of mathematical theory, as Laplace's great *Théorie Analytique des Probabilités* (1814, first published in 1812) showed. Yet it was on the whole a body of work with but little practical application,[7] and one which appeared largely stagnant in nineteenth- century Britain. Perhaps British mathematicians, as Boyer (1968, 621) suggests, preferred to avoid fields that had been thoroughly developed by the Continental giants like Laplace. Certainly, although all British mathematicians would have been acquainted with at least elementary probability theory,[8] few chose to devote much time to the development of the theory. A sporadic controversy took place over the philosophical foundations of the subject (see chapter 8), but the Cambridge mathematician Isaac Todhunter was well able to end his classic compendium of the mathematics of probability theory (1865) with the work of Laplace.

So in mid nineteenth-century Britain there was no tradition of statistical theory.[9] There was a London (from 1887, Royal) Statistical Society, but it remained firmly in the mould of the 'statistical movement' from which it had emerged:

> Although there were a few mathematicians among the original

members, there were many more economists, politicians, peers, government officials, and doctors of medicine: their object was politically useful information about society, not, say, the development of mathematical method.

(Abrams 1968, 14)

In the fifty years from its foundation in 1834, only two per cent of the papers read to it dealt with statistical method (*ibid.*, 16). It remained largely irrelevant to the development of statistical theory in Britain until well into the twentieth century. In the period 1909 to 1934, the percentage of papers on statistical method had risen only to seven per cent (Royal Statistical Society 1934, 205).

In 1865, then, statistical theory as a scientific specialty was effectively non-existent in Britain. The small amount of work on the subject to be found on the Continent – chiefly that of the Belgian astronomer and statistician Quetelet – had had but little direct impact in Britain.[10] Statistical theory was not taught as a university subject, nor for that matter outside the universities. There was no journal devoted to it. Yet by 1930 all this had changed. There was an active group of researchers working on statistical theory. At University College, London, there was a department largely devoted to teaching and research in the field, while at the Rothamsted agricultural research station a second centre had developed. There was a journal, *Biometrika*, a large proportion of whose articles were contributions to statistical theory. Many crucial theoretical advances had been made, and statistical theory could claim to be a rapidly maturing scientific specialty.

Central to this dramatic change were three individuals: Francis Galton (1822–1911), Karl Pearson (1857–1936) and R. A. Fisher (1890–1962). To centre on these three is not to deny the talent and valuable work of other statisticians of the period such as Francis Ysidro Edgeworth and George Udny Yule. Rather it is to concentrate on the men at the focus of three different periods of development, on the institutional and intellectual leaders of the emerging community of statistical theorists.

Sir Francis Galton is probably the best-known of the three. Cousin of Charles Darwin, Victorian gentleman scientist, explorer, pioneer of the use of fingerprints as a method of personal identification, in his work in statistical theory he was, for all his fame, intellectually isolated until quite late. From the late 1860s to the 1880s he worked on statistical problems with occasional help from mathematicians but with no real collaborator. Yet in this period he achieved a theoretical breakthrough of enormous significance: with his concepts of regression and correlation he extended the range of statistical theory from its effective restriction to problems involving only one variable to problems involving more than one.

By the 1890s Galton's work on statistical theory was beginning to find followers. The most important of these was Karl Pearson. Unlike Galton, he was a professional mathematician, and he developed and systematised Galton's insights while making many important contributions of his own. The standard formula for the correlation coefficient and the widely-used 'chi-square' test of the goodness of fit between observations and theoretical predictions are both named after him. From the mid-1890s to the First World War he dominated statistical theory in Britain. He became the first head of the first university department in which statistical theory was a major concern. He was primarily responsible for establishing and editing *Biometrika*, which from 1901 onwards became the major vehicle for the publication of the work in statistical theory done by him, his pupils and collaborators. He built up a coherent group of researchers – the 'biometricians' or 'biometric school', as they were known – and taught the first advanced courses in statistical theory in Britain.

With Sir Ronald Aylmer Fisher we approach the present day. Fisher's statistical theories and methods still form the basis of much contemporary teaching and research. At the Rothamsted research station he pioneered a new role for the statistician – that of active involvement in agricultural and biological experiments. He was also responsible for a reshaping of the basis of statistical theory that remains controversial, and for some major contributions to biology. Much of his work belongs to a period later than that covered here, but I have chosen 1930 as the closing date in my title because that was the year of the publication of the last work to be considered in any detail in these pages, Fisher's *The Genetical Theory of Natural Selection.*

My intention is *not* to provide a simple description of the developments in statistical theory of the years from 1865 to 1930.[11] Many important innovations will receive little or no attention in these pages, perhaps most obviously the work of Jerzy Neyman and Egon Pearson that was just coming to fruition by 1930. Rather, I want to *use* the history of statistical theory in this period to throw light on the general issues discussed in previous sections. My aim, in short, is to examine the relationship between statistical theory and British society in this period.

One specific set of social purposes was common to the work of Galton, Karl Pearson and R. A. Fisher. All were eugenists. They claimed that the most important human characteristics, such as mental ability, were inherited from one generation to the next. People's ancestry, rather than their environment, was crucial to determining their characteristics. The only secure long-term way to improve society, they argued, was to improve the characteristics of the individuals in it, and the best way to do this was to ensure that those in the present generation with good characteristics (the 'fit') had more children than those with bad characteristics (the 'unfit').

The eugenic objectives of Galton, Pearson and Fisher were closely connected to their science. In his biography of Galton, Karl Pearson concluded:

> There was a unity underlying all Galton's varied work . . . which only reveals itself when, after much inquiry and retrospection, we view it as a whole and with a spirit trained to his modes of thought . . . From 1864 to 1911 Galton achieved in many fields, yet in 1864 he had realised his life-aim – to study racial mass-changes in man with a view to controlling the evolution of man, as man controls that of many living forms.
> (Pearson 1914–30, *3A*, 434–5)

For Karl Pearson, the aim of 'the master in whose footsteps I had trod' (*ibid.*, 433) became his aim. As head of the Department of Applied Statistics at University College he bore the title Professor of Eugenics. In the case of Fisher, too, eugenics was vitally important. His first known scientific paper was read to the Cambridge University Eugenics Society, and in *The Genetical Theory of Natural Selection* (1930) biological science and its eugenic applications were explicitly related.

As eugenists, Galton, Pearson and Fisher were contributing to a body of ideas that has become notorious and controversial. The debates of the last decade about race, class and IQ have in many ways merely recapitulated themes to be found in the period discussed here. Galton was the first person to argue systematically, clearly and repeatedly that intelligence was an almost entirely inherited individual characteristic. He and Pearson developed many of the methods – twin studies, the examination of correlations between relatives, and so on – that are at the centre of modern controversies. Fisher developed the first measure of the 'heritability' of a human characteristic.

The next chapter of this book turns, therefore, to the eugenics movement, to its history, its social composition and the nature of its propaganda. I suggest a theory of the relationship between eugenic beliefs and the social structure, and argue that this makes sense of much of what is known about the history of eugenics. Eugenics was – and is – an ideology expressing particular social interests.

In part, subsequent chapters examine the plausibility of this general argument about eugenic beliefs and the social structure in the light of evidence about the particular cases of Galton, Pearson and Fisher. But they also discuss these men's science, in particular their statistical theory, but also their biology. I argue that eugenics did not merely motivate their statistical work but affected its content. The shape of the science they developed was partially determined by eugenic objectives.

Chapter 3 takes up this argument for Francis Galton. It begins by placing Galton in his very specific social context: the group of influential nineteenth-century families that made up what has been called the 'intellectual aristocracy'. His development of the concepts of regression and correlation is then examined and, following the pioneering work of Ruth Schwartz Cowan (1972a) and Victor Hilts (1973), its connection to Galton's eugenics is discussed. Galton's work on regression and correlation has been claimed by some to have been largely anticipated by previous mathematicians. working with very similar mathematical formalism but with quite different goals. This claim is assessed at the end of chapter 3 in order to ascertain the precise effect of eugenic objectives on the content of Galton's statistical theory.

In chapter 4 I turn to Karl Pearson. In some ways he is the most fascinating of the figures discussed here. His writings range far beyond the confines of mathematics and statistical theory. He was a political thinker of some note, well-known as a socialist but also singled out by Hobson (1905) as a leading scientific apologist for imperialism. His *The Grammar of Science* (1892a) became a famous work of the philosophy of science, attacked by, among others, Lenin (1970). He was an early feminist and close friend of Olive Schreiner, the South African writer whose work is now being rediscovered by the women's movement. This chapter tries to show that his thinking in various crucial areas was an exceptionally clear manifestation of the social interests of the class to which he belonged.

Karl Pearson's 'biometric school' is the topic of chapter 5. It shows how Pearson built up the first research institute devoted to statistical theory and its applications. I discuss the crucial connections between it and eugenics, but also show that in the process of 'institutionalising' his science Pearson had to involve individuals and organisations whose goals were very different from his and Galton's. The connection between statistics and eugenics was not indissoluble, and after his retirement, much to his dismay, his department was in fact split up, with the formation of separate departments of statistics and eugenics.

In its heyday, roughly from 1900 to 1914, the work of the biometric school nevertheless can be seen as closely reflecting eugenic objectives. This connection is perhaps most clearly revealed by the two major controversies in which the biometric school engaged in this period. The first is the bitter and much-discussed 'biometrician-Mendelian' controversy, which set Pearson and his collaborators against William Bateson and the early Mendelian geneticists. Pearson refused to accept that Mendel's principles should form the basis for the study of heredity. In chapter 6 I argue that more was at stake than simply technical issues of biology. Differing ways of doing biology, and differing social interests, can be seen as involved in the clash.

The second controversy is much less well known. It concerned how best to measure statistical association, and set Pearson and his followers against Pearson's former pupil George Udny Yule. On the face of it, this was a purely technical disagreement on an esoteric issue. However, in chapter 7 it will be argued that the differing approaches to association adopted by the two sides reflected different goals in the development of statistical theory, and that these different goals can be related to different attitudes to eugenics. The biometric school's commitment to eugenic research, and Yule's distaste for eugenics, were important factors in the divergence of the two theories of association.

In chapter 8 I turn to the third central figure of the period, R. A. Fisher. I describe his early involvement in eugenics, its relation to social interests and its role in his decision to begin work on statistical theory and statistical biology. His claimed 'resolution' of the biometrician-Mendelian controversy is examined and, finally, the beginnings of his revolutionary work in statistical theory are discussed.

The conclusion draws together some of the threads of the previous chapters and returns to the issues raised in the first part of this introduction. What does this case-study imply for our traditional image of mathematical science as 'discovery'? Should it rather be seen as 'invention', fully affected by the goals of the communities of scientists involved in it? What are these goals, and can they be related to social interests? What does this study imply for our understanding of the present state of statistical theory?

2

Eugenics in Britain

. . . . .
. . .
.

What is Eugenics?

In drafting his will endowing a Professorship of Eugenics in the University of London, Francis Galton defined 'eugenics' as 'the study . . . of agencies under social control that may improve the racial qualities of future generations either physically or mentally' (Pearson 1914–30, *3A*, 225).[1] Yet eugenics was by no means simply an academic study. The thrust of Galton's definition – 'agencies *under social control*' – pointed to the fact that eugenic theory was intended as the basis for eugenic practice. Around the central figure of Galton, but going far beyond his immediate circle and surviving him, a social and political movement developed. The core of this movement in Britain was the Eugenics Education Society, founded in 1907 and surviving to this day as the Eugenics Society.

The eugenics movement can be seen as engaged in two basic activities: (a) constructing and drawing upon an account of British society according to which the characteristics of that society were fundamentally the result of the measurable hereditary make-up of the individuals composing it; and (b) devising, and acting as a pressure group for, particular policies designed to improve the hereditary make-up of future generations. While there was an obvious overlap between these two activities, it was far from total. Many people were convinced by the characteristic eugenic model of society, but had moral scruples about, or practical objections to, explicit eugenic policies. Conversely, there were those who saw sense in particular measures proposed by the eugenists, but had quite different images of society.

To give some indication of the flavour of these two types of activity I will give one brief example of each. The first is a lecture by

Francis Galton delivered to the Anthropological Institute in 1901 (Galton 1909, 1–34). Here can be found the most explicit statement by the founder of eugenics of the eugenic theory of society. The second example is drawn from the end of the time period discussed here. It is the particular eugenic policies suggested by Major Leonard Darwin (1926), who as President of the Eugenic Education Society from 1911 to 1929 was the public figurehead of the eugenics movement in the years following Galton's death. Obviously two examples cannot capture the full range of positions within the movement, but they do represent what was arguably the dominant strand in eugenic thinking in Britain.

'The natural character and faculties of human beings differ at least as widely as those of the domesticated animals', said Galton. 'Whether it be in character, disposition, energy, intellect, or physical power, we each receive at our birth a definite endowment'. These various 'natural qualities' or 'talents' 'go towards the making of civic worth in man'. Much of Galton's earlier work (e.g. Galton 1869) had been devoted to the argument that they were *inherited* qualities. 'Experience shows', said Galton, that they follow the 'Normal Law of Frequency', so that if, as in figure 1, we plot along the horizontal axis varying degrees of genetic worth, and along the vertical axis their relative frequency, we obtain the well-known bell-shaped normal curve. Most individuals have middling amounts of inherited talents (groups r and R); large quantities of these talents (groups T, U and V) are found in smaller proportions of people; very small quantities (groups t, u and v) are also relatively rare.

So the first premise of the eugenic theory of society is that individuals each possess a relatively fixed quantity of the socially important characteristics that go to make up 'civic worth'. Galton was vague as to the exact meaning of this latter term. He himself had earlier made equivalent use of the concept of 'natural ability', and later eugenists showed an increasing tendency to build their model of society almost exclusively around the intelligence quotient (IQ). Galton's assumptions that 'civic worth' was a quantitative characteristic that was relatively fixed, and that it was normally distributed, were, indeed, assumptions. He never claimed to have measured 'civic worth'; his was an *a priori* model deriving a great deal of its plausibility simply from the analogy with human *physical* characteristics, such as height, which are measurable, relatively fixed in adults, and do approximately follow a normal distribution.

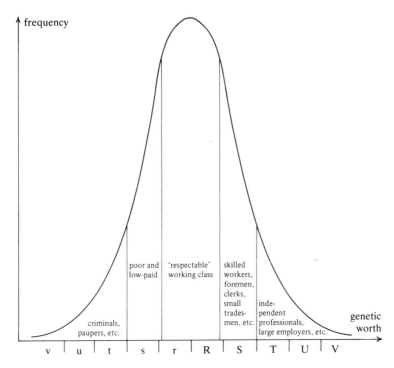

Figure 1. Galton's view of British social structure

The second step in the construction of his eugenic model of society was equally *a priori*. He turned to Charles Booth's social survey of London, and proceeded to map Booth's *social* categories onto his own *natural* ones. Booth's lowest social strata corresponded, Galton assumed, to the groups with the smallest quantities of 'civic worth'. At the very bottom, group v and some of group u, are 'criminals, semi-criminals, loafers and some others'. They are followed by the rest of group u and group t: 'very poor persons who subsist on casual earnings, many of whom are inevitably poor from shiftlessness, idleness or drink'. 'Classes t, u, v and below are undesirables', concluded Galton (1909, 11).

Next come those 'supported by intermittent earnings' – 'they are a hard-working people, but have a very bad character for improvidence and shiftlessness' – and those in regular but very low-paid employment: these 'correspond to the whole of s combined with the lower fifth of r'. Above them, forming the numerically enormous central bulk of the distribution, are the 'mediocre class' of ordinary, respectable workers with regular and moderately large wages. Then follow classes of increasing worth that together form the top fifth of R and the whole of S: first 'better paid artisans and foremen', then 'the lower middle class of shopkeepers, clerks and subordinate professional men, who as a rule are hard-working, energetic and sober' (*ibid.*, 10–11).

Finally, come those of highest 'civic worth'. In a sentence that effectively sums up the eugenic theory of society, Galton (*ibid.*, 11) claimed that 'the brains of our nation lie in the higher of our classes'. They are the large and successful entrepreneurs and the leaders of the professions:

> They found great industries, establish vast undertakings, in-crease the wealth of multitudes and amass large fortunes for themselves. Others, whether they be rich or poor, are the guides and light of the nation, raising its tone, enlightening its difficulties and imposing its ideals. (*ibid.*, 12)

So the eugenic theory of society, as elaborated by Galton, is a way of reading the structure of social classes onto nature. People differ according to their innate qualities and capacities; those at the top of the social hierarchy have, according to this model, the greatest quantity of good qualities and capacities – the largest amount of 'brains'. The lower the social class, the smaller the innate 'civic worth' of the individuals comprising it. This model underwent various modifications. Sometimes it was said that the social hierarchy did not exactly match the natural hierarchy and that it should be altered to do so: the precise social composition of the natural élite was questioned. The model was also elaborated. As Norton (1978d) has shown, attempts were made by psychologists sympathetic to the eugenics movement to give the model an empirical basis by testing the 'intelligence' of individuals in different classes. The essence of the eugenic theory of society remained, however, unchanged. And on the basis of this theory, particular social policies were put forward.

The aim of eugenic policy proposals was, in the words of Leonard Darwin (1926, 138),

> to promote the fertility of the better types which the nation contains, whilst diminishing the birth rate amongst those which are inferior . . .

Following the eugenic model of society, the 'better types' and the 'inferior' could be translated into social class categories. The 'better types' were the higher social classes: 'positive eugenics' was thus largely a matter of boosting their fertility. The 'inferior' were to be found predominantly at the bottom of the class hierarchy: 'negative eugenics' to a great extent meant stopping the lowest social groups from having children. In these twin eugenic policies lay the path to the 'improvement of the race'. Environmental improvements such as better schooling, housing and nutrition were ultimately less important than the improvement of the 'human raw material' on which these worked. The former did not in any case effect a significant permanent improvement in the latter: any good effects that environmental reforms had on individuals were simply 'acquired characteristics' that were not inherited to any important degree.[2]

Eugenists were, however, aware that putting these ideas into practice might prove difficult. Leonard Darwin was perhaps the one person amongst them who gave most thought to these problems, and it is worth examining his schemes in some detail. He drew an important distinction between what he called 'individual' and 'mass' selection. 'Individual' selection was a strategy of negative eugenics: he doubted its practicality for positive eugenics. Certain individuals were defined as 'feebleminded', 'habitual criminals', 'insane', etc.[3] Darwin knew that these were *social* definitions:

> there is every grade of insanity, and yet it is necessary for legal authorities to declare one man to be insane whilst holding another man, nearly as abnormal, not to be so (*ibid.*, 169).

Nevertheless the eugenist could make use of them to 'eliminate' various 'inferior types'. Darwin rejected the 'lethal chamber' (gas chamber, as it became known) as a means for doing so. A more 'humane' method was 'segregation': 'detention combined with as little suffering as may be, the sexes being kept apart' to prevent propagation (*ibid.*, 217). About surgical sterilisation and contraception Darwin, like most British eugenists of the early period, had scruples, the most serious being that these methods might lead to an increase in 'promiscuous sexual intercourse' (*ibid.*, 177). Nevertheless, he was prepared to endorse both with reservations. Sterilisation, however, would have to be purely voluntary 'until popular prejudices have been overcome' (*ibid.*, 184).

To take one example of individual selection: in chapter 13 of his book Darwin indicated how he would deal with the habitual petty criminal. The 'mentally defective' among accused persons would be sent – without trial – 'to proper institutions for their care, and consequently the prevention of procreation on their part' (*ibid.*,

207). As to the others, after their fourth or fifth conviction they would come up before a 'properly qualified court', which would consider such factors as their 'family history' and 'mental and bodily defects'. If this court judged that the descendants of such individuals were a 'racial danger' they should be 'permanently segregated under the most humane conditions possible' (*ibid.*, 225).

Mass selection, where individuals with particular socially-identified 'defects' could not readily be isolated, posed greater problems than individual selection. One method of mass selection would be to use IQ and scholastic achievement tests as the basis for the regulation of fertility. But it would be a long time, thought Darwin, before people would accept that the number of children they had should depend on their IQ: this would be seen by the 'ignorant' as a 'proposal of cranks and theorists' (*ibid.*, 262). More practical would be to rely on the correlation between genetic worth and social position as measured by earnings. Darwin admitted that this correlation was at present still only approximate, but was confident that it would grow more exact 'as we continue to make social progress'. For both eugenic and environmental reasons 'it would be advantageous if the birth rates of the different sections of the nation were to become proportionate to the average income earned' (*ibid.*, 164). Lest the reader imagine that Darwin was contemplating a proposal that would put millionaires under great strain, it should be noted that his emphasis in this sort of discussion was on *earned* income (wages, salaries, professional fees, etc.), and returns on personal savings, not on inherited wealth:

> . . . it is earnings and not the possession of wealth which should be held in view in eugenic reform; for certainly we do not assert that individuals who have great inherited wealth are likely on that account to be characterized in an exceptional manner by the goodness of their qualities . . . (*ibid.*, 263–4)

The advantage to the eugenist of this focus on earnings was that social and economic policies and institutions that had been developed for quite other reasons could be manipulated for eugenic purposes. Thus the fact that the very poor had to rely on state benefits or private charity could be used. 'Conditions as regards parenthood' could be attached to 'grants of public assistance' (*ibid.*, 381). A list should be kept of all those who had been continuously in receipt of public assistance – including free school meals and sickness benefit – for a given period. 'All parents on the list who had had two or more children should be warned that no more should be allowed to appear, and of the consequences of a neglect of this warning' (*ibid.*, 385). These consequences would be an 'immediate cessation of all public assistance' and the placing of the family under a 'special watch' to see whether children were being brought up under 'decent conditions'; should the family prove 'to be living an uncivilized life, all its members should be segregated in some suitable institution'. 'To mitigate the severity of this procedure', Darwin continued, the family could be released if 'it seemed probable that they could re-establish themselves in decent surroundings without public assistance, or if the man consented to be sterilized' (*ibid.*, 386).

Similarly, the problem of positive eugenics effectively became that of finding means to 'stimulate the fertility of the well-to-do' (*ibid.*, 165). One method considered by Darwin was the use of family allowances; this will be briefly discussed in chapter 8 in the context of the work of its major advocate, R. A. Fisher. Another was the use of income tax allowances for children. In the period discussed here very few manual workers paid income tax; increasing income tax allowances for children was thus a measure intended to stimulate the fertility of the middle class. Allowances should not simply be extended on a flat-rate basis, argued Darwin: there should be larger allowances for the better-off. Public relations problems arose, notably that of how to avoid 'the *appearance* of favouring the rich' (*ibid.*, 439; his emphasis). Nevertheless, the Eugenics Education Society did campaign for eugenic reform of the income tax (see, for example, E.E.S. 1914, 7).

All these policies were of course legitimated by the appeal to nature. Thus, discussing his draconian plans for those dependent on public assistance, Darwin commented (*ibid.*, 338):

> All this sounds very hard, and it is hard; but its hardness is solely due to the fact that in some matters nature is absolutely inflexible.

Much of Darwin's book was an account of nature as he saw it, and presented many of the scientific methods and theories that will be discussed below. But before turning to these and their relations to eugenics, it is important to locate the eugenics movement in the social context in which it developed.

The Social Composition of the Eugenics Movement

The Eugenics Education Society was founded in late 1907. Before the first years of the twentieth century eugenics in Britain had no definite institutional form; it was simply an idea to be found in the writings of Galton and a number of other men and women. From 1907 to 1913/14 the Eugenics Education Society grew in strength and numbers: in 1914 it and its provincial branches had 1047 members and associate members (Farrall 1970, 211). Membership declined during the First World War and the 'twenties, recovered during the Depression to 768 in 1932/33 (Searle 1979, 160), but declined again thereafter.

The most straightforward answer to the question, 'who were the eugenists?', is provided by examining the membership of the Eugenics Education Society in the key years just before the First World War: nearly all leading British eugenists were members of the Society. Lyndsay Farrall (1970, 218–27) has examined the occupations of members of the Council of the Society from 1908–20, and of a random sample of 60 members and associate members of the Society from 1912–13. His results for the Council members are shown in table 1 – 'well-documented number' is his term, and refers to those for whom definite biographical information was available; it excludes, for example, those who are classed as 'medical' simply on the grounds of their use of the title 'Dr'. Table 2 shows the occupations of those people in the random sample that he was able to identify.

The most immediate problem posed by this data is the number of people whose occupation was not ascertained. It *could* be, for example, that these were all manual workers, who are of course

Table 1. Occupations of the Members of the E.E.S. Council

Occupation	Total	Well-documented number
Medical	26	10
Academic	18	16
Politicians	4	3
Clergy	3	3
Social Work	3	3
Scientists	2	2
Writers	2	2
Military Officers	2	1
Lawyers	1	1
Housewives	2	2
Not Known	48	0
Totals	111	43

Table 2. Occupations of a random sample of
Members and Associate Members

Occupation	no.	Occupation	no.
Academic	6	Wife	5
Medical	3	Lawyer	1
Social Work	2	Director of Art Museum	1
Writer	2	Local Government	1
Clergy	1	Part-time Author	2
Military Officer	1	No Information	35
		Total	60

much more difficult to identify from the standard biographical
sources than are professionals. To check Farrall's conclusion, I
decided to examine a sub-group of the individuals investigated by
him, and to see whether they could *all* be identified. I chose the 41
elected members of the Council for 1914, and in fact it proved
possible to identify all but one of them. Their occupations are listed
in table 3, and details of the individuals are given in appendix 2.

Table 3.

University teachers and researchers	11
Doctors[4]	9
Lawyers	4
Politicians[5]	2
Non-university scientists[6]	2
Writers	2
Headmasters	1
Clergymen	1
Other[7]	8
Unknown	1
Total	41

Farrall's analysis is thus confirmed by this more detailed investigation. At least as far as the 1914 Council is concerned, the group
that he had failed to identify does not conceal any substantial
involvement of non-professionals in the Eugenics Education Society. So it seems safe to conclude that the Society's activists were
drawn almost exclusively from the professional middle class (the
Council is revealed by the Society's records and Annual Reports to
have been a working, rather than decorative, body), and to suggest

more tentatively that a broadly similar conclusion holds for its wider membership.[8] Businessmen and the hereditary aristocracy (as distinct from ennobled commoners) were only rarely to be found in the eugenics movement; as far as we know, no manual worker ever joined the Eugenics Education Society. Further, it is also clear that eugenists were not recruited equally from all sections of the professional middle class. The universities, science and medicine were relatively heavily represented; law and the church much more sparsely.[9]

It is however by no means obvious what conclusion should be drawn from such evidence on the social composition of the eugenics movement. Farrall identifies eugenics as a form of the 'middle class radicalism' described by Parkin (1968). Members of 'welfare and creative' professions join reforming bodies in order to obtain the psychological satisfaction to be found in moral reform; professionals tend to be do-gooders. Thus:

> . . . the members of the eugenics movement found emotional satisfaction in expressing their personal beliefs in action rather than seeking specific material improvement in their status within society. (Farrall 1970, 293)

As a statement about the psychological state of eugenists this may possibly be correct. Eugenists may genuinely have believed that their aim was not 'specific material improvement in their status within society' but disinterested moral reform. What is at issue, however, is not simply their motivation and psychological state, but also the social nature of the theory and policies of the movement they built.

An inspection of these rapidly reveals that disinterested moral reform is hardly an adequate account of them. Take taxation, for example. A constant theme of eugenic propaganda was the way in which income tax oppressed the 'fit' and led them to reduce the size of their families. The eugenic demand for increased tax allowances for children was one which, if obtained, would clearly have benefited the professional middle-class families from which the eugenists were drawn. (Interestingly, Leonard Darwin's tax proposals would not have benefited *all* the well-to-do: he suggested to the Royal Commission on Income Tax that higher taxes on inherited wealth were eugenically acceptable, as Searle (1976, 129) notes.)

To see this as consciously calculated economic class interest would probably be wrong. To some extent at least the burden of taxation would simply have shifted to middle-class bachelors and spinsters, and in any case there were almost certainly more direct and efficacious ways of seeking to reduce one's income tax liability than joining the Eugenics Society.[10] Yet this policy was clearly a public statement both of the worth of the professional middle class and of dissatisfaction with its situation. In the same way, the Eugenics Education Society's successful move to join with leading professional bodies and institutions to set up a 'Professional Classes War Relief Council' at the outbreak of the First World War (E.E.S. 1915, 4–5), while it may not have been *motivated* by self-interest, at least reveals a certain degree of 'class consciousness'. Indeed, as Searle (1976, 59) points out, it would not be unfair to conclude that in eugenic propaganda the 'professional middle classes and the intelligentsia' were the 'heroes of the play'. Not only was the working class denigrated, but it was often implied that professionals were superior to an aristocracy and business class sapped by injudicious marriage for wealth rather than genetic worth. Thus during the debates on the reform of the House of Lords, Karl Pearson wrote to *The Times* to deny that the hereditary principle exemplified by the Lords was eugenically adequate. In the Upper House were to be found 'mere plutocrats', 'political failures' and 'men who have not taken the pains necessary to found or preserve an able stock' (31 March 1910; Pearson Papers, 23A, *2*, 86–87). 'Hereditary honour should follow ability in the stock and not be granted to a preordained individual' (Pearson 1914–30, *3A*, 33–34; he is paraphrasing Francis Galton's views).

So there is at least a *prima facie* case for regarding eugenics – whatever the motives of the eugenists – as a system of beliefs and practices that, while presented as an objective description of nature and a set of policies in accord with nature, reflected *social interests* and *social relationships*. Let us begin to examine this possibility by looking at the social situation of the professional middle class from which the eugenists were drawn.

The Professional and the Social Structure

The social stratum referred to loosely as the 'professional middle class' has been the object of much impassioned but indecisive sociological debate. Some have seen it as largely analogous in its social position to shopkeepers and artisans, and have located it in the 'new petty bourgeoisie' (Poulantzas 1975). Others have claimed it to be a 'new class' destined to sweep aside the old bourgeoisie and exercise benevolent dominance over the manual working class

(Gouldner 1978). Others still have argued that its structural position is fundamentally contradictory, 'objectively torn' between the basic antagonistic classes of capitalist society (Wright 1978). And there are many more positions that have been taken.[11]

This debate has been curiously sterile. One problem has undoubtedly been that nearly all of those who write about the professional stratum belong to it. While this sometimes brings sensitivity to its situation, it can also lead to idealisation of, for example, the professionals' 'careful and critical discourse' (Gouldner 1978). More seriously, the debate has usually been conducted more in the spirit of the taxonomist than that of the historian: writers have primarily been concerned to find the right pigeon-hole into which to fit the professionals, and have had little sense of class as an emerging phenomenon that is as much cultural as structural.[12] In other words, we have no 'Making of the English Professional Class' to parallel E. P. Thompson (1968). Abstract conceptualisation, rather than theoretically-informed concrete studies, has been the order of the day.

So there is no fully satisfactory historical or theoretical account we can turn to. All we can do is to raid this literature for the insights it undoubtedly contains into the social situation of the professional, and attempt to use these to throw light on our subject matter. In the absence of a clearly superior alternative, I shall continue to use the term 'professional middle class' to describe this group. At least this is an 'actor's category' that the people about whom I am writing would have recognised: indeed, the senior author of the first major study of British professions was a leading member of the Eugenics Society (Carr-Saunders and Wilson 1933). But it should be clear that in talking in these terms I am not implying that this is a separate social class in the Marxist (or any other) sense. That question remains open.

Some general features of the social situation of professionals can fairly readily be seen. First, they occupy a position that is intermediate between the bourgeoisie and proletariat. They differ from the bourgeoisie (and aristocracy) in that they typically do not own or control substantial quantities of capital (or land). They differ from the proletariat in that their work is defined as mental labour, brain work, and is held to be superior to manual labour.[13] Secondly, recruitment to the professional middle class is generally not automatic, but has to be achieved through the educational system. Being the child of a professional obviously helps, but cannot *guarantee* success in the same way that being the child of a millionaire guarantees personal wealth. So as B. and J. Ehrenreich (1976) suggest, the life of professionals is often hedged round by worries about 'class reproduction': will they be able to ensure that their children (in practice, usually, their sons) obtain professional status. This anxiety, the fact that 'ordinary experiences of life' such as 'growing up, giving birth, childraising' (*ibid.*, 29) are intertwined with worries about educational success and future jobs, has been noted by many observers of the professional middle class. Banks (1965) suggests that it was particularly acute in late Victorian Britain, where the expense associated with 'class reproduction' – school fees, etc. – was strongly felt, especially by those with middle-class status but not real capitalist wealth.

Thirdly, the absolute and relative number of professional jobs, and their social prominence, tends to increase with the development of capitalist economies. This process is, however, not uniform. Thus Hobsbawm (1968, 267) suggests that, in some respects, it was relatively slower in Britain than in Germany or France. Further, it is at least arguable that these jobs and the fortunes of their incumbents are not tied to the continuance of a specifically capitalist economic order, and that the responsibilities and rewards associated with them might in at least certain cases be no less, or even greater, in a socialist state (see Gouldner 1978).

What strategies does the professional middle class typically employ in pursuit of its interests? Historically, the most significant has of course been 'professionalisation' itself. The rationale of professionalisation is to give an occupation special status by implying that its work is based on its accredited possession of a body of systematic knowledge, to erect barriers controlling access to this knowledge and to membership of the occupational group, and to free the group as much as possible from control by outsiders or 'laymen', while claiming it can be relied upon to provide disinterested service to the community. The strategy of professionalisation thus reflects the crucial role of accredited knowledge in differentiating the professional middle class from the bourgeoisie and the proletariat. Professional autonomy and control over access to membership of the profession are also important in alleviating the difficulties of 'class reproduction'. The high rate of self-recruitment to be found in the medical profession is evidence of the degree to which this strategy can bear fruit.

When we turn to more general political strategies, we find, however, a certain indeterminateness. The professional middle class is a relatively privileged group within capitalist society, and yet many professional jobs are not bound intrinsically to a capitalist order. A professional's conservatism and a professional's socialism are both possible. What does seem likely, however, is that both the conservatism and the socialism will be expressed in terms of an ideology of the 'expert' and of 'meritocracy'. Harold Perkin (1972, 258) writes of the British professional middle class:

> Their ideal society was a functional one based on expertise and selection by merit. For them trained and qualified expertise rather than property, capital or labour, should be the chief determinant and justification of status and power in society.

Charting the growth of the professional middle class in Britain is difficult. Problems in the occupational classifications in the census, and the general difficulty of deciding when a particular occupation became in the full sense a 'profession', make even rough estimates of numbers difficult.[14] But most historians would agree with Perkin's (1972, 254–5) conclusion:

> With urbanisation and the rise of living standards, doctors, lawyers, writers, and even the clergy (including dissenting ministers) found an enlarged demand for their services, which reduced their dependence on the few rich and increased that on the many comfortable clients of their own social standing. The transition enabled them to acquire a greater measure of self-respect, and to demand corresponding respect from society . . .
>
> At the same time new professions proliferated, and organised themselves to demand the same kind of status and independence as the old.

It seems reasonable to talk (at least by the latter part of the nineteenth century) of the emergence of an established professional middle class. Of course, there were important lines of division: between self-employed professionals and the newer group of professional employees; between the older professions such as law and the church, and the new, initially more marginal ones; between male professionals and women seeking, or having succeeded in achieving, entry to the professions. Despite this, it would appear that the late Victorian and Edwardian professional middle class did have some common sense of identity and social position (Perkin 1972, 254–61).

The Professionals and the Eugenic Theory of Society

We can now begin to see why the view of society put forward by British eugenists was attractive to many professionals. The core of this view was the idea that social position was (or at least should be) the consequence of individual mental ability. There was a natural hierarchy of talent which could be translated into a social hierarchy of occupations. At the top were the professions, with leading businessmen sometimes admitted into the élite: they represented the pick of the nation's brains. Below them were useful but increasingly dull-brained groups: small businessmen, clerks, shop-keepers, foremen, skilled workers. These were socially valuable, if not as valuable as the professional. Finally, there came strata who were typically stupid or worse: the unskilled, the unemployed and the outcast. The eugenic theory of society thus provided the reassurance that those below the professionals fundamentally lacked the ability to do professional jobs adequately. Naturally a handful would rise from the working class to professional status each generation, but it would be primarily the children of the existing professional class who would fill, and who would deserve to fill, their parents' jobs.

The eugenic theory of society could also be directed in the opposite social direction: upwards. Professionalism, with its emphasis on knowledge and 'service', was a 'tacit claim to *technical and moral superiority* over the old class, implying that the latter lack technical credentials and are guided by motives of commercial venality' (Gouldner 1978, 169). Eugenics provided a *natural* basis for this claim. For the old criteria of wealth and honour it substituted mental ability. The bourgeoisie and aristocracy could gain entry to the eugenic élite only on the professionals' terms: accredited knowledge. A few progressive, scientifically-minded businessmen and those aristocrats who won membership of the Royal Society would pass. The rest ran the risk of condemnation as plutocrats and drones.

Again, this does not mean that the eugenic theory of society was elaborated as a conscious and cynical celebration of the professional. All those eugenists that I have studied in detail believed it with patent sincerity and without question. Perhaps one reason for this was that it can be seen as in fact corresponding to certain aspects of the typical experience of the professional. The actual role played by family wealth, sexism, personal contact, string-pulling, class prejudice and discrimination in guaranteeing success was largely hidden. The public version – and one that seems to have been believed by many young intending professionals – was that the path to achievement was performance in competitive examinations followed by individual demonstration of competence in one's professional role. Success *did* appear to flow from individual cognitive ability, failure to be the consequence of its lack. The schoolboy Karl Pearson wrote to his mother from his 'crammer's' in 1874:

> He [his father] must remember that I shall try my best, and if I should prove to be dull, it is the fault of my intellect & not that I have not endeavoured to work well. (Pearson Papers, CIIDIE)

For people in other classes less dependent on the formal educational system this view of success – and consequently the eugenic view of society – would have had less immediate appeal. Manual workers were more aware of the influence of impersonal and collective forces on life-chances. The impact of economic boom and recession, of technological change, of the success or failure of trade union action, were less easily put down to individual mental ability. The successful businessman was certainly likely to believe he owed his success to his individual qualities, but these would perhaps be *virtues* – independence, ambition, self-denial, thrift and so on – rather than the *abilities* that appeared to make for success in examinations. The aristocrat and the eugenist both held the importance of 'birth', but in the aristocratic ideal this was most likely to be manifest in such qualities as honour, savoir-faire and the intuitive grasp of statesmanship.

So the eugenists' insistence of the *individual* determinants of success perhaps indicates the difference between the situation of the professional and the manual worker, and their emphasis on its *cognitive* determinants may reflect their being professionals rather than businessmen or landowners. Certainly eugenics was not blind to personality traits other than mental ability. Eugenists did attempt to prove these too to be inherited, and suggested, for example, that deficiencies in inherited moral qualities typically played a role along with sheer stupidity in such 'types' as the habitual petty criminal. Ability, too, ought to be combined with 'energy', 'perseverance', etc. But – especially with the twentieth century development of eugenics – it was ability, and increasingly the intelligence quotient, that dominated eugenic accounts of society (see Norton 1978d).

Certainly the reality and the metaphor of the examination was peculiarly important in the thought of the founder of eugenics,

Francis Galton. In *Hereditary Genius* he wrote that he looked upon 'social and professional life' as a 'continuous examination'. Candidates in life's examination 'achieve success in proportion as the general estimate is large of their aggregate merits'. The 'chain of proofs' Galton deployed against 'pretensions of natural equality' was 'the experiences of the nursery, the school, the University, and of professional careers'. The schoolboy 'competes in the examinations of school and college, over and over again with his fellows, and soon finds his place among them'. The large spread of marks in the Cambridge Mathematical Tripos examination indicated 'the enormous difference between the intellectual capacity of men'. The youths at Cambridge and Oxford 'include the highest youthful scholastic ability of all England'; the Senior Wrangler (winner of the Mathematics Tripos Examination at Cambridge), 'is the chief of these as regards mathematics'. On leaving university, the youth merely 'enters a larger field of competition' where after much experience of success and failure he finally comes to realise the limits of his ability, 'and finds true moral repose in an honest conviction that he is engaged in as much good work as his nature has rendered him capable of performing' (Galton 1869, 6–7 and 14–21).

So I would argue that the eugenic theory of society[15] corresponded in its main features to certain important aspects of the social interests and typical social experience of the professional middle class. Of course, much remains to be done to move from this overall correspondence to detailed connections, and this argument will be further developed in the discussion in later chapters of our three key statistical eugenists, Galton, Pearson and Fisher. Nevertheless, there are several more general questions about eugenics that should be answered before we begin to look at individual writers.

Eugenics and Capitalism

The British professional middle class did not confront other groups in a social vacuum. British society was by the period we are discussing dominated, despite the remnants of pre-capitalist institutions, by capitalist social relations. This inevitably raises the question of the relation of eugenics to capitalism. In the United States this relationship is reasonably manifest, if still under-researched: sectors of the American bourgeoisie supported and funded eugenics (see Allen 1975b, 1976). Yet in Britain matters are less clear. Big business did not play a major role in supporting and funding eugenics. And as we have seen, the eugenics movement was often critical of existing élite groups, some eugenists indeed calling themselves socialists. Nevertheless, it would be a mistake to argue that connections between eugenics and capitalism did not exist. To see this, we need to make two distinctions. The first is between different kinds of professionals, the second between capitalists and capital.

If we adopt for a moment a European perspective, one of the most striking aspects of the British professional middle class is its relative political quiescence. In pre-1914 Britain we do not find anything other than pale shadows of the Russian intellectuals who became social-revolutionaries or Bolsheviks, of the Austro-Marxist theoreticians, even of the French Dreyfusards (Hobsbawm 1968, 255–6). Of course, there are undoubtedly reasons for this in the relative social and political stability of Britain. There is, however, a more immediate possible cause that deserves consideration: the close integration of the élite of the British professionals into the ruling class. In an essay that has not received the attention it deserves, N. G. Annan (1955) describes the development in nineteenth-century Britain of an 'intellectual aristocracy'. This group emerged from sectors of the eighteenth and early nineteenth-century bourgeoisie. The children of marriages within this group tended to abandon direct involvement in business for the world of scholarship, education and the professions. They rapidly rose to dominant positions in the universities, public schools, science, literature and the increasingly professionalised civil service. Continuing intermarriage and a common set of cultural and political assumptions kept the group tightly knit. To list their family names is to give a roll-call of many of the leading figures of the nineteenth and twentieth-century British intelligentsia: Macaulay, Booth, Trevelyan, Arnold, Huxley, Darwin, Galton, Butler, Keynes, Sidgwick, Cornford, Balfour, Pease, Haldane, Hodgkin, Stephen, Bell, Strachey, Vaughan, Venn, Lubbock . . . . Numerically, it was not a very large group, but its influence was out of all proportion to its size.

Here then we have an élite of professional families. It was not an isolated élite. It was tied by continuing family wealth and by kinship to capital – respectable and old-established wealth rather than that of the nouveau-riche – and government. To take only one example, the descendants of the Newcastle merchant, William Scott, include: Lord Eldon, Fellow of the Royal Society and Lord Chancellor, who when he died left a fortune of £700,000 and 'much land' (Rubinstein 1977, 118); John Burdon Sanderson, Regius Professor of Medicine at Oxford; Lord Haldane, Lord Chancellor, Secretary for War and

F.R.S.; John Scott Haldane, the physiologist; John Burdon Sanderson Haldane, of whom more in chapter 8; Naomi Mitchison, the novelist; and the present Professor of Zoology of the university in which this book is written, J.M. Mitchison.

Eugenics was born within this élite. As I shall argue in the chapter on Francis Galton, eugenics can be seen as, initially, the practice and experience of the intellectual aristocracy read onto nature. While support for eugenics was not restricted to the members of this élite, they remained fully represented in the eugenics movement: Leonard Darwin, for example, belonged to the intellectual aristocracy. And the distinctive politics of this group, as described by Annan, can also be found in the style of the mainstream of British eugenics: a cautious commitment to modernisation and efficiency, to the gradual reform of existing institutions, to 'insider politics'. British eugenists were *not* (in general) 'cranks': had they been so, it is doubtful if the eugenics movement could have attracted the support of such people as the twin architects of the mid-twentieth-century British 'consensus', John Maynard Keynes and William Beveridge.[16]

It would be grossly mistaken to see the intellectual aristocracy as opposed to capitalism, apart perhaps in the case of an occasional individual and in the heady days of the 1930s and the war in Spain. Similarly, in no way can the majority of British eugenists be regarded as wishing to alter fundamentally a society based on capital. Yet loyalty to capital is quite compatible with a low opinion of capitalists, especially if seen as idle, philistine plutocrats. The intellectual aristocracy – and the eugenists – were committed to change within the framework of capitalism. To seek to make the state more efficient, capital more productive and the labour force 'fitter' might well involve opposing the vested interests of placemen and backward capitalists, but it was not opposition to capital.

So, despite the superficial anti-capitalist rhetoric of some eugenists, eugenics as a system of thought was thoroughly saturated with assumptions derived from the experience of living in a privileged position in a society based on capital and wage-labour. As Abrams (1968) has argued, eugenic thought was in close continuity with the classical ideology of the British bourgeoisie, liberal political economy, and with its biological variant, social Darwinism. The eugenic view of society was fundamentally individualistic and atomistic: it was to the individual, with his or her strengths and weaknesses, that the eugenists ultimately looked. Economic failure and social disorder resulted not from anything one might call 'the system', but from the faults of individuals. Poverty, crime and stupidity arose from the hereditary weakness of the poor, the criminal and the mentally-defective.

Further, the eugenists' typical view of human nature (the person as largely the sum of a number of potentially measurable abilities and personality traits) and of human populations (as manipulable aggregates of such abilities and traits) is that to be expected in a society in which the ultimate criterion of a person's worth is quantitative. 'The rate of wages', wrote Leonard Darwin (1926, 271), 'may be made to offer some indication of the innate qualities of the wage-earner'. In Francis Galton's eugenic utopia (Pearson 1914–30, 3A, 413–24), people would judge each other according to their 'marks' in a 'eugenic examination'. This reduction of people to numbers can surely be seen as a version of the tendency in capitalist societies described by Lukács (1971) as 'reification', thing-ification, the treatment of people and social processes as if they were things. Indeed Levidow (1978) argues that the modern notion of intelligence – largely the product of eugenically-minded psychologists – is rooted in the process of alienation by which human labour power is defined as a quantitative thing, as 'abstract labour power' for capital. The person becomes an 'abstract individual', the 'proprietor of abilities, technically defined, ordinally comparable, and valued instrumentally' (ibid., 64–5). Human capacities become commodities: 'it must be remembered', commented Leonard Darwin (1926, 275), 'that it is not only inanimate objects, but human beings also, which differ in regard to their capital values'.

What though of those eugenists who called themselves socialists? They were never large in number, but they should not therefore be neglected. Apart from Karl Pearson, who will be discussed in subsequent chapters, those who appeared to owe allegiance to both socialism and eugenics included the leaders of the Fabian Society: Beatrice and Sidney Webb, George Bernard Shaw and H. G. Wells.[17] It is possible, as Geoffrey Searle has emphasised, that their use of eugenic rhetoric was sometimes tactical, as in Sidney Webb's attempt to gain the support of the Eugenics Education Society for the Minority Report on the Poor Law on the grounds that it had been 'drawn on strictly eugenic lines' (Searle 1978, 14). Nevertheless, even their very willingness to use eugenics in this way seems surprising: why should socialists seek so hard to steal, and masquerade in, their enemies' clothes?

The answer appears to be that the Fabians were rather peculiar, though fascinatingly interesting, 'socialists'. As Eric Hobsbawm (1968) has shown, the social composition of the Fabian Society was 'overwhelmingly non-proletarian', with journalists, writers, university and school teachers, doctors, clergy and public officials the most common occupations of its members. There were wide political differences between the Fabians and the majority of working class socialists:

> The Fabians, alone among socialist groups, opposed the formation of an independent party of labour, supported imperialism, refused to oppose the Boer War, took no interest in the traditional international and anti-war preoccupations of the left, and their leaders took practically no part in the trade union revivals of 1889 or 1911. (*ibid.*, 253)

But the chief concern of the Fabians was not with the working class as the agency of social change. Fabian ideology (especially as expressed by the Webbs) pivoted round the salaried middle class:

> They are the trained, impartial and scientific administrators and expert advisers who have created an alternative court of appeal to profit. (*ibid.*, 258)

The Fabians saw in the ethos of professionalism 'a working alternative to a system in which men worked in proportion only to their financial incentive' (*ibid.*, 258). The professional middle class as a whole would come to realise, as the Fabians had done, that a socialist society 'really suited them just as well if not better than the capitalist' (*ibid.*, 259).

What, precisely, was it in capitalism that was objectionable? Not exploitation: Fabian economics rejected the labour theory of value. Not the lack of worker's control: the Webbs, for example, had strong doubts about the desirability of that. Rather, what was wrong was *laissez-faire*, the hallowed principle according to which state activity should be kept to a minimum, and capitalists allowed to go on with their business as they pleased. The Fabians' socialism was above all opposition to *laissez-faire*; their demand, in a myriad of detailed technical forms, was the growth of state regulation and intervention; their success-story was the reformed, rationalised and centralised London County Council.

It was this, argues Hobsbawm, that explains Fabianism's appeal to the professionals. The growth of job opportunities for them was much slower in Britain than in, say, the Germany of Bismarck's 'state socialism'. *Laissez-faire* restricted the scope for their talents, as for example in the relative paucity of state support for science. The 'experts' were being held back by the dogmas of an archaic social system. The state – apparently a neutral body standing above society – was to be their tool. Poverty, disease, inefficiency, industrial strife and inadequate national defence were all problems to be solved by the experts once the state was freed from the chains of *laissez-faire.*

A parallel between eugenics and Fabianism thus emerges, which enables us to see why it was possible to adhere to both simultaneously. In the words of Searle (1978, 13), 'the leading Fabians, with their general commitment to the notion of a planned society, were clearly attracted by the possibility of *genetic* planning, and they were not by temperament squeamish about the sort of bureaucratic interference in family life which such planning would indubitably involve'. There were tensions that were to prise apart Fabianism and eugenics (Searle 1978). Nevertheless, there remains a strong sense in which both ideologies were responses – different but overlapping – to the situation of the professional middle class within British capitalism. The Fabian critique of capitalism was, at root, one limited to an attack on those aspects of capitalism that were barriers to the full use of the professionals' expertise. It was never generalised to those deeper features – the hierarchical division of labour, and so on – that I have analysed as underlying the eugenic theory of society. So, at least at this level of generality, eugenics and Fabian 'socialism' were quite compatible. And, in their common emphasis on the need for state intervention and planning, on the desirability of a fit and efficient population, on the social importance of brain-work, the two movements seemed to be working towards similar objectives.

Eugenic Social Policies
and the Twin Crises of Reproduction

Discussing the conditions for the continuing existence of capitalist society, Karl Marx wrote (1976, 718):

> The maintenance and reproduction of the working class remains a necessary condition for the reproduction of capital. But the capitalist may safely leave this to the worker's drives for self-preservation and propagation.

British eugenists were fully aware of the point made in Marx's first sentence, but they would have disagreed emphatically with his second claim: the reproduction of the working class could not safely be left to 'the worker's drives for self-preservation and propagation'.

Opponents of eugenics sensed that behind it lay a desire to create a labour force fully suited to the needs of capital. 'At root', wrote G. K. Chesterton (1922, 137), 'the Eugenist is the Employer'. What the eugenist 'is really wanted for', he continued, 'is to get the grip of the governing classes on to the unmanageable output of poor people'. The core of eugenics, he implied, was 'the idea of ultimately herding and breeding the workers like cattle' (*ibid.*, 141 and 147). Vehemently opposing the second reading of the Feeble-Minded Persons (Control) Bill in the House of Commons, J. C. Wedgwood (1912, col.1474) complained that the 'horrible' Eugenics Education Society was 'setting out to breed the working classes as though they were cattle' with the aim of turning people 'into better money-making machines'.

These attacks contain an element of over-statement. When Leonard Darwin, for example, contemplated the idea of breeding a 'docile human beast of burden' he rejected it, though admittedly only on the grounds of its 'demoralising effect' on superior classes (1926, 258–9). More importantly, however, eugenists were perfectly well aware that they could never get away with plans literally to 'breed the working classes as though they were cattle': the rejection of the 'methods of the stockyard' was a consistent theme in public statements by leaders of the eugenics movement. The actual direction of eugenic social policies for the reproduction of the working class was more realistic. To set it in context, we must look at how established society typically regarded the working class in the latter part of the nineteenth century and early twentieth century.

Obviously, generalisation on a point like this is bound to be problematic and hedged round with exceptions. Nevertheless, it can be said with reasonable confidence that middle-class fears of the industrial working class declined during the middle part of the nineteenth century. Francis Galton had been working in the Birmingham General Hospital during the Chartist disturbances. Though his comment on these was typically detached – 'it was curious to observe the apparent cleanness of the cuts that were made through the scalp by the blow of a policeman's round truncheon' (1908, 30–1) – he must have been as well aware as his contemporaries of the threat to social order posed by the working class in the early years of the nineteenth century. Yet by 1869 he could quote with agreement Chadwick's judgement on the 'typical modern British workman':

> . . . great bodily strength, applied under the command of a steadily persevering will, mental self-contentedness, impossibility to external irrelevant impressions, which carries them through the continued repetition of toilsome labour, 'steady as time'.

The 'artisan part of our population', Galton commented, 'is slowly becoming bred to its duties' (1869, 346–8).

This complacency about the bulk of the working class did not, however, extend to all of it. As Jones (1971) has emphasised, confidence in the 'respectable' working class co-existed with concern for, and more importantly fear of, the poor of the large city slums:

> The most characteristic image of the working class was that of increasingly prosperous and cohesive communities bound together by the chapel, the friendly society, and the co-op. Pitted against the dominant climate of moral and material improvement however was a minority of the still unregenerate poor: those who had turned their backs on progress, or had been rejected by it. This group was variously referred to as 'the dangerous class', the casual poor or most characteristically, as 'the residuum'. (*ibid.*, 10–11)

In other words, the perceived problem of social control was no longer the working class as a whole, but only a 'residual' section of it. The largest concentration of the 'residuum' was in London. The *Quarterly Review* summed up middle class attitudes as early as 1855:

> . . . the most remarkable feature of London life is a class decidedly lower in the social scale than the labourer, and numerically very large, though the population returns do not number them among the inhabitants of the kingdom, who derive their living from the streets . . . for the most part their utmost efforts do little more than maintain them in a state of chronic starvation . . . very many have besides their acknowledged calling, another in the background in direct violation of the eighth commandment; and thus by gradations imperceptibly darkening as we advance, we arrive at the classes who are at open war with society, and professedly live by the produce of depredation or the wages of infamy.

> (quoted by Jones 1971, 12)

The worst situation was in the East End:

From the end of the 1860s to the First World War, the East End
was a by-word for chronic and hopeless poverty, and endemic
economic malaise. (*ibid.*, 99)

There was thus a definite 'social problem' in London. The residuum
were not, it is true, radical or revolutionary. They were, however,
politically volatile, and, pressed by extreme hardship, they were
liable to riot.

Social control was not the only problem. Middle-class observers
felt that the poor were physically and mentally degenerate as well as
dangerous. The urban slum dweller was characteristically compared
with the healthy and strong agricultural labourer. It was widely
believed that urban conditions caused the degeneration of immi-
grants from the country, whether by the direct effect of environment or by the selection of the worst types. Francis Galton (1869,
340) wrote:

It is perfectly distressing to me to witness the draggled, drudged,
mean look of the mass of individuals, especially of the women,
that one meets in the streets of London and other purely
English towns. The conditions of their life seem too hard for
their constitutions, and to be crushing them into degeneracy.

Increasingly the problem of urban degeneration was seen in the
context of imperialism. A degenerating population was serious
enough under any circumstances, but it could be fatal to a British
Empire faced with increasing foreign economic competition, colo-
nial war and the ultimate threat of inter-imperialist war. The early
reverses suffered by British troops in the Boer War (1899–1902)
gave concrete form to these misgivings. It was put about, and widely
believed, that up to 60 per cent of working-class volunteers for the
army had had to be rejected because they failed to meet the army's
minimum standards of physical fitness (Gilbert 1966, 84–91).

The problem, then, was seen to be a section of the working class
that lacked moral fibre (i.e. was outside social control) and was
physically unfit. The growth of large cities had broken the older
forms of social control based on direct personal contact between
rich and poor. The most important early attempt at a solution was
the Charity Organisation Society, set up in 1869, which sought to
re-impose social control through organised, selective charity and
trained social workers (Jones 1971, 241–61). With the deepening
urban crisis of the 1880s and the serious rioting of 1886–87, there
was a conscious search for new responses to the problem. Crucial to
these was the distinction between the respectable working class and

the residuum: the residuum must be isolated from the working class as a whole (even at the price of concessions to the bulk of workers) and neutralised or eliminated. Fabians, Tories and Liberal Imperialists could find common ground in agreement that a solution to the problem of the urban residuum was a prerequisite of imperial survival. This became one of the bases for social imperialism, the linking of imperialism and social reform that loomed large in British politics between the 1880s and 1914, and, as Farrall (1970) points out, provided a favourable context for eugenic schemes.[18]

The eugenists had a biological explanation of the residuum and a biological solution to the problem it posed. The suspension of natural selection through the operation of charity, medical science and sanitary reform had led, they claimed, to the flourishing, in the hearts of the great cities, of a group of people tainted by hereditary defect. Members of this group were unemployed because they lacked the health, ability and strength of will to work. Hereditary weakness turned them towards crime and alcohol. Their constitutions inclined them to wasting diseases such as tuberculosis. The residuum was outbreeding skilled artisans and 'respectable' workers in general. The eugenists warned that although natural selection was largely suspended within British society, competition between different nations went on. Britain was engaged in a struggle for survival that was normally commercial but might at any time become military. National fitness for this struggle was necessary. Under the conditions of modern civilisation, a replacement for natural selection had to be found in conscious eugenic selection. The working class had to be 'purged' by isolating the residuum in institutions where parenthood would be made impossible. Negative eugenics was, in large part, the elimination of the residuum.

It is important to realise that this eugenic policy was not *exceptionally* severe when judged in the context of other proposals for the treatment of the residuum. Thus, Charles Booth, famous as a documenter of London poverty, envisaged solving the problem by moving the poor out of the slums into labour camps. Should they refuse to go, they could be encouraged by 'making life otherwise impossible'; 'State Socialism' had to take 'charge of the lives of the incapable' (quotations from Jones 1971, 307). Rather, the eugenic solution stood out because of its thoroughgoing naturalism. The residuum was, according to the eugenists, not a social category, or even primarily a moral category, but a *natural* category, a degenerated variety, or collection of varieties, of the species *homo sapiens*.

This naturalism implied limitations on the efficacy of other strategies for dealing with the residuum proposed by other élite groups. There really was not much point preaching to the residuum, attempting to save their souls and convert them to a decent and hard-working Christian life, if they differed naturally from respectable workers. The eugenic strategy was one that placed a premium on the skills of the scientific 'expert' rather than those of the priest: the solution lay with the biologist's and doctor's knowledge of heredity, with the statistician's survey, the social worker's case-report, and ultimately the psychiatrist's custodial care or the surgeon's scalpel.

'Negative eugenics' in Britain was thus in large part a strategy for dealing with a crisis in the reproduction of labour power. The residuum was a section of the working class surplus to capital's requirements. They were indeed only temporarily so: with the First World War the 'genetically unemployable' were suddenly to be found in steady jobs (Jones 1971, 336). But this was not foreseen before 1914. The residuum were forced to rely in part on charity, state aid and petty crime to support themselves, and they appeared to be reproducing themselves in ever-increasing numbers. They were the prime perceived obstacle to the creation of an entirely pliant, healthy and adequately skilled working class. In promising to eliminate them, the eugenic professionals felt they were pointing part of the way to the creation and maintenance of an imperial race.

But only part of the way. There was another crisis of reproduction to be faced, and this one nearer home. The class from which the eugenists were drawn was threatened by a declining birth-rate that seemed to imply its eventual failure to replenish itself from within its own ranks, and thus its swamping by the lower orders. Exact and reliable figures were difficult to obtain because of technical problems such as the use of different occupational classifications in different official statistical series, but all observers were agreed that the middle class birth-rate had fallen drastically since mid-Victorian times, and that it was much lower than that of the working class, especially of the unskilled.[19] To a believer in the eugenic theory of society, this implied that Britain's 'national intelligence' was threatened. Leonard Darwin complained that 'our professional classes in fact almost certainly form a group that is dying out' (Darwin 1926, 323; cited by Searle 1978, 18).

Much of 'positive eugenics' in Britain was a straightforward response to this situation. The eugenists sought to diagnose the causes of it, and to find ways of encouraging parenthood amongst the professional middle-class groups to which they belonged. Some of their solutions have been discussed above. A clear conviction of their class's genetic worth runs through them. Yet it is possible that another conflict, as well as that between classes, manifests itself in the concern for middle-class fertility.

'Middle-class fertility' of course meant in practice the fertility of middle-class women. And the period of the rise of eugenics was also the period of the growth of feminism in Britain. It is difficult to avoid the suspicion that amongst the social interests sustaining 'positive eugenics' may have been that of professional men in having women – especially the growing number of women professionals – return to their traditional roles and stop 'shirking' motherhood. One such male professional asked in the *Eugenics Review* of 1911 whether the 'new woman's . . . knowledge of mathematics, or even her efficiency in athletics' made her 'intrinsically a better mother than the natural, bright, intelligent girl interested in frills, dances and flirtations?'. 'Womanliness', perhaps the result of 'Natural Selection', was 'rightly or wrongly associated with certain passive qualities, such as sympathy and tenderness . . . which best find their expression in the domestic sphere and more particularly in the role of wife and mother' (Dr R. Murray Leslie, quoted by Davin 1978, 20–21; see also McLaren 1978, 147 for further examples of anti-feminist eugenic argument).

Yet eugenics was a double-edged weapon for anti-feminists. The eugenic argument could be turned on its head, and the legal and financial independence of women from men justified on the grounds that only under those circumstances would women be free to select the 'fit' to father their children.[20] Those who argued for eugenics but against birth control could be accused of inconsistency, and Marie Stopes's pioneer 'Society for Constructive Birth Control and Racial Progress' indicates by its very name the way eugenic arguments could be used in defence of contraception. Sexual inconoclasm and eugenics could, and did, go together in the work of writers such as Havelock Ellis and George Bernard Shaw (McLaren 1978, 254). The Council of the Eugenics Education Society contained several of the 'new women' objected to by Murray Leslie, and in 1913 women outnumbered men amongst the members and associate members of the Society (Farrall 1970, 211n.).

In the combination of eugenics and feminism lurked a contradiction, but it was not one that was always apparent.[21] The feminists sought *women's* control of their own fertility, the eugenists *state* control of, or at least influence on, women's fertility. These different goals sometimes allowed common action. Both feminists and eugenists could agree that Marie Stopes's work in improving working-class women's access to contraception was beneficial, the feminist on the grounds that it increased their control over their own bodies, the eugenist on the grounds that it would reduce the birth-rate of the working class. The Eugenics Society could thus enjoy 'long-standing and cordial relations with the Family Planning Association and the International Planned Parenthood Federation', and its Council could under the terms of her will 'control' the Marie Stopes Memorial Foundation (Schenk and Parkes 1968, 142, 154).

It is in fact this sort of linking of eugenics to other publicly quite non-eugenic causes that is of particular interest in understanding the history of eugenic social policies after the period discussed in this book. With the exception of Waterman (1975) and Searle (1979), existing studies of British eugenics have focused on the pre-1914 period, when British eugenics seemed closest to achieving direct influence on state policy. So any statements about the development of eugenics after the First World War must be tentative. Nevertheless, several general points can be made. The eugenic theory of society continued to enjoy considerable, indeed growing, success, in the form of the cult of intelligence. As Simon (1971, 10) has emphasised, the twentieth-century British school system 'was shaped by a selective process based on classification by Intelligence Quotient'. Clearly the eugenists did not themselves bring this about; wider social forces did. But psychologists and psychological ideas nurtured within the eugenics movement played a major role in legitimating the selective process: the work of Sir Cyril Burt is the most notorious example. The building of a system of education on the assumption that the extent to which a child could benefit from education was determined by a single number that was highly correlated with parental occupational position – the children of professional and managerial parents 'having' the highest average IQ – represented to a large degree the *institutionalisation* of the eugenic model of society. As Henderson (1976) argues, the professional middle class were able to define the terms on which working-class children could achieve social mobility.

Positive eugenics, in the sense of the deliberate encouragement of professional middle-class fertility, however, lost much of its rationale as the birth-rates of other classes fell to the level (or even below the level) of the professional middle class. The pro-natalist policies of positive eugenics were never successful. If the eugenists themselves did not practice what they preached – and, with the exception of R. A. Fisher, I have come across few eugenists who had particularly large families – it was not very likely that their fellow professionals would. So eugenic attention focused more and more strongly on negative eugenics. But in the inter-War period the form taken by the perceived crisis in the reproduction of labour power altered. 'Responsible' eugenic scientists such as Julian Huxley continued to argue as late as 1931 that state benefits should be given only to those of the unemployed who ceased to reproduce:

> Infringement of this order could probably be met by a short period of segregation in a labour camp. After three or six months' separation from his wife he [an unemployed man] would be likely to be more careful the next time.
> (quoted by Werskey 1978, 42)

When the unemployed numbered in the millions this sort of policy was, however, scarcely feasible this side of fascism. Direct state intervention in the reproduction of a relatively small and stigmatised section of the working class was one thing; subjecting huge numbers of workers to the kind of coercion envisaged by Huxley was quite another, and would certainly have provoked massive resistance.

So in one sense the crisis faced by the eugenics movement in the middle and late 1930s was implicitly present before Hitler came to power. *Either* the eugenists had to give up old-style negative eugenics, *or* they had to embark on a policy that could only be conducted by a state apparatus prepared to employ the harshest authoritarian measures. An editorial in Britain's leading scientific magazine *Nature* (Crew 1933)[22] noted that the new National Socialist rulers of Germany had passed a Bill for 'the avoidance of inherited disease in posterity', providing for the sterilisation of sufferers from 'congenital feeblemindedness, manic depressive insanity, schizophrenia, hereditary epilepsy, hereditary St. Vitus's dance, hereditary blindness and deafness, hereditary bodily malformation and habitual alcoholism'. Given that *Nature* had welcomed not wholly dissimilar proposals from British eugenists (Werskey 1969), it would have been less than consistent to do other than note that 'the Bill, as it reads, will command the appreciative attention of all who are interested in the controlled and deliberate improvement of human stock'. But the Bill gave prison governors the power 'to recommend that a prisoner shall be sterilised', and a further Bill provided for the 'compulsory emasculation of dangerous criminals'. With Germany's jails full of political prisoners, *Nature* commented that 'it is impossible to avoid the thought that here is provided a most frightful opportunity for those politically strong at present to outrage the politically oppressed'.

With the anti-fascist movement in Britain gathering strength, and with the stream of exiled intellectuals making it clear that fascism boded ill for the freedom of the professional, most British eugenists stopped short of support for Hitler's campaign to purify the race. The British Union of Fascists made eugenics part of its platform (Rowbotham 1973, 151), and several British eugenists ardently defended the 'German experiment' (Searle 1979). George Pitt-Rivers, Secretary of the International Federation of Eugenic Societies, joined the British Union of Fascists and was interned during the Second World War (Werskey 1972b, 252). But the main-stream of British eugenists stopped short of fascism, and, as Searle (1979) emphasises, the leadership of the Eugenics Society took considerable pains to distance themselves from the Nazis.

The taint of fascism was nevertheless one that it was hard for British eugenists to avoid. Between 1932 and 1956 the total membership of the Eugenics Society fell from 768 to 456. The conclusion was obvious, if apparently resisted by die-hards within the Society. In the words of its Honorary Secretary, C. P. Blacker, in a 1957 memorandum on the Society's future, 'the Society should pursue eugenic ends by less obvious means, that is by a policy of crypto-eugenics, which was apparently proving successful with the u.s. Eugenics Society'[23] (quoted by Schenk and Parkes 1968, 154). Though a proposal to change the Society's name to the more neutral 'Galton Society' failed, public propaganda was ceased. It was agreed in 1960 that 'crypto-eugenics' should be 'pursued vigorously'; the Family Planning Association, International Planned Parenthood Federation and Society for the Study of Human Biology were specially mentioned in this context. A series of successful symposia was organised following a 1963 decision that the 'main activity' of the Society should be on 'the common ground between the biological and social sciences', 'to bring together for the mutual exchange of ideas and information those interested in genetic as contrasted with environmental influences' (Schenk and Parkes 1968, 155–6). In 1977 the Society had a small but influential[24] membership of 370, and assets of £82,000, which were about to be supplemented by almost £150,000 following the voluntary liquidation of the Marie

Stopes Memorial Foundation Limited and the Society for Constructive Birth Control Limited, and the transfer of their assets to the Eugenics Society (Eugenics Society 1977a,b).

Opponents of Eugenics

Even in its heyday, eugenics was never unopposed. To understand fully the social basis of eugenics, it is important to begin to identify the sources of systematic opposition to it. While this is a topic on which work has scarcely begun,[25] some tentative generalisations are perhaps possible, even if they stand open to future refutation.

Eugenics, I argue, represented certain interests and experiences of the professional middle class *within capitalism*. Hence we should expect to find the potential for opposition to eugenics amongst those who were capable of a wider vision. This is precisely what we do find; and this opposition took two forms. The first was from those who went beyond the Fabians' state-socialist antagonism to *laissez-faire* to a socialism of a more fundamental and far-reaching nature. One such person was Lancelot Hogben. As Werskey (1978) emphasises, Hogben was the *only* major British biologist prior to the 1930s to mount a clear and consistent campaign against eugenic science. Although he accepted that 'those who insist on social control of production can raise little serious objection to some measure of social control in reproduction' (Hogben 1919b, 154), he was sharply aware that in human genetics there was a danger 'that social bias will enter into the actual selection and interpretation of data' (1919b, 155–6) and he became the most effective critic of the eugenists' 'social bias'.

The fact that the article from which these quotes are taken appeared in the Independent Labour Party's *Socialist Review* indicates that Hogben's attack on eugenics had a political context. His socialism was clearly to the left of the Fabians' – he had in fact succeeded in 'de-Fabianising' the Cambridge University Fabian Society, transforming it into a Socialist Society (Werskey 1978, 64) – and earlier in the same volume of the *Socialist Review* he had talked of 'the triumph of the Russian proletariat' (1919a, 60). The first pupil from a London County Council secondary school to win an open scholarship to Trinity College, Cambridge, and an imprisoned First World War conscientious objector, Hogben in the 1920s channelled his socialism into scientific opposition to the assumptions of eugenics, particularly to the eugenists' over-facile separation of heredity and environment (Werskey 1978, 62–5 and 105–9).

46

There were also those who condemned capitalism not in the name of the future but of the past. By far the most comprehensive of these was G. K. Chesterton. *Eugenics and other Evils* (Chesterton 1922) savaged eugenics, 'scientific officialism', the 'scientifically organised State', capitalist industrialism and Fabian socialism in the name of tradition:

> Far into the unfathomable past of our race we find the assumption that the founding of a family is the personal adventure of a free man . . . (1922, 9–10)

Others managed to combine these two different forms of attack. Josiah Wedgwood, MP, was a 'Liberal-Anarchist' and follower of Henry George's socialist land-tax scheme (C. V. Wedgwood 1951).[26] Though a distant relation of Charles Darwin and Francis Galton, he had moved far from the characteristic style and beliefs of the intellectual aristocracy. In his opposition – already noted above – to the eugenically-inspired Feeble-Minded Persons (Control) Bill, he attacked the 'dictum of the specialist', 'the inevitable two doctors to decide whether a man is to be free or not', 'government by specialists' and the eugenists' 'gross materialism' and denial of the 'soul' as well as the Bill's discrimination against the poor and women (1912, cols. 1470–1, 1474, 1476–7).

Another group of opponents of eugenics shared Chesterton's and Wedgwood's opposition to the militant scientism of eugenics without sharing their critique of capitalism. Traditional sectors of the professional middle class, notably clerics and lawyers, were much under-represented in the eugenics movement compared to the scientific professions. And some traditional professionals, most notably Catholic clergy, openly attacked eugenics: in December 1930 the Catholic Church issued a solemn and formal condemnation of eugenics and associated practices in the encyclical *De Casti Connubii*.[27] The Church, especially the Catholic Church, had always considered matters of the family, marriage, sex and reproduction to fall firmly within its distinctive sphere of competence. Eugenics represented the invasion of this sphere by alien, naturalistic, 'materialist' forces.

Slightly more surprising than these forms of opposition to eugenics is opposition from 'within the ranks of the "modern", professional middle class' (Searle 1978, 10): from Medical Officers of Health, some other types of doctor, and from those involved in 'philanthropy, social work and social reform' (*ibid.*, 7–17). As this seems on the face of it to cast doubt on the hypothesis that professional middle-class interests sustained eugenics, it is worth examining in slightly more detail.

What happened in the case of the Medical Officers of Health seems clear. The hereditarianism of at least some eugenists was taken to imply the conclusion that preventive medicine was both useless, in that the most important causative factors in, say, tuberculosis were hereditary, and even detrimental, in that it lowered the death-rate of the unfit. Eugenists were seen as implying that their particular occupation was futile. As I shall argue in chapter 4, in this case a particular occupational interest can be seen as cutting across a more general 'class' one.

The case of the medical profession as a whole is a little more complicated, and one of the great values of Searle (1978) is that he begins to unravel the complexity. Eugenics, he emphasises, drew its support primarily from the élite of the medical profession, its scientifically most advanced sectors: specialists in hereditary diseases, 'leading surgeons and consultants associated with the big teaching hospitals or holding university appointments', and medical journalists (ibid., 9). The bulk of ordinary family doctors, ignorant of statistics and genetics, awed by the possibility of having to decide fitness for parenthood, sometimes Roman Catholic in their religion, and alienated by tactless suggestions by eugenists that medical effort to prolong the lives of the 'unfit' was misplaced, were not eugenic enthusiasts (ibid., 9–10). This pattern – the scientific élite being readier to support eugenics than the more traditionalist rank-and-file, who were sometimes openly hostile – is quite in line with what would be expected on the basis of the analysis suggested here.

What, though, of those involved in 'philanthropy, social work and social reform'? Here surely we touch on the major systematic pole of opposition to eugenics – environmentalism. It is indeed true that there was a clear divide between eugenics and traditional philanthropy: the eugenic experts had no time for the rich dowager salving her conscience, or for the parson attracting the poor with soup and charity. But surely with the growth of social work and of reform movements based on social science we have the emergence of a group, equally as professional as the eugenists, possessing their own anti-eugenic theoretical position. Further, is Searle (1978) not right to assert that it was in this direction that the true interests of the professional lay? For environmentalism, to put it crudely, implied more jobs for professionals than did eugenics. The scalpel of a single surgeon could remove the necessity for a host of teachers, social workers and psychiatrists, or so the eugenists claimed.

The problem lies in assessing the extent to which eugenics and environmentalism really were opposites. It is indeed orthodox, at least since the work of Pastore (1949), to conceive of a 'nature-nurture controversy' in which eugenics and environmentalism faced each other as mutually exclusive and exhaustive options. But the most recent writing on this topic has begun to throw doubt on this orthodoxy. Briefly, it has been suggested that what unites eugenics and mainstream environmentalism is in many ways more significant than what divides them.[28]

Thus Werskey (1978, 30) suggests that eugenics and environmentalism should be seen as 'two different forms of biological engineering' with a common goal: to produce 'a population fit and clever enough to preserve the existing social order'. Rose (1979, 33-7) argues that the influential Fabian-inspired Minority Report of the Poor Law Commission was based not on environmentalism as against eugenics, but on a conjunction of eugenic and environmentalist strategies. Levidow (1978) and Harwood (1979) have each, in their different ways, shown the surprisingly large extent of the common ground shared by hereditarian and environmentalist sides of the IQ debate of the 1960s and 1970s.

It is in this context that the distinction made at the start of this chapter between the eugenic theory of society and particular eugenic policies becomes relevant. For it appears that mainstream environmentalism has not challenged the fundamental eugenic model of society as an actual or potential individualist meritocracy. Those basic assumptions that I have analysed as arising from the social interests and experience of the professional middle class within capitalism are precisely what the environmentalist critique has left untouched. At least in those versions that have received detailed attention, environmentalism has softened the hard genetic determinism of the eugenists, but (in the words of Harwood 1979, 246) still seen 'the ideal society as allocating rank on grounds of a measure of intellect'. Existing IQ tests are criticised as not fully adequate measures of ability, and the heritability of IQ is said not to be as high as hereditarians claim. But the assumptions that ability is an individually possessed 'thing' that can at least potentially be measured, and that the results of this process ought to bear an important relation to an individual's social position, survive intact.

On the other hand, if eugenics and environmentalism are seen not as social theories, but as social policies, as strategies for social control, then an obvious difference does emerge. Nikolas Rose (1979) puts the point neatly. The strategy of eugenics is segregation; the strategy of environmentalism is socialisation, re-attachment of marginal or disaffected groups to the social order. Eugenics seeks control by exclusion and the tightening of boundaries; environmentalism by integration.[29]

This then is how I would suggest we regard the divide between eugenics and mainstream environmentalism. Both involve similar meritocratic social theories, and thus at this level both reflect professional middle-class interests and experiences. But they involve different strategies of control: eugenics is hard, environmentalism soft. They thus differ in their tactical appropriateness to ruling groups in different situations (see Harwood 1979). And they may well be differentially attractive to different types of professional according to the skills they call for.

Professional middle-class adherence to environmentalism, as documented by Searle (1978), is thus, in this perspective, fully compatible with the view that professional interests sustained eugenics (and especially the eugenic model of society). The difference between eugenics and environmentalism is less a fundamental divide than a localised and, in an important sense, tactical disagreement. Certainly, for most of the twentieth century in Britain environmentalism has had a tactical advantage. It was more suitable for the needs of the gradually emerging pattern of social accommodation that crystallised in post-1945 welfare capitalism. But as that accommodation comes under threat in the 1980s, it would not surprise me if the tactical balance begins to shift back towards eugenics. If that happens, then this present study of the origins of eugenic science will perhaps have more relevance than its author imagined when he began it.[30]

3

Francis Galton

· · · · ·
· · ·
·

That Galton's statistical theory was connected to his eugenics is not a new conclusion. Pearson (1914–30), Cowan (1972a) and Hilts (1973) all deduce it by different routes and in somewhat different forms. My aim here is to develop their analyses in two directions so as to make clear in what sense we can see Galton's work as a case-study in the social construction of scientific knowledge.

The first direction is to display Galton's work in its social context. The biographical focus of many writers on Galton might easily lead one to imagine him as an individual genius in isolation. It is indeed true that in many areas he was a founder of movements rather than a joiner of them: eugenics is the obvious example. Yet eugenics did not spring into his head from nowhere. It is my argument that Galton's eugenics was tied in two ways to the social group to which he belonged. First, Galton's early eugenic theorising drew on his social experience as a resource, the form of his eugenic thought reflecting the form of organisation of his social group, and at the same time legitimating it. Secondly, his eugenics can very clearly be seen as part of the wider movement in thought known as scientific naturalism – a movement that has been analysed as expressing the social interests of scientific professionals. So in this double respect, the case of Galton represents an individual instance of the connection between eugenics and the professionals suggested in chapter 2. Without necessarily arguing that his motive was a desire to advance professional interests – this is dubious – his eugenic thought was a celebration of the work of the professional élite and was also a bold attempt to colonise intellectual territory previously occupied by science's rivals.

The second task of this chapter is to examine in detail the nature of the connections between eugenics and statistical theory to be found in Galton's work. Sometimes these connections are taken to be at the level of motivation. Thus Cowan (1972a, 528) ends her study with the conclusion that Galton's 'eugenic dreams had provided him with the motivation and the mental perseverance that he needed to unlock the secrets of probability'. In fact, though, Cowan's own work shows that a stronger conclusion is possible: that the needs of eugenics in large part determined the content of Galton's statistical theory. So most of this chapter will be concerned with the transformation of statistical theory achieved by Galton. If the immediate problems of eugenic research were to be solved, a new theory of statistics, different from that of the previously dominant error theorists, had to be constructed.

Eugenics, the Intellectual Aristocracy and Naturalism

In chapter 2, I pointed out that the British professional middle class contained an identifiable élite: the intellectual aristocracy, to use the term suggested by Annan (1955). Francis Galton could well be taken as an archetypal member of this group. He was born into one of its leading families (the Wedgwood/Darwin/Galton family) and married into another (the Butlers). From birth to death, his social world was, with occasional exception (notably his travels abroad), that of the intellectual aristocracy. His relatives, his friends, the clubs and other organisations he joined – none of these took him much outside its ambit.

Galton himself informs us that his experience of kinship links amongst the professional élite was a source of his initial hereditarian convictions.[1] He wrote in his autobiography (1908, 288; see also Galton 1869, v):

> I had been immensely impressed by many obvious cases of heredity among the Cambridge men who were at the University about my own time.

The method of his initial studies of heredity (1865, 1869) was a simple generalisation of his observations of his contemporaries. He traced kinship links amongst those acknowledged to be of exceptional mental ability. By this means he showed that achievement ran in families: the closeness of kinship links amongst the eminent was far greater than would be expected if eminence was distributed at random in the population. This Galton interpreted as proof of the inheritance of mental ability, and he went on to argue (1865, 319–20) that 'the improvement of the breed of mankind is no insuperable difficulty'. The careful, early and fertile marriage of the most able would greatly increase the stock of ability in the population.

Galton's work clearly legitimated the elevated position of the professional élite to which he belonged. His argument was that it was a natural élite, not merely a social one. A chapter of *Hereditary Genius* (1869, 37–49) was devoted to justifying the twin propositions that the most eminent were exceptionally well-endowed by nature, and that there were no overwhelming barriers to the most able achieving eminence, even if they were born outside the élite. So membership of the professional élite was deserved, and those outside it had no reason to complain. People like him – he included both his own and his wife's families amongst his examples of the inheritance of ability – were innately superior.

At the end of his life Galton wrote a novel, *Kantsaywhere*, in which he described his eugenic utopia.[2] This reads, in many respects, as a direct description of the practice and ideals of the intellectual aristocracy. The island of Kantsaywhere is dominated by a benevolent oligarchy; the Eugenic College, that administers it along the lines suggested by Galton's early articles. The College examines eugenic fitness, encourages the early marriage of the 'fit', and deports or segregates the 'unfit'. The population has fully accepted the rule of the College, and 'everyone is classed by everybody else according to their estimate or knowledge of his person and faculties'. The College is trusted and looked up to:

> The Trustees of the College are the sole proprietors of almost all the territory of Kantsaywhere, and they exercise a corresponding influence over the whole population. Their moral ascendancy is paramount. The families of the College and those of the Town are connected by numerous inter-marriages and common interests, so that the relation between them is more like that between the Fellows of a College and the undergraduates, than between the Gown and Town of an English University. In short, Kantsaywhere may be looked upon as an active little community, containing a highly-respected and wealthy guild. (quoted by Pearson, 1914–30. *3A*, 414)

Competitive examinations determine status, the intellectually gifted intermarry, and the dominance of society by the titled and extremely wealthy has been replaced by the dominance of the intellectual élite. In short, the relaxed social control of the university, passing and 'plucking', has been extended over the whole of society.

Utopia aside, eugenic reform necessitated precisely the sort of social change that a rising professional middle class desired:

The best form of civilisation in respect to the improvement of the race, would be one in which society was not costly; where incomes were chiefly derived from professional sources, and not much through inheritance; where every lad had a chance of showing his abilities, and, if highly gifted, was enabled to achieve a first-class education and entrance into professional life, by the liberal help of the exhibitions and scholarships which he had gained in his early youth . . . (Galton 1869, 392)

These policies were precisely those that, according to Annan (1955), the intellectual aristocracy was pressing for, such as the abolition of religious tests and of patronage, and their replacement by competitive examination as a means of allocating jobs. Confident of their own superiority, they assumed that such reforms would open up to them and their children spheres such as the Civil Service that had previously been the province of others.

The hereditarian and meritocratic elements of Galton's eugenic thought thus reveal one aspect of its connection to the social situation of the professional middle class. The naturalism of Galton's eugenics reveals another aspect. From his very first eugenic article, Galton made it quite plain that eugenics was based on a view of human psychology that reduced the mind to a collection of natural abilities and personality traits, and excluded all supernatural concepts such as that of the 'soul':

Most persons seem to have a vague idea that a new element, specially fashioned in heaven, and not transmitted by simple descent, is introduced into the body of every newly-born infant. Such a notion is unfitted to stand upon any scientific basis with which we are acquainted . . . the terms *talent* and *character* are exhaustive: they include the whole of man's spiritual nature so far as we are able to understand it. (Galton 1865, 322)

That basic work of Victorian scientific naturalism, *On the Origin of Species* (Darwin 1859), 'made a marked epoch in my own mental development' (Galton 1908, 298): 'Its effect was to demolish a multitude of dogmatic barriers by a single stroke, and to arouse a spirit of rebellion against all ancient authorities whose positive and unauthenticated statements were contradicted by modern science'.

Galton stood very close to the centre of the Victorian battle between naturalism and traditional religion. When Thomas Henry Huxley and Bishop Wilberforce debated the theory of evolution at the 1860 meeting of the British Association, he was there (Forrest

1974, 84). In the clubs and scientific societies of London his life constantly criss-crossed with those of the other leading naturalistic thinkers: Huxley, Tyndall, Clifford. The role of Galton's eugenics in this battle of cosmologies was perfectly clear. What struck contemporaries as noteworthy about Galton's *Hereditary Genius* was not so much its hereditarianism as its uncompromising naturalism (the Galton Papers, 120, contain a number of interesting responses to it). Galton certainly did little enough to placate the clerics, as when he commented that 'the chief peculiarity in the moral nature of the pious man is its conscious instability' (Galton 1869, 281), or when he claimed to have demonstrated the lack of any statistical evidence for God's intervention on behalf of His representatives on earth. But even had Galton been more tactful, it would have been hard to hide the fundamentally naturalistic thrust of eugenics. Areas of traditional religious authority – the human mind and conscience, the holy sacrament of marriage, the relation of parent to child – were being invaded by science. Galton even saw in eugenics an *alternative* to Christianity – eugenics was to be a naturalistic religion in which individuals would find their places as manifestations of the immortal germ plasm (see, e.g., Galton 1869, 376).

As F. M. Turner (1974a, b and, especially, 1978) has made clear, the Victorian conflict between naturalism and traditional worldviews should not be seen as a purely abstract battle of ideas. What was at stake was *who* should have authority to pronounce on the cosmos, society and people, and who would gain the very wordly advantages that flowed from possession of that authority. If science was to gain the respect due to it, and its practitioners to get the jobs they needed, clerical authority had to be drastically restricted – so reasoned the proponents of scientific naturalism. Naturalism, concludes Turner (1978), was the cosmological weapon of professionalising scientists. By denying the *super*natural, by reducing the universe to what was knowable by science, it established the indispensability and sufficiency of science as a cultural form.

This 'professional dimension' of the conflict between science and religion is quite explicit in Galton's writings. The near monopoly of the church in comfortable professional positions must, he felt, be ended, and an adequately-supported profession of science established. The scientists' role should not be a mere technical one. They should form 'a sort of scientific priesthood throughout the kingdom, whose high duties would have reference to the health and wellbeing of the nation in its broadest sense' (Galton 1874, 260).

Eugenics – as a social practice and as a surrogate religion – can well be seen a system of belief tailored to the needs of just such a 'scientific priesthood'.

To impute to Galton *motives* of calculative self-interest in advancing eugenics is quite unnecessary. It would indeed probably be wrong: he was rich enough never to have to worry about personal job prospects, salaries or fees. Nevertheless, the naturalism of eugenics fitted well the interests of the rising scientific sector of the professional middle class. By the time the Eugenics Education Society was established, mainstream British Christianity (though not Catholicism) had reached an accommodation with science. It was then possible for a churchman like Dean Inge to sit on the Society's Council, and for a leading eugenist such as R. A. Fisher to be a practising Anglican. Later eugenics thus never bore the aggressive tone of Galton's naturalism. Yet it remained a thoroughly naturalistic doctrine, claiming for science the right to a decisive say in matters of marriage and parenthood. In laying the foundations of eugenics, Galton was providing the scientific expert with a potentially fruitful source of power and legitimacy.[3]

Galton's Breakthrough

In order to understand the way eugenic objectives affected statistical theory in Galton's work, it is first necessary to examine the tradition of thought from which Galton initially drew many of his conceptual tools: error theory. This had developed in the eighteenth and nineteenth centuries largely as a mathematical adjunct to sciences such as physics and astronomy. Scientists in these fields had had to acknowledge that it was impossible to measure anything with complete accuracy and exactitude. Measurement was always subject to a degree of error that was – for a given level of observational and experimental technique – irreducible. However, it was normally possible to make a given measurement more than once. The goal of error theory was to take advantage of this to reduce as far as possible, and to give a reliable estimate of the likely amount of, the error in any given quantity.

Thus the error theorists showed that the best estimate of a quantity being measured would usually be the mean of the various measurements of it, and that these measurements typically followed the mathematical distribution they referred to as 'the law of frequency of error' or 'error curve' – the distribution we would now call the 'normal' (see appendix 8). The likely amount of error could be estimated by a quantity they called the 'probable error'. Helen Walker explains (1928, 50):

> The term probable error originated among the German mathematical astronomers who wrote near the beginning of the nineteenth century. The early use of the term is in certain memoirs dealing with astronomy, geodesy, or artillery fire, where the writer is attempting to make the best possible determination of the true position of a point from a series of observations all of which involve an element of error. A deviation from the true position of the point, or more commonly from the mean of the observations, of such a magnitude that, if the number of observations be indefinitely increased, one half of the errors may be expected to be numerically greater and one half numerically less than this value, is then termed the 'probable error'.

These concerns formed the basis for a reasonably major tradition of mathematical work. By 1877 Merriman was able to list 408 books and memoirs in the field, dealing with such topics as attempts to 'prove' the law of frequency of error and the associated 'method of least squares' for finding which straight line best fitted a set of simultaneous measurements of two quantities. Error theory was primarily a Continental specialty. Only 14 per cent of the works listed by Merriman were published in Britain, and a mere handful of British mathematicians devoted much attention to the field.[4] Nevertheless, the basic techniques of error theory were widely known and used in Britain, and it was natural that Galton should turn to them when seeking statistical tools, particularly since the Belgian astronomer and statistician Quetelet had already successfully applied them to human data, showing, for example, that several human physical measurements followed the law of frequency of error.[5]

In *Hereditary Genius* (1869) Galton followed Quetelet in applying the law of error to human beings. He invented no new statistical tools at this stage of his work. His innovation was rather his argument that mental characteristics, as well as physical ones, followed the law of error. Long before the invention of IQ tests, Galton decided that intelligence must follow a Gaussian distribution:

> This is what I am driving at – that analogy clearly shows there must be a fairly constant average mental capacity in the inhabitants of the British Isles, and that deviations from that average – upwards towards genius, and downwards towards stupidity – must follow the law that governs deviations from all true averages. (Galton 1869, 32)

In this analogical extension, the inadequacies of error theory techniques for Galton's purposes were already becoming apparent.[6] For the error theorists, variability ('error') was something to be eliminated, or at least in practice to be controlled and measured. The goals of error theory thus militated against the treatment of variability as a phenomenon in its own right. For Galton, as a eugenist, human variability was the potential source of racial progress. Galton's eugenics thus led in his statistical work to an orientation towards variability as an intrinsically important phenomenon. In the light of this orientation, error theory concepts appeared to be restrictive and misleading, even absurd (Galton 1875a, 35). Most basically, was it really useful to think of an exceptionally able person as a large *error* by nature?

Galton's break with the error theory approach to variability became fully apparent in his paper 'Statistics by Intercomparison' (1875a). In it he sought replacements for the error theory measures of central tendency (the mean) and of variability (the probable error). He did this by the use of relative rank rather than absolute value as the basis of his statistical analysis. He later justified this approach by explicit reference to the characteristics of social life (1889c, 474):

> Relative rank is, however, on the whole, a more important consideration than the absolute amount of performance by which that rank is obtained. It has an importance of its own, because the conditions of life are those of continual competition, in which the man who is relatively strong will always achieve success, while the relatively weak will fail. The absolute difference between their powers matters little.

Galton would rank-order a set of individuals or objects by comparing them one against the other according to some quality.

> The object then found to occupy the middle position of the series must possess the quality in such a degree that the number of objects in the series that have more of it is equal to that of those that have less of it. In other words, it represents the *mean* value of the series in at least one of the many senses in which that term may be used. (1875a, 34; Galton's emphasis)

This value Galton was later (1883, 52) to term the 'median value'.[7] To measure variability Galton used what were later called the quartiles: those objects such that one-quarter and three-quarters of the objects had smaller values of the quality in question. Half the inter-quartile distance was then a useful measure of the variability of the objects. Although Galton generally continued in his published work to use the terms 'mean' and 'probable error', in his actual calculations the median and inter-quartile distance are more frequent (see, for example, Galton 1888b).[8]

Galton's negative evaluation of error theory and his introduction of rank-ordering methods in statistics can therefore be traced to his having goals different from those of error theory. They can also be taken as indicators of a new approach to the statistics of distributions. Even though his followers such as Pearson preferred, for reasons of mathematical tractability, to use the earlier formulae (mean instead of median, etc.), this shift of focus was to continue. Thus there was a gradual transition from use of the term 'probable error' to the term 'standard deviation' (which is free of the implication that a deviation is in any sense an error), and from the term 'law of error' to the term 'normal distribution'.[9]

Galton himself became aware of the divergence between his approach and that of the error theorists, and of the reasons for it. He wrote in his autobiography that some of his applications of the law of error seemed 'to be comprehended with difficulty by mathematicians'.

> The primary objects of the Gaussian Law of Error were exactly opposed, in one sense, to those to which I applied them [sic]. They were to get rid of, or to provide a just allowance for errors. But these errors or deviations were the very things I wanted to preserve and to know about. (1908, 305)

Galton's work represents, however, much more than a shift in general focus in statistical theory. The error theorists had worked predominantly with distributions of one variable or, at most, of mutually independent variables.[10] Galton provided, in the concepts of regression and correlation, the key tools for the treatment of two dependent variables, and made the advance to the general treatment of any number of dependent variables a relatively easy technical problem. His work in this area arose directly from his eugenic concerns.

In the last chapter of *Hereditary Genius*, Galton discussed the relationship between parent and offspring generations. He envisaged the development of a predictive, quantitative theory of descent. It might be possible, for example, to deduce the average contribution of each ancestor to the hereditary make-up of a child:

> Suppose, for the sake merely of a very simple numerical example, that a child acquired one-tenth of his nature from

individual variation, and inherited the remaining nine-tenths from his parents. It follows, that his two parents would have handed down only nine-tenths of nine-tenths, or 81/100 from his grandparents, 729/1000 from his great-grandparents, and so on; the numerator of the fraction increasing in each successive step less rapidly than the denominator, until we arrive at a vanishing value of the fraction. (1869, 371)

At first Galton felt that this theory could be developed by physiological theorising, in particular by the use of Charles Darwin's 'provisional hypothesis of pangenesis' (Darwin 1868, 2, 357–404, especially 374). According to this, there circulated in the body bearers of hereditary characteristics called 'gemmules', which came together in the sperm and ova. Galton tried to test the theory in rabbits. If it were true, he reasoned, the offspring of a rabbit that had received a massive transfusion of the blood of another rabbit should show a tendency to resemble the latter rather than the former. Galton was unable to find any such effect, and concluded that the theory was untrue.[11] He put forward his own corrected version of pangenesis, without freely circulating gemmules (Galton 1875b). This alternative theory had the additional feature of effectively denying the possibility of the inheritance of acquired characteristics, a possibility that had been affirmed in Darwin's original theory of pangenesis and that Galton had apparently never liked.[12] While Galton's new theory made possible what is arguably the first clear statement of what is now called the genotype/phenotype distinction (*ibid.*, 94), it did not lead to the development of a mathematical law connecting parent and offspring generations. To find this, Galton had to turn to direct experiment.

Ideally, Galton would have preferred to use human data; however, these were as yet unavailable, and he turned to a more convenient alternative. He began work on sweetpea seeds, though

> It was anthropological evidence that I desired, caring only for the seeds as means of throwing light on heredity in man. (Galton 1885a, 507; quoted by Cowan 1972a, 517)

His scheme was to grow sweetpeas from seeds of a measured size, and to measure the seeds produced by these plants. The second generation of seeds could be considered the offspring of the first. Galton would thus have the data for a direct numerical examination of the relationship between two generations connected by heredity. He began the experiment by taking several thousand sweetpea seeds and weighing them individually, thus obtaining the mean and probable error of the distribution of weight. He then made up several sets of seeds. Each set consisted of seven packets, each packet containing ten seeds of exactly the same weight. The weights were chosen so that one packet contained very small seeds (with weights given by the population mean minus three times the probable error), the next slightly larger (weight equal to the population mean minus twice the probable error) and so on up to a packet with giant seeds (weight equal to the population mean plus three times the probable error). Nine of these sets were made up, and Galton sent them to friends to grow. Two sets failed, but he obtained the produce of the other seven sets.

He presented the results of the experiment in a lecture delivered at the Royal Institution on 9 February 1877 (Galton 1877; the data on which the statements in this lecture were based were never fully published).[13] Galton said that an exceedingly simple law connected parent and offspring seeds. Let the mean of the parent generation be M and its probable error be Q. Then the parent seeds fall into the seven categories $M-3Q$, $M-2Q$, $M-Q$, M, $M+Q$, $M+2Q$, $M+3Q$. The offspring of each category of parent had weights distributed according to the law of frequency of error, and the probable error of each group of offspring was the same: the offspring of the smallest seeds were no less variable than the offspring of the largest seeds. But the *mean* weight of each class of offspring was less extreme than that of their parents. As Galton put it, 'reversion' had taken place. Further, this reversion was linear. That is, the seven parent categories gave rise to seven offspring classes with means $M-3bQ$, $M-2bQ$, $M-bQ$, M, $M+bQ$, $M+2bQ$, $M+3bQ$, where b is a positive constant less than one.[14]

A hypothetical example may make this clearer. Suppose the parent generation to have mean 100 units and probable error 20 units. Then we have seven sets of seeds of weights 40, 60, 80, 100, 120, 140, 160 units. The mean weight of the offspring of the parent seeds weighing 40 units is not 40 units but 70 units; the offspring of the parents weighing 60 units have mean weight 80 units; of those weighing 80 units, 90; of those weighing 100, 100; of those weighing 120, 110; of those weighing 140, 120; of those weighing 160, 130. In this case $b = \frac{1}{2}$; the average offspring seeds differ from the mean by only half as much as their parents.

On the face of it, this is an odd result. Does it not mean that the offspring generation will be clustered round the mean much more closely than the parent generation? Galton was, of course, well aware that the curve representing the distribution of a particular character in a species ordinarily remains virtually identical from one generation to another (Galton 1869, 27). He argued that linear reversion to the mean was in fact part of the process by which the stability of the distribution was maintained from generation to generation. The 'compression' of the distribution due to reversion would be balanced by the 'expansion' due to fraternal variability (that is, to the variability *within* groups of brothers and sisters). [Galton suggested that this process could be seen as having, in theory, two parts. We start with a parent generation with probable error c_1. Reversion we imagine as 'compressing' this distribution to one with a probable error of bc_1 (b is less than one). We now imagine each parent as tending to breed true to the (reverted) parental type, but the offspring of each parentage having a probable error f. The 'error' of the offspring generation (c_2) will thus be the resultant of the two independent 'errors' bc_1 and f, and, according to a well-known error theory result:

$$c_2{}^2 = b^2 c_1{}^2 + f^2$$

Parent and offspring generations can then have equal variability ($c_1 = c_2$) provided $f^2 = (1 - b^2)c_1{}^2$: this is a quantitative statement of the balancing of fraternal variability and the reduction in variability due to reversion.]

Unlike sweetpea seeds, human offspring have more than one parent. Galton found a neat device for handling this problem: the mid-parent. The mid-parent was a fictitious amalgam of the characteristics of father and mother. Thus the mid-parental height was the mean of the paternal and maternal heights, with female height adjusted to allow for the greater mean and probable error of male height. Offspring could now be considered as descended by uni-parental inheritance from this mid-parent. The population of mid-parents has, because of its construction, a smaller variability than either paternal or maternal populations. [To see why this is so, let paternal height be x, let maternal height (adjusted to make it comparable with paternal height) be y, and let the probable error of the paternal generation (which is equal to the probable error of the adjusted maternal generation) be c. The formula for mid-parental height is simply $\frac{1}{2}(x + y)$. Using the same error theory result as before, the square of the probable error of the mid-parental population is given by $\frac{1}{4}(c^2 + c^2)$ if we can assume paternal and maternal height to be independent (that is, no assortative mating). This gives a probable error for the mid-parental population of $c/\sqrt{2}$, not c.]

In retrospect, this paper (Galton 1877) can be seen as the first stage of Galton's revolution in statistical theory: his first development of the concept that was later to be called linear regression. However, Galton did not at the time see himself as doing anything other than contributing to knowledge about heredity, as is indicated by his use of the biological term 'reversion'. Further, it may appear from the account so far given that the 'law of reversion' was reached purely empirically; that Galton simply looked at the data and deduced the law. This is most unlikely. Galton had a definite prior notion of the kind of law he was looking for: a simple, predictive, mathematical statement of the relationship between parent and offspring generations. There is indeed reason to believe that his data did not unequivocally 'suggest' the law of reversion. Some later comments by Galton indicate this. Thus he wrote (1885c, 259):

> I possessed less evidence than I desired to prove the bettering of the produce of very small seeds.

His data was not even sufficiently good to enable him to give a numerical value for the coefficient of reversion:

> The exact ratio of regression remained a little doubtful, owing to variable influences; therefore I did not attempt to define it. (1885a, 507)

It would therefore seem that Galton was seeking to show order in his data, rather than the data spontaneously manifesting order.[15]

The Bivariate Normal Distribution and Correlation

By the end of the 1870s Galton had broken with the error theory approach to statistics. He had also made the first decisive step, with his law of reversion, in developing a statistical theory of two dependent variables. The 1880s saw him consolidate this early work, develop the theory of the bivariate normal distribution, and move from the concept of reversion to that of correlation.

In the early 1880s Galton began to seek anthropometric data of direct relevance to problems of human heredity. This data could, he felt, be of other than purely scientific use. As the notion that human characteristics were predominantly hereditary became more and more established, it was 'highly desirable to give more attention than has been customary hitherto to investigate and define the capacities of each individual' (1882, 333). With this information, Galton felt that a better fit of individuals and their social roles could be achieved. Galton called for the establishment of 'anthropometric laboratories' in which individuals and whole families could have a wide range of physical and mental traits examined and measured.

In 1884 Galton set up just such a laboratory at the International Health Exhibition held in South Kensington. By 1885 over 9,000 people had paid the small fee and been measured for keenness of sight, colour sense, 'judgment of eye', hearing, highest audible note, breathing power, strength of pull and squeeze, swiftness of blow, span of arms, height standing and sitting, and weight (Galton 1885b). The offer of public prizes for the best-kept 'family records' brought in another body of important anthropometric data (Forrest 1974, 179–80).

With this data Galton was able, in effect, to repeat the sweetpea study on human beings. He revealed his first results in his Presidential Address to the Anthropological Section of the British Association (1885a). On the basis of the family records already obtained he claimed:

> An analysis of the records fully confirms and goes far beyond the conclusions I obtained from the seeds. (1885a, 507)

The particular human trait he chose to investigate was stature. It was easy to measure, relatively constant during adult life, its distribution closely followed the law of frequency of error, and assortative mating according to stature was, Galton argued, negligible. Galton had to hand the stature measurements of 928 adults and of their 205 parentages. For each parentage he calculated the height of the mid-parent by multiplying the mother's height by 1.08 and taking the mean of that and the father's height. He was then able to investigate the relationship of offspring height to mid-parental height.

Galton found that this human data showed clearly the pattern more ambiguously manifested by the sweetpea data. A relationship of linear reversion (or 'regression' as he now called it)[16] existed between offspring and mid-parental heights. A mid-parental deviation of one unit implied an expected offspring deviation of $^2/_3$ of a unit ($b = {}^2/_3$), and the probable error of the offspring of each class of mid-parent was constant.

Galton did not stop at this confirmation of his earlier result. On examining the joint frequency distribution of offspring and mid-parental heights, he noticed some strange patterns:

> I found it hard at first to catch the full significance of the entries in the table, which had curious relations that were very interesting to investigate. They came out distinctly when I 'smoothed'

the entries by writing at each intersection of a horizontal column with a vertical one, the sum of the entries of the four
adjacent squares, and using these to work upon. I then noticed
. . . that lines drawn through entries of the same value formed a
series of concentric and similar ellipses . . . (1885c, 254–5)
Galton guessed that these patterns might be the clue to a deeper
understanding of regression. They might, for example, help him
understand why, when he reversed the direction of his analysis and
examined the distribution of mid-parental heights for a given offspring height, he found a relationship of regression, but with a
coefficient of $^1/_3$ and not $^2/_3$ (1885a, 509).

Galton decided to try to construct, from what he knew of regression, an equation for the joint frequency surface that had displayed
these elliptical patterns. Doubting his own mathematical powers,
he sought the assistance of the Cambridge mathematician, J.D.
Hamilton Dickson. In formulating the problem for Hamilton Dickson, Galton in fact more or less solved it. Hamilton Dickson was
able to write down directly the equation Galton needed (Galton
1886, 63–6) – see appendix 3.

This equation we would now call the bivariate normal distribution, but the modern reader might not immediately recognise it as
such; that is because the formula is now usually written in terms of r,
the coefficient of correlation of x and y. To modern eyes, the step
from 'regression' to 'correlation' seems an obvious one. But Galton
had no immediate motivation to extend his analysis. His eugenic
researches had thrown up specific puzzles, which he had, in his eyes,
adequately solved. It was to take a further impetus to make him
move from 'regression' to 'correlation'.

The stimulus that led to his work on correlation was a system of
personal identification, proposed by the French anthropometrician
and criminologist Alphonse Bertillon, which consisted in compiling
measurements of selected parts of the body. Galton's interest in the
topic of personal identification (another product of which was of
course the fingerprint system) was in part the result of his general
concern with heredity and family likeness:

. . . one of the inducements to making these inquiries into
personal identification has been to discover independent features suitable for hereditary investigation . . . it is not improb-
able, and worth taking pains to inquire whether each person
may not carry visibly about his body undeniable evidence of his
parentage and near kinships. (Galton 1888a, 202)

Bertillon's system was clearly of importance, but one aspect of it worried Galton. Its effectiveness would be reduced to the extent that the component measurements of the system were not independent:

> The bodily measurements are so dependent on one another that we cannot afford to neglect small distinctions. Thus long feet and long middle-fingers usually go together . . . No attempt has yet been made to estimate the degree of their interdependence. I am therefore having the above measurements (with slight necessary variation) recorded at my anthropometric laboratory for the purpose of doing so. (Galton 1888a, 175)

Galton would indeed have been familiar with the well-known biological principle of the interdependence (or correlation) of organs. Thus Darwin had written in *The Variation of Animals and Plants under Domestication*:

> All the parts of the organisation are to a certain extent connected or correlated together; but the connection may be so slight that it hardly exists, as with compound animals or buds on the same tree. (1868, *2*, 319)

In his copy Galton underlined the words 'are to a certain extent' and 'so slight'.[17] With the mass of data from the Anthropometric Laboratory (as well as Bertillon's own measurements), Galton was in a position to investigate the *exact* extent of the correlation of various parts of the human body. The results of the investigation (which examined such measurements as stature and cubit) were for him a happy surprise. As he told the Anthropological Institute on 22 January 1889:

> . . . it became evident almost from the first that I had unconsciously explored the very same ground before. No sooner had I begun to tabulate the data than I saw that they ran in just the same form as those that referred to family likeness in stature, which were submitted to you two years ago. A very little reflection made it clear that family likeness was nothing more than a particular case of the wide subject of correlation, and that the whole of the reasoning already bestowed upon the special case of family likeness was equally applicable to correlation in its most general aspect. (Galton 1889a, 403–4)

The previous month he had presented the results of his work to the Royal Society:

> 'Co-relation or correlation of structure' is a phrase much used in biology, and not least in that branch of it which refers to

heredity, and the idea is even more frequently present than the phrase; but I am not aware of any present attempt to define it clearly, to trace its mode of action in detail, or to show how to measure its degree. (Galton 1888b, 135)

Galton had found that height regressed on cubit, and cubit on height, in the same way as offspring height regressed on mid-parental height. If height and, say, left cubit are both measured from their respective population means, then the mean cubit of individuals with height x would be $\beta_{21}x$, where β_{21} is a constant. Similarly individuals with cubits y would have mean height $\beta_{12}y$. So far so good. But β_{12} is not in general equal to β_{21}, so neither β_{12} nor β_{21} can serve as a measure of the dependence or correlation of height and cubit. The measure must, intuitively, have a property of reciprocity: the correlation of height and cubit must be the same as the correlation of cubit and height. As Galton already knew, the lack of reciprocity of coefficients of regression was due to the different probable errors of the two variables involved ($\beta_{21}/\beta_{12} = \sigma_2^2/\sigma_1^2$, as discussed in appendix 3). Thus the next step was easy – now that Galton had a reason to make it. If he scaled the variables so that σ_1 was equal to σ_2, then β_{21} was made equal to β_{12}:

> These relations [of regression] are not numerically reciprocal, but the exactness of the co-relation becomes established when we have transmuted the inches or other measurement of the cubit and of the stature into units dependent on their respective scales of variability. We thus cause a long cubit and an equally long stature, as compared to the general run of cubits and statures, to be designated by an identical scale-value. The particular unit that I shall employ is the value of the probable error of any single measure in its own group.
> (Galton 1888b, 136)

After each variable had been scaled by division by its own probable error, Galton found that some simple relationships held. Either variable regressed linearly on the other, and the coefficients of regression were equal. This latter result followed of necessity from his procedure, but Galton confirmed it empirically. Galton called the mutual value of the coefficients of regression r. The value of r would always be less than one, he claimed.[18] Finally, Galton concluded that 'r measures the closeness of the co-relation' (1888b, 145).

Much work, of course, remained to be done on the theory of correlation: for example, the invention by Pearson (1896) of an efficient non-graphical method of calculating the coefficient of correlation. The essential breakthrough, however, had been made. Even though direct eugenic concerns were not present in Galton's work on correlation, his interest in personal identification was partly inspired by eugenics, and the intellectual tools used by Galton – the theory of reversion/regression and of the bivariate normal distribution – had themselves been created directly out of Galton's eugenic researches. Galton's eugenics thus accounts at least in part for his invention of correlation.

Galton and the Error Theorists

The preceding two sections have hopefully shown the detailed interconnections of Galton's statistics and eugenics: the way that eugenics informed and guided his statistical theorising. The closeness of this connection is sufficient to suggest that it is reasonable to see Galton's eugenics not merely as providing the motive for his statistical work, but also as conditioning the content of it. Yet a study of his work alone is not sufficient to establish this latter point, for the objection can be raised that others had developed the same theory, even though they had no eugenic concerns. It is thus necessary to enquire a little more deeply and to compare Galton's work with the preceding work that most closely approached it.

This was the work done in the tradition of error theory, notably by a French naval officer, astronomer and physicist, Auguste Bravais (1811–63), and by a Dutch civil engineer, mathematician and military scientist, Charles Schols (1849–97).[19] Bravais and Schols are credited with having discovered the bivariate and trivariate normal distributions (Seal 1967). Karl Pearson, who first drew attention in Britain to the work of Bravais, said that 'the fundamental theorems of correlation were for the first time and almost exhaustively discussed by Bravais' (Pearson 1896, 261). Helen Walker (1929, 96–8) describes Bravais as a kind of Columbus, discovering correlation without fully realising that he had done so:

> . . . it is known that [Bravais] set forth the mathematics of the normal correlation surface three decades before the idea of correlation had been conceived . . . Bravais recognised the existence of a relationship, a 'correlation', between his principal variables, but gave it merely passing notice . . . [he] remained unaware of the stupendous idea in whose vicinity his mind was hovering . . . he might, with one leap of creative imagination, have pounced squarely upon this conception . . .

Lancaster (1972, 293) claims that Bravais 'derived normal correlations', albeit on the basis of somewhat restricted assumptions, but, like Walker, notes that he 'did not define a coefficient of correlation'.

So scientists with very different goals seem to have made effectively the same 'discovery'. Galton's eugenics, or the error theory concerns of Bravais and Schols, seem thus to be relegated simply to the status of factors explaining a particular area of statistical mathematics, and are denied any role in explaining what was found there. Bravais and Schols may admittedly not have 'pounced squarely' on the coefficient of correlation; on the other hand, they, better mathematicians than Galton, were able to give results for three, as well as two, variables. But before admitting the validity of this viewpoint, let us examine in more detail what Bravais and Schols in fact did.

While most error theorists dealt with errors in the measurement of one quantity, on occasion it was necessary to examine two or more simultaneously occurring errors. Thus astronomers or surveyors had not simply to measure the length of lines, but to estimate the positions of points on a two-dimensional plane or in three-dimensional space. This might well involve no fundamental stretching of basic error theory concepts. If the position of a point in a plane could be found by measuring first its coordinate in one direction, and then its coordinate in another, in such a way that these two measurements were independent of each other, no problem ensued. The resultant errors were independent of each other; their joint law of error could be obtained simply by multiplying together their two separate laws of error.

However, as Bravais (1846) pointed out, people like surveyors and astronomers had on occasion to determine the position of a point not by direct measurement of its coordinates but by combining together several basic observations (he called them m, n, p, . . .) to estimate the coordinates x and y. The basic observations m, n, p, . . . may well be mutually independent, but if one or more of them had to be used in the estimates of *both x and y*, then the errors of x and y would no longer be independent. 'Une corrélation' (*ibid.*, 263) would be produced, and the established error theory methods then gave no way of deducing the joint law of error of x and y.

Bravais set to work to derive that law of error. He assumed that the basic observations m, n, p, . . . were independent, and that each followed the law of frequency of error; he further assumed that the equations from which x and y were derived from m, n, p, . . . took a simple linear form. From these assumptions he derived the form of the joint law of error of x and y, showing that it had an extra term not found in the ordinary case when x and y are independent (see appendix 3). The form of his joint law of error – and this is crucial to the interpretations of his work just quoted – was identical to that constructed by Galton and Hamilton Dickson. But thus far Bravais had only the *form* of his law; it contained four unknown coefficients whose value he had then to determine (*ibid.*, 268–9).

The modern statistician, acquainted with Galton's work on the bivariate normal distribution, would be in no doubt what Bravais should have done next. He should have evaluated his coefficients – especially the coefficient of the crucial extra term – in terms of the coefficient of correlation of x and y, or of their coefficients of regression, thus fully displaying the dependence of x on y (and vice versa). Bravais did nothing of the sort. He evaluated his coefficients in terms of the probable errors of the basic observations $m, n, p, \ldots$ and the parameters of the transformation by which x and y had been obtained from these basic observations. His passing reference to the 'corrélation' of x and y was not followed by any attempt to study or measure this 'corrélation'.

In terms of the goals of error theory, what Bravais did makes perfect sense. He evaluated the coefficients in the equation of his law of error using the quantities that the surveyor or astronomer would have had numerical values for: the probable errors of the basic measurements and the parameters of the equations used to construct x and y from these basic measurements. For him to have done what Galton did – examined the dependence of x and y in order to know the influence of one on the other – would have made little sense.

In repudiating his earlier suggestion that Bravais had partially anticipated Galton's work on correlation, Karl Pearson (1920b, 192) notes that Bravais never considered the possibility that basic observations might be other than independent, and claims that the 'same criticism applies to all the treatment of normal surfaces by later writers' in the error theory tradition. However, as Seal (1967) points out, this was not fully true of the work of Schols (1886; first published in Dutch in 1875). His work concerned 'errors' in artillery fire, and he pointed out that one should not assume that errors in different directions would be independent (1886, 174). (Thus overshooting the target might for example be typically associated with the shell landing on the right of it.) Unlike Bravais, who had assumed independent basic errors, he used a model that assumed only that errors in the coordinates of a point in space were the resultant of a large number of small errors.

He followed a rather loose process of analogical reasoning to show that despite the lack of independence of the errors in different directions, axes could be found with respect to which errors could be treated as if they were independent (see appendix 3). He was content with this conclusion, and made no attempt to formulate an expression for the degree of influence of the error in one direction on that in another. Again, this makes perfect sense. He had shown that if you chose your axes correctly, the standard error theory model applied. The problem was then satisfactorily solved.

How, then, should we assess the work of Bravais and Schols? I feel that it makes most sense simply to see them as workers in a tradition whose goals were very different from those of Galton. As Kuhn (1970) would put it, they were doing 'normal science', extending the established mathematics of error theory into a new area, that of dependent errors. Both were concerned to establish a law of error for dependent errors, and both did so, albeit in somewhat different ways. The point is that for neither of them was statistical dependence in itself the focus of attention, as it was for Galton. It was a problem to be solved, or more accurately dissolved, by showing that the existing resources of error theory could, with a little ingenuity, adequately cope with it: by reference back to basic independent observations (Bravais), or simply by choice of the right set of axes (Schols).

By comparison, the demands of eugenics research were such that Galton's work, if it were to be successful, had to develop radically new concepts. As a eugenist, his central concern was with the effect of the characteristics of one generation on that of the next. The statistical dependence of two variables (of, say, offspring height on mid-parental height) thus became crucial to his research. It was no marginal problem to be dissolved by reference to independent variables. Indeed, were offspring characteristics genuinely independent of parental characteristics, then eugenic intervention in reproduction would be pointless: the very basis of eugenics was the belief in the dependence of the characteristics of the child on those of the parent. Eugenics made the understanding and measurement of statistical dependence *as a phenomenon in its own right* a central goal of statistical theory.

So Galton's statistical theorising was informed by a goal absent in the work of the error theorists. This goal – or its absence – affected not merely the choice of area of research but also the detailed technical mathematics employed, as we have seen by comparing Galton's work with that of Bravais and Schols. Further, the presence of this goal has to be explained in terms of the needs of eugenics. And Galton's eugenics reflected the social interests of the group of élite professionals to which he belonged. Hence we have here an instance of the effect of social interests on the conceptual development of statistical theory.

4

Karl Pearson

. . . . .
. : .
.

On the face of it, applying the sociology of knowledge to an individual such as Karl Pearson may seem an unlikely enterprise. In no sense can Pearson be said to be an 'average' late Victorian professional. Few of his contemporaries could match his range of intellectual interests: his publications include poetry, a 'passion play', art history, studies of the Reformation and mediaeval Germany, philosophy, biography and essays on politics, quite apart from his contributions – in the form of over four hundred articles – to mathematical physics, statistics and biology. His commitment to freethought rather than to orthodox religion, his public espousal of socialism and his questioning of the relationship between the sexes in Victorian society all placed him very close to the margin of – though never actually outside – the boundaries of respectable society.

So if we see the sociology of knowledge as necessarily involving propositions such as 'all (or most) believers in situation type z adopt beliefs of type x' (Laudan 1977, 217), then we can hardly hope for it to throw much light on Pearson. But, as explained in the introduction, there is no need to restrict a sociological approach to an empiricist framework such as that. Without claiming that the sociology of knowledge can in any deterministic sense *explain* the beliefs of particular people, we can nevertheless sometimes usefully discuss individual beliefs in social perspective.

Goldmann's work, especially Goldmann (1964), suggests one interesting way of doing this. If our sociology of knowledge proposes tendencies in belief that need not actually be manifest in the majority of individuals most of the time, then we may actually get more insight by looking at exceptional moments in time and at exceptional individuals rather than at normal periods and average people.[1] If we are concerned, say, not with what most workers appear to think most of the time, but with the social determinants of class consciousness, it may well be worthwhile to examine times of particularly intense unrest: processes usually hidden may then be manifest. And if we are looking at normal times, the lives and statements of unusual people may reveal submerged aspects of the situation of the mass.

Certainly this approach has its dangers. The most obvious is to deduce *a priori* what the 'correct' beliefs for a group are, and to dismiss those periods and people in which they are not to be found as instances of 'false consciousness'. The study of the actual dialectic of belief and social experience is then reduced to a sterile tale of continual advances towards, or retreats from, 'ideal' consciousness. Further, it is too easy to slip into thinking of Goldmann's 'exceptional individuals' purely psychologically – for example, to see them as 'exceptionally intelligent'. If we are to proceed, we need ways of thinking that avoid these errors.

One such way may be to remember that all societies of any complexity are structured in more than one way and at more than one level. Thus we can identify within any given society an *overall structure,* such as a class structure, and a *fine structure,* consisting of all sorts of more particular gender, occupational, kinship or genera-tional structures, and of specific institutions such as state appara-tuses, educational institutions, political parties or trade unions.[2] If our theory seeks to relate ideas to the overall class structure, then we must expect the fine structure of the society, insofar as it does not run parallel to the overall structure, to generate particular interests and experiences and thus to cut across and 'suppress' this relation. The fine structure produces 'noise' from the point of view of our overall pattern of explanation. So perhaps we can expect 'excep-tional individuals' to be found in structural locations and historical situations where the 'distorting' effects of the fine structure are least. It is clearly impossible without much study to specify these locations and situations. We can at present identify exceptional individuals only on the basis of their 'thought' – the available record of what they wrote and said. So they cannot provide an independent check on the validity of our theory, nor can we claim to have explained why they believed what they did. But if our theory is correct we should at least expect it to provide a coherent and convincing interpretation of the 'thought' of these individuals.

Below, I investigate the extent to which Karl Pearson's 'thought' can be seen as, in this sense, 'exceptional'. My account is based, ultimately, on the hypothesised structural connection between the social position of the professional middle class, its interests and certain patterns of belief, that was discussed in chapter 2. But I hope that detailed consideration of this individual case may throw further light on this connection.

Pearson's Politics

Karl Pearson's political views seem to have been formulated largely in the period 1879–88. In the former year, aged 22, he was placed Third Wrangler in the Cambridge Mathematics Tripos and subsequently was awarded a Fellowship of King's College that supported him financially until in 1884 he became Professor of Applied Mathematics and Mechanics at University College, London. The intervening years were of travel and study (especially in Germany), thought, lecturing and writing, and were years in which mathematics seemed to concern him much less than his general political, philosophical and historical studies. In 1888 he published *The Ethic of Freethought*, a collection of essays in which his political position emerges clearly.

His childhood was not exceptional for the Victorian professional middle class. The son of a lawyer – an upwardly mobile, independently minded, hardworking, rather stern man – Karl Pearson seems to have been a delicate, serious-minded, academically oriented child.[3] In his undergraduate years he passed through the not unusual experience of a loss of Christian faith: 'I think I have definitely rejected Christianity', he wrote (1877, 33). In 1877–79 he rebelled, individually but ultimately successfully, against compulsory divinity lectures in King's College.[4] Secular, social concerns began to replace religious ones: 'our god is the welfare of the race' (*ibid.*, 40). The poverty and squalor of Victorian England, and the complacent superficiality of Cambridge University, are themes that began to appear in his thought.[5] Yet no clear alternative to the Victorian conventional wisdom emerged in his writing.

The spur to the development of such an alternative seems to have been his contact, in 1879–80, with German social democracy. In Heidelberg, seeking practice in German conversation, he became friendly with Raphael Wertheimer, a social democratic student. The middle-class youth from a Britain still awaiting the 'socialist revival' of the 1880s discovered a new world of radical politics, *Das Kapital*, and police searches.[6] Rapidly, Pearson became acquainted with the range of socialist thought from insurrectionist anarchism to

Bismarckian 'state socialism', and he began to construct his own political position.

This position was expressed in his published and unpublished writings from the early 1880s. In the categories of the time, it was undoubtedly a socialist position. Yet it was by no means a revolutionary one. Pearson saw the socialist movement as split into what we would now call 'revolutionary' and 'reformist' camps, and it was clearly with the latter that he identified himself. *Laissez-faire* capitalism was, he felt, a system of inefficient, anarchic competition. It had to be replaced by a system of state planning, with all capital concentrated in the hands of the state. This change must not be attempted by revolutionary means, but by slow and gradual reform, with the capitalists being compensated for the loss of their property Class conflict should be avoided, and the socialist should instead preach class harmony and the loyalty that all citizens owed to the state. There was no question of the state 'withering away' under socialism: it was envisaged as still a power over society, a body of officials charged with planning and administration.

Of course, this was a political position that was soon to become prominent in Britain with the formation of the Fabian Society – though it must be emphasised that Pearson's views were developed independently of, and prior to, its establishment. Pearson never, to my knowledge, joined the Fabian Society, yet he was politically closest to it. He was a personal acquaintance of leading Fabians such as Sidney Webb and George Bernard Shaw, and in his published writings (especially Pearson 1890) showed considerable sympathy for the Fabians' cause.

As suggested in chapter 2, Fabianism can, following the work of Hobsbawm (1968), be analysed as a political expression of the interests of the emerging stratum of white-collar and professional employees. Frustrated by *laissez-faire,* they turned to socialism, but to the élitist socialism of planners, administrators and experts, involving no 'transfers of class allegiance', no commitment to the manual working class.

Pearson's early writings form interesting evidence for this point of view. Pearson described the existence of four major social classes, based respectively on 'birth', 'capital', 'learning' and manual labour (1881–82, 2). He further divided the working class into 'the better class of working man' and 'the dumb, helpless masses of our great towns, the Proletariat pure and simple' (1881b, 269). Pearson's viewpoint had two major poles. The 'positive' pole was the class based on 'learning', a class whose interests were quite distinct from those of the classes based on 'birth' and 'capital': 'the man who earns his money by his brains has just as little capital as the workman' (1881–82, 6). The 'negative' pole was the 'Proletariat pure and simple'. It was to be despised for its degeneracy, but also – even more importantly – to be feared because of its insurrectionary potential.

In the tension of these two poles Pearson's political position was worked out. An article for the *Cambridge Review* entitled 'Anarchy' (Pearson 1881b) reveals this particularly clearly. The London poor were seen as a revolutionary threat:

> Those emaciated beings, weak and feeble as they look, have power to break the half-inch of glass which separates them from the weapons they require . . . (*ibid.*, 269)

The consequence of such a revolution would be catastrophic: 'night, blackest night'. To ward it off, 'the revolution must be carried through from above'. A society stratified in terms of wealth could perhaps be replaced by one stratified in terms of 'education and culture':

> . . . while power material shall be divided as equally as may be between the various classes, power intellectual shall form a scale on which the necessary graduation of society may take place. Power intellectual shall determine whether the life-calling of a man is to scavenge the streets, or to guide the nation. (*ibid.*, 270)

But it was unlikely, Pearson concluded pessimistically, that 'the ruling Bourgeoisie' would easily accept a change from plutocracy to meritocracy. 'We seem as it were drifting helplessly onward to the brink of a terrible and unexplored abyss . . . (*ibid.*, 270)

Elsewhere (1886b, 407), Pearson called for a common front of professionals and manual workers against the idle rich:

> . . . how little is the conception of comradeship between the hand-worker and the brain-worker generally grasped! When will the two unite to expel the drone from the community . . . ?

Intellectuals in Britain should follow the example of their Russian counterparts and ally themselves to popular movements. The rationale of this alliance was, as the Russian author quoted by Pearson claimed, self-interest rather than altruism:

> If the peasants prosper, the educated classes will prosper also; if the peasants become masters of their destinies, enjoy freedom and real and not fictitious self-government, the educated

men will acquire all the political and social influence due to their capacity as managers, teachers and political representatives of the masses.

(S. Stepniak, quoted by Pearson 1886b, 407)

There was a governing class in Britain, Pearson argued (1888, 348), which was composed of the 'owners of land and owners of capital'. The 'educative' and 'productive' classes were excluded from power by this governing class. Pearson called for the transition from a social system based on wealth to one based on labour. But this did not mean simply manual labour:

> The man who puts cargo into a ship is no more or less a labourer than the captain who directs her course across the ocean; nor is either of them more of a labourer than the mathematician or astronomer whose calculations and observations enable the captain to know which direction he shall take . . . (*ibid.*, 353)

Because all kinds of labour are necessary parts of an integrated division of labour, it must be an 'axiom' of socialism that 'all forms of labour are equally honourable'. Nevertheless, there was little doubt in Pearson's mind that head work was, in the long run, more important than hand work.

> There is labour of the hand, which provides necessaries for all society; there is labour of the head, which produces all we term *progress*, and enables any individual society to maintain its place in the battle of life – the labour which educates and organises. (*ibid.*, 355)

So Pearson's socialism in no way implied a shift of identification to the working class. It was to the class of 'head workers' that he owed allegiance. He was no egalitarian, and his socialism might well be described, like that of the group of German *Katheder-Socialisten* that he admired, as a 'socialism of professors'.[7]

Pearson's political position can thus be analysed as one appropriate to the interests of a rising professional middle class. It was a strategy for containing revolutionary pressure by a process of gradual reform, while slowly edging the bourgeoisie out of positions of power, and replacing a society based on wealth by one based on knowledge and mental skills. Further, in its full development, Pearson's position can in a certain sense be seen as more consistent than the Fabianism of the Fabian Society. Thus, one crucial issue on which Pearson differed from the majority of Fabians was that of political democracy and the extension of the franchise: the Fabians saw universal suffrage as the path to socialism, but Pearson did not.[8]

Reviewing the first edition of *Fabian Essays,* he wrote (1890, 198):

> Personally dreading an uneducated democracy as much as a prejudiced aristocracy . . . we cannot but deprecate this identification of socialist and social-democrat.

Instead, Pearson's ideal was, as he expressed it elsewhere (1888, 322), 'the cautious direction of social progress by the selected few'.

What are we to make of this divergence? Aside from this point, Pearson's views on socialist strategy coincided almost exactly with the Fabians'. It was not the case that Pearson had a more jaundiced view of the working class than did most Fabians. For example, in 1889 the Fabian journal *Today* did not merely approve Booth's plan to force the chronic poor into labour colonies, but enthused about it as a harbinger of the collectivist change Fabians desired (Jones 1971, 314). Rather, the difference is best seen as an instance of the 'exceptional' nature of Pearson's thought. The Fabians were seeking political influence, first through the Liberal and later the Labour Party: an extension of the franchise, they calculated, could only increase the pressure for social reform, and thus strengthen their position. The 'fine structure' of British politics dictated that they support the extension of political democracy, even though critics of the Fabians sensed that their commitment to democracy was less than total. 'At heart [their] principal leaders are bureaucrats not democrats', one wrote (quoted by Hobsbawm 1968, 264). Pearson's writing, on the other hand, had nothing to do with calculations of particular political advantage. In this sense, he was more consistent than they were: his position reflects only the 'overall' structure of classes; theirs reflects also the fine structure of institutions.

Pearson's Philosophy

To see 'politics' as relating merely to the 'party-political' issues discussed in the previous section would be to adopt a narrow perspective. Pearson's philosophical thought can also be seen as political, and as reflecting particular social interests. It was by no means idle speculation, nor an abstract choice of methodology, but the active forging and controversial use of theories of morality and of knowledge.

The germs of Pearson's philosophy can, like those of his socialism, be found in his early study and thinking, especially in Germany. Again, no passive 'influence' model can account for its development. As his 'Common-Place Books' and correspondence with his closest friend, Robert Parker, show, Pearson exposed himself to a wide range of philosophies, and actively chose among them.[9]

Pearson developed a moral philosophy that can be summed up in his two maxims (1888, 117 and 122):

> Morality is what is social, and immorality what is anti-social . . .
> The ignorant cannot be moral.

He had rejected – not altogether painlessly – all systems of absolute morality. Neither Christianity, nor the ethics of Kant or the neo-Hegelians, satisfied him. Instead, he put forward not an ethical relativism, as might be assumed from the statement 'morality is what is social', but an ethical naturalism. Morality was not simply the following of group norms. The truly moral actor had to take into account not only the existing state of society but also the direction of its evolution:

> One thing only is fixed, the direction and rate of change of human society at a particular epoch. It may be difficult to measure, but it is none the less real and definite. The moral or good action is that which tends in the direction of growth of a particular society in a particular land at a particular time.
> (1888, 428)

This is why 'the ignorant cannot be moral'. Only the individual who has knowledge of science and history, and is therefore acquainted with the scientific laws of social evolution, can know which course of action is moral.

By discarding traditional systems of morality, this ethical theory undermined the power of the priests and their allies within philosophy, the 'emotionalists, mystics and metaphysical idealists' (Pearson, as quoted by Norton 1978a, 26). By the premium it placed on action based on knowledge of social evolution, it enhanced the role of the possessors of this knowledge. By making nonsensical any talk of 'rights', it could be used to oppose the rhetoric of those who sought to whip up emotions in pursuit of over-rapid change. Talk of 'rights' led too easily to revolutionary upheaval, Pearson felt: it was 'the enthusiasm of the market place'. Consideration, instead, of the laws of social development led to moderation and the avoidance of revolutionary agitation, to the intellectually-sound 'enthusiasm of the study' (1888, 115–34).

If scientific knowledge decided what was and was not moral, Pearson clearly needed to demarcate the boundary between proper scientific knowledge and mere belief. The key to his epistemology was the construction of just such a boundary. His philosophy of science emerged gradually, from early reflections on Kant through contact with the ideas of Clifford and Mach (see Norton 1978a, 14–15 and 24–6). But in its mature presentation in *The Grammar of Science* (Pearson 1892a) it constituted an important and impressive contribution to positivist and phenomenalist thought.

All knowledge, Pearson argued, was based on sense-impressions; it was impossible meaningfully to discuss the unknown and unknowable 'things-in-themselves' that metaphysicians saw as lying behind sense-impressions. The task of science was simply to describe as economically as possible the 'routine of perceptions'. Concepts that were firmly based on experience, and those that contributed to economy of description, were allowable, others were to be banished. The sphere of science as thus delimited was co-extensive with the sphere of all valid knowledge. Certainly, there were types of phenomena that had yet to be satisfactorily described by science, but there were no phenomena to which the scientific method was not applicable. What was not science was simply not knowledge.[10]

Pearson's theory of knowledge, like his theory of morality, belongs firmly in the tradition of Victorian scientific naturalism. Its positivism and phenomenalism were *weapons* in the ideological battle – still not wholly won – to establish science as the sole arbiter of rational belief, to dethrone theology, and to banish from within the camp of science systems of thought that gave aid and comfort to the theistically-inclined. Thus in his polemic against the conservative philosopher-politician Arthur Balfour (for whom see Jacyna 1980), Pearson was attacking both Balfour's philosophical anti-naturalism *and* his defence of 'authority'. Reason – the positivist rationalism of the 'progressive' scientist – had to supplant traditional sources of authority as the final court of appeal. For 'the race of life is now to those who educate and foster thought – to the reasoners among the nations' (1897, *1*, 224). The ultimate test of philosophies was the struggle for existence. That struggle, Pearson was confident, would prove the merit of his version of reason and would bring to power the scientific intellectuals whose practice embodied it.

Pearson's Darwinism

It is not surprising that Karl Pearson should have been an ardent Darwinian. To be a Darwinian was to ally oneself with progress against reaction, with the secular against the religious, and with the rising scientifically-based professions against the still powerful

Established Church. Despite the availability of a whole range of intermediate positions between Darwinian naturalism and scriptural anti-Darwinism (Turner 1974a), Darwinism remained a potent cultural symbol. Pearson embraced that symbol ardently. Interestingly enough, however, he did not do so until the mid-1880s (*after* his first writings on politics and philosophy), and the manner in which he finally came to Darwinism is of some significance.

Pearson came to Darwinism not as a biologist – he showed almost no interest in biology as such until the 1890s – nor even, primarily, as a freethinker seeking a weapon against revealed religion. To him, Darwinism's prime importance was as a theory of history. 'The philosophy of history is only possible since Darwin', he wrote (1888, 430). During the early 1880s Pearson devoted a good deal of time to historical studies, particularly early German history. As these proceeded he began to claim that evolutionary theory provided a means of integrating them and drawing the general lessons from them.[11]

From the beginning, then, Pearson's Darwinism was explicitly a social Darwinism. The laws of social development that were to be the basis for moral action had to be derived, Pearson felt, from a Darwinian study of history. He drew two major conclusions from this study, one of them orthodox, the other less conventional. Both, however, can be seen as fitting closely his earlier political thought. Nature was being developed as a resource in social and political argument.

Pearson's orthodox conclusion concerned natural and social change. As a political thinker, he had already firmly decided against revolution and in favour of gradual and orderly change. Indeed, he saw a key aspect of the role of the intellectual to be the defence of this conclusion:

> There are mighty forces at work likely to revolutionise social ideas and shake social stability. It is the duty of those who have the leisure to investigate, to show how by gradual and continuous change we can restrain these forces within safe channels . . . (1888, 7)

In part, he argued for this conclusion from descriptive historical studies, most notably his vivid account of the failure and terrible fate of the millennial communist 'Kingdom of God' in Münster (1888, 263–314). But he also appealed to continuity and gradualism in nature as an argument against revolution in society:

> Human progress, like Nature, never leaps . . . (1888, 122)

> . . . *no great change ever occurs with a leap* . . . is as much a law
> of history as of nature. (1888, 363)

Pearson never employed the Fabian slogan of 'the inevitability of
gradualness', but it was a principle that underlay his thinking about
both nature and society.

Pearson's other conclusion concerned the way in which natural
selection operated on contemporary human societies. Social Dar-
winists of the previous generation (e.g. Spencer 1873) had typically
employed the notion of selection operating on individuals as an
argument for *laissez-faire* and against state intervention as inter-
fering with the destruction of the less fit. To Pearson this was a
politically unacceptable conclusion. Darwinism had to be rescued
from the *laissez-faire* individualists and turned into a legitimation of
collectivism and a strong state.

The way in which he did this was simple. He argued that the chief
locus of the struggle for existence was no longer the individual but
the group. The spur to efficiency was not individual competition,
but inter-group struggle: survival went to the fittest group, not the
fittest individual. In inter-group struggle, the social organisation of
the group counted for as much, or indeed more, than the individual
fitnesses of the individuals comprising the group. The internal competition that resulted from *laissez-faire* capitalism weakened a nation in international struggle. A class-divided nation, with an unfit
and disaffected proletariat, could hardly hope to compete successfully with a well-organised and united state.[12]

Pearson was by no means the only individual who, in the 1880s,
was seeking to modify the individualistic thrust of previous social
Darwinism (see, e.g., Ritchie 1889). It was, of course, natural that
those who formed the 'socialist revival' of the 1880s should seek to
show that Darwinism need not be individualist and *laissez-faire* in its
social implications. But another factor may also have been at work:
the growth, both in reality and as a factor in popular consciousness,
of imperialism. The 'internal' social Darwinism of Spencer could be
used to justify a competitive capitalist order within one nation. The
new 'external' social Darwinism could be used to justify the economic and military competition of advanced nations and their ruth-
less exploitation and extermination of 'inferior' peoples.[13]

These two explanations of the transition in social Darwinism in
the 1880s should not be taken as contradictory. We now tend to
think of socialism and imperialism as opposites. But in the period
1880 to 1914 socialism of certain brands, such as Fabianism, was

closely linked to imperialism. Collectivist social reform was needed, it was argued, to secure national efficiency in the inter-imperialist struggle; the profits of imperialism could, in turn, finance social reform. As the First World War was to demonstrate, many state-socialist demands could be won under the pressure of a threat to national survival (Marwick 1967).

In his book on 'social-imperialism', this conjunction of imperia-lism and social reform, Bernard Semmel (1960; see also Semmel 1958) takes Karl Pearson as a key example of a social-imperialist thinker. Pearson's social Darwinism, with its emphasis on maxi-mising group efficiency for the struggle between groups, was a perfect legitimation of social-imperialism. Again, Pearson was put-ting forward in particularly coherent fashion an ideology expressing the interests of his social group. Imperialism vastly broadened the job opportunities for professionals (Gollwitzer 1969, 86), and social-imperialism, with its emphasis on technocratic, collectivist reform, was an attractive short-cut to power for the rising profes-sional experts. Thus Pearson's *National Life from the Standpoint of Science* (1901a) employed social-imperialist arguments to bolster its conclusion that scientific expertise should determine the path to national survival. State socialism and a rationalised imperialism were, for Pearson, necessary allies, not enemies:

> No thoughtful socialist, so far as I am aware, would object to cultivate Uganda *at the expense of its present occupiers* if Lanca-shire were starving. Only he would have this done directly and consciously, and not by way of missionaries and exploiting companies. (1897, *1*, 111; Pearson's emphasis)

Pearson's Eugenics

Pearson saw two great social movements as crucial to the develop-ment of British society of his time. The first, of course, was the socialist movement, and the second was the women's movement. From early on Pearson was in sympathetic contact with feminism. He was a member of a small circle of men and women who came together in the 1880s to discuss the relation of the sexes, the 'Men's and Women's Club'. His essays of this period show him prepared to take seriously, if not to endorse unequivocally, radical proposals such as for 'free unions' to replace conventional marriage (Pearson 1888, 442–3).

Pearson had reservations about feminism paralleling closely those he had about socialism. 'We cannot possibly check' the women's movement, he wrote, but the implication was not that it should be supported uncritically but that an endeavour should be made to 'direct' it so that it should not undermine social stability (1897, *1*, 243). Nevertheless, Pearson's contact with feminism brought him in touch with thinking far different from that conventional in Victorian Britain. In particular, sexual morality was for him an open, rather than a closed, question.

His answer was, given the rest of his thinking, not surprising: '. . . the test is the social or antisocial effects of the act'.[14] A major possible effect of the sexual act between men and women is the production of children, and it was to this that Pearson's contributions to the Men's and Women's Club began to turn. During the middle and late 1880s he became a eugenist. 'Shall those who are diseased, shall those who are nighest to the brute, have the right to reproduce their like?', he asked (1888, 391), and answered firmly in the negative. Part of the 'socialistic solution' to the sex problem was 'state interference if necessary in the matter of child-bearing' (*ibid.*, 445). The 'anti-social propagators of unnecessary human beings' (*ibid.*, 433) had to be restrained.

Eugenics became more and more prominent in Pearson's writings as earlier themes became less so. His earlier concerns were *condensed* into his eugenics.[15] He saw his eugenics as integrally linked to his politics; at the same time it was an application of his moral philosophy to human reproduction and a science to be developed along the lines decreed by his epistemology. Finally, the necessity of a programme of national eugenics was, he felt, a direct consequence of the application of evolutionary theory to the contemporary world of international competition.

For example, he saw socialism and eugenics as inseparable. Natural selection had to be replaced by artificial selection to ensure that the 'unfit' did not outbreed the 'fit' in a socialist nation. At the same time, socialism was arguably a precondition for eugenics. A eugenic policy was unlikely to be successful under *laissez-faire* capitalism, chiefly because capitalists desiring large supplies of cheap unskilled labour had an interest in maintaining the rate of reproduction of the 'unfit' at home and permitting large-scale immigration of the 'unfit' from abroad. In sum:

> The pious wish of Darwin that the superior and not the inferior members of the group should be the parents of the future, is far more likely to be realised in a socialistic than in an individualistic state. (1897, *1*, 138)

Pearson may well seem to be making common cause with arch-reactionaries when he pointed to the anti-eugenic effects of the abolition of child labour in turning a child from an economic asset to a straightforward expense amongst the 'better class' of workers (1909e, 7–9). But it is important to realise that in such matters he was *not* calling for a return to the past.

> Do I therefore call for less human sympathy, for more limit-
> ed charity, and for sterner treatment of the weak? Not for a
> moment . . . (1909c, 25)

What he wanted was rationalisation, planning, conscious state inter-vention – as he understood it, socialism – applied to matters con-cerning human reproduction.

> . . . I demand that all sympathy and charity shall be organised
> and guided into paths where they will promote racial efficiency,
> and not lead us straight towards national shipwreck. (*ibid.*, 25)

Pearson's eugenics embodied assumptions about social class that are already familiar to us from chapter 2. Practical eugenics, he wrote (1909e, 22), is concerned with two fundamental problems:

> (i) The production of a sufficient supply of leaders of ability
> and energy for the community, and
> (ii) The provision of intelligent and healthy men and women
> for the great army of workers.

'Leaders' would have to be recruited predominantly from the exis-ting middle class. It was true that individuals of ability could be found in the manual working class, but these were few, and

> It is cruel to the individual, it serves no social purpose, to drag
> a man of only moderate intellectual power from the hand-
> working to the brain-working group. (1902b, x)

It was both 'undesirable' and 'impossible' to 'subject every indi-vidual in the nation to a test of fitness for every possible calling'. Instead it had to be recognised that class was an approximate but useful indicator of innate ability. 'With rough practical efficiency a man's work in life is settled by his caste or class'. In particular:

> . . . the middle class in England, which stands there for intel-
> lectual culture and brain-work, is the product of generations of
> selection from other classes and of in-marriage.
> . . . [working-class] county council scholars are on the average
> not up to the mean middle-class intelligence. It is very rarely
> that one could not pick out for any given post better, often
> many better, middle-class candidates. (*ibid.*, x)

So the social divide between 'hand-work' and 'brain-work' was seen by Pearson to correspond at least roughly to a natural divide between different innate abilities. The manual worker was to be educated in such a way as to become 'an intelligent instrument for his allotted task', but in a quite different way from the professional:

> We need a system of education for the bulk of men, who follow, entirely independent of the system requisite for the minority, who organize and lead. (*ibid.*, xvi)

Evidence such as this can be taken as indicating that a general analysis of professional middle-class interests as sustaining eugenics holds in Pearson's case. One then has the problem of accounting for the bitter controversies between Pearson and other leading eugenists. However, it may be that in Pearson's thought professional middle-class interests were being more consistently expressed than in that of his eugenic opponents. Thus, two major strands can be seen as running through these disputes. First, Pearson distrusted the Eugenics Education Society and the 'wilder' eugenists such as George Bernard Shaw. Caution, expertise, a 'Fabian' approach, were what he called for instead (1914–30, *3A*, 260–1). He felt that other eugenists were taking dangerous shortcuts; eugenics had to be kept under the control of properly trained scientific experts, and out of that of 'cranks'. Secondly, several leading eugenists found Pearson too rigorous in his hereditarianism, particularly in his scepticism that parental alcoholism had a direct inherited effect on children and in his criticism of environmental, rather than eugenic, measures against tuberculosis.[16] Here, perhaps, the fine structure of institutions and occupations cut across the overall structure of class interests, as far as Pearson's opponents were concerned. They were hereditarians in general, but wished to maintain particular exceptions to eugenic principles because of particular commitments: to the temperance movement, in the case of the controversy over alcoholism, and to environmental health programmes and sanatorium treatment in the case of tuberculosis. Pearson, free of these conflicting commitments,[17] was able to develop a consistent hereditarianism unaltered by particularistic exceptions.[18]

Pearson's Statistical Biology

In the areas discussed up to now – Fabian socialism, scientific naturalism, Darwinism and eugenics – Pearson's writings can largely be seen as a *combination*, as the bringing together into a sharp and coherent form, of ideas to be found relatively frequently in the professional middle class. His originality, his real transformation rather than re-ordering of knowledge, is to be found in his work in statistical biology, where he took Galton's insights and made out of them a new science. It was the work of his maturity – he started it only in his mid-thirties – and in it can be found the flowering of most of the major concerns of his youth.

His growing involvement in it can be divided roughly into four phases. The first, preliminary, phase is that up to the beginning of 1891. Given Pearson's mathematical skills, and given his growing interest in eugenics, it was natural that he should turn to the work of Francis Galton. In 1889 he read a paper to the Men's and Women's Club discussing the eugenically-inspired statistical analyses of Galton's latest book, *Natural Inheritance*. Pearson found Galton's work substantively convincing:

> The general conclusion one must be forced to by accepting Galton's theories is the imperative importance of humans doing for themselves what they do for cattle, if they wish to raise the mediocrity of their race. (1889, 34)

But he had serious methodological doubts:

> Personally I ought to say that there is, in my own opinion, considerable danger in applying the methods of exact science to problems in descriptive science . . . the grace and logical accuracy of the mathematical processes are apt to so fascinate the descriptive scientist that he seeks for sociological hypotheses which fit his mathematical reasoning. . . . (*ibid.*, 2)

In any case, Pearson's energies were at this time taken up with the preparation of *The Grammar of Science*; while he was attracted to Galton's eugenics, he was not yet ready to begin work in a new scientific field.

The second phase began after the appointment in December 1890 of W. F. R. Weldon to the Chair of Zoology at University College, London. Weldon was also interested in what Galton was doing. Unlike Pearson, it was Galton's statistical method rather than eugenic conclusions that attracted Weldon: he saw in Galton's work a way of making biology, especially evolutionary biology, more rigorous (see chapter 5). He needed the help of a professional mathematician, and approached his colleague Pearson. In their collaboration Pearson's methodological doubts about Galton's approach were overcome: he realised that statistical analyses could be seen as exemplifying, rather than contradicting, the positivist and phenomenalist criteria of valid knowledge of the *Grammar*. Using statistics, the biologist could (apparently) measure without theorising, summarise facts without going beyond them, describe without explaining.[19]

Pearson thus began work on mathematical problems suggested by Weldon's work. His first paper on statistics (Pearson 1894) dealt with the dissection of frequency curves into separate normal components, and applied the method to some of Weldon's data on crab shells. The second (Pearson 1895) discussed the fitting of skew frequency curves to observational data, and developed the well-known method-of-moments or Pearson system of curves: the examples again included the crab measurements, but also a wide range of human, biological and metereological observations.

The work of this second phase might suggest that Pearson was simply interested in applying his mathematical skills to other scientists' problems, irrespective of any intrinsic concern for these problems. This interpretation is, however, shown to be false by his work of the third phase of the transition, which can be dated roughly as 1894 to 1897. Pearson himself wrote of this phase:

> Now, if you are going to take Darwinism as your theory of life and apply it to human problems, you must not only *believe* it to be true, but you must set to, and demonstrate that it actually applies. That task I endeavoured to undertake after the late Lord Salisbury's famous attack on Darwinism at the Oxford meeting of the British Association in 1894. It was not a light task, but it gave for many years the *raison d'être* of my statistical work. (1912b, 11)

Salisbury (1894) had suggested that the process of natural selection could not be demonstrated, but was merely an implausible hypothesis, and he had called for a return to the principle of creative design. The religiously motivated atack on Darwinism from the High Tory peer led to an immediate riposte from Pearson (reprinted in Pearson 1897, *1*, 140–72). He attacked Salisbury as a representative of 'reaction' and the 'new bigotry', and claimed that 'the theory of evolution is likely to become a branch of the theory of chance', and that when this happened views like Salisbury's would obtain 'very poor comfort' as a 'quantitative measure of the rate of natural selection' was found (*ibid.*, *1*, 172 and 167).

Pearson's mathematisation of Darwinism can be seen, then, in part as an attempt to defend the theory of natural selection from its reactionary opponents. He sought to develop an evolutionary science that was philosophically impeccable, according to his own phenomenalism and positivism. This he did not do simply for its own sake, but in order to legitimate its application to the human species, its use as social Darwinism. For Pearson (1900a, 468), the theory of evolution

> ... is not merely a passive intellectual view of nature; it applies to man in his communities as it applies to all forms of life. It teaches us the art of living, of building up stable and dominant nations ...

Such a theory had to be presentable as based on hard, solid, preferably quantitative fact, in order to obtain maximum plausibility and to combat people like Lord Salisbury; hence the necessity to develop it in a statistical form, free from speculative, theoretical elements.

Pearson's third 'Mathematical contribution to the theory of evolution' (1896) serves as an illustration of the nature of his statistical biology and its relation to the rest of his thought. In this important paper Pearson put forward the now standard product-moment expression for the coefficient of correlation and developed a large part of the theory of multiple correlation and regression. These contributions to statistical theory were prompted by the objective of manipulating and showing the interrelations of various concepts from evolutionary biology to which he had given operational, statistical definitions. However, the paper was not simply an abstract piece of mathematical biology. In a real sense it was about human beings in society. The definitions were indeed general, but it is clear that man was the organism to which they were primarily intended to apply. All Pearson's major concrete examples referred to humans, and his introduction to the paper hinted strongly at possible eugenic applications.

Further, in writing this paper Pearson had a particular political purpose. He wished to refute the theory that, should natural selection be suspended and random mating take place, a species would revert to an original 'species type'. This notion, referred to by Pearson as the doctrine of 'panmixia', had been used by Benjamin Kidd in his widely-read *Social Evolution* (1895, first published in 1894) to prove the impossibility of the long-term success of a socialist society: with the struggle for survival suspended, degeneration would automatically follow. Pearson had responded to Kidd with a defence of socialism in the *Fortnightly Review* of July 1894 (reprinted in Pearson 1897, *1*, 103–39), and his later mathematical paper provided more precise substantiation of his argument. The efficacy of selection was greater and more permanent than the theory of panmixia allowed, he argued. The suggestion that regression took place to a fixed racial mean was almost certainly mistaken, he suggested; instead, the focus of regression shifted with selection. Adopting this view, it could be shown mathematically that as little as five generations of selection could lead to the establishment of a stable new breed (Pearson 1896, 317).

Thus, it can be clearly seen that Pearson was not simply providing a mathematical apparatus for others to use. To make his point, he was quite happy to modify an essential substantive part of the theory of regression developed by Galton, for it was Galton who had held that the focus of regression was stable. And Pearson's point was essentially a political one: the viability, and indeed superiority to capitalism, of a socialist state with eugenically-planned reproduction. The quantitative statistical form of his argument provided him with convincing rhetorical resources, which he employed mercilessly against Kidd (e.g. Pearson 1897, *1*, 105).

By the end of this third phase, Pearson's transition to work on statistical biology was essentially complete. From 1897 onwards, a fourth phase of consolidation was entered into: a period of gradually building a 'research institute', of initiating major projects on his own account rather than using others' data, of work on the numerous particular statistical and other problems thrown up by his research programme. This phase naturally involved Pearson in work less obviously and directly connected to his central political, philosophical and eugenic concerns, and he collaborated with many people who did not share these concerns. Nevertheless, it can still be argued that Pearson's work of this mature period, and that of his 'research institute', continued to reflect these concerns, as we shall see below.

Pearson and the Professional Middle Class

Pearson's overall intellectual position was unique. While many late Victorian professionals may have shared elements of it, the overall mix is not to be found, to my knowledge, in any other person. The central point made in this chapter – which distinguishes the approach to the sociology of knowledge associated with Lukács and Goldmann from any empiricist, statistical approach – is that this uniqueness in no way invalidates the analysis of Pearson's system of belief as one appropriate to the professional middle class of late Victorian Britain. Indeed, I have suggested that part of the reason for its uniqueness – for example for Pearson's difference from most

Fabians and most eugenists – lies in the fact that Pearson's thought reflected professional middle-class interests uncomplicated by particularistic commitments. I have claimed that Pearson was in this sense an 'exceptional' individual.

The point being made is not a psychological, motivational one. I am not claiming, for example, that Pearson deliberately and consciously set out to create a professional middle-class ideology. Nor is it one that rests on a sociological determinism. I am not claiming that Pearson's social background, for example, caused his ideas. If my analyses of Pearson's writings and of the interests of the professional middle class are accepted, then all we have is an instance of a 'match' of beliefs and social interests. Explaining why this 'match' came about exactly when it did, and why the particular individual Karl Pearson should have manifested it, is beyond the present capacity of the sociology of knowledge. In the last analysis, it is not necessarily a sociological problem.

This does not mean that all we can do is to point to this one instance of a 'match'. It is possible to look at the relationship between the historical fate of a system of belief and that of the class to which it is claimed to be appropriate. Ideologies are of course context-bound, and there is no reason to expect a permanent attachment of particular ideas to particular classes in changing cultural and historical circumstances. Nevertheless, at least some regularities can surely be expected. Take Fabianism, for example. Since 1914 the professional middle class, and state bureaucracy and social intervention, have grown rapidly. Fabianism has changed from a minority belief to a dominant ideology. It is no longer radical to talk of experts, scientific administration and politics, or selection on merit, nor, up to a few years ago, was it particularly radical to demand an expansion in the role of the state. Similarly with eugenics. While negative eugenics as a programme of social control proved context-bound, many of the eugenists' psychological ideas became widely accepted. The relatively recent reaction against them within sectors of the professional middle class, itself an interesting problem for the sociology of knowledge, should not blind us to the ideological success of hereditarian theories of mental ability. A reaction has also set in against scientific positivism of the Pearsonian kind, but the claims for science found in *The Grammar of Science* would not be wholly unacceptable to many contemporary scientists. The particular form of Pearson's reaction against individualistic social Darwinism is outdated, but the notions of collectivism, and of the development of internal cohesion against external threat, have enjoyed considerable twentieth-century success.

It would, therefore, not be correct to dismiss Pearson's ideas as simply those of an idiosyncratic individual. It is too easy to focus on aspects that were discarded and now seem outlandish, and to forget those that became the commonplace beliefs of the professional middle class of at least the recent past. On the whole, the ideas embraced by Pearson were ideas growing, rather than declining, in their historical importance. This growth can surely be attributed to the growth of the professional middle class and its social role: Fabianism, the 'IQ cult', positivism in a general sense, and so on, grew as professional administrators, teachers and psychologists, social and natural scientists became more important. On the other hand, Pearson as an individual, while at least moderately famous as a general intellectual in the Edwardian period, never enjoyed a cult status amongst the professional middle class. In full accord with his own views on the correct strategy for the scientific intellectual, Pearson eschewed opportunism. He never made the compromises that would have been necessary to become leader of a social movement such as Fabianism or eugenics. That does not mean, however, that the ideas he put forward should be seen as unsuccessful ideas.

The analysis of Pearson presented here does differ in its nature from that by Goldmann (1964) of Pascal and Racine, in which Goldmann's sociology of knowledge is best developed. Goldmann's argument rests, ultimately, on a claimed structural homology between Jansenism, as expressed by Pascal and Racine, and the social situation of the class, the *noblesse de robe,* to which Jansenism is imputed. The analysis of Pearson does not depend on structural parallels, but rather on notions of class interest. Further, Goldmann makes much of the aesthetic coherence of the ideas of his principal subjects. The coherence found in Pearson's work is not of this nature: it refers instead to what I claim to be the relative freedom of Pearson's thought from the 'noise' generated by particularistic interests. These two reservations aside, I would hope that this chapter has shown that the type of analysis pioneered by Goldmann can be of use in understanding aspects of the relationship between individual thinkers and social classes. A sociological approach need not be restricted to relatively large-scale movements but can also be used to analyse the work of unique individuals such as Karl Pearson.

5

The Development of Statistical Theory
as a Scientific Specialty

· · · · ·
· · ·
·

Up to this point, my discussion of statistical theory has been focused almost exclusively on only two men, Francis Galton and Karl Pearson. Certainly they were central to the development of British statistics but, in order to give a rounded picture of the context in which they worked, it is necessary to consider other, less prominent, individuals, and also organisational developments. It has been convincingly argued (notably by Ben-David and Collins 1966) that good and productive ideas alone are not sufficient for the foundation of a new scientific specialty. Several things must happen before we can talk of the emergence of a new specialty: a network of scientists interested in the new field must develop; means of communication between them, both formal and informal, must be established; a mechanism must be devised for recruitment to, and training in, the field, and this mechanism must be given some stable form; and sufficient financial and other resources must be obtained to permit the foregoing.

Over the last few years a considerable literature has developed which employs this perspective in the discussion of the growth of scientific specialties,[1] and useful provisional summaries of it are given by Edge and Mulkay (1975) and in the introduction to Lemaine et al. (1976). Perhaps the most useful way to conceptualise the problem is to see the development of a new discipline as analogous to the development of a new political party. Seen in this light, some of the points raised in this literature become strikingly familiar. Compare, for example, Griffith and Mullins (1972) with Lenin (1947): both works emphasise the crucial role of tightly knit and coherent groups, even if small, in promoting revolutionary change.

Consider the above list of necessary conditions for the development and institutionalisation of a new discipline. Do they not apply also to the development of a new political party? It too must be based on a network of committed individuals, who must develop means of communication with each other. It too needs to recruit, and to develop the ideological and other competences of those it recruits. Notoriously, it too requires material resources. However, the analogy of the political party suggests that it may well be misguided to search for a single set of factors governing the development of scientific specialties. Political environments differ. Factors that promote the successful growth of a party in one environment (for example, a highly centralised internal structure) may hinder its growth in another. Funds may be most readily available from one source (business concerns, say) in one situation, and from another (mass subscriptions) in another. Similarly with scientific disciplines. Access to graduate students, say, may be necessary for growth under the normal conditions of the scientific enterprise in industrialised societies, but it can hardly be a universal factor. The creation of a new journal may sometimes be necessary, sometimes not.

So the perspective taken here will not be an attempt to list a set of factors that are present or absent in the development of British statistics. Rather, Galton and Pearson will be considered as the nucleus of a scientific 'party', attempting to build networks, to establish adequate means of communication, recruit and train others and to gain resources to do so. An attempt will be made to understand the situation in which they operated, and how particular contexts and connections helped and hindered their enterprise. Further, lest this framework be thought too voluntaristic, attention will be paid to the 'side bets' (Becker 1960) involved in the process. Interests extraneous to the original enterprise became involved in it and transformed its nature, independently of the conscious intention of those who initiated it. The process of the formation of 'side bets' is, of course, familiar to students of politics. In attempting to promote change, reformers frequently develop a stake in the very institutions they have set out to alter or destroy. Nothing as complete as this happens in the case of British statistics, but it is clear that the enterprise that developed largely as a result of the efforts of Galton and Pearson was not shaped by their initial intentions alone.

Galton and the Mathematicians

In 1892 Francis Galton wrote to the former Senior Wrangler, W. F. Sheppard:

What is greatly wanted is a clean elegant *résumé* of all the

theoretical work concerned in the social and biographical problems to which the exponential law has been applied. I believe the time is ripe for any competent mathematician to do this with much credit to himself. I am *not* competent and know it. . . I have often considered what seems wanted and been very desirous of discovering someone who was disposed to throw himself into so useful and such high-class work. He might practically *found* a science, the material for which is now too chaotic.
(quoted in Pearson 1914–30, *3B*, 486–7; Galton's emphasis)

Galton had tried long and hard to generate consistent interest by a 'competent mathematician' in the mathematical and statistical aspects of the problems on which he was working. Up to 1892 he had sought to develop active collaboration with at least seven such men: H.W.Watson, Donald MacAlister, J.D.Hamilton Dickson, John Venn, S.H.Burbury, W.F.Sheppard, and Francis Ysidro Edgeworth. While none of these collaborations was sterile, none produced the fruitful results of Galton's contact with Karl Pearson. It is, therefore, worth contrasting these former with the latter, and also to discuss one further mathematician, Arthur Black, who, although he never met or corresponded with Galton, might have contributed more than any of the others apart from Pearson, had his career not been terminated by his suicide in 1893.

Galton's relationships with the first six are discussed in appendix 4. All six were Cambridge graduates, and all were highly placed in the Tripos examination in mathematics. Only Hamilton Dickson pursued a career exclusively in university teaching and research in mathematics. The others spent at least part of their lives in the established professions: Watson and Venn, the church; MacAlister, medicine; Burbury and Sheppard, the law. One might indeed suspect that men like this, academically trained but marginal to any established career structure in mathematics, might be ideally suited to the role of innovator in an applied mathematical field. This may have been the case, but, with the partial exception of Sheppard, they all seem to have lacked commitment to Galton's particular project. The pattern in each case is similar. Each became interested in a particular problem or aspect of Galton's work, investigated it mathematically, and having done so dropped it and returned to his own pursuits. In modern parlance, their role was almost that of the 'consultant', except that it was the chance to display their mathematical competences on an interesting problem – and perhaps the flattering contact with a highly prestigious man like Galton – that motivated them, rather than financial reward.

Galton's contact with W. F. Sheppard, although it was productive of a much larger body of work than his contact with the other five, was not qualitatively dissimilar. Sheppard's initial interest in Galton's work may have been sparked by its eugenic applications, but his prime motive seems to have been simply that, in first Galton's and then Pearson's work, he found an excellent area for the application of his particular skills. Where Galton and Pearson had provided the key concepts, he followed with detailed investigation and tabulation. He was particularly competent in what would now be called numerical analysis: for example, he drew up the first modern tables of the normal curve using the standard deviation as the argument (Sheppard 1903). He did prove a moderately important theorem in bivariate normal correlation, which is now sometimes known as Sheppard's theorem on median dichotomy, and also made a major contribution to methods of evaluating probable errors (Sheppard 1898b). In general, though, it can be said that it is not unfair to the man, with his great concern for precision and numerical accuracy, that his name should have gone down in the history of statistics primarily as the inventor of a correction formula: Sheppard's formula for the correction of moments estimated from grouped data, first presented in Sheppard (1897b).

Unlike these six mathematicians, Francis Ysidro Edgeworth (1845–1926) began work on statistical theory independently of Galton.[2] Apparently self-taught in mathematics, he was educated in classics at Trinity College, Dublin, and at Oxford, and seems to have then spent some years practising law. In 1880 he became Lecturer in Logic, and in 1888 Professor of Political Economy, at King's College, London. In 1891 he was appointed Drummond Professor of Political Economy at Oxford.

Utilitarianism formed the basis of his early work, notably Edgeworth (1877, 1881). His utilitarianism was, however, not at all radical in its thrust. Thus Edgeworth claimed that when

> . . . we calculate the utility of pre-utilitarian institutions, we are impressed with a view of Nature, not, as in the picture left by Mill, all bad, but a first approximation to the best. We are biased to a more conservative caution in reform. And we may have here not only a direction, but a motive, to our end. For, as Nature is judged more good, so more potent than the great utilitarian has allowed are the motives to morality which religion finds in the attributes of God. (1881, 82)

Edgeworth appears to have first made use of Galton's work in order to justify the removal of any egalitarian implications from the utilitarian goal of maximising happiness. Edgeworth argued that individuals differed in their capacity for happiness and that to maximise total happiness more of the 'means of happiness' should be given to those most able to enjoy them. Lest anyone be so foolish as to imagine that the proletariat had a large capacity to be happy, Edgeworth hastened to point out that 'the higher pleasures are on the whole most pleasurable . . . those who are most apt to enjoy those pleasures tend to be most capable of happiness' (*ibid.*, 58).

Edgeworth then had to answer the objection that the capacity for happiness might be the result of education. He argued that this would be incompatible with 'what is known about heredity' (*ibid.*, 59). Citing Quetelet and Galton, he claimed that the distribution of capacity for happiness was normal, and that the offspring of parents with a given capacity for happiness would have capacities for happiness distributed normally round those of their parents (*ibid.*, 69–70). To maximise happiness in the next generation, those with a low capacity for happiness should not have children, concluded Edgeworth, and he commented favourably on Galton's notion of a refuge for the 'weak' in celibate monasteries (*ibid.*, 71–2).

Edgeworth did not take this idea any further: it must be suspected that he was interested in eugenics only in so far as hereditarian ideas helped him in the production of a conservative utilitarianism. He worked on statistical theory from the 1880s onwards, but it was not along the lines of Galton's research programme. Edgeworth's general aim was the construction of a 'mathematical psychics' with two main subdivisions: the study of utility, which led him into his well-known work in mathematical economics; and the study of belief, which led him into research in statistical theory, in particular in those parts closely connected to the foundations of the subject, as in Edgeworth (1883a,b, 1884, 1885, 1887). His work in this latter area was obscurely presented and had little impact at the time. Even those parts that might have been of use to other British statisticians, such as his work on the 'Edgeworth expansion' generalising the normal distribution or on the 'method of transformation', were not taken up.[3]

In the 1880s Edgeworth was the only person in Britain, with the exception of Galton, doing anything approaching serious and sustained general work in statistical theory.[4] Accordingly, Galton appears to have tried on more than one occasion to recruit Edgeworth to work on the statistics of heredity.[5] In the early 1890s Edgeworth finally turned to a problem suggested by Galton's work, that of generalising the bivariate normal distribution constructed by Galton and Hamilton Dickson to an indefinite number of variables. Edgeworth's papers on correlation (1892a,b, 1893a,b,c,d) show clearly that he solved the problem in essence, even though they are marred by occasional errors, misprints and obscurities.[6] Edgeworth, however, did no further statistical work along Galton's lines. Instead, in the words of Karl Pearson, he 'ploughed always right across the line of [the biometricians'] furrows' (quoted by Kendall 1968, 262); Edgeworth thus stood aside from the main line of development of statistical theory in Britain.

The next figure to be discussed never met Galton, though he knew of at least some of Galton's work, and his own studies may have been in part inspired by it. Arthur Black[7] (1851–93) was the son of David Black, solicitor and coroner in Brighton; his sister Constance, later Constance Garnett, was to become famous for her translations of the novels of Tolstoy and Dostoyevsky. Arthur took a BSc degree of the University of London by private study, graduating in 1877, and was a 'favourite pupil' of the leading mathematician and scientific naturalist ideologist, W. K. Clifford (Weldon to Galton, 4 June 1894, Galton Papers 340/c). Subsequently he earned a rather precarious living as an army coach and tutor in Brighton, while pursuing his mathematical and philosophical interests. His marriage was fraught and unhappy, and he finally died by his own hand in very sad circumstances (*The Times*, 20 and 21 January 1893).

He left behind him a large, and apparently fairly complete, manuscript on the *Algebra of Animal Evolution*. This was sent to Karl Pearson, who was personally known to Black's sister Constance; they moved in similar circles of radical intellectuals. Pearson started to read it, but realised immediately that it discussed topics very similar to those he was working on, and decided not to read it himself but to send it to Francis Galton for his advice. Galton was clearly impressed by it, and recommended its publication. Cambridge University Press agreed to publish it, with Weldon acting as an editor. Problems seem to have arisen, however, in finding a mathematician to act as co-editor and finally all concerned agreed that part of the mathematical work should be extracted and published. M. J. M. Hill, Professor of Mathematics at University College, London, took responsibility for this.

Unfortunately, it has proved impossible to locate the manuscript of the *Algebra of Animal Evolution*. However, Black's surviving notebooks, together with the material extracted from the *Algebra* by Hill as Black (1898), give some indication of the scope and nature of Arthur Black's work. Like Pearson, Black was a convinced Darwinian. He took the side of scientific naturalism against its theological opponents. The main focus of his work seems to have been an attempt to use his considerable mathematical skills to develop a quantitative theory of evolution. One incomplete notebook, probably part of a draft of the introduction to his larger manuscript, is entitled:

> *An Algebra of Evolution*, being an essay on the quantitative mathematical treatment of rate of change of specific types, as affected by severity of competition, extent of deviation from the average, longevity, fecundity, tendency to deteriorate, and pure chance.

Another notebook, entitled *The Theory of Deviation from an Average*, states:

> ... the aim is to put the theory of variation of specific characters in course of time by natural selection upon a mathematical footing: the advantages of which will be to exhibit such parts of the theory as admit of proof in a demonstrative form, and to estimate quantitatively those tendencies to change which evolutionists describe ... the actual application of the results to special cases will not be entered upon. The data are probably not yet accumulated for that task.

The work extracted by Hill from the *Algebra of Animal Evolution* was an evaluation of the multiple integral

$$\int V \exp(-U)\, dx_1\, dx_2 \ldots dx_n$$

'where U and V are homogeneous quadratic functions of the n variables $x_1, \ldots, x_n$ and a constant x_0, and all the integrations are from $-\infty$ to $+\infty$, it being further supposed that U is essentially positive' (Black 1898, 219). This is a very competent solution of a problem of some difficulty, but tells us little of the more statistical side of Black's work. On this the notebooks are more revealing.

Buried amongst a large bulk of unorganised material, nearly all of it rough working, are a couple of quite striking fragments. The first occurs during a discussion of problems to do with the probabilities of survival and reproduction. In investigating such problems Black naturally turned to the multinomial distribution and its properties.

The most interesting aspect of this investigation is his derivation of what would now be called the chi-square approximation to the multinomial distribution. Of course, as Black was not thinking in terms of expected and observed frequencies, we cannot credit him with anticipating Pearson's invention of the chi-square goodness-of-fit test.[8]

The second interesting fragment constitutes an apparently independent derivation of what is now called the Poisson distribution, though it perhaps should not strictly be attributed to Poisson (David 1969, Sheynin 1971b). This comes in a notebook entitled *Problems relating to the Mathematical Treatment of Statistics: Periodicity and Deviation*. Black obtained the distribution to give the probability of an incident occurring 0, 1, . . . times in a given interval of time, when the average of its occurrence in a small unit interval has some small value, say Y. He showed that

> . . . the rule is write certainty in the form $e^Y e^{-Y}$, and expand e^Y in powers of Y by the exponential theorem. The successive terms are the probabilities of 0, 1, . . . incidents.

It is clear, then, that Black was an able mathematical statistician, and what we know of his more general goals indicates very similar sympathies to those of Pearson. But he was quite without influence on the development of statistical theory. His case is not radically different from those of the other mathematicians we have examined. The intellectual 'ripeness' of statistical theory – clearly perceived by Galton[9] – was not in itself sufficient to create a scientific specialism. Individual workers, however talented and committed, could not do this on their own, even were they blessed with happier circumstances than was Arthur Black. What was needed was the establishment of a framework that would give continuity and coherence to work that previously, as we have seen, had been the ephemeral result of temporary collaboration or isolated endeavour.

The Biometric School

In 1892 Karl Pearson and W. F. R. Weldon began the collaboration that was to grow into the biometric school.[10] From 1894, when Pearson began teaching his first advanced course in statistical theory, until the 1920s, when Fisher began to establish an alternative centre at Rothamsted Experimental Station, the biometric school was the only institution in Britain providing an advanced training in modern statistical theory. Even in the 1890s, the first decade of its existence, the biometric school was already producing around half the papers in statistical theory published in Britain.[11] Ben-David (1971, 151n.) notes that:

> Those who actually taught [at University College] include 5 of the 15 persons named as the most important contributors to the development of present-day statistical method in the *International Encyclopedia of Social Science*.

Biometrika (the 'house journal' of the biometric school) was for a long period the major publication outlet for work in statistical theory in Britain, and it remains one of the world's foremost statistical journals. All in all, in discussing the biometric school we are a long way from the sporadic individual contributions discussed in the last few pages. The nucleus of a new discipline was coming into being.

For all the biometric school's importance to the development of statistical theory, the latter was a subsidiary part of its activity as far as its financial and organisational backing was concerned. Two developments came together to create the biometric school: a move from within the community of biological scientists to quantify biology, and the tradition of eugenic research begun by Francis Galton. The first development was crucial to the school's formation, the second to its continuing existence and growth.

The move from within biology to quantify its subject matter can be traced to a crisis within the dominant tradition of professional evolutionary biology in Britain, the school of evolutionary morphology centred round F.M.Balfour at Cambridge. The aim of this school was to establish phylogenetic relations (evolutionary trees) between classes of organism by comparative study of their forms, relying in particular on the hypothesis that 'ontogeny recapitulates phylogeny'. In 1886 one young member of the school, William Bateson, wrote:

> Of late the attempt to arrange genealogical trees involving hypothetical groups has come to be the subject of some ridicule, perhaps deserved. (quoted by Provine 1971, 37)

There seems to have been, at least amongst the younger practitioners of descriptive evolutionary morphology, a general openness to new, and hopefully more rigorous, methods of investigation.[12]

Galton's statistical studies, although focused on human heredity rather than general problems of evolutionary biology, offered a possible exemplar of just such a new method. W.F.R.Weldon (1860–1906) saw in Galton's work a way of reconstructing evolutionary biology on a sounder basis than that offered by the morphological approach in which he had been trained. Weldon, who in December 1890 became Professor of Zoology at University College, London, demonstrated in a series of four papers (1890, 1892, 1893, 1895) the applicability of Galton's methods to populations of crabs and shrimps. The first paper showed that measurements made on several local races of shrimp followed the normal distribution. It was sent to Galton to referee, and brought Weldon and Galton into personal contact, Galton aiding Weldon in revising the statistical analysis (Pearson 1906, 282–3). The next two papers applied Galton's correlation techniques, using a non-graphical method of determining the coefficient of correlation devised by Weldon himself. Weldon (1895) attempted the ambitious task of demonstrating natural selection at work in a population of crabs.[13]

As Professors of Zoology and Applied Mathematics in University College, Weldon and Pearson were able to build up a small group of students and co-workers that were either independently supported or in posts associated with the two professorships. Thus, Pearson's first course on advanced statistics had an audience of two: George Udny Yule, Pearson's demonstrator, and Alice Lee, a lecturer in Bedford College. Weldon recruited several postgraduates, first at University College and then, from 1899, at Oxford; notable among these were Ernest Warren, Arthur Darbishire and Edgar Schuster.[14]

The work of Weldon and his postgraduates demonstrates the early importance of the move within the biological community to a statistical methodology. The fact that Weldon's group did not survive his early death indicates, however, biometry's lack of implantation within biology. It was work that required a relatively unusual combination of training; professional biologists were suspicious of the new methodology; the biometrician/Mendelian controversy may have led some biologists to identify biometric methods with hostility to Mendelism.[15] Whatever the causes, biometry as a specialty within professional biology must be judged a failure.[16]

With the waning of biometry as a biological specialty the overt connection between statistics and eugenics became of increasing importance in the development of the biometric school. In the early 1900s Pearson began the transformation of his still relatively haphazard and informal group into an established research institute. In this process, some resources were available to him simply through his university professorship and the general reputation of his work.[17] Other funds, however, came specifically for eugenics. In February 1905 Francis Galton gave the University of London £1500 to establish a Eugenics Record Office, and from then until his death he gave £500 per year for eugenics research (Farrall 1970, 131). At the end of 1906 Galton asked Pearson to take over the direction of the Eugenics Record Office, which became known as the Galton Laboratory of National Eugenics (Farrall 1970, 111). The Eugenics Laboratory, together with a 'Biometric Laboratory' established from Pearson's other resources and oriented more towards statistical theory as such, became the beginnings of a solid base for the biometric school.

This base was further extended when Galton died in 1911. In his will he left the residue of his estate to the University of London for the establishment of a 'Galton Professorship of Eugenics' with 'a laboratory or office and library attached thereto', and recommended that the post be offered to Karl Pearson (K. Pearson 1914–30, 3A, 437–8). A public appeal was launched for funds for a building for the Eugenics Laboratory, and supported in a *Times* leader in October 1911:

> The state of morals and of intelligence disclosed by the recent strikes, the state of health of the rising industrial population as disclosed by the medical inspections of schools are alike in showing the need for the study and the application of Eugenics, and in affording support to the appeal which we bring before our readers. (quoted by E. S. Pearson, 1936–38, part 2, 190)

The appeal seems finally to have brought in some £2300.[18] Most of the money was provided by friends and relatives of Galton and members of the Eugenics Education Society: there were no very large donations from businessmen.[19] A much larger sum of money, however, was provided (though it was apparently not initially earmarked for eugenics) by a donation to University College from a businessman, Sir Herbert H. Bartlett.[20]

The money from Galton, Bartlett and the subscribers to the appeal fund made possible the provision of a building intended to house the Biometric and Eugenic Laboratories, which were now jointly called the Department of Applied Statistics, and enabled Pearson to give up his onerous teaching duties as Professor of Applied Mathematics and become Galton Professor of Eugenics. Thus, the first university department in Britain committed to advanced teaching and research in statistical theory was established, with the funds for its establishment coming in part from the connections between statistics and eugenics.

It should be emphasised that the use by Pearson of the 'eugenic connection' to obtain support for statistical research was not a cynical or opportunist strategy, but reflected both his personal position on the relationship of eugenics and statistics and their actual coupling in the practice of the Biometric and Eugenic Laboratories. Pearson believed that eugenics had to have a statistical form to be properly scientific and a sound basis for social action: he was, for example, reluctant to become Professor of Eugenics unless allowed to carry on the direction of the Biometric Laboratory, with its programme of teaching and research in statistical theory (Pearson 1914–30, *3A*, 436). At the same time the needs of eugenics figured large in his work in statistical theory. In his last report to the Worshipful Company of Drapers, who had provided regular funds for the Biometric Laboratory, Pearson warned of the need to keep statistical theory 'in touch with practical needs' (Pearson 1936–38, part 2, 230) and there is no doubt that in his mind eugenics – as 'the main, if not the sole, safeguard for future national progress' (Pearson 1909d, 39) – was the source of the most central of these practical needs. In reality, there seems to have been little clear demarcation between the Biometric and Eugenic Laboratories, which shared personnel, methods and problems. The Laboratories are best seen as a unified research institute pursuing, at least in the period up to 1914, a multi-faceted but still integrated research programme.

The biometric school was a coherent social group under the clear leadership of Pearson. Much of its work was collaborative. To the extent that the nature of this work tended to involve large numbers of measurements, and a very large amount of detailed arithmetical calculation, this was inevitable. Despite the division of labour involved, Pearson seems to have kept a close eye on the progress of work. He would frequently assist subordinates in the preparation of their work for publication. Ethel Elderton wrote that he 'always had time to sit down and discuss an individual problem. We did not go to his room, but he came round at least once a day to see everyone' (quoted by Pearson 1936–38, part 2, 182). W. S. Gosset wrote:

> ... I gained a lot from his 'rounds': I remember in particular his supplying the missing link in the probable error of the mean paper – a paper for which he disclaimed any responsibility ... at 5 o'clock he would always come round with a cup of tea ... and expect us to carry on till about half past six.
> (quoted *ibid.*, part 2, 182–3)

This social situation led naturally to a high degree of intellectual coherence, which was reinforced by the fact that the group possessed its own organs for publication (*Biometrika*, and the various series of Biometric and Eugenic Laboratory publications) over which Pearson exercised direct control. Yule claims that *Biometrika* was 'surely the most personally edited journal that was ever published' (Yule 1936, 100).

Within the group strong personal ties were formed, and a considerable *esprit de corps* seems to have existed. Yule writes that, 'in the old days', Pearson and he 'spent several holidays together' (1936, 101). When Weldon moved to Oxford, the biometricians would meet in a country cottage for a working weekend (Pearson 1906, 309–10). Yule informs us that there was much social intercourse between Pearson and his students, and that '... the influence of [Pearson's] striking and dominating personality went far beyond the class-room walls' (1936, 100).

There seems to have been a strong sense of the correctness of the scientific approach of the biometric school, and conversely of the weakness of much of the work done outside it. In Karl Pearson's lectures, writes Egon Pearson, 'we were told of the sins of many people' (1936–38, part 2, 207). Pearson was a fierce controversialist, and on occasion personally cold and hostile to those with whom he disagreed. This attitude does not seem to have sprung from psychological disposition: Yule, who had often been the object of Pearson's anger, conceded that Pearson was in non-intellectual matters unfailingly courteous and friendly (Yule 1936, 101). Perhaps it makes more sense to see Pearson's attitude as the response of the man at the centre of a small group of researchers, pursuing what he felt to be work of the greatest scientific, social and moral importance in a world he interpreted as prejudiced, indifferent and hostile. In any case, the consequence was a further tightening of the group boundary. Those members, or former members, of the biometric group who espoused what Pearson considered to be error were cut off from the group. As the letters between Yule and Greenwood in the period immediately before 1914 indicate, those 'expelled' had a definite sense of a bounded group from which they had been excluded (Yule Papers, box 1; Yule-Greenwood Letters).[21]

Individual Careers and the Social Institution

The biometric school was a social institution, using the term in a wide sense to include not merely formal organisations but the whole range of relatively stable, trans-individual patterns of social behaviour (see, e.g., Berger and Luckmann 1971, 65–109). As indicated above, it had an internal social life involving collaborative work, a clear leadership role, non-work socialising, and a strong sense of boundary between insiders and outsiders. It was also involved in society outside it. From outside, it received funds and other forms of support. To the outside, it presented a public face largely in the enormous stream of papers and monographs that its members produced.

When discussing the relationship of Galton to the mathematicians with whom he collaborated, questions of individual motives and commitments, of personal aims and goals, were naturally foremost. For these were haphazard one-to-one contacts, not set in any clear pattern. But when we analyse the biometric school we are talking about an entity that, because it was an institution, had an existence over and above that of the particular individuals that comprised it. Their careers were (at least for a time) lived within the institution, but that institution was more than the simple sum of their aims and motives.

To see this, it is most useful to consider the relationship of statistics to eugenics. Central to the corporate existence of the biometric school was the link between statistics and eugenics. Its funds largely derived from that link, and as we shall see in the next two chapters, its published work largely reflected it. The connection of statistics and eugenics was thus an *institutionalised* one, a public aspect of the biometric school and what it did. Yet this by no means implies that the individuals comprising the biometric school were all committed eugenists.

A large number of people worked, at least for a short period, in the Biometric and Eugenic Laboratories at University College. From 1911 onwards the Laboratories had a joint staff of between six and twelve (Farrall 1970, 320–1), and postgraduates and others with their own sources of finance also came to the Laboratories to study and do research. Over forty individuals are known to have worked with Pearson in the years from 1900 to 1914.[22]

On the available evidence, it is impossible to tell why these individuals came to work with Pearson. Some, such as the future social-democratic political theorist, H.J.Laski, appear to have come because of their enthusiasm for eugenics.[23] Others probably had no interest in eugenics, but came to learn specific skills that would be useful to them in other contexts. In most cases, however, the motives of the individuals concerned are quite unknown.

More information is available on the subsequent careers of those who passed through the Laboratories. Two main career paths seem to have been followed by those who, in their time at the Laboratories, became sufficiently skilled in statistics to engage in independent publication. A minority became full-time eugenic or biometric researchers, or took up teaching and research in statistical theory. Some of these, notably Ethel Elderton, obtained permanent employment at University College (Love 1979). The others found employment elsewhere. Raymond Pearl and J. A. Harris returned to academic careers in biometry in the United States, while Greenwood and Soper went on to statistical careers in Britain. The majority of those trained by Pearson, however, found employment outside academic research and teaching or in non-statistical academic work. Heron became chief statistician to the London Guarantee and Accident Co. Ltd (Pearson 1970a). Edgar Schuster eventually became Assistant Secretary to the Medical Research Committee, forerunner of the Medical Research Council (Paton and Phillips 1973). Leon Isserlis became statistician to the Chamber of Shipping (Irwin 1966). E. C. Snow became Director of the United Tanners Federation (White 1960). W. P. Elderton never left employment as an actuary (Menzler 1962). John Blakeman became head of the Mathematics Department of Leicester College of Technology and subsequently Principal of Northampton College of Technology (*Who was Who*, 1914–30).

Employment opportunities thus did exist for Pearson's highly trained students. These opportunities were, however, not such as to permit the easy diffusion of the particular type of eugenically-oriented statistical theory pursued at University College. Finding employment nearly always meant turning to other kinds of work. Thus, Pearson complained in a letter to Galton in 1909:

> You must remember that at present the training in statistics does not lead to paid positions. It is beginning to, but the posts available are few . . . In the last four or five years I have had at least two or three really strong men pass through my hands, but I could not frankly say: 'Stick to statistics and throw up medicine or biology because there is some day a prize to be had'. I feel sure, however, with a future, such men will naturally turn to Eugenics work. Only this last winter one of my American students said: 'I wish I could go in for Eugenics, but my bread and butter lies in doing botanical work. I know that definite posts are there available'. And that was precisely the case with

Raymond Pearl, who has now got the control of an Agricultural State Breeding Station – he was far keener on man than on pigs and poultry, but the public yet has not realised that it needs breeding also! . . . At present the biometrician is the man who by calling is medical, botanical or zoological, and he dare not devote all his enthusiasm and energy to our work. The powers that be are against him in this country.

(Pearson 1914–30, *3A*, 381)

So, as one might expect, it appears that individuals were recruited to the biometric school for a variety of reasons, and, when they had to leave it, were subject to competing pressures. What, however, happened to them while they were in it? Did the social institution mould them, or did they use it for their own purposes? Again, no complete answer can be given, but it is interesting to look at a few individual cases to get some idea of the range of different ways individual careers and the social institution interacted.

'Insiders': Elderton, Heron and Greenwood

In some cases the institutional connections between statistics and eugenics were internalised: individuals belonging to the biometric school adopted its public, eugenic, objectives as their own, private, aims. They were fully in tune with the institution; they were 'insiders' in the full sense. Three such cases were Ethel Elderton, David Heron and Major Greenwood.

The career of Ethel Elderton (1878–1954) has recently been described by Love (1979). In 1905 Elderton left her job as a school teacher to become assistant to Francis Galton in his Eugenics Record Office (the forerunner of the Eugenics Laboratory). She 'then became successively Secretary to the Eugenics Record Office, Galton Research Scholar in the Eugenics Laboratory, then Galton Fellow, and is now [1930] Assistant-Professor in that Laboratory' (Pearson 1914–30, *3A*, 258). She 'early impressed everyone with her enthusiasm for the eugenist cause' (Love 1979, 148). Twenty-two articles in *Biometrika* from 1909 to 1935 bear her name, as do several of the most important Eugenics Laboratory publications. 'Much of her work', writes Love (*ibid.*, 152), 'examined important social issues of the day from the eugenist viewpoint that social problems were to be related to factors inherent in the individual'. While she certainly could put an individual slant on her work – Love tentatively suggests that some of it may have been informed by feminism – it remained technically and politically within the boundaries of the biometric school's statistical eugenics.

David Heron (1881–1969) was educated in a Scottish village school, Perth Academy and St Andrews University before coming to London as a postgraduate in 1905 (Pearson 1970). He started work with Pearson on statistical eugenics, writing the first *Study in National Deterioration* (Heron 1906) in which the statistical methods developed by the biometric school were used to point to the eugenically disastrous differential in fertility between lower and upper social classes. He was taken on to the staff of the Eugenics Laboratory as Galton Fellow and worked in close association with Pearson until in 1915 he began an extremely successful career in insurance. Like Elderton, he seems to have been fully in tune with the dominant approach of the biometric school, standing at Pearson's side in the major controversies to be described in chapters 6 and 7. He remained loyal to the biometric school during his subsequent career, each Christmas presenting Karl Pearson with a cheque 'to be used as the latter might think best for the good of his Laboratories' (Pearson 1970, 289). And his eugenic convictions appear to have remained unshaken (see Heron 1919).

The case of Major Greenwood (1889–1949) is rather more complicated than those of Elderton and Heron. A typewritten autobiographical note in the Pearl Papers (filed with Greenwood to Pearl, 4 April 1926), describes his background and early contacts with Pearson. Inspired by Pearson's *The Grammar of Science*, Greenwood – a medical student in the early 1900s – developed for its author what he described as 'an almost school-girl passion' (Hogben 1950, 140). While still an undergraduate he began biometric work, drawing Darwinian conclusions from a study of healthy and diseased organs (Greenwood 1904, 73). When his father allowed him to work with Pearson after his graduation, Greenwood studied furiously to catch up with the more mathematically-competent members of the biometric school. He was soon publishing studies claiming an important hereditary factor in tuberculosis (Greenwood 1909, especially 267) and writing in the *Eugenics Review* (Greenwood 1912, 289–90) of a hereditary type 'physiologically inferior to the normal' comprising 'the tuberculous, the criminal, the mentally ill-balanced' and so on.

Yet by the time of publication of the latter paper doubts had already set in about the correctness of the position he had embraced. In 1910 Greenwood had been appointed statistician at the Lister Institute of Preventive Medicine, and began a distinguished career in medical statistics, particularly epidemiology and public health (Hogben 1950). In this new occupational setting, concerned with environmental measures to prevent the spread of disease, hard-line eugenics was scarcely appropriate, given that it implied limited efficacy (and even eventual harmful consequences) for precisely the type of measures that Greenwood's colleagues and employers were advocating. His letters to his close friend George Udny Yule reveal a growing ambivalence about eugenics:

> All this chatter about nutrition having no relation to, not the *Anlage* of intelligence – that is something we know nothing about – but the manifestation of the *Anlage* as shown in the shaping of the child at school either in work or in the impression he produces on the teacher is manifest balderdash. Give a dog a protein-free diet and he will become a corpse after a certain number of days, give him protein but not enough to keep him in nitrogenous equilibrium and he will equally become a corpse in a rather greater number of days. Now we know that many of the kids are not in nitrogenous equilibrium (Rowntree etc. *ad nauseam*). All this is not just medical dogma but hard solid experimental fact. Really if this is all we statisticians can do towards the solution of social problems . . . (Greenwood to Yule, 30 June 1913, Yule Papers, box 1)

By 1914, he was prepared to join with Yule in publicly attacking some of Karl Pearson's published work in eugenics (Greenwood and Yule 1914).

Greenwood's case clearly shows that the experience of passing through the biometric school did not permanently stamp even those who fully accepted its assumptions. In a different environment, where a different approach was needed to 'make out' (Barnes 1971), the politics and (as we shall see in chapter 7) the techniques of the biometric school could be judged unduly restrictive.

The 'Outsider': 'Student'

W. S. Gosset (1876–1937) came to the biometric school already established in a different environment.[24] An Oxford science graduate, Gosset began work in 1899 for Arthur Guinness and Son, the famous Dublin brewers. Guinness was an early example of an 'agribusiness' monopoly, operating on a scale that came near to dominating the economy of Southern Ireland: thus in 1880 Guinness bought over half the Irish barley crop (Lynch and Vaizey 1960, 221). By the end of the nineteenth century its management had begun to see the potential for the use of science to rationalise the brewer's traditional art and to improve the production of the raw materials needed for brewing. Gosset was one of a number of science graduates taken on for this task.

Gosset quickly accepted the commercial environment in which he found himself.[25] Although offered at least one academic job (McMullen 1939, 357), he chose to remain with Guinness, rising to become in 1935 the manager of the newly established Guinness brewery in London. He does not appear to have disagreed with the practical and profit-oriented demands of his employment (Pearson 1939, 366 and 373), nor does he even seem to have chafed at having (apparently because of a company regulation) to publish under his famous pseudonym of 'Student'.

The most mathematical of the scientists taken on by Guinness (McMullen 1939, 355), Gosset became involved in work on the problems posed by the results of experimental trials. To this work he brought a knowledge of the theory of errors; E. S. Pearson (1939, 363) indicates that he used the three well-known textbooks Airy (1861), Merriman (1901) and Lupton (1898). Gosset soon found, however, that error theory was not fully adequate for the kind of work that had to be done in the brewery.

One problem was the assumption made by the error theorists of the independence of observations (see chapter 3). As Gosset was later to put it, in the brewery situation, where many variables could not be controlled, 'secular change' could lead to 'successive experiments being positively correlated' (1908a, 12). He concluded (presumably as a result of direct experience) that the standard methods of combining independent errors were inapplicable (Pearson 1939, 364–5). He was at this stage unaware of the work of Galton and Pearson on correlation, and could not entirely to his satisfaction solve the problem of how 'to establish a relationship between sets of observations' (ibid., 366).[26] A second difficulty was, in essence, a problem of decision theory. In a report to his board of directors in 1904 he pointed out that because of the large-scale processes used in brewing, and the difficulties of exact control of them, accurate experimentation was not possible, and any conclusions drawn were necessarily probabilistic rather than certain (ibid., 363–4). The question was, then, that of the 'degree of probability to be accepted as proving various propositions' (ibid., 365). Gosset soon realised that there was no single answer to this question:

... in such work as ours the degree of uncertainty to be aimed at must depend on the pecuniary advantage to be gained by following the result of the experiment, compared with the increased cost of the new method, if any, and the cost of each experiment. (*ibid.*, 365–6)

The error theorists, working in astronomy and such fields, had not faced difficulties of this nature. This problem was the first posed by Gosset to Karl Pearson when he consulted him in July 1905, contact having been made through Vernon Harcourt, an Oxford chemist (*ibid.*, 365).

What advice, if any, Pearson was able to give Gosset on this question is unknown. Pearson was, however, able to solve Gosset's problem with non-independent observations by introducing him to the correlation coefficient. On his return to Dublin, Gosset enthusiastically applied the new method. As Egon Pearson puts it (*ibid.*, 367):

It became possible to assess with precision the relative importance of the many factors influencing quality at the different stages in the complicated process of brewing, and before long the methods of partial and multiple correlation were mastered and applied [by Gosset].

A further problem had, however, already arisen by the time Gosset met Pearson, and this was one for which there was no solution in either error theory or biometric statistics.

I find out the P.E. [probable error] of a certain laboratory analysis from n analyses of the same sample. This gives me a value of the P.E. which itself has a P.E. of P.E.$/\sqrt{(2n)}$. I now have another sample analysed and wish to assign limits within which it is a given probability that the truth must lie. E.g. if n were infinite, I could say 'it is 10:1 that the truth lies within 2.6 of the result of the analysis'. As however n is finite and in some cases not very large, it is clear that I must enlarge my limits, but I do not know by how much. (*ibid.*, 366)

Error theorists such as Merriman (on whose work Gosset seems to have been drawing in this instance) were certainly aware that formulae such as that for the probable error of a probable error were strictly valid only for large numbers of observations. Nevertheless, they continued to use them: Merriman (1901) gives probable errors based on five, seven and eight measurements. In practice, of course, the error theorists were concerned chiefly with giving a fairly rough indication of the reliability of a result. It may not have worried them that exact probability statements based on the law of error were not valid for probable errors obtained from small numbers of observations. But it did worry Gosset, perhaps because of his 'decision theory' orientation. Furthermore, Gosset soon realised that precisely the same problem arose with the biometric methods that he had so recently learnt:

> Correlation coefficients are usually calculated from large numbers of cases, in fact I have only found one paper in *Biometrika* of which the cases are as few in number as those at which I have been working lately. (*ibid.*, 367)

That Gosset should have found this is not surprising. Biometric statistical theory was designed to apply to large samples from plant, animal, and human populations. Pearson was not happy unless he could work with sample sizes of at least several hundred, as the following footnote (Pearson 1896, 273) indicates:

> Of course 200 couples give graphically nothing like a surface of correlation, nor can any section of it be taken as a fair normal curve. We assume *a priori* that 1000 couples would give a fair surface.

Biometric statistical theory typically relied (notably in its methods for evaluating probable errors) on the assumption that sample statistics could safely be substituted for population parameters, an assumption that was itself based on an appeal to the behaviour of sample statistics as sample size became large:

> . . . in a considerable number of cases [the] sampled population is unknown to us . . . What accordingly do we do? Why, we replace the constants of the sampled population by those calculated from the sample itself, as the best information we have. And the justification of this proceeding is not far to seek . . . (Pearson 1922, 186–7)

And Pearson went on to argue that sample and population constants differed on average by terms of the order $1/\sqrt{n}$, where n is the sample size (and thus that the difference would tend to zero as n became large).

So we have here a very basic aspect of biometric statistical practice. Indeed, it was one that was enshrined in their notation. They never systematically distinguished between population parameters and the corresponding sample statistics, using the same letters for both (e.g. r for both sample and population correlation coefficients, σ for both sample and population standard deviations). Further, the reliance on large sample sizes does not seem to have been seen as an irksome restriction on their theory, for Karl Pearson at least appears to have felt that small sample work was unsafe and should be placed outside the boundary of proper statistical practice (Pearson 1939, 378).

The biometric school could of course afford to take this attitude. While they, like anyone else, sometimes had difficulty obtaining data, they did usually succeed in amassing large samples. For Pearson's major study of human heredity (described in chapter 7) he collected data on nearly 4000 pairs of siblings. Gosset, on the other hand, could hardly expect his employers to wait while he had a large-scale trial in the brewery repeated several hundred times. As he put it himself (*ibid.*, 373), 'if the Brewery is to get all the possible benefit from statistical processes' techniques valid for small samples had to be devised.

So when Gosset was allowed leave for the year 1906–07 to study and research with the biometric school, he came with goals, derived from his working environment, that were different from those embodied in biometric theory. He took full advantage of the resources he found at University College, but he used them for his own (or rather the brewery's) ends, quite indifferent to the objectives of the research programme that was being pursued around him.

The result was two remarkable papers: 'The Probable Error of a Mean' (1908a) and 'Probable Error of a Correlation Coefficient' (1908b).[27] The objective of these papers was clear:

> . . . it is sometimes necessary to judge of the certainty of the results from a very small sample, which itself affords the only indication of the variability. Some chemical, many biological, and most agricultural and large-scale experiments belong to this class, which has hitherto been almost outside the range of statistical enquiry. (1908a, 12)

The first paper, from which this quotation is drawn, showed how these problems could be overcome in working with sample means drawn from very small samples. Without claiming mathematical rigour, Gosset derived 'the distribution of the distance of the mean of a sample from the mean of the population expressed in terms of the standard deviation of the sample for any normal population' (*ibid.*, 18),[28] making possible what is now called Student's *t*-test. With this, he claimed, inferences could safely be drawn about samples of sizes as small as four. The benefit was clear: 'it can be judged whether a series of experiments, however short, have given a result which conforms to any required standard of accuracy or whether it is necessary to continue the investigation' (*ibid.*, 34)

The second paper dealt with the corresponding problem in the case of correlation coefficients. Gosset worked largely empirically, studying the actual distribution of sample correlation coefficients in small samples artificially generated from a known population. He found a result that, he claimed, 'probably represents the theoretical distribution of r [the sample correlation coefficient] when samples of [size] n are drawn from a normally distributed population with no correlation' (1908b, 41).[29]

With the benefit of hindsight, these two papers can be seen as the beginning of a revolution in statistical theory that was based on ascertaining the exact distribution of sample statistics without relying on assumptions about large sample sizes. Gosset's use of different letters to denote sample (s) and population (σ) standard deviations, and sample (r) and population (R) correlations, is a simple but important indicator of his conceptual break from the biometric approach. Much of twentieth-century statistical theory (for example the work of Fisher described in chapter 8) was to take off from the type of problem first clearly spelt out by Gosset.

The reaction of the biometric school was, however, largely one of indifference. Gosset's practical objectives were for them unimportant. In correspondence with Gosset about how best to estimate the population standard deviation (whether to divide the sum of squared deviations by n or $n-1$, where n is the sample size), Pearson playfully chided Gosset that 'only naughty brewers take n so small that the difference is not of the order of the probable error!' (Pearson to Gosset, 17 September 1912; quoted by Pearson 1939, 368). Pearson was not hostile to what Gosset was doing: he helped Gosset in his work, and had the results published in *Biometrika*. But he could see small sample work as important only when its results bore on the validity of the biometric school's own techniques. The only aspect of Gosset's work that was taken up by the biometric school was that of the distribution of the correlation coefficient (Soper 1913, Soper *et al.* 1917). The reason for this is almost certainly that they realised that the sampling distribution of the correlation coefficient could diverge so much from the normal that their standard assumptions might be invalid even for the large samples they typically used. Even when Gosset's work was made rigorous and more general by R. A. Fisher, Pearson was interested only in so far as this work 'solved distributional problems'; 'as to the possible uses of t and r in small samples he always remained sceptical' (Pearson 1967, 350).

From Eugenics to Statistics

Gosset's use of the resources of the biometric school for very different objectives indicates the ultimate vulnerability of the tight connection between statistics and eugenics that the school embodied. Techniques that had been produced for the needs of eugenics, or for biometric biology more generally, could be used for other purposes. That was precisely what Gosset did, drawing on biometric achievements such as the theories of correlation and regression, and the Pearson system of curve-fitting, to satisfy the practical needs of applied research in an industrial context.

Up to the First World War, however, individual use of biometric techniques for different objectives in no way threatened the institutionalised link of statistics and eugenics. On the eve of the War, indeed, the plans of Galton and Pearson for the establishment of a scientific 'party' in which eugenics and statistics would be unified seemed about to come to full fruition. Egon Pearson writes (1936–38, part 2, 195):

> . . . in the early summer of 1914 the auspices for the future of biometry and eugenics were good . . . A spacious new building was nearing completion . . . funds for its equipment were in the bank . . . Courses of public lectures were well attended; though sometimes hidden behind a screen of controversy and of journalistic popularisation of the concept of eugenics, a growing body of opinion was learning to appreciate the value of statistical method.

The War changed everything. The biometric school's research was interrupted as the Laboratories' computing skills were employed in ballistics research. Pearson found it difficult to retain trained staff as new openings for statisticians opened up in government service. Wartime inflation ate away the Department's funds. Perhaps most serious of all, by the end of the War the enthusiasm for eugenics that had characterised the years before 1914 had largely passed. While the long-term credibility of the eugenic theory of society was relatively unaffected, and particular eugenic policies were to regain popularity by the end of the 'twenties (Searle 1979), the immediate post-war years saw a marked decline in the work of the Eugenics Society (Searle 1979, 160) and in the directly eugenic research of the biometric school (Pearson 1936–38, 205–6).

Karl Pearson fought against the tide. Despite, for example, discouragingly poor audiences at public lectures on eugenics, Pearson established in 1925 a new journal, *Annals of Eugenics*, devoted 'wholly to the scientific treatment of racial problems in man' (Pearson 1936–38, part 2, 217). The journal survives to the present, though under the title *Annals of Human Genetics*. But despite Pearson's efforts – and those of Ethel Elderton, who helped edit *Annals of Eugenics* – the old pre-war momentum of eugenic statistics could not be regained. Increasingly, the statistical work of the Department (notably that of Karl Pearson's equally-renowned son, Egon Pearson) began to take quite a different direction.

On Pearson's retirement in 1933 the authorities of University College organisationally severed the link of statistics and eugenics. The Department of Applied Statistics was split in two, establishing separate chairs: Eugenics, to which R.A. Fisher was appointed, and Statistics, to which Egon Pearson was appointed. A legacy from W.F.R. Weldon's widow made possible the establishment of a third chair, that of Biometry, to which J.B.S. Haldane was appointed. Despite this increase in the number of senior posts, Pearson felt that the division of his Department constituted a fragmentation that negated his life's work, and he bitterly opposed it (Pearson 1936–38, part 2, 231–2).

So the unification of statistics, eugenics and biometry in Pearson's programme did not survive. Eugenics in the University College context became human genetics, largely lacking the political thrust of Pearson's eugenics. New factors came to be of importance in the development of statistical theory. Yet the statistical techniques of the biometric school were, in many cases, integrated, albeit in a changed interpretation, into the new statistical theory. The Department created by Pearson survived, although it was divided. Pearson's students carved out careers for themselves in these changed circumstances. Perhaps the best way to conceptualise this process is, as suggested at the beginning of this chapter, in terms of the formation of side bets. The aim of Pearson and, before him, Galton, had been to create a scientific specialty and a research institute in which statistical research into heredity and evolution would be pursued, with the ultimate aim of the application of the knowledge gained in a eugenic programme. In pursuing this aim, they had recruited others to this programme, funded and established a new University department, and so on. But in doing so, interests, individuals and bodies extraneous to the initial aim became involved. The most systematic and advanced training then available in mathematical statistics was offered. It attracted those who had no interest in eugenics as such, and took on a momentum of its own. To give the research institute a stable setting, it was established within University College: this committed the College authorities to it, but gave them power over it. These, and other similar side bets, meant that the institutional development started by Pearson and Galton was no longer tied to their initial purposes alone. As eugenics waned, the side bets became more prominent until they came to dominate the initial purposes.

But while the unification of statistics and eugenics persisted it was of prime importance. In the next two chapters I hope to show that it affected the scientific knowledge generated by the biometric school at the most fundamental level. The method I have chosen is to examine the two most important scientific controversies in which the biometric school engaged.

6

Biometrician versus Mendelian

· · · · ·
· · ·
·

The best-known of the controversies involving Karl Pearson and his co-workers is that with the early Mendelian geneticists led by William Bateson. It was marked by the shattering of personal friendships, by heated public debate, by suggestions of fraud and by long-standing divisions within the British scientific community. Pearson suggested that the early death of his co-worker Weldon could be attributed in part to the strain of the controversy (1906, 311). At stake was nothing less than the validity of the theory that became the core of modern genetics: Mendelism. Accordingly, the debate has received much attention from modern historians of biology.[1]

Green Peas, Yellow Peas and Greenish-Yellow Peas

In 1900, Mendel's work on heredity was 'rediscovered' by three Continental biologists, Hugo de Vries, Carl Correns and Erich von Tschermak.[2] The Cambridge biologist William Bateson (1861–1926) seized eagerly on the new approach. He became the leading British Mendelian, and played a crucial role in developing the new 'paradigm' and extending it into different fields. He coined the term 'genetics', and the new discipline it refers to owed a great deal to his work. Much of the terminology of Mendelian genetics is his, and many early examples of the successful use of Mendelian explanations are to be found in his work and that of his group of co-workers, of whom R. C. Punnett (1875–1967) was the most prominent.

Bateson and the Mendelians operated with a theoretical model of the process of heredity, at the basis of which were discrete, elementary genetic factors. These latter we have come to call 'genes', but that term is somewhat misleading because we tend to think of the gene as a physical thing, while at the beginning of the period discussed here the Mendelian factor was a purely theoretical entity. William Bateson, for example, never fully accepted the notion of the Mendelian factor as a material particle and disliked the chromosome theory on which this imputation was based (Coleman 1970).

Mendelian factors were held to pass unchanged from parent to offspring: pairs of factors underwent segregation and random distribution, but no blending of factors took place. Using elementary probability theory, together with assumptions about, for example, the dominance of one factor over another in the visible manifestation of the factors in the offspring, theoretical accounts of processes of heredity could be produced. These accounts were applied to the inheritance of characteristics such as, classically, the green and yellow colourations, and smooth and wrinkled forms, of pea seeds.

The biometricians, on the other hand, did not use a developed, explicitly theoretical model of heredity. If we were to seek a single exemplar as typical of their approach, it would be the treatment of quantitative, easily measured characteristics such as height. Galton's 'typical laws of heredity' (1877) were descriptions of statistical regularities in the relationship between parental and offspring characteristics. Pearson (1896, 259) formalised this approach with his operational definition of heredity as the correlation between the characteristics of parents and offspring (see p.168 below). The concept of heredity predominant in the work of the biometric school was thus that of the degree of similarity in the observed characteristics of different generations of the same organism.

The biometricians' approach pre-dated the 'rediscovery' of Mendelism. Their reaction to the latter was by no means simple,[3] but in its public aspect was primarily one of scepticism and hostility. Biometric criticisms of Mendelism met with fierce rebuttals from the Mendelian camp and a vehement debate about the validity of Mendelism began, which reached its public climax at the 1904 meeting of the British Association. Over thirty years later R.C. Punnett remembered the occasion:

> We adjourned for lunch[4] and on resuming found the room packed as tight as it could hold. Even the window sills were requisitioned. For the word had got round that there was going to be a fight . . . Weldon spoke with voluminous and impassioned eloquence, beads of sweat dripping from his face . . . (quoted by Provine 1971, 86)

Even the report in *Nature* (1904) could not but catch some of the drama of the occasion. Weldon was quoted as describing the Mendelians' hypothetical mechanism of heredity as 'cumbrous and un-demonstrable'. Bateson in reply argued that the Mendelian theory 'had begun to co-ordinate the facts of heredity, until then utterly incoherent and contradictory. The advance made in five years had been enormous . . .' Pearson accused the Mendelians of producing figures 'without making any attempt to show that the figures were consonant with the theory they were supposed to illustrate'. He suggested further investigation rather than mere 'disputation', but remembered the meeting ending with Bateson 'dramatically hold-ing aloft the volumes of this Journal [*Biometrika*] as patent evi-dence of the folly of the [biometric] school, and refusing the offer of a truce in this time-wasting controversy'.[5]

The sudden death of Weldon in 1906 brought an end to the most open phase of controversy, but by no means an end to disagree-ment. As late as 1930 Karl Pearson (1914–30, *3A*, 288) could still describe Mendelism as a largely unproven theory, long after nearly all professional biologists had accepted it. Fundamentally, the two sides in the debate were operating with different approaches to heredity, approaches that were (to use the terminology of Feyer-abend 1962 and Kuhn 1970) 'incommensurable'. To put it crudely, they did not agree on the nature of the problem they were trying to solve, and so there was no clear basis for the assessment of the relative merits of different solutions.

The Mendelians believed that the prime aim of the science of heredity should be the development of a theoretical model of the process of heredity – the development of an account of the passage from parent to offspring of the factors that determined the obser-vable characteristics of organisms, of the 'genotypes' that led to the observable 'phenotypes'. The biometricians – especially Pearson – were primarily concerned with detailing and measuring the resem-blances of these 'phenotypes'. These goals sound complementary rather than conflicting, but in practice they translated into sharply different judgements. Thus the Mendelians felt that they possessed the key to a theoretical understanding of heredity. Believing that, they saw the vast range of phenomena for which generally accep-table Mendelian explanations had not been found – a range that included at the time we are discussing all but a handful of human characteristics – as simply puzzles awaiting resolution in the future. But the biometricians saw matters quite differently. Their primary goal being the description of phenotypic resemblance, they judged different approaches according to their success in this task. 'Mendelism is only a truth so long as it is an effective description', wrote Pearson (1914–30, *3A*, 288). The simplicity of early Mendelism was a point against it, not for it. What appears to be Pearson's earliest discussion of Mendelism[6] considered Mendelism as a description of patterns of resemblances and concluded that it was unlikely to fit all the cases of inheritance of characteristics such as eye-colour and coat-colour, much less more complex characteristics.[7] The flexible descriptive apparatus of biometry seemed much more hopeful as a descriptive tool than the apparently perilously narrow Mendelian model.[8]

The two sides could not always agree even on the facts that stood in need of explanation or description. Mendel's experiments were predicated on the unproblematic classification of peas into different classes (yellow/green, smooth/wrinkled, etc.). He deliberately used only characteristics that he felt to 'permit of a sharp and certain separation' (1865, 45). But the biometricians doubted that this sharp differentiation was possible, even for the characteristics that Mendel had chosen. Weldon (1902a) argued that pea seeds did not fall naturally into Mendel's classes, but shaded gradually from yellow to green through intermediate tones, and from smooth to wrinkled by various degrees. He presented photographs of pea seeds to prove his point.[9] In reply Bateson argued that Weldon's key cases were 'mongrel' peas, rather than the 'pure' variety needed to manifest Mendelian phenomena unequivocally (1902, 188–9). But the very notion of the 'purity' of a variety was itself a theoretical Mendelian concept, not a simple empirical description (*ibid.*, 129). Further, Bateson argued that even if pure-bred peas were used, anomalous results could be produced by such contingencies as accidental crossing, 'sporting' and environmental factors.

The dispute between the biometricians and the Mendelians could not, to use Kuhn's phrase, 'be unequivocally settled by logic and experiment alone' (1970, 94). There was nothing *illogical* in arguing, as Pearson did, that the best approach to heredity was that which best described the regularities of phenotypic resemblance, nor in placing *a priori* confidence in a theoretical model and being unabashed at its inability initially to explain anything other than a small range of observed phenomena, as the Mendelians did. Nor could experimental studies of heredity have resolved the issue, even if the two sides had been able to agree on the interpretation of a given result. An undisputable experimental demonstration of a predicted Mendelian ratio would not have converted Pearson and

Weldon to Mendelism: they could simply have pointed to the vast range of phenomena not adequately described by Mendelism. Nor, *a fortiori*, would the failure of Mendelism in a particular case have caused the Mendelians to jettison their basic model. In fact, attempts at 'crucial experiments' did not in any case reach any definite conclusions, but largely degenerated into disputes about the competence and honesty of the experimenters (Provine 1971, 73–80 and 87–8).

The incommensurability of the two positions did lead to difficulties of understanding and communication. 'Mr Bateson and I do not use the same language', wrote Karl Pearson (1902a, 331). This was particularly the case with the different interpretations of Galton's 'law of ancestral heredity'. As Froggatt and Nevin (1971a,b) emphasise, disputes over the validity of this 'law' were prominent in the controversy. Galton had primarily intended the law, first pointed to in his 1865 paper on 'Hereditary Talent and Character' (1865, 326), to summarise the degree of influence of ancestors of each degree on the height, say, of an individual:

> . . . the influence, pure and simple, of the mid-parent may be taken as $1/2$, of the mid-grandparent $1/4$, of the mid-great-grand-parent $1/8$, and so on. (1885c, 261)

Pearson interpreted the law as one of phenotypic resemblance, and attempted to recast it in terms of the theory of multiple regression: as a linear equation giving the predicted height of an individual, in terms of its deviation from the mean height of that individual's generation, as a function of the heights of that individual's ancestors, in terms of the deviation of their heights from the means of their generations (Pearson 1898, 1903a).

At first sight, Mendelism contradicted Galton's law. Once the genetic characteristics of the parents were known, knowledge of distant ancestry was redundant in predicting offspring characteristics. Thus Weldon could write (1902a, 252):

> The fundamental mistake which vitiates all work based upon Mendel's method is the neglect of ancestry . . . not only the parents themselves, but their race, that is their ancestry, must be taken into account before the result of pairing them can be predicted.

Bateson appeared to agree that a fundamental divergence existed between Mendelism and the 'ancestrian' approach:

> We note at once that the Mendelian conception of heredity effected by *pure* gametes representing definite allelomorphs is

quite irreconcilable with Galton's conception in which *every* ancestor is brought to account in reckoning the probable constitution of every descendant.

(Bateson and Saunders 1902, 157)

The two sides were, however, talking about different things. The Mendelians had in mind not phenotypic resemblance, but genetic structure. It was true that on a Mendelian view, distant ancestry was irrelevant, in the sense that what mattered was the composition of the zygote: all individuals with the same zygote were genetically identical, irrespective of where the particular factors had come from. When, however, it came to predicting on a statistical and phenotypic basis the characteristics of offspring, then even on a Mendelian view the characteristics of an individual's ancestry *were* relevant, as these helped indicate the (unknown) parental genetic make-up. As Pearson (1904a, 1909a,b) was able to demonstrate, a multi-factorial Mendelian model in fact led, at the phenotypic level, to a multiple regression equation similar to the law of ancestral heredity.

This last development illustrates that difficulties of understanding and communication, while they did exist, were surmountable. In spite of their incommensurability – or, rather, *because* of it, because the two approaches were on different ontological levels – there was no absolute formal barrier to a synthesis of the two approaches. Sporadic attempts at reconciliation were indeed made from early on (e.g., Yule 1902). But the major participants in the controversy chose to maintain it as a controversy, to highlight rather than to gloss over or eradicate the differences in their approaches. Logic did not force them to do this – it was a choice they made. And, to a large extent, it was not a choice made in ignorance. Pearson and Weldon, for example, were perfectly capable of understanding Mendelian work; both sides knew of Yule's work. So the incommensurability of the two positions cannot be taken as explaining the controversy – in fact it is itself something to be explained. We must not stop at the demonstration of incommensurability, but seek to explain the initial generation and continued maintenance of divergent positions.

Mathematics and Biology

Perhaps the most obvious factor that might account for the differences between the two approaches is to be found in the different sorts of skills employed by the two sides. Thus Bateson appears to have felt that the biometricians did not possess (or, in the case of Weldon, were not using) the competences of trained biologists. He lamented the fact that Galton and Pearson 'were not trained in the profession of the naturalist' (1902a, xii). The connection between theoretical Mendelian factors and the observed properties of organisms was not such that anyone could immediately 'see' what was going on. A naive approach, which failed to take account of the complexities of the relationship between theory and the results of particular experiments, could mislead. Even classification of peas into categories – green or yellow, smooth or wrinkled – could not be done mechanically, as Bateson felt the biometricians did it, but was a difficult task requiring experience (see Bateson to Yule, 28 November 1922; Yule Papers, box 22). The statistical approach of the biometricians was quite inadequate, Bateson told the 1904 meeting of the British Association, in dealing with subtleties of, for example, the creation of new stocks in practical breeding:

> Operating among such phenomena the gross statistical method is a misleading instrument; and, applied to these intricate discriminations, the imposing Correlation Table into which the biometrical Procrustes fits his arrays of unanalysed data is still no substitute for the common sieve of a trained judgment. For nothing but minute analysis of the facts by an observer thoroughly conversant with the particular plant or animal, its habits and properties, checked by the test of crucial experiment, can disentangle the truth. (Bateson 1928, 240)[10]

Conversely, the biometricians, particularly Pearson, felt themselves to be practising a more rigorous form of biology, which employed exact definitions and mathematical argument. Bateson and the 'old school' of biologists operated with 'confused and undefined notions', the biometricians with 'clear and quantitatively definite ideas' (Pearson 1902a, 321). The lack of mathematical training of the majority of biologists was blamed by Pearson for what he saw as their indifferent or hostile response to biometry. In the theory of evolution, and some other fields of biology, 'without mathematics, further progress has become impossible':

> . . . mathematical knowledge will soon be as much a part of the biologist's equipment as today of the physicist's. (*ibid.*, 344)

Thus, the participants themselves viewed the controversy as, at least in part, a clash of traditional biological and mathematical skills. How far is it possible to build this insight into an acceptable account of the controversy? One possible approach would be to start with the training individuals receive and their early disciplinary experiences, and to regard these as having a conditioning effect on their future scientific work. This approach is, in effect, that employed by de Marrais (1974). He argues that the mathematical perspective of Galton and the biometricians, in particular their continual use of the normal curve, constrained their perception. It was impossible logically to move from continuous variation to determine a finite number of underlying factors.

> . . . by its very nature the Frequency Law prohibits the discovery of the real (i.e., finite number of) causal agencies determining a trait's distribution pattern or 'type'. (*ibid.*, 154)

By comparison, Bateson, who was a notoriously weak mathematician, was not constrained in this way.

> The nonmathematical basis of William Bateson's (and all the early Mendelians') thought represented not so much a cause of his Mendelism as an absence of the mainstay holding together the bundle of inhibitory relations that held back the biometricians. (*ibid.*, 169)

However, the model of the operation of training and early experiences implied in arguments such as this seems implausible. To use Wrong's phrase, it would seem to involve an 'oversocialised conception of man' (Wrong 1976). Without supporting theory or evidence, it is difficult to imagine why individuals should be trapped in this manner by their disciplinary socialisation. After all, there are plenty of instances of individuals breaking with the approach of their training: thus both Weldon and Bateson broke, in different ways, from the morphological and embryological approach to biology of their Cambridge training (Pearson 1906, Coleman 1970). An individual is not necessarily programmed for life by his or her training. Yet training obviously is important. Can these two points be reconciled?

The internal social structure of science is, as Hagstrom (1965) argues, competitive. Prestige and reward follow in part from the recognition, by their fellows, of scientists' work as correct and interesting. In this 'market', the scientists' resources include the skills relevant to the performance of successful scientific work that they possess. No-one is all-competent. Individuals' competences are competences to use particular techniques, to work within the framework of particular theories, to handle particular materials. Thus, we can expect there to arise a tendency to evaluate new theoretical developments, new techniques, and so on, in terms of their effects on the value of scientists' existing skills. Other things being equal, we would expect scientists to be favourably inclined to developments that enhance the value of their skills, and hostile to those that devalue them. Training provides individuals with skills, and these skills can affect a scientist's evaluations because of their role as resources in a competitive market for scientific knowledge.[11]

On this view, it is certainly possible to understand the hostility shown by traditional biologists to biometry. If the biometric approach came to dominate biology, as Pearson and Weldon clearly and publicly hoped, then traditional biological skills would be devalued. E. Ray Lankester wrote (1896, 366):

> You can not (it seems to me) reduce natural history, as Prof. Weldon proposes, to an unimaginative statistical form, without either ignoring or abandoning its most interesting problems, and at the same time refusing to employ the universal method by which mankind has gained new knowledge of the phenomena of nature – that, namely, of imaginative hypothesis and consequent experiment.

One of Bateson's favourite bits of advice to young biologists was to 'treasure your exceptions' (Bateson 1928, 324). But there seemed to be little room in the biometric approach for the skilled attention of the biologist to the individual case. Biometry would, at least in part, substitute the skills of the mathematician for those of the biologist, and Bateson (along with many of his colleagues) was no mathematician. Bateson publicly admitted that 'his [Pearson's] treatment is in algebraical form and beyond me' (1902, 110n.).

Conversely, this view helps us to understand the widespread acceptance of Mendelism by the new generation of professional biologists following the rapid development, by T. H. Morgan and others, of the Mendelian chromosome theory in the period 1910–15 (Allen 1975a, 56–65; see also Allen 1978). This new generation had been trained in an experimental and mechanistic approach to biology. Initially they were sceptical of the Mendelian approach, which they found too speculative (Allen 1975a, 53). The establishment of the Mendelian chromosome theory, by the use of the fast-breeding *Drosophila* and the development of techniques such as chromosome mapping, changed their attitude completely. The techniques of Morgan's 'fly room' made the problem of heredity experimentally approachable. Mendelism then became the key to extending the scope of experimental biology: it was a theory that enhanced the value of the competences of experimental biologists, by showing that the use of these competences could throw new light on traditional areas of biological investigation (Allen 1968, 138).

Thus, it is perhaps useful to see the scientists involved in the controversy as being faced with competing bases of judgement that embodied different technical competences (those of the traditional biologist, of the experimentalist, of the mathematician, etc.). So as to avoid the 'devaluation' of their competences, they typically rejected bases of judgement involving alien competences and adhered to those involving the use of familiar skills. Take, for example, one instance of a particular scientific judgement: that of the adequacy of Mendelian categories such as 'yellow' and 'green', or 'hairy' and 'glabrous' (hairless). Bateson was confident that a skilled biologist could reliably classify plants and animals into categories such as these, even if an untrained observer would find it a difficult or impossible task. His judgement that these Mendelian categories should be used thus rested on the biologist's competences. The biometricians, on the other hand, criticised these Mendelian categories as 'ambiguous', as 'leading to the accumulation of records, in which results are massed together in ill-defined categories of variable and uncertain extent' (Weldon 1902b, 55). Rather than use the category 'hairy', say, they argued for the keeping of detailed records of the numbers of hairs per unit area. Should records be kept in this form, the necessity for the use of mathematical and statistical competences would immediately be clear.

In other words, the detailed technical judgements made by the two sides reflect at least in part the social interests of groups of scientific practitioners with differing skills. Is this all they reflect? Before answering that question, it is worth examining another aspect of the controversy that went beyond the issue of the validity of Mendelism.

Heredity and Evolution

The central figures in the two sides of the dispute (Bateson, Weldon and Pearson) were already involved in controversy before the 'rediscovery' of Mendelism provided the debate with its best-known focus. This wider controversy had various manifestations: Weldon's (1894) review of Bateson (1894); argument over the origins of the cultivated *Cineraria*; attacks by Bateson on Weldon's work on crabs and on Pearson's work on 'homotyposis'. A single central thread ran through all these particular disagreements (which are fully described in Provine 1971 and Norton 1973). That thread was the issue of the nature of evolutionary change.

The biometricians (Pearson, Weldon and their co-workers, but not Francis Galton) believed that evolution was a process of gradual change, taking place by the selection of continuous differences. If height conferred a selective advantage, then the mean height of a population would rise gradually from one generation to the next, because each successive generation would be formed by proportionately more offspring of tall parents than of short parents. In this, the biometricians were following Darwin (1859). The orthodox view had never gone unchallenged, even within the community of evolutionists: both T. H. Huxley and Francis Galton had doubted that evolution worked in this way, and had suggested a greater role for discontinuous variations ('sports' or 'saltations'), which differed markedly from the parental generation (Provine 1971, 10–24). Thus, Galton had felt that evolution might not proceed smoothly, but might 'jerk' from one position of 'stability' to another (1869, especially 367–70 and 375–6). Those opposed to Darwinism also took up the issue of discontinous variations, although, unlike Huxley and Galton, they tended to suggest that a 'nonmaterial directive agency' was guiding the production of these variations (Provine 1971, 24).

This long-standing thread of opposition to orthodox Darwinian selectionism was given new force in 1894, with the publication of William Bateson's *Materials for the Study of Variation*. The book is indeed mainly a catalogue of a large number of instances of variation. The subtitle, however, conveyed the import of these examples: *Treated with Especial Regard to Discontinuity in the Origin of Species*. Bateson argued that the morphological approach to evolutionary theory (in which he, like Weldon, had been trained), had proven to be barren: attention had to shift to the empirical study of variation. This empirical study revealed clearly that large, discontinuous variations did occur in nature. Further, he concluded that it was this type of variation (and not quantitative individual differences) that was of evolutionary significance. Species were discontinuous entities, differing qualitatively from each other: environments, by comparison, shaded continuously one into the other. The source of specific discontinuity could not, therefore, be the environment (whether acting in a direct Lamarckian or indirect selectionist fashion): it had to lie in variation, in the 'raw material' for evolution. Although Bateson said, cautiously, that 'inquiry into the causes of variation is as yet, in my judgement, premature' (1894, 78), he did suggest that the source of discontinuity should be sought 'in the living thing itself', and that the key to its understanding lay in the phenomena of pattern: symmetry and merism (Coleman 1970, 250).

In the following decade, Hugo de Vries published his *Die Muta-tionstheorie* (1901–3), which was in part stimulated by Bateson's work (Allen 1969, 65). Like Bateson, de Vries thought that large discontinuities were the key to the evolutionary process:

> The object of the present book is to show that species arise by saltation and that the individual saltations are occurrences which can be observed like any other physiological process. (quoted by Allen 1969, 59–60)

While Bateson's work had had an impact amongst only those biologists with clear evolutionary concerns, that of de Vries received wide and generally favourable attention (Allen 1969, 65–9).

Thus, overlapping the controversy over the validity of Mendelism was this further dispute over the nature of evolutionary change. The equation of Mendelism with a discontinuous, anti-Darwinian view of evolution was not, it is true, a logically necessary one. For example, Morgan's work from 1910 onwards on mutant *Drosophila* convinced him that mutations could have small phenotypic effects (no greater than the usual limits of continuous variability): he simultaneously upheld Mendelism, a Mendelian mutation theory, and a view of evolution as a gradual process (Allen 1968; see also Allen 1978, 314). Conversely, de Vries, although one of the three 'rediscoverers' of Mendelism, denied that progressive mutations obeyed Mendelian laws (Allen 1969, 61), and became disenchanted with Mendelism (Provine 1971, 68). But, for all this absence of a *necessary* connection, the two issues became closely bound together, especially in Britain.

In one sense, Bateson came to Mendelism as a result of his belief in the role of discontinuities in evolution.[12] In the years following the publication of the *Materials*, he set himself the task of discovering how discontinuous variations might be passed on to successive generations (a key issue in the development of a 'saltationist' theory of evolution). The method he chose was experimental plant hybridisation, the crossing of closely related varieties and the examination of the characteristics of sets of offspring of such crosses (Coleman 1970, 250–1). Bateson was travelling by train from Cambridge to London, to deliver a lecture on the preliminary results of his investigations, when he first read Mendel's paper on peas; he immediately incorporated the results into his lecture (Bateson 1928, 73). He had been 'made ready' for reading Mendel by his own work on discontinuous variations and their heredity. He reacted enthusiastically, and interpreted Mendelism as supporting his own 'saltationist' evolutionary views. He wrote (*ibid.*, 223):

The discovery of Mendelian elements admirably coincided with and at once gave a rationale of these facts.

Pearson and Weldon also felt there to be a connection between Mendelism and a discontinuous view of evolution; but this, for them, was a reason to reject Mendelism, not to embrace it. Pearson wrote (1906, 306):

To those who accept the biometric standpoint, that in the main evolution has not taken place by leaps, but by continuous selection of the favourable variation from the distribution of the offspring round the ancestrally fixed type, each selection modifying *pro rata* that type, there must be a manifest want in Mendelian theories of inheritance. Reproduction from this standpoint can only shake the kaleidoscope of existing alternatives; it can bring nothing new into the field. To complete a Mendelian theory we must apparently associate it for the purposes of evolution with some hypothesis of 'mutations'.

Thus, the biometricians' opposition to Mendelism can be seen, at least in part, as an opposition to the saltationism with which they associated it.

So the problem of explaining the biometrician/Mendelian controversy is one of explaining these divergent views of evolution, at least in so far as we wish to explain the prior dispute between the biometricians and Bateson, and its continuance into the later phase of the controversy over Mendelism proper. These divergent views on evolution did not arise in any simple way from experimental evidence, but rather took the form of basic assumptions. Thus Bateson (1901) separated variation *by definition* into the two classes of 'specific' variations (which were discontinuous and of evolutionary significance) and 'normal' or 'continuous' variations (which *a priori* were not), and criticised Pearson *et al.* (1901) on the grounds that the biometricians had not done so. And, as the quotation above indicated, Pearson took the continuous view of evolution as 'the biometric standpoint', i.e. fundamentally as a presupposition.

Factors internal to the social system of science, such as professional competences, may again be examined as a possible grounding for these different views of evolution. Allen (1969) shows how de Vries's mutation theory appeared initially to solve some of the problems that troubled the Darwinian theory (see also Darden 1976). Biologists might then be expected to take up the new theory as a promising area for innovative work. In particular, the mutation theory gave new relevance to experimental work in the form of attempts to demonstrate mutations in plants and animals reared in experimental conditions. Mayr (1973, 149) states of the period immediately after 1900:

> I am not aware of a single experimental . . . biologist who championed natural selection.

Old-fashioned field naturalists, by comparison, tended, according to Mayr, to remain faithful to orthodox Darwinism.

It would therefore seem plausible to suggest that the assessment of evolutionary theories by experimental biologists was informed by judgements of the relative scope offered by these theories for experimental work, and that it was in part for this reason that they preferred the mutation theory to orthodox Darwinism. An instance of this would appear to be C. B. Davenport. Davenport had introduced Pearsonian biometry to America, but following the 'rediscovery' of Mendelism and the publication of the *Mutationstheorie* he 'defected'.[13] Davenport had considerable experience as an experimentalist, and had introduced the teaching of experimental morphology to Harvard. A 'painfully ambitious' man, he was from 1902 to 1904 engaged in a campaign to persuade the Carnegie Institution to set up a station for the experimental study of evolution. He therefore approached the mutation theory with a strong interest in the experimental studies it made possible. In 1902 he toured Europe, visiting the Marine Biological Stations there 'to better fit myself for the work of directing the Station for Experiments on Evolution, whenever the Carnegie Institution establishes it' (quoted by MacDowell 1946, 19). On his return Davenport wrote (1903, 46):

> The most important events relating to the study of variation that have occurred during the past two years have been the establishment of the journal *Biometrika*, the foundation in America of a Society of Plant and Animal Breeding, the completion of the first volume of de Vries's 'Mutationstheorie', and the rediscovery of Mendel's Law of Hybridity. Especially the latter two events have awakened a strong tendency toward the experimental study of evolution.
>
> During the last four months the recorder has visited many of the experimental evolutionists of Europe. While the total work

on this subject in Europe is of the greatest importance, it is carried on under conditions that greatly hamper the work and make it impossible to start experiments that require to be carried on for a long period of years. Everywhere the hope was expressed that in America a permanent station for experimental evolution would be founded, and it was believed that the Carnegie Institution would be the proper organisation to initiate and maintain such a station.

Thus, we can claim that for Davenport the mutation theory and Mendelism made it possible to *do* more (within his desired occupational role) than the Darwinism of the biometricians. In 1904 he did indeed achieve his aim of becoming Director of a Laboratory set up by the Carnegie Institution at Cold Spring Harbor, and the work done under his direction was Mendelian and mutationist in tendency. As he wrote (1905, 369), reviewing the work of de Vries:

> The great service of de Vries's work is that, being founded on experimentation, it challenges to experimentation as the only judge of its merits. It will attain its highest usefulness only if it creates a widespread stimulus to the experimental investigation of evolution.

Such an attitude to mutation was incompatible with collaboration with Pearson, and relations between Pearson and Davenport deteriorated rapidly.[14]

Disciplinary skills seem once again to have been important in the overall dispute about evolution. However, most of the evidence about their role concerns the relevance of experimental skills (as against those of field naturalists, for example). As far as these are concerned, the two groups most centrally involved in the dispute in Britain do not seem to have differed too radically. For example, both Bateson and Weldon were arguably closer in their skills to the field naturalist than to the new experimentalists. When Bateson finally began to concede some validity to the chromosome theory, he felt that he would have to import the necessary skills in cell biology from outside his group:

> Cytology here [in the United States] is such a commonplace that every one is familiar with it. I wish it were so with us . . . we must try to get a cytologist . . . (Bateson 1928, 143)

And Weldon was described by Pearson (1906, 297) as 'essentially a field naturalist' in his 'tastes' and 'emotional nature'. So, again, it is wise not to close the enquiry at this point.

Nature and Society : Biometry

On the surface, the biometrician-Mendelian dispute was about the correct way of studying and interpreting the processes of heredity and evolution – it was between two different views of nature. Digging a little deeper, we have found reason to suspect that the vested interests of scientists with different types of skill partially sustained this dispute, particularly those aspects of it that concerned method. And when we extend our investigation from the micropolitics of science to the macropolitics of the wider society, we begin to find hints of the possible operation of a quite different set of factors.

The study of heredity and evolution in Victorian and Edwardian Britain was an activity loaded with social and political meaning. As the credibility of religion declined, it was increasingly to nature, rather than to God, that people turned to advocate and defend their political views. To argue for a state of society as natural began to become more common than to argue for it as divinely ordained. While scientific fields such as geometry (Richards 1979) and physics (Wynne 1979) were by no means immune from use for purposes of legitimation, the biological sciences were the rhetorical resources most often drawn upon. As Young (1969) has documented, the result was that no strict boundaries can be drawn between Victorian biological and social thought, especially in the key field of evolution. While the motivation of particular key thinkers such as Darwin remains a matter of dispute, there is ample evidence that theorising about nature was informed by metaphors drawn from the social world, and that disputes about social policy were frequently carried on in the idiom of biology.[15]

It would be surprising, then, if such a major dispute as that between the biometricians and Mendelians – even if it did take place well after the first bitter debates about evolution and its social meaning – was found not to have some wider social significance. Yet this possibility received but little attention from the historians of biology who documented so thoroughly the course of the controversy. It is indeed true that a social message is not always fully explicit. But perhaps one can be 'decoded' – and perhaps evidence can be found to help check the plausibility of this decoding.

Consider biometry, especially as developed by Pearson. In his crucial third 'Mathematical Contribution to the Theory of Evolution' we find the following statement of a typical biometric research task:

We, therefore, require a generalised investigation of the following kind: Given $p+1$ normally correlated organs, p out of these organs are selected in the following manner: each organ is selected normally round a given mean, and the p selected organs, pair and pair, are correlated in any arbitrary manner. What will be the nature of the distribution of the remaining $(p+1)$th organ?

. . . If the p organs are organs of ancestry – as many as we please – and the $(p+1)$th organ that of a descendant, we have here the general problem of natural selection modified by inheritance. (Pearson 1896, 298; emphasis deleted)

'The general problem of natural selection modified by inheritance' was, for the biometricians, that of constructing a descriptive and predictive model of the process of evolution. In this model, factors such as heredity, natural and artificial selection operated in measurable fashion on biological populations to produce definite effects on succeeding generations. The biometricians' key goal, we might say, was the development of techniques to permit the prediction of the overall incidence of characteristics within biological populations.

It did not appear to the biometricians that their enterprise was in any particular sense goal-oriented. They identified their goals as simply those of any properly scientific study of heredity and evolution. Yet from another perspective the biometricians can be seen as oriented to *particular* goals. Their enterprise was, as suggested above, organised round problems of what we would now call phenotypic resemblances. They studied evolution as a mass process involving gradual, measurable changes in the characteristics of successive generations of whole populations. Their statistical techniques were, as Bateson saw, ill-suited to the identification of suddenly-arising new varieties of evolutionary significance; just as Bateson's techniques were inadequate for the study of mass secular change. The biometricians sought to predict population changes by predicting the characteristics of individuals and summing these for the population. Biological populations were thus seen as individualistic and aggregative, and so as subject to Darwinian selection of continuous differences. 'Holistic' views of biological populations, which saw these as having a stability beyond that of the sum of individual characteristics, were explicitly rejected by the biometricians.[16]

Successful prediction and the potential for control are closely linked. Had the biometric enterprise been fully successful, fully reliable techniques for the prediction of the effects of intervention in one generation on the measurable characteristics of subsequent generations would have been produced. This might indeed have helped the plant or animal breeders, especially had they been concerned with slow improvement of the quantitative characteristics of stock, rather than with the rapid formation of qualitatively new varieties. But it would particularly have helped those eugenists concerned with the planned improvement of whole populations.[17] For there was a strong parallel between the predictive goals of biometry and the interventionist aims of this type of eugenics. The eugenists wanted to alter patterns of reproduction so as to improve the mental and physical characteristics of future generations. Whole human populations were considered, but as aggregates of the individuals composing them. Eugenics was to proceed by identifying 'unfit' individuals, and preventing them reproducing, and/or by identifying 'fit' individuals and encouraging their reproduction. Through the process of heredity, the aggregate 'phenotypic' characteristics of future generations would then be improved; attempts to prove this eugenic assumption were based largely on demonstrating correlations between the incidence of key characteristics in successive generations. Eugenic intervention was social improvement by artificial selection, paralleling almost exactly biological evolution by natural selection as conceived by the biometricians.

In the light of the evidence discussed in the previous chapters of this book, this formal parallelism between biometry and eugenics is hardly surprising. In the origins of biometric methods in the work of Galton,[18] and in their subsequent development and institutionalisation by Karl Pearson, eugenic concerns figured large. The ties of the natural to the social within biometry were present from the beginning. *A priori,* it could be argued that the biometricians first developed their science, and only then saw its social implications – this, indeed, is how they would doubtless have presented matters. But the historical record renders this view unlikely.

Take, for example, the issue of evolutionary change. That evolution was a continuous process, not involving large jumps, was a belief that Pearson had formed well before his involvement in biological research. It was a view that was peculiarly appropriate to the job of justifying gradual, planned social change. As shown in chapter 4, this was indeed precisely the purpose for which Pearson used it; for him, it was a key legitimation of the social role of the intellectual and scientific expert. And it was a view to which he held firm throughout the vogue of discontinuous, mutationist theories of evolution, and was one of the key bases of his criticism of them. Arguably, then, this view represents a channel by which social interests – those of the professional middle-class expert – were brought to bear on the construction of biological knowledge. Further, the chronology – that Pearson's political use of the idea preceded his biological defence of it – effectively disposes of the notion that the course of events was of the later discovery of the social implications of biological theory.

The biometric school's detailed arguments against Mendelism yield further evidence of the connections of biometry and eugenics and of the role of social interests in the evaluation of knowledge. One of the most interesting statements of these arguments is to be found in a comment in a work on human albinism (Pearson, Nettleship and Usher 1913, 491; see Pearson 1936–38, part 2, 169–70). It is worth quoting in full:

> The problem of whether philosophical Darwinism is to disappear before a theory which provides nothing but a shuffling of old unit characters varied by the appearance of an unexplained 'fit of mutation' is not the only point at issue in breeding experiments. There is a still graver matter that we face, when we adduce evidence that all characters do not follow Mendelian rules. Mendelism is being applied wholly prematurely to anthropological and social problems in order to deduce rules as to disease and pathological states which have serious social bearing. Thus we are told that mental defect, – a wide term which covers more grades even than human albinism, – is a 'unit character' and obeys Mendelian rules; and again on the basis of Mendelian theory it is asserted that both normal and abnormal members of insane stocks may without risk to future offspring marry members of healthy stocks. Surely, if science is to be a real help to man in assisting him in a conscious evolution, we must at least avoid spanning the crevasses in our knowledge by such snow-bridges of theory. A careful record of facts will last for ages, but theory is ever in the making or the unmaking, a mere fashion which describes more or less effectually our experience. To extrapolate from theory beyond experience in nine cases out of ten leads to failure, even to disaster when it touches social problems. In all that relates to the evolution of man and to the problems of race betterment, it is wiser to admit our present limitations than to force our data

into Mendelian theory and on the basis of such rules propound sweeping racial theories and inculcate definite rules for social conduct.

That the biometric school's evolutionary theory was designed to be applicable to society as well as nature did not simply constrain the *content* of biology by ruling out theories, such as those referred to in the first sentence of this quotation, that formulated evolution as a discontinuous and unpredictable process. It also constrained its *form*, as the rest of the quotation indicates. To be credible, social programmes such as eugenics had to be seen as based on sure knowledge, not knowledge that was subject to future retraction and contradiction. This was taken to mean that a theory of evolution and heredity had to be developed from observational data, and from these alone. Knowledge of the 'facts' was stable and a safe basis for social action. Theory which went beyond the facts was, however, subject to 'fashion', to change. Thus, evolutionary biology should be phenomenalist, not theoretical, in its form.

The biometric school claimed that their own approach met this criterion. As outlined above, their notion of heredity was primarily a phenotypic, phenomenalist one. Biometry attempted to 'display' evolution as measurable mass change in population distributions. The mathematical apparatus developed by Pearson (1896), for example, took observational data and analysed it according to multiple regression models. The law of ancestral heredity, according to Pearson, was derived from observational data, and enabled the apparently theory-free prediction of offspring characteristics from ancestral characteristics. The effects of eugenic intervention were predictable, without any biological theory of heredity, because the biometric concept of heredity simply summarised what happened in the 'passage' of a characteristic from given individuals in one generation to those in the next. Theory-free control, as well as theory-free prediction, was thus apparently possible.

Early Mendelism, by comparison, was obviously theoretical. A simple exemplar was being imaginatively and sometimes rashly deployed, and was being modified in what often seemed an *ad hoc* fashion. Pearson wrote (1906, 306):

> The simplicity of Mendel's Mendelism has been gradually replaced by a complexity as great as that of any description hitherto suggested of hereditary relationships . . . The old categories are, as Weldon indicated, being found insufficient, narrower classifications are being taken, and irregular domi-

139

nance, imperfect recessiveness, the correlation of attributes, the latency of ancestral characters, and more complex determinantal theories are becoming the order of the day.

With hindsight, we can identify this as creative science, as simply the growth of genetic knowledge. But for those who sought in the study of heredity the basis of an applied social science of evolution, this process could have scandalous consequences.

The most serious of these was when Davenport (1910) suggested that feeblemindedness was a simple Mendelian recessive, and went on (Davenport 1911) to argue that a whole range of characteristics of eugenic importance were of a similar nature. Davenport drew from this what seemed to Pearson to be not merely a foolish, but an immoral conclusion:

> Weakness in any characteristic must be mated with strength in that characteristic; and strength may be mated with weakness. (1910, 25)

A devastating criticism of Davenport's work was produced by the biometrician David Heron, who showed how Davenport's methods were biased towards producing the simple Mendelian results he sought. It concluded (Heron 1913, 62):

> The future of the race depends on the strong mating with the strong, and the weak refraining from every form of parenthood. Nothing short of this rule will satisfy the true Eugenist.

In the course of time, Mendelians themselves came to reject Davenport's simplistic analyses. Bateson was always doubtful (Bateson 1928, 341n), although in the 1920s Punnett still assumed that feeblemindedness was a simple recessive trait (Punnett 1925, 705). Pearson's point, however, was that unjustified theoretical extrapolations, even if subsequently retracted, could have disastrous antieugenic consequences. Eugenics could not be based on a fallible theory: it had to be based on 'hard fact', reliable prediction, and thus unerring control.

Norton (1975a,b) has suggested that Pearson's phenomenalism should be seen as a cause of his rejection of Mendelism. It seems to me that he is right to point to the importance of phenomenalism in connection with the biometric school's assessment of Mendelism, but that it is not necessary – and perhaps wrong – to see Pearson's judgements as determined by an abstract philosophical position. For it is easy to point to instances of Pearson making judgements (for example about the desirability of underlying-variable theories, as described in chapter 7) that scarcely comply with strict phenomenalism. Rather than see phenomenalist philosophy as a kind of straitjacket within which Pearson's mind was confined, it is perhaps better to consider it as a rhetorical resource that he could employ where it was appropriate. As we have seen in chapter 4, his philosophical phenomenalism was a useful weapon in general arguments against the anti-naturalist opponents of scientific expertise: phenomenalist criteria could be used to argue that speculative theorising about the supernatural was *a priori* unsound. Similarly, phenomenalist criteria could be brought be bear to condemn Mendelians who were engaging in rash (and, as Pearson or Heron would put it, anti-eugenic) theorising. Phenomenalist philosophy legitimated what the biometric school was doing – producing apparently theory-free predictive models of population processes – and, more generally, legitimated the naturalistic scientist's claim to privileged knowledge. But to say that it *legitimated* these is not to imply that it *caused* them.[19]

So far I have not attempted to distinguish between the individual positions held by different members of the biometric school. In some cases, for example those of David Heron (see p.110 above and Heron 1913) or H.J.Laski (1912), these individual positions seem indistinguishable from that of Pearson. It was not, however, the case that all members of the biometric school were committed eugenists. But, as explained in chapter 5, individual lack of commitment to eugenics did not affect the fact that there were *institutionalised* connections between biometry and eugenics. In particular, the fact that some biometricians lacked enthusiasm for eugenics does not refute the notion that the goals of biometry were seen as peculiarly appropriate for eugenics.

Consider the case of the most important biometrician who was not a eugenist: W.F.R.Weldon. Weldon's position on the use of biology in political argument is perhaps best summed up in a letter he wrote to Pearson during the Boer War (21 January 1901; Pearson Papers, 625). He is referring to Pearson's major social-imperialist tract, *National Life from the Standpoint of Science* (1901a):

> After talking to invalids in Madeira, who will tell one something about the Army, your lecture seems even more necessary than it did before. I hope you will go on doing work of this kind, as you can do it so well.

Weldon was not hostile to Pearson's social use of science: it was 'necessary'. But it was Pearson, not himself, that he felt should engage in it. His own biological work can hardly be seen as a

141

response to the needs of eugenics: he even pointed out that heredity and environment were not separable factors (as the eugenists assumed), and annoyed Galton by doing so (Weldon to Pearson, 16 October 1904; Pearson Papers, 625). Yet in defending biometry, he was able to draw upon the connection between biometry and eugenics:

> Dr Mercier [a critic of Galton], and those who think with him, object, first of all, that the actuarial [i.e., in this context, biometric] method is faulty, because it does not account for the phenomena of inheritance ... [But] the actuarial method does not pretend to account for anything. It does pretend to describe a large number of complex phenomena with a very fair degree of accuracy, and for this reason it is admirably adapted for the purposes of Eugenic Inquirers. As I conceive the matter, the essential object of Eugenics is not to put forward any theory of the causation of hereditary phenomena, but to obtain and diffuse a knowledge of what those phenomena really are.
> (Weldon 1905, 56)

So despite the lack of evidence that eugenics was an important factor in Weldon's motivation,[20] the biometry-eugenics link, constructed and sustained by others, was available to him as a resource in argument. The link was more than a private obsession of Pearson's, it was a public aspect of biometry. While some eugenists wished to deny the special connection of biometry and eugenics,[21] they had to fly in the face of the public position of the founder of their movement, Francis Galton (e.g. 1909, 72–99).

Nature and Society : Bateson

It would be foolish to try to attribute a single political colouring to a theory such as Mendelism, which was to be found in many different countries and contexts. Nevertheless, the group around William Bateson – the biometricians' most central opponents – is well worth investigating from the point of view of the relation of images of nature to social interests.[22] It is my suggestion that Batesonian biology carried, in the context we are discussing, a social message radically different from that carried by biometry, and can perhaps be seen as sustained in part by social interests quite at odds with those sustaining biometry.

Happily, much of the groundwork of this investigation has already been carried out, in the form of Coleman's penetrating study of the thought of William Bateson (Coleman 1970). While some aspects of Coleman's account may be open to challenge,[23] the overall picture he draws is convincing. His approach is not a sociological one, in that he does not seek to relate the pattern of Bateson's thought to the social factors that might have sustained it. Nevertheless, it is one crying out for sociological interpretation.

Following the usage of the term by Mannheim (1953), Coleman characterises Bateson's thought as 'conservative'. Here I shall, however, describe it as 'romantic-conservative', as the meaning of 'conservative' in Mannheim's sense is easily mistaken by those for whom it conjures up, for example, the image of the British Conservative Party. Indeed, romantic-conservatism is best seen as an *oppositional* stance. It is a critique of bourgeois society, although not from the point of view of a socialist future, but from that of an idealised past. Its chief characteristics can be defined precisely as the negations of the major tenets of the 'natural-law' style of thought characteristic of a progresssive bourgeoisie.

For example, romantic-conservative thinkers typically oppose rationalist individualism (of which utilitarianism would be the best British example). They would elevate being over thinking, the whole over the parts, the particular over the general, the traditional over the progressive. Romantic-conservatism, if Mannheim is correct, is an anti-atomistic style of thinking: holism, organic unity, the qualitative rather than the quantitative, would be romantic-conservative preferences. Because romantic-conservativism is in a sense defined by what it opposes, Mannheim emphasises that the work of a single romantic-conservative need not be expected to possess all these characteristics – to negate one or two key aspects of natural-law thought may be sufficient to signal opposition to bourgeois society.

Mannheim's original work concerned romantic-conservatism in Germany as it defined itself in opposition to the ideologies associated with the French revolution. Potential analogues in Britain are, however, easy to suggest: the 'culture and society' tradition identified by Raymond Williams (1968); Perkin's (1972, 237–52 and 262–4) upholders of the 'aristocratic ideal'; the Christian Socialists as discussed, for example, by Levitas (1976). Romantic-conservative opposition to rampant individualism, to the depredations of capitalist industry, to the destruction of patriarchal order and deference – all these are surely to be found in Victorian Britain.

It is, however, perhaps a little surprising to see a leading professional scientist described as a romantic-conservative. Yet it is precisely in this way that Coleman suggests we characterise Bateson's thought. Coleman's argument rests chiefly on the 'style' of Bateson's science, on what he claims to be its emphasis on experiential concreteness and on the aesthetic, on pattern and form and on visual metaphors. Rather than discuss this general characterisation, I will concentrate instead on more specific instances of overt connections of the social and the biological in Bateson's work. Before doing this, it is, however, necessary to discuss one immediate and obvious objection to any characterisation of Bateson's science as romantic-conservative.

On Mannheim's schema, atomism is a general characteristic of natural-law thought, and not of romantic-conservatism, which typically counterposes holism to atomism. Yet Bateson was a Mendelian, and surely Mendelism is the archetype of reductionist atomism? The interesting point about Bateson, at least on Coleman's analysis, is, however, precisely Bateson's reluctance to accept the chromosome theory, which most fully developed the atomic metaphor in Mendelism by, in effect, reducing the gene to a material particle. As against this literal atomism, Bateson developed an alternative metaphor that, while still mechanical, emphasised holistic ordering rather than 'billiard ball' materialism. Animals and plants are not matter, wrote Bateson, they are 'systems through which matter is continually passing'. On this view:

> The cell . . . is a vortex of chemical and molecular change . . .
> We must press for an answer to the question, How does our vortex spontaneously divide? The study of these vortices is biology, and the place at which we must look for our answer is cell division. (quoted by Coleman 1970, 274–5)

Coleman (*ibid.*, 264–9) makes the interesting suggestion that the source of Bateson's alternative metaphor was the ethereal, non-material vortex atom of the Cambridge physicists. The latter have themselves been analysed by Wynne (1977, 1979) as exhibiting a romantic-conservative style of thought.

Holism played an important part in Bateson's biological thinking. His son Gregory writes of him (Bateson 1973, 349):

> In the language of today, we might say that he was groping for those orderly characteristics of living things which illustrate the fact that organisms evolve and develop within cybernetic, organisational and other communicational limitations.

Early letters to his sister Anna, taken together with the *Materials*, reveal William Bateson's early evolutionary thinking as centring on his dissatisfaction with what he saw as the impoverished view of the organism in orthodox Darwinism and on his search for an alternative way of conceptualising the organism as an integrated, patterned whole.[24] Orthodox Darwinism he criticised as a 'utilitarian view of the building up of Species' (1894, 11). The manifest lack of utility of many specific characteristics, such as plumage, and the fact that many useful characteristics could be useful only if perfect (and thus could not have arisen gradually), were for him strong arguments against this 'utilitarian' selectionism.

It would perhaps be too speculative to place much weight simply on Bateson's choice of the term 'utilitarian' to describe what he opposed in accepted evolutionary theory.[25] It is interesting, however, that at precisely the time when Bateson was developing his opposition to orthodox Darwinism he was conducting his major campaign in Cambridge University politics. He was a leader of the opposition to the abolition of the compulsory entrance qualification in classical Greek. It may seem strange that a man who was a scientist and not a classical scholar should choose such an issue to devote his energies to, but for Bateson compulsory Greek was of enormous symbolic importance. At stake was the 'Classical System' as against mere 'Technical Education'. Mathematics was, he felt, compulsory for the wrong reasons: it was useful 'in trade and professions for the making of money' (quoted by Crowther 1952, 252). Greek, by comparison, was a means of social control and enculturation:

> In the arid mind of many a common man there is an oasis of reverence which would not have been there if he had never read Greek. For Society it would be dangerous, and for the common man it would be hard, if he had never stood thus once in the presence of noble and beautiful things.
>
> (Bateson 1928, 48)

Those who came to Cambridge from 'the Black Country of the commonplace' had to be exposed to the 'side of life which is not common' (*ibid.*, 48). To remove the entrance qualification in Greek would lead to the selection for Cambridge of those who, in the words of his wife, had 'educational aims . . . so utilitarian as to be properly placed outside the University pale' (*ibid.*, 49).

Bateson's broadsheet on compulsory Greek suggests a conscious connection between his attacks on utilitarianism in education and in biology. He admitted – even boasted – that the Classical System was 'useless'. However,

> . . . from grim analogies in Nature it must be feared that it is in just this 'uselessness' that the unique virtue of the [Classical] System lies. (*ibid.*, 48)

It seems possible that there was a link between Bateson's social defence 'of the things which are beautiful and have no "use"' (*ibid.*, 48) and his attack on a biological utilitarianism that held that

> . . . living beings are plastic conglomerates of miscellaneous attributes, and that order of form or Symmetry have been impressed upon this medley by Selection alone.
> (Bateson 1894, 80)

The link may have been a common concern for the necessary conditions of holistic order and stability, whether social or biological, as against exclusive concern for the 'useful'; for 'physiological co-ordination' rather than 'malignant individualism' (Bateson 1928, 315).

One expression of Bateson's hostility to orthodox Darwinism was thus his development of a holistic view of the organism, which emphasised those aspects of it, the phenomena of pattern and symmetry in particular, that could not be seen as 'useful'. The publicly more prominent aspect was, of course, his championing of discontinuity. Here again, the social and the biological intermingled in his writings. He opposed, both socially and biologically, the biometric view of evolution as an orderly, predictable process based on gradual changes in the aggregate. Real advance came, he felt, from rare and largely unpredictable discontinuities, whether the appearance of a 'sport' in biology or an exceptional 'genius' in society. The 'genius' and the 'sport' were indeed identified:

> It is upon mutational novelties, definite favourable variations, that all progress in civilisation and in the control of natural forces must depend. (*ibid.*, 353)
>
> . . . we have come to recognise that evolutionary change proceeds not by fluctuations in the characters of the mass, but by the predominance of sporadic and special strains possessing definite characteristics . . . (*ibid.*, 354; see also 296 and 309)

Given the crucial role of eugenics in expressing the connection between society and biology in the work of the biometric school, Bateson's position on eugenics takes on particular interest. He was just as much of a hereditarian as any of the eugenists, and quite happy to interpret class differences in genetic terms. He showed no compassion for most of those on whom the practice of negative eugenics was proposed, and wrote of the 'feebleminded':

> The union of such social vermin we should no more permit than
> we would allow parasites to breed on our own bodies.
> (*ibid.*, 306)

Eugenics disquieted him, however. Its reforming nature was alien
to his pessimistic conservatism:

> The kind of thing I say on such occasions [talks on eugenics] is
> what no reformer wants to hear, and the Eugenic ravens are
> croaking for Reform. . . . (*ibid.*, 388)

He disliked what he saw as the narrowly middle-class values of the
eugenics movement:

> Consistent and portentous selfishness, combined with dulness
> of imagination are probably just as transmissible as want of
> self-control, though destitute of the amiable qualities not rarely
> associated with the genetic composition of persons of unstable
> mind. (*ibid.*, 374)

He would 'shudder', he said, when he read Galton's condemnations
of 'Bohemianism'. He suggested that Galton had too much respect
for 'material success'.

> In the eugenic paradise I hope and believe that there will be
> room for the man who works by fits and starts, though Galton
> does say that he is a futile person who can no longer earn his
> living and ought to be abolished. The pressure of the world on
> the families of unbusinesslike Bohemians, artists, musicians,
> authors, discoverers and inventors, is serious enough in all
> conscience . . . Broadcloth, bank balances and the other appur-
> tenances of the bay-tree type of righteousness are not really
> essentials of the eugenic ideal . . . I imagine that by the exercise
> of continuous eugenic caution the world might have lost Beet-
> hoven and Keats, perhaps even Francis Bacon, and that a
> system might find advocates under which the poet Hayley
> would be passed and his friends Blake and Cowper rejected.
> (*ibid.*, 374–5, 377)

Bateson, then, was torn. Eugenic measures might well be in the
interests of the 'intellectual and professional class' (*ibid.*, 387) to
which he belonged. Yet their success might merely continue the
process of the encroachment of utilitarian rationalisation and modernisation against which he had set himself. Whatever his private
motives for opposing eugenics – several of those to whom I talked in
seeking information about Bateson told me that his own pedigree
was eugenically dubious – the stated grounds for his opposition fit in
well with his overall romantic-conservatism.

It is important to state clearly that in describing Bateson as a romantic-conservative I am not saying that he was simple a Tory. That is not the case. In fact in his youth he actively supported a Liberal parliamentary candidate, though later he became disillusioned with party politics. Unlike the fiercely imperialist Pearson and conventional Weldon, Bateson opposed the Boer War and the vulgar commercialism that he felt lay behind British involvement: Bateson 'is a fanatical pro-Boer', wrote Weldon to Pearson (16 February 1902; Pearson Papers, 625). The personal tragedy of the loss of a son in the First World War did not turn him into an anti-German jingo: he bravely upheld scientific internationalism and reserved his scorn for the 'army contractors' and 'newspaper patriots' (Bateson 1928, 374). Bateson thus shared many of the strands of left-wing opposition to capitalist imperialism.

Yet his distaste for the 'sordid shopkeeper utility' (*ibid.*, 433) characteristic of capitalism did not make him a socialist. When his sister Anna was thinking of setting up a market garden, he chided her in a letter: 'I think it always a "regrettable incident" when persons whose parents have got clear of trade, relapse into it' (31 July 1889; quoted by Cock 1979, 61). As Cock suggests, he may have been teasing, but the assumption that lay behind the tease – that 'trade' was to be despised – surfaces again and again in Bateson's writing. Industrial capitalism he condemned as socially unnatural – it made too many concessions to egalitarianism – and ecologically doomed in its dependence on fossil fuel. Instead, 'we recognise in the feudal system a nearer approach to the *natural* plan' (Bateson 1928, 456; emphasis added):

> We have abolished the Middle Age conception of the State as composed of classes permanently graded, with the ladder of lords rising from the *minuti homines* below to the king on his throne, and yet to such stratification, after each successive disturbance, society tends to return. (*ibid.*, 354)

Is it possible to give a precise social location for British romantic-conservatism, such as that exemplified by Bateson? In the German situation discussed by Mannheim it seems that, as one might expect, the landed aristocracy formed the ultimate 'market' whose ideological needs were satisfied by romantic-conservative intellectuals. But at least in the period discussed here, the British aristocracy was predominantly in a situation of accommodation with, rather than opposition to, the bourgeoisie (see, for example, Barrington Moore 1967, 3–39). An attack on industrial capitalism was hardly in the interests of late nineteenth-century British land-owners, most of whose income depended directly or indirectly on industry.

In any case, Bateson himself cannot realistically be seen as a propagandist for the aristocracy. He held the old aristocracy in high regard, believing it to have been superior to the middle class (Bateson 1928, 312), but had no illusions in it as a contemporary social force:

> The old aristocracy has largely gone under, not because it had not great qualities, but because those qualities were not of a kind that count for much in the modern world. (*ibid.*, 417)

Nor was his social background aristocratic, though it certainly was élite. Both his grandfathers were Liverpool businessmen,[26] and his father, W.H.Bateson, was Master of St John's College, Cambridge, and a leading university reformer and Liberal.

If Bateson's romantic-conservatism can be linked to an actual social institution it must in fact surely be Cambridge University. This formed the background of his life from birth – his father had already been Vice-Chancellor of Cambridge University before William was born – to his forty-ninth year, when he finally left Cambridge for the security and resources provided by the Directorship of the John Innes Horticultural Institution. The political energies of Bateson's prime were to a significant degree channelled into defending Cambridge University's integrity and élite, anti-utilitarian ethos.[27] His defence of traditional Cambridge was in spite of the fact that his personal career in the University was largely unsuccessful. He never reached the prominent position of his father, and for a long time relied on marginal posts (such as the Stewardship of St John's College) in order not to have to seek employment outside the University.

It is clear that several options were open to Bateson. He could, for example, have chosen to press for Cambridge University to 'move with the times', become 'relevant', and so on, and in doing so could have hoped that this would have improved his own insecure position. In adopting an anti-utilitarian, anti-reforming conservatism, he can be seen as making a genuine choice.[28] Nevertheless, it was a choice between options that were themselves formed by the social structure. He was choosing to defend, rather than reform, a given social institution. He was choosing opposition to, rather than furtherance of, a given process of industrialisation and modernisation. So it makes sense to see his romantic-conservatism as socially conditioned, as one response to a given set of social circumstances, even if not, at the level of Bateson as a concrete individual, socially determined. Although the generality of the conservative response is not crucial to this argument, it is interesting to note that Wynne (1977, 38–9) finds it to be prominent amongst Cambridge dons of Bateson's generation.[29]

Sociobiologies in Competition

In the first part of this chapter, we found evidence to suggest that the biometrician/Mendelian dispute was partly grounded in the 'internal' social structure of science. Groups of scientists with large investments in particular skills would typically be reluctant, it was suggested, to accept scientific approaches that implied the devaluation of these skills. This may explain, for example, the clash of 'mathematical' and 'traditional biological' methodologies. In the second part of the chapter, it was suggested that a further factor of importance was that the theories of heredity and evolution put forward by the two sides carried, in the context of the time, particular social 'messages'.

A few final words about this second facet of the controversy are perhaps in order. Both Pearson and Bateson were following what might be described as a *sociobiological* strategy: both were advocating or defending particular social arrangements as in accord with nature. It was Bateson who commented (Bateson 1928, 334) that 'the knowledge needed for the right direction of social progress must be gained by biological observation and experiment', but there is no evidence that he was uttering anything other than a commonplace. Certainly, while one can find participants in the controversy who seem to have been *indifferent* to the sociobiological strategy (Weldon, for example), I have found none that condemned the strategy as *invalid*.[30]

The point of my account is that the lack of clear challenge to the general sociobiological strategy did not extend to agreement on what nature was like or on what social arrangements were actually in accord with nature. Further, this disagreement was patterned. On the one hand, we find in the writings of the biometric school the view of nature as orderly, predictable and in gradual mass progress alongside the advocacy of orderly, predictable and gradual collective social change, particularly through eugenic improvement of the innate characteristics of entire human populations. On the other hand, in the writings of Bateson we find the view of biological evolution as the result of the sporadic appearance of qualitatively different varieties alongside the claim that all that is socially worthwhile springs from the unpredictable appearance of genius; the view that the organism is holistically ordered alongside the view that society ought to be similarly ordered; even the view of evolution as loss[31] alongside the condemnation of what the conventional called progress.

It can thus simply be noted that the biometric school and Bateson constructed different biologies and used them in defence of different social arrangements. Sometimes the role of this context of use in the detailed construction and assessment of knowledge is explicit, as in the biometric school's judgement of the eugenic potential of Mendelism. At other times we may find clues – such as Bateson's use of the term 'utilitarian' to describe what he disliked in both biological theorising and social organisation – but at present lack sufficient evidence to make definitive statements. Nevertheless, I feel that on balance there is a good case for the conclusion that the scientific judgements of those involved in the controversy cannot properly be understood in isolation from the sociobiological use of the knowledge they produced.

Further, these two competing sociobiologies have been analysed as expressing the interests of different social groups. Gradual and orderly reform, made predictable by the guidance of experts and exemplified by cautious eugenic intervention was, I have argued, an appropriate programme for the rising class of professional experts. And defence of the individual genius against the mediocre mass, and of the value of stable hierarchy and tradition, was what one would expect from the romantic-conservative critics of bourgeois progress.[32]

As has been argued elsewhere (Barnes 1977, 58–63), this is a structural rather than an individual imputation. It is not my claim, for example, that all individual biometricians were rising professionals motivated by meritocratic ambitions. All I suggest is that biometry was an appropriate worldview for such a professional group, and that it was actually used in furtherance of this group's interests. Similarly, my claim is merely that Bateson's biology was an appropriate account of nature for romantic-conservatives, and that it was used to advocate a form of society congenial to their interests. I do not feel justified in going beyond these claims into the realm of the explanation of individual behaviour or the imputation of individual motives. Nevertheless, if these claims are true, and if the sociobiological context of use did indeed structure the produc-

151

tion and evaluation of knowledge, then we have here another instance of the detailed connection of social interests and scientific knowledge.

7

The Politics of the Contingency Table

. . . . .
. . .
.

In the years when the biometrician/Mendelian dispute was reaching peak intensity, another controversy involving the biometric school was just beginning. Much more esoteric in its nature, it never attracted the attention of more than a few specialists and has been relatively little studied by historians.[1] What was at stake – the correct way to measure the association of data arranged in contingency tables – was on the surface an abstruse and merely technical question. Yet the controversy touched the very heart of the biometric programme of eugenic statistics.

The Issue

By 1900 British statisticians had reached apparent consensus on how to measure the correlation of those variables, such as height and weight, for which a measurement scale with a valid unit of measurement existed. In his concepts of regression and correlation Francis Galton had provided the basic technology for dealing with these 'interval' variables.[2] F. Y. Edgeworth, S. H. Burbury and Karl Pearson had extended the theory from two to any number of variables, and Pearson had provided the now standard product-moment formula for the coefficient of correlation. Aside from some private disagreement[3] as to the extent to which Galton's theory, developed for normally-distributed variables, could be applied to non-normal variables, the problem seemed solved for interval-level variables. From 1900 onwards attention shifted to nominal variables – those in which no unit of measurement was available, and classification into different categories was all that was possible. The two main attempts to develop a theory of the association of nominal variables were by Karl Pearson and George Udny Yule (1871–1951).

Let us consider Yule's work (Yule 1900) first. His approach was extremely direct. Consider a set of N objects, classified according to two nominal variables A and B. Each object is classed as either A_1 or A_2, and either B_1 or B_2.[4] Thus A_1 might be 'survived an epidemic', A_2 'died in the epidemic', B_1 'vaccinated', B_2 'non-vaccinated'. If a is the number of those vaccinated who survived the epidemic, b the number of those unvaccinated who survived, etc., the data are most conveniently presented in the following way (the so-called 'contingency table'):

	B_1 (vaccinated)	B_2 (unvaccinated)	Total
A_1 (survived)	a	b	$a + b$
A_2 (died)	c	d	$c + d$
Total	$a + c$	$b + d$	N

Yule argued that a coefficient of association for such a table must have three properties. Firstly, it should be zero if and only if A and B are non-associated or independent. In the above example, survival and vaccination (A and B) would be said to be independent if the proportion of survivors was the same amongst the vaccinated and the unvaccinated. This can be expressed symbolically as:

$$\frac{a}{(a + c)} = \frac{b}{(b + d)}$$

or $\quad ab + ad = ab + bc$

or $\quad ad - bc = 0$

Working backwards through this chain of thought, it can be shown that $ad - bc = 0$ implies that A and B are non-associated. Thus the first desideratum will be satisfied by a coefficient that has the value zero if and only if $ad - bc = 0$.

The second property is that the coefficient should be $+1$ when, and only when, A and B are completely associated. There are two possible senses of complete association here. The first is the strong sense in which A and B are said to be completely associated only when all A_1's are B_1's and all A_2's are B_2's (i.e. $b = c = 0$). In the above example, this would mean that all those who were vaccinated survived and all those who were not vaccinated died. There is also a weaker sense of complete association, according to which A and B are completely associated if either all A_1's are B_1's or all A_2's are B_2's. Either of the following two contingency tables thus displays complete association in this sense:

	B_1 (vaccinated)	B_2 (unvaccinated)
A_1 (survived)	a	0
A_2 (died)	c	d

	B_1 (vaccinated)	B_2 (unvaccinated)
A_1 (survived)	a	b
A_2 (died)	0	d

In the first table none of the unvaccinated survive (even though some of the vaccinated die). In the second none of the vaccinated die (even although some of the unvaccinated live). Yule chose to use this weaker definition of complete association; thus, his second criterion was that the coefficient should be $+1$ if and only if either $b = 0$ or $c = 0$.

The third property is that the coefficient should be -1 when A and B are completely associated in a negative sense. Again, there is a strong and a weak meaning of complete negative association, and Yule chose the weak meaning. A and B are completely associated in the negative sense when either all A_1's are B_2's or all A_2's are B_1's.

	B_1	B_2
A_1	0	b
A_2	c	d

or

	B_1	B_2
A_1	a	b
A_2	c	0

Thus the coefficient should be -1 if and only if either $a = 0$ or $b = 0$.

Yule then examined the coefficient $Q = (ad - bc)/(ad + bc)$. Clearly, if $ad - bc = 0$, then $Q = 0$. Conversely $Q = 0$ implies $ad - bc = 0$. So Q satisfies the first condition. If either $b = 0$ or $c = 0$, then $bc = 0$, and $Q = ad/ad = +1$. Also if $Q = +1$, then $ad - bc = ad + bc$, hence $bc = 0$, and so either $b = 0$ or $c = 0$. So Q satisfies the second condition. Finally, if either $a = 0$ or $d = 0$, then $ad = 0$, and $Q = -bc/bc = -1$; conversely $Q = -1$ implies $ad - bc = -ad - bc$, hence $ad = 0$, and so either $a = 0$ or $d = 0$. Q thus satisfies all three conditions, and Yule put it forward as a measure of association in two-by-two tables. However, as Yule was aware, Q has no *special* justification. There is an unlimited number of functions that satisfy Yule's three conditions – for example Q^3, Q^5, and so on. Further, as Pearson was later to show, two different tables could be ranked in one order as regards strength of association by one of these functions, and in a different order by another.

Pearson's approach (Pearson 1900b) was to produce, by a much tighter but more precarious theoretical argument, a coefficient of association that I shall denote by r_T (Pearson denoted it simply by r). The crucial assumption at the base of the derivation of r_T is that the observed contingency table can be regarded as having arisen in the following fashion. The observed categories A_1, A_2 and B_1, B_2 are taken to correspond to ranges of more basic interval variables y and x: A_1 corresponding, for example, to $y \leq k'$, A_2 to $y > k'$, B_1 to $x \leq h'$, B_2 to $x > h'$. It is further assumed that y and x jointly follow a bivariate normal distribution, with x having zero mean and standard deviation σ_1, and y zero mean and standard deviation σ_2. Geometrically this can be shown as in figure 2, where we see the bivariate normal frequency surface (see appendix 8) rising above the plane of x and y. This plane is divided into four quadrants by lines through the point (h', k') – the four quadrants corresponding to the cells of the four-fold table. The volume above the top left of these quadrants corresponds to the frequency with which $x \leq h'$ and $y \leq k'$, and thus corresponds to the frequency a in the original table.

Pearson had thus provided a model of a statistical distribution assumed to underly the given two-by-two table. The model has three parameters, h'/σ_1, k'/σ_2, and r, the correlation of x and y. There are three independent parameters in the given table (not four, as the total, N, is regarded as fixed and $a + b + c + d = N$). The model can be fitted to any four-fold table, as the equations relating the model and the observations are always soluble, although the solution requires the use of numerical methods (see appendix 5). A value for r, the correlation of the underlying variables, can thus be found.

This correlation of the underlying variables was what Pearson called the 'tetrachoric coefficient of correlation', r_T (from the Greek words *tetra*, four, and *chōrā*, region). While Pearson was clearly aware that the mathematical derivation of this coefficient involved the assumption of an underlying bivariate normal distribution, and was also aware that this assumption could not usually be tested, he referred to r_T as *the* correlation in the title of his paper and in other places. He did consider other, empirical, coefficients of association, including Yule's Q, but treated them only as approximations to r_T, with the advantage of much greater ease of calculation, but the disadvantage of deviating by a greater or lesser extent from r_T.

One last point has to be made before the further developments of the different approaches are considered. Yule's and Pearson's coefficients have been presented as if the data to which they were

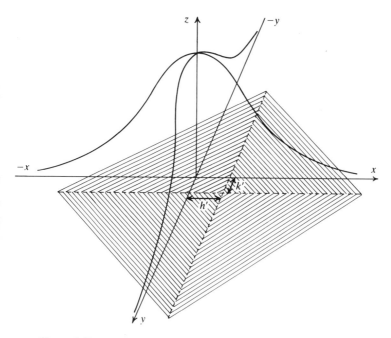

Figure 2. Pearson's model of underlying variables.
Compare the example of a bivariate normal distribution
given in appendix 8. Here, for the sake of simplicity, the
x-axis and y-axis are drawn so that the centre of the 'bell'
is directly above their mutual zero-point, rather than
away from it, as in appendix 8.

applied were always entire populations. In this I am remaining
faithful to the work of Yule and Pearson, who did not systematically
distinguish between sample statistics and population parameters.
Yule and Pearson were of course aware that the data to which they
applied Q and r_T were often drawn from samples, but, apart from
calculating the 'probable errors' of their coefficients, they did not
address themselves generally to the problems posed by this.

Further Developments in Pearson's and Yule's Approaches

The invention of the tetrachoric coefficient by no means concluded
Pearson's theoretical work on the measurement of association.
Indeed, this area was a major focus of his work in mathematical
statistics from 1900 to 1922. Pearson was fully aware of the short-
comings of r_T – in particular, its restriction to two-by-two tables.

While continuing to champion the use of r_T, he attempted to find an approach to the problem of the measurement of association that would allow the direct analysis of larger tables (those in which objects are classed as $A_1, A_2, \ldots, A_p$ and $B_1, B_2, \ldots, B_q$) and would, if possible, avoid the assumptions involved in the derivation of r_T.

The most important of these attempts was his development of the coefficients of contingency. This derived from the application of his own χ^2 (chi-square) test to two-way tables (Pearson 1900c). For any such table it is possible to work out the expected frequencies in each cell on the assumption that the two variables are independent, and then to measure the divergence between observed and expected frequencies by means of χ^2. Reference to the distribution of χ^2 then gives a measure of the probability of such a divergence from the expected frequencies, on the assumption of independence. The value of χ^2 itself was of little direct interest to Pearson. He wanted not simply to reject the hypothesis of no association, but to measure the strength of association. The value of χ^2 cannot serve as such a measure, because multiplying the frequencies in each cell of a table by a constant (which presumably does not alter the strength of association) multiplies the value of χ^2 by that constant. This problem is, however, easily avoided. If the value of χ^2 is divided by N, the total number of cases in the table, then the resultant coefficient clearly remains unaltered by multiplication of each cell in the table by a constant. This coefficient, $\phi^2 = \chi^2/N$, Pearson (1904b, 6) referred to as the mean square contingency.

A measure based on χ^2 has clear attraction. It is free from any need to assume underlying variables, and it can be applied to any size of table. It is even independent of the ordering of the categories of each variable. The problem is, which particular measure based on χ^2 should be used? Once again, Pearson solved this problem by reference back to the correlation of normally distributed interval variables. He supposed any given table to have arisen by splitting these continuous variables into categories. He then found a relationship between the mean square contingency for such a table and the coefficient of correlation of the underlying variables, r. In the limiting case that the number of cells in the table tends to infinity, he showed (*ibid.*, 7–8) that:

$$r = \pm \sqrt{\frac{\phi^2}{1 + \phi^2}}$$

He then proposed the coefficient

$$C_1 = \sqrt{\frac{\phi^2}{1 + \phi^2}}$$

which he called the 'first coefficient of contingency' (*ibid.*, 9).[5] If the two-way table had arisen by categorisation of an underlying bivariate normal distribution, and if the number of cells in the table was large, then C_1 approximated to the coefficient of correlation of the underlying variables. Because C_1 is a monotonic function of the value of χ^2 for the table from which it is calculated, it has also a certain justification quite apart from the validity of these assumptions.

C_1 did not displace r_T in Pearson's affection. Pearson felt that C_1 was best used only in larger tables (of about 25 cells), because for small tables the limit relationship between C_1 and r did not hold, and thus C_1 was a bad estimate of the correlation of underlying variables.

> Hence the new conception of contingency, while illuminating the whole subject . . . does not do away with the older method of fourfold division. (*ibid.*, 9)

Pearson's fundamental criterion was still the relationship between a coefficient of association and the correlation of underlying variables: he still sought a coefficient of association directly comparable with the correlation coefficient of interval variables.

Other developments of the theory of association by Pearson (e.g. Pearson 1910a, 1912a, 1913a,b) follow broadly the same lines. The desire for comparability with the interval-level coefficient of correlation can be seen in such comments as 'in order that our results shall agree fairly closely with the results for Gaussian distributions we select . . . our scale . . .' (Pearson 1912a, 24). One major aim of this work was to 'improve' C_1 by various corrections, the most important being the class-index correction, described in Pearson (1913a). Again, the basis of the correction is the assumption of underlying continuous variables, and the purpose of the correction is to improve the estimate of the correlation of these variables by taking account of the fact that C_1 is calculated from a finite number of cells rather than the infinite number presupposed by the limit relationship between C_1 and r. Uncorrected, C_1 has a tendency to underestimate the 'true' correlation: the typical effect of a class index correction on a five-by-five table is to boost C_1 by about 0.05.

The final attempt Pearson made to find a 'perfect' solution to the problem of the measurement of association was to derive an iterative method for fitting a bivariate normal distribution to a two-way table (in effect, to find a counterpart to r_T for tables larger than two-by-two). A solution to this problem was published in a joint paper with his son Egon Pearson (K. and E. S. Pearson 1922). But the resultant 'polychoric coefficient', while representing in a sense the logical conclusion of Karl Pearson's approach to the problem, was in that pre-computer age defeated by the sheer laboriousness of its mode of calculation.

Yule developed two further coefficients, the 'product-sum coefficient', r_{PS}, and the 'coefficient of colligation', w. These two coefficients did not represent any fundamental break with the approach lying behind his earlier work. Both satisfy his three criteria for a coefficient of association, the only difference being that, while Q and w take the value 1 for perfect association in the weak sense (either b or c zero), r_{PS} takes this value only for positive association in the strong sense (both b and c zero). The product-sum coefficient is the ordinary interval-variable coefficient of correlation applied to a two-by-two table, not on Pearson's sophisticated model, but 'naively', by making the assumption that the two categories correspond to the values 0 and 1 of a discrete variable. It can be shown that this yields the value:

$$r_{PS} = \frac{ad - bc}{\sqrt{(a+c)(b+d)(a+b)(c+d)}}$$

Yule referred to r_{PS} as 'the correlation-coefficient for a [two-by-two] table' although he did not suggest it displaced Q.[6] The coefficient of colligation (Yule 1912) links Q and r_{PS}. The formula for it is

$$w = \frac{\sqrt{ad} - \sqrt{bc}}{\sqrt{ad} + \sqrt{bc}}$$

and Q and w are related by a simple equation

$$Q = \frac{2w}{1 + w^2}$$

When the given two-by-two table is reduced to a standardised symmetrical form by multiplication and division of the rows and columns by constants until each marginal total equals $\frac{1}{2}N$, w for the original table equals r_{PS} for the standardised table. So w and r_{PS} are also related. But the inter-relatedness of Q, w and r_{PS} is much weaker than the inter-relatedness of Pearson's coefficients, all of which bear some reference to the single theoretical standard of the interval-variable coefficient of correlation. Q, w, and r_{PS} give different values when applied to the same table, and Yule gave no general rules as to which to use in a given case.

The Controversy

The fundamental issues at stake in the controversy were implicit in the two original papers that Pearson and Yule published in 1900. Neither openly attacked the other, however, and personal relations between the two men seem to have remained good. Open conflict began only in late 1905. On 7 December, Yule read to the Royal Society of London two papers (Yule 1906a,b) critical of some aspects of Pearson's work, in particular throwing doubt on the validity of the assumptions underlying Pearson's use of the tetrachoric coefficient. Pearson replied to these criticisms in an article in *Biometrika* (Pearson 1907). At this stage, the controversy was still not generalised to all aspects of the competing approaches to the measurement of association. This happened only when Yule published his textbook *An Introduction to the Theory of Statistics* (1911), in which he gave an account of his measures Q and r_{PS}. Pearson's collaborator David Heron wrote a sharply-worded warning to the readers of *Biometrika* on the 'danger' of Yule's formulae (Heron 1911). Yule in his turn read to the Royal Statistical Society a long paper defending his position and attacking Pearson's (Yule 1912). Pearson and Heron replied in a paper covering 157 of the large pages of *Biometrika* (Pearson and Heron 1913; see also Pearson 1913b). This paper effectively marked the end of the overt phase of the controversy (though see also Greenwood and Yule 1915). It was, however, unresolved. Pearson and Yule no doubt felt they had fully stated their positions, but neither had succeeded even partially in convincing the other. Yule's obituary notice of Pearson refers to the controversy and comments, 'Time will settle the question in due course' (Yule 1936, 84).

The main focus of Yule's attack on the tetrachoric coefficient was on the assumptions involved in its derivation and use. He wrote (Yule 1912, 140):

> The introduction of needless and unverifiable hypotheses does not appear to me a desirable proceeding in scientific work.

When dealing, for example, with vaccination statistics (an area where biometricians had applied the tetrachoric method), Yule argued that 'vaccinated', 'unvaccinated', 'survived' and 'died' constitute naturally discrete classes:

... all those who have died of small-pox are all equally dead: no one of them is more dead or less dead than another, and the dead are quite distinct from the survivors. (*ibid.*, 139–40)

To apply here a coefficient that had as its basis an assumption of underlying continuous variables was absurd:

At the best the normal coefficient [r_T] can only be said to give us in cases like these a hypothetical correlation between supposititious variables. (*ibid.*, 140)

There were cases, Yule conceded, where the assumption of underlying continuity was 'less unreasonable'. In these cases, however, the hypothesis that the underlying distribution is bivariate normal was frequently doubtful. Pearson had often used the tetrachoric coefficient in two-by-two tables that had been obtained from larger tables by the amalgamation of adjacent classes. Indeed until his invention of the coefficient of contingency he was forced to do this, as he had no method of analysing larger tables. In these larger tables, unlike two-by-two tables, it was possible to test the validity of the hypothesis of an underlying bivariate normal distribution.

This could be done in two ways. First, if the hypothesis is true it should not matter, from the point of view of the calculation of r_T, which precise way one chose to amalgamate classes. The value of r_T should be at least approximately independent of the boundary line chosen between the two final classes. Yule was thus able to test Pearson's hypothesis by calculating r_T in several different ways for the same large table. He showed (*ibid.*, 144) that, at least in certain cases given by Pearson, the values obtained varied considerably, ranging for example from 0.27 to 0.58 in a table on the resemblance between fathers and sons in eye-colour. Secondly, if a large table has in fact arisen according to Pearson's hypothesis, then it should display the property Yule termed 'isotropy'. Consider any four adjacent frequencies, n_1, n_2, n_3 and n_4, extracted from a larger table.

	n_1	n_2	
	n_3	n_4	

The table is called 'isotropic' if the sign of $n_1 n_4 - n_2 n_3$ is the same for all similar 'sub-squares' of the table. In his first published criticism of Pearson's work, Yule tested for 'isotropy' tables on which Pearson had, after amalgamation of classes, used r_T. He found (Yule 1906a) that many were not 'isotropic'.

Pearson (1907) defended himself by arguing that Yule's isotropy criterion was invalid because he had failed to evaluate the probable error of $n_1 n_4 - n_2 n_3$. Because a given table is only a sample from a larger population, a failure of isotropy may occur through random fluctuation alone. Pearson accepted that the variation in values of r_T obtained in different ways from the same table showed that in certain cases the assumption of underlying normality did not appear to be tenable. But he had been aware of this, he said, and the method of contingency had been developed to deal precisely with those cases. When coefficients of contingency were worked out for the tables in question, they were found to agree 'sensibly' with the tetrachoric coefficients, and Pearson claimed that his conclusions thus held, despite the flaws in the method by which they had been obtained.

The basis of the attack on Yule's approach mounted by Pearson and Heron was that, for the same table, Yule's various coefficients did not agree in value, and further that for tables formed from genuine bivariate normal data none agreed with the ordinary correlation coefficient. For one table given by Yule, Heron found that $Q = 0.91$ while $r_{PS} = 0.02$. For bivariate normal data Q did not differ very much from the correlation coefficient so long as divisions were taken near the medians, but for more extreme divisions the divergence could be large (e.g. $r = 0.5$, $Q = 0.97$). For such data, Q varied in value according to exactly where the divisions were taken; the same is true of r_{PS} (and indeed of w).

Pearson and Heron claimed that Yule was reifying his categories. Only in rare cases – such as that of Mendelian theory, where the categories of a two-by-two table correspond to the presence or absence of a Mendelian unit and thus the two variables genuinely are discrete (factor present = 1; factor absent = 0) – was the use of such methods justified. In these cases r_{PS} was the correct way to extend the ordinary theory of correlation, as it assumed just such discrete variables. In general, however, treating categories in this way was mere empty formalism.

> And here we will at once emphasise the fundamental difference between Mr Yule and ourselves. Mr Yule, as we will indicate later, does not stop to discuss whether his attributes are really continuous or are discrete, or hide under discrete terminology

163

true continuous variates. We see under such class-indices as 'death' or 'recovery', 'employment' or 'non-employment' of mother, only measures of continuous variates – which of course are not *a priori* and necessarily Gaussian . . . (Pearson and Heron 1913, 161)

The controversy between us is much more important than an idle reader will at once comprehend. It is the old controversy of nominalism against realism. Mr Yule is juggling with class-names as if they represented real entities, and his statistics are only a form of symbolic logic. No knowledge of a practical kind ever came out of these logical theories. As exercises for students of logic they may be of educational value, but great harm will arise to modern statistical practice, if Mr Yule's methods of treating all individuals under a class-index as identities become widespread, and there is grave danger of such a result, for his path is easy to follow and most men shirk the arduous.
(*ibid.*, 302)

Pearson and Heron justified the biometric position by arguing that it was necessary to make *some* hypothesis about the nature of the continuous frequency distribution of which the observed classes were groupings. In practice, they argued, methods based on the normal distribution almost always gave adequate results. The unique advantage of these methods seemed to them to outweigh the difficulties involved:

The coefficient of correlation has such valuable and definite physical meanings that if it can be obtained for any material, even approximately, it is worth immensely more than any arbitrary coefficients of 'association' and 'colligation'.
(*ibid.*, 300)

The General Character of the Two Approaches

Pearson's work was dominated by its reference to an existing achievement of statistical theory, the interval-level theory of correlation and regression. For Pearson, this theory was an exemplary instance of the way statistics enhanced the scope of prediction. Thus, regression was the theory of how best to predict the value of one variable from that of another, in situations where there was no one-to-one correspondence. The correlation of two variables was, for Pearson, that constant, or set of constants, that was sufficient to describe how the expected value of one variable depended on the value of another (Pearson 1896, 256–7). In one case only had the correlation in this sense been fully specified: that of two variables that followed a bivariate normal distribution. Given the correlation coefficient for two such variables, it was possible to state immediately the expected value of one variable associated with any value of the other.

Pearson's approach to the association of nominal variables was based on the analogy between the association of such variables and the correlation of interval-level variables with a joint normal distribution. This correlation had a clear meaning in terms of prediction, and this meaning made it uniquely suitable as the criterion for judging the strength of association. Use of this basic reference point was the foundation of Pearson's attempt to construct a unitary theory of association and correlation, and of his negative evaluation of the work of Yule.

The derivation of r_T shows that Pearson initially *defined* association as the correlation of the hypothetical underlying bivariate normal distribution. In the later work on contingency this literal superposition of the two cases was partially discarded: Pearson accepted that the assumption of an underlying bivariate normal distribution might not be factually correct. But the analogy still operated, as can be seen in the way that the bivariate normal model was used to choose the particular functions of χ^2 that were selected to be the coefficients of contingency. Measures of association were thus seen by Pearson as ways of estimating the correlation of an actual or notional underlying distribution. This was, in effect, simply what Pearson meant by 'measuring association', and the way in which he described r_T as 'the coefficient of correlation' indicates the taken-for-granted nature of the metaphor. For Pearson, the basic criterion of the validity of coefficients of association was their usefulness in the estimation of this underlying correlation.

This criterion of validity was typically put into operation in the following way. Interval data that followed a bivariate normal distribution would be taken, and from this data a two-by-two or larger table would be constructed. Thus, if the data referred to the height and weight of individuals, a two-by-two table could be constructed by classifying those individuals over six feet as 'tall', those under as 'short', those over 150 pounds as 'heavy', those under as 'light'. A coefficient of association would then be applied to this table. If the value of the coefficient approximated well to the interval-level correlation of height and weight, this was a point in its favour. If the values of a coefficient did not tally with the coefficient of correlation, then this was an argument for its rejection.

The tetrachoric coefficient passed this test; its ability to do so was of course guaranteed by its method of construction. So did the coefficient of contingency, at least for sufficiently large tables. Yule's coefficients, on the other hand, all failed abysmally. Not only were they on the whole poor approximations to the coefficient of correlation, but the values they took depended on where the arbitrary divisions between 'tall' and 'short' and 'heavy' and 'light' were taken.[7]

Given the basic goal of maximising the nominal/interval analogy, Pearson's use of the bivariate normal model makes sense. It was not that he was obsessed by the normal distribution. Quite the opposite: he was one of the first statisticians to point to the non-normal nature of many empirical distributions (Pearson 1895), and had sought, albeit unsuccessfully, to develop a theory of correlation for non-normal variables that would fully take into account their non-normality.[8] Pearson's position was pragmatic. If correlation is taken, as Pearson took it, to depend upon the specification of the function that best predicts the value of one variable from that of another, then something about the joint distribution of the two variables must be assumed. Only one joint distribution was, Pearson felt, sufficiently well known for this kind of analysis to be possible: the bivariate normal. So if one had to use a model, Pearson felt that the bivariate normal was best. Further, some model *was* necessary if the nominal/interval analogy was to have any validity. For consider Yule's Q as an example of a coefficient not based on an explicit model. Values of Q are not comparable with those of the coefficient of correlation. Nor can comparability of the nominal and interval cases be achieved by reducing the interval data to two-by-two tables and applying Q, for the value of Q depends on the process by which this is done. Indeed, comparison of the values of Q from one two-by-two nominal table to another becomes, on this perspective, a process which is very difficult to justify. Without some model of the situation to give a meaning to coefficients of association, their comparative use appeared to Pearson dangerously arbitrary.

Pearson's approach to the theory of association was thus tightly structured by the analogy between the association of nominal variables and correlation employed as a tool for interval-level prediction. Yule's approach was much looser. A coefficient of association in the nominal case (or, indeed, a coefficient of correlation in the interval case) was for him a measure of statistical dependence that need satisfy only general formal criteria (be zero for independence, one for complete dependence, and so on). Just to know that two variables are associated (that vaccination and survival, for example, are not independent) is obviously of some use, and Yule was not primarily concerned to be able to draw tighter inferences than this. Specific problems of prediction in specific contexts of use did enter into Yule's choice of particular coefficients (for example, between Q, w and r_{PS} in any particular instance) but did not structure Yule's overall formulation of the problem of association.[9] Yule can thus be seen as putting forward a general, formal theory of association, which left a great deal of room for elaboration in specific instances. He did not seek a single best measure of association. Just as there are different measures of central tendency (mean, median, mode, and so on) there were, Yule felt, different ways of measuring association, which would yield different values for the same table. The superiority of one to the other could not be guaranteed in advance of the consideration of particular applications. Attempts to do so on the basis of contentious assumptions (such as that of underlying distributions) were, Yule claimed, simply dangerous and misleading. When working with nominal data the statistician had to accept the limitation implied by the level of measurement: one was dealing with cases classed into categories, and nothing more. In short, the interval/nominal analogy had, for Yule, no force.

These differing goals of Pearson's and Yule's work led to their two positions being incommensurable.[10] Logic and mathematical demonstration alone were insufficient to decide between them, we might say. Their concepts of 'measuring association' were different: for Pearson, it meant seeking to estimate an underlying correlation; for Yule, it meant simply trying to summarise the degree of dependence manifest in the given nominal data. And the same mathematical result would be interpreted differently by the two sides in the light of their different objectives.

Thus, both sides knew that for any given table Yule's three coefficients, Q, r_{PS} and w, would normally not agree, and sometimes would differ wildly in their values. For Pearson, this was sufficient to damn Yule's system utterly, for how could there be three different values for the association of the one table? For Yule, on the other hand, this was fully to be expected, for Q, r_{PS} and w were simply different ways of summing up the observed data. Similarly, both sides accepted that the value of the coefficient of contingency was affected by the size of the table to which it was applied. For Yule, this was a severe weakness of the coefficient of contingency. Under certain circumstances its value reflected the number of cells in the table as much as the association of the data. For Pearson, on the other hand, this property was only to be expected. The coefficient of contingency was equal to the coefficient of correlation only in the limit case where the number of cells in the table became infinite. Therefore it was not surprising that the value of the coefficient of contingency should be affected by table size; on the assumption of an underlying normal distribution this could be corrected for. To take another instance, it was not disputed by either side that when applied to genuinely continuous binormal data, the value of Yule's Q differed considerably according to where the division (for example, between tall and short) was taken. For Pearson this invalidated Q. For Yule any property that Q had when artificially applied to interval data did not affect its use for nominal data, because he rejected Pearson's basic model of an underlying distribution.[11]

Eugenics and the Measurement of Association

The differing goals manifested in the work of Pearson and Yule on association were not accidental. They can be related to different objectives in the development of statistical theory, and perhaps ultimately to differing social interests.

Pearson's work in statistical theory continued the link, initially forged by Galton, between the mathematics of regression and correlation, and the eugenic problem of the hereditary relationship of successive generations. In his first fully general discussion of the statistical approach to the theory of evolution, Pearson defined 'heredity' as follows (1896, 259):

> Given any organ in a parent and the same or any other organ in its offspring, the mathematical measure of heredity is the correlation of these organs for pairs of parents and offspring . . . The word organ here must be taken to include any characteristic which can be quantitatively measured.

Two pages earlier Pearson (*ibid.*, 256–7) had explained that the correlation of two variables (he used the terms 'organs') was what defined the function allowing the prediction of the value of one from that of the other. Put together, these notions of heredity and of correlation indicate what Pearson was doing. He was constructing a mathematical theory of descent, in order to be able to predict from the knowledge of an individual's ancestry the characteristics of that individual. Galton had solved the problem for the individual's parentage; Pearson wished to go further back and consider grandparents, great-grandparents, and so on.

Pearson's paper reveals two aspects of his position on correlation and its measurement. His notion of correlation, as a function allowing direct prediction from one variable to another, is shown to have its roots in the task that correlation was supposed to perform in evolutionary and eugenic prediction. It was not adequate simply to know that offspring characteristics were dependent on ancestral characteristics: this dependence had to be measured in such a way as to allow the prediction of the effects of natural selection, or of conscious intervention in reproduction. To move in the direction indicated here, from prediction to potential control over evolutionary processes, required powerful and accurate predictive tools: mere statements of dependence would be inadequate. Secondly, the prominence of correlation in his statistical thought can be seen to be related to the role of correlation as measuring the 'strength of heredity'. To define heredity as the correlation of parents and offspring indicates the *a priori* nature of Pearson's hereditarianism; that the correlation could be due to the similarity of parental and offspring environments was not even considered in this paper.[12] It also indicates the possibility that the direct linking of correlation and heredity could well be the motivation of Pearson's work on the theory of correlation. If the study of heredity was to be increased in its scope, the theory of correlation had to undergo parallel development. In this paper of 1896, the move from consideration of parentage to entire ancestry was clearly associated with the development of the theory of correlation from Galton's two-variable case to an indefinite number of variables.

The major restriction on Pearson's studies of heredity in the late 1890s was their limitation to measurable characteristics. Many characteristics, such as the colouration of animals and plants and the eugenically crucial mental characteristics of man, were not immediately susceptible to quantification (this period, of course, predates the introduction of the Binet-Simon scale of 'intelligence'). All that was possible for these characteristics was classification of individuals into categories, and as the resulting data could not be analysed by an interval-level theory of correlation, there was no direct way of estimating the 'strength of heredity' for these characteristics. To extend research in heredity from interval to

nominal characteristics required, given Pearson's operational definition of heredity, the extension of the theory of correlation from
interval to nominal variables.

That this is the correct interpretation of the origins of Pearson's
work on the theory of association is suggested by Pearson's own
description of his problem situation:

> Many characters are such that it is very difficult if not impos-
> sible to form either a discrete or a continuous numerical scale
> of their intensity. Such, for example, are skin, coat, or eye-
> colour in animals, or colour in flowers . . . Now these characters
> are some of those which are commonest, and of which it is
> generally possible for the eye at once to form an appreciation.
> A horse-breeder will classify a horse as brown, bay or chestnut;
> a mother classify her child's eyes as blue, grey or brown without
> hesitation and within certain broad limits correctly. It is clear
> that if the theory of correlation can be extended so as to readily
> apply to such cases, we shall have much widened the field
> within which we can make numerical investigations into the
> intensity of heredity, as well as much lessened the labour of
> collecting data and forming records.

(Pearson and Lee 1900, 324–5)

Pearson's research on heredity did not simply provide the motivation for the development of his theory of association. It also conditioned the nature of that theory. Pearson already had what he felt
to be a satisfactory means for the investigation of the inheritance of
interval characteristics, by the use of which he had accumulated a
considerable body of 'coefficients of heredity'. In order to maximise
the value of information on the inheritance of nominal characteristics, it was necessary to devise a 'coefficient of heredity' for them
that paralleled that for interval characteristics. Therefore, the direction of development of the theory of association was, in the case
of Pearson, determined by the need to maximise the analogy between the association of nominal variables and the correlation of
interval variables. Pearson wanted to be able to say 'the coefficient
of heredity for human mental ability is r', and to compare that with
the already calculated 'coefficients of heredity' for height and other
similar characteristics. A coefficient of association such as Yule's Q
would not have enabled him to do this. As explained above, values
of Q cannot be compared with that of the coefficient of correlation;
nor can both height and mental ability data be analysed by the use of
Q, because of Q's dependence on the arbitrary boundary between

'tall' and 'short'. For interval/nominal comparison to be plausible, Pearson needed a coefficient that, when applied to dichotomised height data, would yield a value as close as possible to that of the coefficient of correlation: hence Pearson's construction of r_T, and hence also his fundamental criterion of evaluation of coefficients of association.

Pearson had in fact begun collecting a set of primarily nominal data of great relevance to eugenics even before he had devised, in r_T, the necessary means of analysing it. Parent-child correlations were difficult to collect; Pearson however reasoned that the correlation of siblings (a term he introduced for pairs of brothers or sisters irrespective of sex)[13] were of equal theoretical value as measures of the strength of heredity.[14] By circularising teachers he obtained information on nearly 4,000 pairs of siblings, including interval physical characteristics such as the cephalic index, nominal physical characteristics such as eye colour, and a range of nominal mental characteristics such as 'ability' and 'conscientiousness'. The study was begun in 1898; by 1903 Pearson felt able to give a comprehensive survey of the results obtained in his Huxley Lecture to the Anthropological Institute (Pearson 1903c; some early results were presented in Pearson 1901b). This was Pearson's major contribution to the hereditarian theory of mental characteristics, and the forerunner of many later more sophisticated attempts to prove the dominance of nature over nurture.[15] It is also his most central attempt to use r_T, and the one which most strongly drew Yule's criticism.

Pearson's analysis of mental ability can be taken as an example of his procedure. He had asked teachers to classify each of a pair of siblings into one of the following classes: quick intelligent, intelligent, slow intelligent, slow, slow dull, very dull and inaccurate-erratic. 'Very dull', for example, was defined as 'capable of holding in their minds only the simplest facts, and incapable of perceiving or reasoning about the relationship between facts' (Pearson 1903c, 209). To permit the use of r_T these seven categories were reduced to two, 'quick intelligent' and 'intelligent' forming one category, and the rest the other. Two-by-two tables were then drawn up, and from these tables values of r_T were calculated. A typical table for pairs of brothers, which is reconstructed from Pearson's data (*ibid.*, 236), appears at the top of the next page. In this case $r_T = 0.46$.

Pearson found from these data measures of the 'strength of inheritance' for nine mental and nine physical characteristics, and

Second Brother	First Brother		
	QI & I	Other	Totals
QI & I	526	324	850
Other	324	694	1018
Totals	850	1018	1868

was also able to bring into the comparison other previously produced estimates of the correlation of physical characteristics in pairs
of siblings. Central to his argument were two assumptions, only
partly explicit: the comparability of the coefficients of correlation
for interval data and the value of r_T for nominal data; and the
interpretation of these coefficients as measures of the 'strength of
heredity'. On the basis of these assumptions, he was able to claim a
remarkable finding: the strength of inheritance for a wide range of
human mental and physical characteristics was virtually identical at
around 0.5. Further, he claimed that environment played no significant part, and thus presumably assumed that residual effects (the
fact that the correlation was only 0.5 and not 1.0) were simply the
result of chance variations. Environment could, Pearson felt, be
discounted because his series of characteristics included eye colour.
It was accepted that environment played no part in determining eye
colour, and yet the strength of inheritance for eye colour was very
close to the common 0.5. If environment played no part in the case
of eye colour, Pearson deduced that it therefore played no part in
the other cases. Pearson's conclusion (*ibid.*, 204) was a strong
affirmation of hereditarianism:

> We are forced, I think literally forced, to the general con-
> clusion that the physical and psychical characters in man are
> inherited within broad lines in the same manner, and with the
> same intensity . . . We inherit our parents' tempers, our
> parents' conscientiousness, shyness and ability, even as we
> inherit their stature, forearm and span.

Pearson thus had, by use of the tetrachoric coefficient, been able
to forge a connection between physical and mental human characteristics along which inductive inferences could pass. It was, he felt,
widely admitted that human physical characteristics were largely
determined by heredity. By use of this channel of inference an
identical conclusion could be drawn for mental characteristics. The
polemical possibilities that this opened up for eugenists were obviously important. Pearson was able to further extend them by bring-

ing coefficients of heredity for various characteristics in animals into the argument. In other species 'the resemblance of parent and offspring is again roughly .5' (*ibid.*, 204). Thus, the generally accepted conclusion that in animal species 'good stock breeds good stock' (*ibid.*, 206) could be extended to man.

At the end of the Huxley Lecture Pearson drew out the political conclusions that followed from his analysis. He talked of Britain's failure in imperialist competition with Germany and the United States, and the lack of intelligence and leadership that was, he claimed, the cause of it. His work, he argued, showed that the only solution was 'to alter the relative fertility of the good and the bad stocks in the community'.

> That remedy lies first in getting the intellectual section of our nation to realise that intelligence can be aided and be trained, but no training or education can *create* it. You must breed it, that is the broad result for statecraft which flows from the equality in inheritance of the psychical and the physical characters in man. (*ibid.*, 207)

Given the contemporary concern for 'national efficiency' these were words in season, and were not without impact outside the scientific community. Pearson's lecture was quoted at some length by the Inter-Departmental Committee on Physical Deterioration (1904, 38–9), which had been set up by the Conservative Government as a result of the scare following early defeats of the British by the Boers in the South African War. Few of Pearson's contemporaries would have fully understood the mathematics of the tetrachoric coefficient, and few seem to have subjected his argument to close scrutiny, but the conclusion he was able to draw struck home.

Yule, on the other hand, had no commitment to eugenics. There is no record of his ever having made a public statement of his attitude to eugenics, nor do his letters to Karl Pearson, for example, reveal his opinions. Nevertheless, in his correspondence with the man who was perhaps his closest friend, Major Greenwood, it is possible to discover evidence of Yule's private views. These appear to have been a mixture of indifference and hostility, as the following quotations[16] indicate:

> . . . votes for women is to me nearly as loathworthy [*sic*] as eugenics.
> The Eugenics Congress is rather a joke. . . .
> I've just got the letter from the Eugenics Ed[ucatio]n Soc[iety] asking me to lecture. I do not altogether like it. . . .

I am not a eugenist, and I am not in the least keenly interested in eugenics.

When Yule's academic work touched on subjects of eugenic importance, a certain distance from the standard eugenic positions is apparent. On the issue of heredity versus environment he was cautious:

To take an example from the inheritance of disease, the chances of an individual dying of phthisis depends [sic] not only on the phthisical character of his ancestry, but also very largely on his habits, nurture, and occupation. (Yule 1902, 228)

A major topic of Yule's early statistical work was pauperism, which the eugenists claimed to be a symptom of hereditary degeneracy. Yule, however, eschewed such arguments, and concentrated on the way administrative reforms, notably the abolition of out-relief, reduced the observed rate of pauperism (see Yule 1895–96, 1896, 1899).[17]

Even while he was a student of Pearson, Yule gave signs that he was to develop in an independent direction from his teacher.[18] In 1893, aged 22, he became Pearson's demonstrator, assisting in the teaching of mathematics to engineering students and forming, along with Alice Lee, the audience for Pearson's first advanced course in mathematical statistics. In 1895 he was elected to, and became an active member of, the Royal Statistical Society. The concerns of this body, rather than Pearson's social Darwinism, form the context of application for much of Yule's statistical work. While Yule's work was technically far in advance of what the Royal Statistical Society was accustomed to, in subject, style and, indeed, in political assumptions, it would have been familiar. Thus, the Fellows were accustomed to an ameliorative orientation towards pauperism, and to Yule's focus on administration rather than the economy or social structure, even if the technical apparatus Yule employed was new.

It is possible that Yule may have come to realise the need for a measure of association while studying another favourite topic of the Royal Statistical Society, vaccination statistics. In 1897, during a discussion at the Society of an anti-vaccinationist paper, he made a long and highly critical comment on the author's use of statistical technique (Yule 1897b). Consideration of the frequently dubious use of statistics in the vaccination debates then raging[19] might well have prompted him to seek a standardised measure of the association between vaccination and survival during an epidemic, and objectives associated with this may have played a minor role in structuring Yule's work on association.[20] They did not, however, generate a search for a single measure of association as a unique property of the data. At most, the requirements of the vaccination question placed but loose constraints upon the evaluation of measures of association. For example, a shared convention was needed that would distinguish between intervention being totally without effect (no association) and intervention being totally effective (complete association). But no more general inductive inferences needed to be drawn. Yule's use of formal rather than substantive criteria in the construction of coefficients of association, his development of an empirical rather than a unitary theoretical approach, and his preference for dealing with nominal data as they were given, would all make sense in the light of this situation.

It was not, however, that Yule was developing a general theory of association while Pearson was developing one with only a limited sphere of application. Pearson strongly felt that his was a general theory, and applied it even to Yule's favourite cases such as vaccination statistics; Yule most strongly criticised the application of Pearson's theory to inheritance data.[21] Both sides felt the theory of the other was *wrong,* and not merely *misapplied.* It was, rather, that the eugenic concerns embodied in Pearson's work led to a sophisticated and elaborate theory constructed round a specific goal, while in Yule's work more diffuse concerns led to a looser approach that embodied goals of a more general nature.

Further Aspects of the Controversy

Up to this point I have treated the controversy as if it were simply a dispute between two individuals, Pearson and Yule. While these two were overwhelmingly the most active participants, it is important to look at the involvement of others in the British statistical community. The group of scientists contributing to the development of statistical theory in Britain in the period 1900 to 1914 was small. A list produced using Kendall and Doig's *Bibliography of Statistical Literature* (1968) consists of 26 individuals who can be seen as having in some sense an active ongoing interest in the development of statistical theory.[22] Of these, twelve can be regarded as members of Pearson's biometric school, since they had close ties to the Biometric and Eugenic Laboratories at University College, London, and their preferred medium for publication seems to have been *Biometrika.* The other 14 had a wide variety of affiliations, and included civil servants, administrators and one industrial scientist, as well as university staff.[23]

Ten of the twelve biometric school members either took part in attacks on Yule on this topic (Pearson, Heron), contributed to the theoretical discussion or development of the Pearsonian approach (J. Blakeman, W. P. Elderton, Everitt, Heron, Pearson, Snow, Soper) or used the tetrachoric coefficient in empirical work (E. M. Elderton, A. Lee, E. H. J. Schuster and all the above except possibly Blakeman and Soper). In the remaining two cases (Galton and Isserlis), I have not been able to find evidence of attitudes. Galton died in 1911, before the controversy came to a head; the work of Isserlis on the theory of statistics was just beginning at the end of this period, and in any case his connections with the biometric school were much looser than those of the above.

This overall pattern is as one would expect. The tetrachoric method and the related later developments were part of the distinctive approach of the biometric school, were widely applied to empirical data, primarily in the eugenic field, and were the focus of theoretical attention. As described in chapter 5, the biometric school was a tightly knit, coherent group. Its research was often a team activity in which data collection, the development of the necessary mathematical theory, computation, and so on, were closely integrated under the personal supervision of Karl Pearson. So it is hardly surprising that the opponents of Pearson's approach to the measurement of association should perceive themselves as attacking no mere technique but a central dogma of a disciplined sect. Along with his letter of 8 November 1913 (Yule Papers, box 1), Major Greenwood sent to Yule the following fantasy:

Extracts from *The Times*, 1 April 1925

G. Udny Yule, who had been convicted of high treason on the 7th ult., was executed this morning on a scaffold outside Gower St. Station. A short but painful scene occurred on the scaffold. As the rope was being adjusted, the criminal made some observation, imperfectly heard in the press enclosure, the only audible words being 'the normal coefficient is —'. Yule was immediately seized by the Imperial guard and gagged. The coroner's jury subsequently received evidence that death had been instantaneous. Snow was the executioner and among others present were the Sheriff, Viscount Heron of Borkham and the Hon. W. Palin Elderton.

Up to the time of going to press the warrant for the apprehension of Greenwood had not been executed, but the police have what they regard to be an important clue. During the usual morning service at St. Paul's Cathedral, which was well attended, the carlovingian creed was, in accordance with an imperial rescript, chanted by the choir. When the solemn words, 'I believe in one holy and absolute coefficient of four-fold correlation' were uttered a shabbily dressed man near the North door shouted 'balls'. Amid a scene of indescribable excitement, the vergers armed with several volumes of *Biometrika* made their way to the spot, but one of them was savagely bitten in the calf by a small mongrel and in the confusion the criminal escaped.

Major Greenwood's own loss of faith in r_T is itself interesting. In 1909, while still fully integrated into the biometric school, he wrote a paper in which r_T was described – almost in the way he was later to parody – as the 'exact' and 'true' method of measuring association (Greenwood 1909, 259). In this paper r_T was used in the typical manner of biometric eugenics to argue the importance of the hereditary factor in tuberculosis. In 1910, however, Greenwood left the biometric school for a job in public health. As described in chapter 5, he began to have increasing doubts about eugenics. And soon he became a private, and then a public, critic of r_T.[24]

What the available information about the biometric school, eugenics and the measurement of association indicates, it seems to me, is that r_T and the other Pearsonian coefficients were part of the approach to statistical theory that was characteristic of the biometric school. r_T was a social institution. Further, it was a social institution that can be explained in terms of the connection between biometric statistics and eugenics: r_T and the other coefficients were needed for the school's eugenic work. Again, my argument is not about individual motivations. I have not the slightest idea whether P. F. Everitt, say, who drew up tables of 'tetrachoric functions' to permit easier calculation of r_T, was motivated by a desire to further eugenics. The point, however, is that he was working to overcome a difficulty that had arisen within the context of an integrated, institutionalised research programme in which the demands of eugenic research generated, and conditioned the solution of, particular technical problems.

What of those statisticians who were not members of the biometric school? Of these only one, John Brownlee, seems to have been an enthusiast for the tetrachoric method. He was a member of the Glasgow Branch of the Eugenics Education Society.[25] Yule, Green wood and Brownlee apart, only two 'non-biometric' statisticians seem to have publicly committed themselves on the measurement of association: F. Y. Edgeworth and R. H. Hooker. Neither, as far as I am able to tell, was a eugenist.[26] Both were members of the Royal Statistical Society, and it was at a meeting of the Society that they gave at least qualified support to Yule (Edgeworth 1912, Hooker 1912); the Society seems, in fact, to have been the closest Yule came to having an 'institutional base'. Clearly it was in no way comparable to Pearson's Biometric and Eugenic Laboratories, with their own publications and journal, but at least the Society provided Yule with a sympathetic hearing and a place to publish his major attack on Pearson as well as other more minor writings on association.

Thus, consideration of British statisticians other than Pearson and Yule seems to confirm in broad terms the association of Pearson's approach with the needs of eugenic research and that of Yule with the broader and less specific needs of general applied statistics. However, before concluding, it is necessary to consider other possible explanations of the controversy, and to examine briefly the history of the measurement of association after 1914.

It might be argued that Pearson's philosophical views account for his attitude to the measurement of association. However, it would seem that his approach, with its use of hypothetical underlying variables, violates rather than exemplifies the positivist and phenomenalist programme of *The Grammar of Science* (Pearson 1892a). The practical demands of his research proved stronger than his formal philosophy of science. His characterisation (Pearson and Heron 1913, 302) of the dispute as between his 'nominalism' and Yule's 'realism' can indeed be turned on its head. In their concepts of correlation Pearson was the 'realist' and Yule the 'nominalist'. Pearson's Huxley Lecture argument, for example, rests on the interpretation of a correlation as the measure of a real entity, as a strength of heredity, and largely collapses if a correlation is seen as merely the name for an observed pattern of data. Pearson's general cosmological bent towards continuity and variation rather than homogeneity and discrete entities (Norton 1975a) may in part account for his rejection of methods such as r_{PS} (which involved treating individuals in a given category as in a certain sense identical), but cannot, it seems to me, account for the specific features of Pearson's methods of measuring association.

Psychological explanations (such as a clash of personalities) also seem inadequate. Personal relations between Pearson and Yule seem to have been soured as a result of disagreement, rather than disagreement being caused by personal antagonism.[27] The divergence of views was already present in the perfectly amicable papers of 1900. Even if Pearson and Yule had remained the best of friends they would still have measured association differently, and this difference would still have to be explained.

A third possible explanation might be that non-eugenic biometrical concerns were of equal or greater importance in leading to Pearson's development of the tetrachoric method. It is certainly true that Pearson used r_T to measure the 'strength of inheritance' in organisms other than man. But to separate a 'neutral' biometry from an 'ideological' eugenics would be ahistorical and would fail to capture the integral nature of Pearson's thought. The results of the biometric studies of heredity in animals were used in Pearson's eugenic argument: the channel of inference from the animal world to human physical characteristics to human mental characteristics was crucial to Pearson's position.

How did the controversy end? Debate virtually ceased at the time of the First World War, and two factors may have been involved in this. After 1918 the huge amount of data on inheritance of human and animal characteristics flowing into the Biometric and Eugenic Laboratories was much reduced. 'The post-war years were not favourable to the spread of Galton's eugenic creed' and in Pearson's work 'eugenics was for the moment set aside' (Pearson 1936–38, part 2, 205, 206). Thus, the immediate importance of the problem for Pearson was reduced, and much less theoretical and practical work on the measurement of association was done at the Biometric and Eugenic Laboratories. Secondly, a new approach to eugenics and statistics was developing, most notably in the work of R. A. Fisher, which focused attention on different problems. Fisher devised a new way of measuring the 'strength of heredity', to be described in chapter 8 below. The emphasis in this was on a theoretical Mendelian model, rather than on the direct comparison of correlation coefficients. So while Fisher did not reject Pearson's work on the inheritance of mental characteristics, his own research programme made the problem of the measurement of association a relatively marginal one.

The controversy was not, however, resolved. Contemporary statistical opinion tends to deny that any one coefficient has unique validity. To take one influential example, Goodman and Kruskal

(1954–59, part 1, 763) argued that measures of association 'should be carefully constructed in a manner appropriate to the problem in hand' in such a way as to have operational interpretations. This type of theoretical pluralism seems to be sufficiently widespread to allow us to conclude that the general approach of modern statisticians is closer to that of Yule than that of Pearson. Yule's Q remains a popular coefficient, especially amongst sociologists (see, for example, Davis 1971). But one aspect of Pearson's approach – the construction of models to fit the data – has if anything gained importance since his day, and indeed his tetrachoric coefficient has not completely disappeared. Its main use appears to be in psychometric work (for example, Castellon 1966). It is interesting to speculate whether its contemporary use in this field can be attributed to the continuing influence of eugenics, but this point could be established only by an analysis of the contemporary literature, which is outside the scope of this study.

The Controversy and Social Interests

Finally, can we connect the controversy to social interests in the same way as was done with the biometrician/Mendelian debate? As far as biometry is concerned, a very similar argument can indeed be put forward. The biometric approach to association was the result of the needs of eugenics, and eugenics can, I have argued above, be seen as ultimately sustained by professional middle-class interests. So, in crude summary, I would suggest that the biometric mathematics of association reflected the influence of social interests on statistical theory, as mediated through the connections between statistics and eugenics.

The case for an analysis of Yule's work along the lines of the analysis of Bateson's is, however, much weaker. It is difficult to identify very specific goals informing this work, and the most one can clearly point to is the *absence* of the crucial eugenics/statistics connection. It is just possible – I claim no more – that this absence may reflect a similar dynamic to that discussed above in chapters 2 and 6: traditionalist opposition to eugenics.

Unlike Pearson, Yule was ordinarily reticent in matters of philosophy or politics. What one can perhaps glean from his letters, from the comments of those who knew him well, and from occasional passages in his writings, is a position that might be described as, in general terms, conservative. Major Greenwood wrote of Yule that 'politically, even in university politics, he is a stern, unbending

Tory' (Greenwood to Pearl, 19 August 1926; Pearl Papers, Greenwood file). In later life, Yule turned to religion (Yule to Greenwood, 2 February 1936; Yule-Greenwood letters). Yet, while Yule's position certainly lacked the radicalism of Bateson's romantic-conservatism, there was a degree of detachment and scepticism about it that stopped it being merely conventionally Tory.

On some crucial issues Yule's position does indeed remind us of that of Bateson, and certainly contrasts sharply with that of Pearson. As against Pearson's orthodox Darwinism, Yule advocated the anti-Darwinian and mutationist views of J. C. Willis (Yule 1924; see Willis 1922). Like Bateson (see, e.g., Bateson 1928, 91–2), Yule was wary of too close a connection between 'pure' science and its applications. His ideal of the scientific researcher was of a 'loafer of the world', free from contracts and ties (Yule 1920). And, as against Pearson's positivism, Yule was suspicious of the cult of measurement (Yule 1921, 106–7).

Further, there are some interesting similarities between Yule and his supporters Edgeworth and Hooker. All three came from old-established élite families, but ones that were in decline. Yule came from a family of army officers, Indian civil servants and orientalists. Both his father and his uncle had been knighted. The family's wealth does not, however, seem to have been transmitted to Yule. In the absence of a sufficiently well paid statistical job he was forced, during most of the period discussed here, to take an administrative position in a board examining apprentice craftsmen and technicians and to lecture in the evenings to clerks. R. H. Hooker was the son of Sir Joseph Dalton Hooker and grandson of Sir William Hooker, both Directors of the Royal Gardens at Kew; he himself had a humbler career as a civil servant in the Board of Agriculture (Yule 1944). Francis Ysidro Edgeworth came from an old and distinguished family of Anglo-Irish gentry (Edgeworthstown, County Longford, was their family seat), but one that was in particularly sharp decline. Although Edgeworth was the fifth son of a sixth son, he was the last in the male line of the Edgeworths, and by the time he had inherited it the family estate had sunk into neglect (Keynes 1926, Bowley 1934).[28]

It is difficult to know what to make of this. It is possible that the Royal Statistical Society, with its strong 'establishment' connections, was particularly attractive to men like Yule, Hooker and Edgeworth – that they may have formed a 'reactionary' statistical sub-culture that would have seen positivist, meritocratic eugenics as vulgar. But this is merely speculation, and certainly it must be remembered that there were other grounds for opposition to eugenic policies: occupational commitments in the field of public health, for example, as evidenced by the career of Greenwood. Until further evidence can be uncovered, we may simply note the possibility that specific social interests sustained the non-eugenic statistics of Yule and his supporters.

8

R. A. Fisher

. . . . .
. : .
.

With Sir Ronald Aylmer Fisher (1890–1962) we come to a recognis-
ably modern figure. Galton and even to a degree Karl Pearson were
Victorian gentlemen-scientists, but Fisher's scientific style and research activity belong much more closely to the twentieth century.
His ideas form much of the basis of the courses in statistics taught in
many British and American universities. His students occupy many
of the leading positions in statistical and genetic research. His books
– notably the many editions of *Statistical Methods for Research
Workers*, *The Genetical Theory of Natural Selection* and *The Design
of Experiments* – have become classics. He contributed centrally to
the modern theory of experimental design, and played vital roles in
the establishment of population genetics and in the study of blood
groups in human beings.

To examine the life and work of Fisher in its entirety is far beyond
the scope of this book; those interested can turn to the 500 pages of
Joan Fisher Box's excellent biography (Box 1978).[1] My purpose
here is more modest: to situate Fisher in terms of the preceding
tradition of work associated with Galton and Pearson, and to examine the extent to which the analysis developed above can throw
light on at least his early work. I shall argue that the bitter personal
controversy that developed between Karl Pearson and R. A. Fisher
has obscured a fundamental fact about Fisher: the extent to which
his work was in continuity with that of Karl Pearson, and with that
of Galton before him. Despite Fisher's different approach to many
statistical problems, despite his acceptance of Mendelism, despite
Fisher's support for the Conservative Party and adherence to the
Anglican religion, Fisher and Pearson shared many common goals.
Both saw in the science and political programme of eugenics the
path to national salvation, and both saw in statistics not merely a

technical adjunct to research but a new methodology of real philosophical importance. And, in different ways, the thought of each
man can be seen as reflecting the interests of the professional middle
class.

Fisher, Eugenics and the Professional Middle Class

As with Karl Pearson, it would certainly be false to claim that Fisher
was an 'average' or conforming member of the professional class. It
is true that he came from a family straddling the professional and
business class, and, although his father's business as a prestigious
auctioneer collapsed, that Fisher enjoyed the educational benefits
of preparatory school, Harrow, and Gonville and Caius College,
Cambridge. But he spent the last of his postgraduate Cambridge
scholarship travelling to Canada to work on a farm, and it was
several years after leaving Cambridge before he settled into a steady
job. He was keen on subsistence farming and used to annoy his
more conventional neighbours by keeping goats. He was always
absent-minded and unconventional in dress, and his personality was
marked by an extreme egocentricity and violent temper. In interviews with students of his, I was told many anecdotes about his
disregard for convention and his eccentricity: for example, when
bored in conversation, he had the habit of removing his false teeth
and cleaning them.

Yet, despite the friction surrounding Fisher's contact with the
individuals and institutions of the professional middle class, he had
a strong conviction of its fundamental worth and – perhaps a result
of his family's financial difficulties – an acute sense of its 'crisis of
reproduction' (see chapter 2). His plans for the professional middle
class were more modest and less radical than Pearson's schemes for
state-socialist meritocracy, but they were perhaps more practical.
Fisher sought to promote – in early articles and in the writing and
political activity of his maturity – social policies designed to benefit
the professional middle class and ensure its reproduction in the face
of a threatening situation:

> The protection afforded by professional societies undoubtedly
> renders the professions more favourable ground for men of
> intellect and honour, but the status and dignity to which some
> of the professions have laboriously reached can only be main-
> tained by a succession of persons duly qualified to justify that
> trust in their wisdom and integrity to which, in the long run, the
> respect paid to lawyers and doctors is due. (Fisher 1917, 207)

From his undergraduate times onwards Fisher was an active eugenist. His eugenics was often played down in accounts of his work written in the decade after his death, but with the discovery of the records of the Cambridge University Eugenics Society in the library of the Eugenics Society in London, and with Box's use of unpublished material in the Fisher papers in Adelaide, we can now begin to see the centrality of eugenics in Fisher's work. For Fisher, the worth of the professional middle class was primarily *genetic* worth; if national degeneration was to be avoided, the genes of the professional middle class had to be transmitted to the next generation, and must not be swamped by those of the lower orders. This was not merely an abstract conviction: 'His large family . . . reared in conditions of great financial stringency, was a personal expression of his genetic and evolutionary convictions' (Yates and Mather 1963, 96). When his eldest son, George, was killed in a Second World War plane crash, Fisher seems to have made widespread inquiries to see if 'among the girls George had known' he 'might have left a son' to carry on his 'line' (Box 1978, 397).

A 1917 article on 'Positive Eugenics' clearly reveals the connection in Fisher's thought between eugenics and the professional middle class. Fisher argued that the Eugenics Education Society should 'put itself in direct and sympathetic touch with the special aspirations of professional bodies' (1917, 212). A profession, he wrote (*ibid.*, 207):

> . . . must have power to select its own members, rigorously to exclude all inferior types, who would lower both the standard of living and the level of professional status. In this process the eugenist sees a desirable type, selected for its valuable qualities, and protected by the exclusive power of its profession in a situation of comparative affluence.

It was important that an 'exclusive profession' should 'offer advantageous prospects to the sons of its members' by, for example, 'requiring the nominations of each candidate by a number of members of the profession'. This would 'give a considerable advantage to the children of the professional men', and lessen the entry of 'new blood' which was 'on the whole, inferior to the professional families of long standing' and which rendered difficult 'the maintenance of a high tradition of professional etiquette' (*ibid.*, 210–11).

There seems little doubt that Fisher's involvement with eugenics was of crucial importance to his choice of scientific career. His work for his degree was in pure mathematics and mathematical physics.

Statistical theory as such was not taught at Cambridge until 1912, the year of Fisher's graduation, when Yule was appointed to a lectureship in statistics; Fisher did spend a further year at Cambridge after graduation, but seems to have attended only one of Yule's lectures. Nor would there have been any academic incentive for a mathematics undergraduate to study biology. So there was little in Fisher's curriculum to turn him in the direction of statistics and genetics.[2] But his formal curriculum took up only a part of his attention. He was a member of a typical Cambridge undergraduate coterie, the 'We Frees', who combined pleasure and philosophical wit and discussion. Only on occasional evenings would Fisher excuse himself from his friends 'to do in two hours the work of two months' (Box 1978, 18–21). It seems most likely that it was in the conversations of the other evenings that Fisher discovered eugenics.

In the Spring of 1911, during Fisher's second year at Cambridge, he and his friend and fellow undergraduate C. S. Stock set up the Cambridge University Eugenics Society.[3] Although it attracted such influential patrons as Lord Rayleigh and the Bishop of Ely, and a wide-ranging academic membership (including J. M. Keynes), the senior members of the Society seem to have played little active part in it. 'We see so little of them, hear so little from them', complained Fisher (1912b). The most regular activity of the Society was the series of discussion meetings held by its undergraduate group. These meetings began in Fisher's rooms in October 1911, when Stock gave a general introduction to 'The Eugenic Field'. At the second meeting on 10 November 1911 Fisher introduced the group to the scientific basis of eugenics, with a paper entitled 'Heredity, comparing the Methods of Biometry and Mendelism' (Fisher 1911). This paper shows that Fisher had already immersed himself in the academic literature relevant to eugenics. He had clearly read widely in the two major competing approaches to heredity, and had thought deeply and in an original fashion about the difficult topic of multifactorial Mendelian models.

The Society itself was shortlived. Its activities seem to have ceased by the outbreak of the First World War (it was revived after the War, but finally ceased to exist in 1923, according to a pencilled note in the file of records). However, the effect on Fisher of his involvement with eugenics was much more long-lasting. Eugenic concerns led him to do the extra-curricular reading – and, we might presume, provided him with the motivation – that was necessary to enable him to do original work in statistics and genetics. In addition, eugenics provided Fisher with vital support during the years of poverty and uncertainty following his departure from Cambridge. Without this support, it is quite likely that his nascent intellectual interests would never have flourished.

The most concrete form this support took was the patronage of the President of the Eugenics Education Society, Major Leonard Darwin. Darwin encouraged Fisher in his scientific work related to eugenics for over twenty years, and in the first years after Cambridge used his influence and wealth to assist Fisher directly. Darwin probably met Fisher when he travelled to Cambridge in 1912 to address the newly-formed University Eugenics Society, and later that year Fisher and his fellow members acted as stewards at the International Eugenics Congress in London over which Darwin presided (Box 1978, 27). In the year after leaving Cambridge Fisher lived in London for a time, and started to become involved in the activities of the Eugenics Education Society. When a teaching job took Fisher away from London, Major Darwin 'appointed him to a part-time position and paid him a salary' to enable him to continue working for the Society (*ibid.*, 50–1). The arrangement, according to a letter from Darwin to Fisher quoted by Box (*ibid.*, 51), seems to have been that Fisher worked 'on the Society's business or, in default of that, on eugenic investigation' for about one day a week.

Fisher's main activity for the Eugenics Education Society for which we have a record is his work for the *Eugenics Review*. He was a frequent contributor and an assiduous book reviewer: the 1916/17 volume, for example, contains twenty reviews by Fisher of political, statistical and biological works of relevance to eugenics. This activity must in itself have been an encouragement to keep in touch with the academic literature. But Darwin also encouraged Fisher's scientific work more directly. By the middle of 1916 Fisher had finished his first really important paper, 'The Correlation between Relatives on the Supposition of Mendelian Inheritance', only to suffer the disappointment of it being rejected by the Royal Society of London. It was through Leonard Darwin's sponsorship – and, it would appear, his financial backing – that the paper finally saw the light of day in the *Transactions of the Royal Society of Edinburgh* (Box 1978, 60). In the *Eugenics Review* Fisher published a simplified account of this work, and acknowledged his

> . . . deep sense of gratitude to the Eugenics Education Society, who have most generously assisted me throughout; and in particular to Major Leonard Darwin whose continual kindness

and encouragement has enabled me to carry through the work. (Fisher 1918b, 220)

Even when Fisher's scientific career was well established, eugenics, while no longer necessary as a support, remained a motivation. Thus, according to Box (1978, 339) his work in the 1930s and 1940s on blood groups was prompted by the realisation that 'blood groups would be of diagnostic importance for eugenic applications'. Fisher did indeed fall out with the Eugenics Society in the 1930s, but his reason for doing so was not opposition to eugenics. He seems to have felt that 'in the absence of scientific leadership, social scientists of an environmentalist persuasion . . . could divert the efforts of the Eugenics Society from their proper study of human inheritance to serve a noneugenic social function' (*ibid.*, 195). Fisher's ally, Major Darwin, was no longer President of the Society, and Fisher attempted, according to Box (*ibid.*, 196), an ultimately unsuccessful coup against the 'environmentalist' tendency. Like Pearson before him, he had come to feel that a eugenics society led by amateurs rather than by hereditarian scientists had become a danger to the cause of eugenics.

Questions about the support and motivation for research are, however, not the same as questions about its content. Much more detailed study is needed before the question of whether the needs of eugenics affected the content of Fisher's biology and statistical theory can be settled decisively. In the rest of this chapter I shall attempt only a provisional answer. We shall see that there are indeed grounds to conclude that Fisher's work in biology was strongly connected to his involvement in the eugenics movement. In the case of statistics, however, I shall suggest that the close relationship between eugenics and innovations in statistical theory to be found in the work of Galton and Pearson is not there in that of Fisher. The explanation of what is novel in Fisher's statistical theory must, in general, be sought elsewhere.

Genetics and Evolution

On the face of it, Fisher's contribution to biology seems different from, indeed opposed to, that of Pearson and the biometricians. What Norton (1978a, 491) calls the 'standard account' of the history of the theory of evolution since Darwin sees Fisher as contributing crucially to the *resolution* of the controversy between biometricians and Mendelians – clearing up the confusion that lay at the basis of this controversy.

There is certainly much truth in the 'standard account'. Fisher (1918a) showed that the statistics of the inheritance of quantitative traits found by the biometricians could indeeed be compatible with the Mendelian theory. Fisher (1930) showed that a theoretical account of evolution by natural selection could be erected on the basis of Mendelism. Yet, where the view of Fisher as *resolving* the biometrician-Mendelian controversy may be lacking is that it fails to see the extent to which the goals of Fisher's biology were identical to those of Pearson's, the extent to which, to quote Hodge, he too was a 'eugenist and a . . . biometrician' (Forbes 1978, 449).[4]

From the very beginning (Fisher 1911) Fisher accepted Mendelism as a theory of heredity. Exactly why, I do not know; perhaps simply that as an undergraduate in the university that was the home of British Mendelism, Fisher took for granted Mendelism's basic validity. This does not imply, however, that the goals informing Fisher's work were different from those informing Pearson's. For, rather than rejecting Mendelism as inadequate for the pursuit of these goals (as Pearson had done), Fisher chose to transform Mendelism into an appropriate tool for a eugenist-biometrician. In short, he sought not to *reconcile* Mendelism and biometry, but to *use* Mendelism to vindicate biometric eugenics.

We can summarise the discussion of Pearson's evolutionary biology in chapters 4 and 6 by identifying five goals that it manifested. Pearson sought to display evolution as a predictable process in which factors such as natural selection produced definite measurable effects on subsequent generations. He sought to display it as a mass process, involving gradual changes in whole populations. He rejected holistic views of biological populations, assuming that to view them as the sum of their individual parts was quite adequate. He sought a theory with special applicability to man and human societies. Finally, he sought a theory that would have potential for the eugenic control of the evolution of human populations. Orientation to these goals pervaded all of the biometricians' biology, from the way in which observations were classified, through the techniques of analysis used to the presentation of their results.

Might it help us to understand Fisher's biology if we were to postulate that similar goals informed it too? For example, might we be able to understand Fisher's disagreements with other biologists in terms of Fisher's pursuit of these goals and their pursuit of other goals? In order to show that there is at least some evidence that the answer to these questions might be in the affirmative, let us turn to

189

Fisher's writings on genetics and evolution, particularly to *The Genetical Theory of Natural Selection* (1930).

Approached with this perspective, the first thing that strikes us about the *Genetical Theory* is the support that it lends to inferring the presence of the fourth and fifth goals listed above. Five of its twelve chapters deal with human beings and society, and the last chapter contains detailed eugenic proposals. In the introduction, Fisher stated explicitly that 'the deductions respecting Man are strictly inseparable from the more general chapters' (*ibid.*, x). At the end of the book he decried the 'divorce between theory and practice', arguing that the thinker should not 'detach himself from the natural outcome, in the real world, of his theoretical researches' (*ibid.*, 264); this 'natural outcome' in Fisher's case was his eugenic policy.

Of course, it could be argued that eugenic implications were not really a *goal* of Fisher's theorising, but merely an accidental by-product of it. This much is implied by Fisher's description of his eugenic ideas as 'deductions' from, and the 'outcome' of, his theorising, although it should, of course, be noted that he would hardly have been likely to present his biological theories as merely legitimations for the policies he favoured. Eugenic considerations, however, figured large from early on in Fisher's discussions of criteria for the judgement of biological theories. Thus Fisher's first paper on biology, his 1911 talk to the Cambridge University Eugenics Society, treated biometry as a eugenic strategy:

> Biometrics then can effect a slow but sure improvement in the mental and physical status of the population; it can ensure a constant supply to meet the growing demand for men of high ability.

'Mendelian synthesis', by comparison, promised quick and 'almost miraculous' results, but Fisher appears to have doubted the practicality of its application to man, dependent as it was on 'experimental breeding'.

In a paper written in 1915 jointly with his fellow Cambridge eugenist, C. S. Stock, Fisher noted the existence of a confused controversy between Darwinians and 'extreme Mendelians'. Fisher and Stock argued (1915, 60):

> It is essential for Eugenists to consider on which side they ought to range themselves. . . .

Closely echoing Pearson, they argued that Mendelism was being rashly applied:

> . . . regrettable things have been done, and more regrettable things have been said in America in the name of Mendel. Direct legislative proposals have been made, and in some cases passed, based upon quite inadequate knowledge. Persons suffering from supposedly Mendelian defects have been advised to mingle with sound stocks, though the result of doing so is clearly to lay up hereditary trouble for the future. (*ibid.*, 59)

Eugenists were thus 'open to all kinds of attack on the side of Mendelism'. By comparison, 'on Darwin's ground they are impregnable'.

> Were all information except that used by Darwin inaccessible, such information would not only allow but compel us to formulate eugenic concepts and proposals. (*ibid.*, 60)

This early paper by Fisher and Stock is worth pondering for a moment. It was an attack on the anti-Darwinism of the French Mendelian, Lucien Cuénot, whose work

> . . . provides just such an account of the tendencies of one school of Biologist as will serve for the 'point d'appui' of certain criticisms which we believe it is very much in the interests of Eugenics to make. (*ibid.*, 46)

It was contemporary anti-Darwinism in general that they were attacking 'in the interests of Eugenics'. William Bateson was not mentioned, but in the light of Fisher's later scathing references to Bateson's evolutionism, it is to be doubted that he would have been exempt.[5] Fisher disagreed totally with the Mendelian rejection of Darwinism. He sought a eugenics that would be applicable to whole human societies in their growth and decay. For this, the details of the mechanism of heredity were less important than the broad view of evolution provided by the Darwinian theory of natural selection:

> Changes in the composition of a mixed population depend primarily upon selection; the existing and possible agencies of selection do at present and must always provide the most fruitful field of eugenic research. (*ibid.*, 60)

This theme – selection – is what most obviously ties Fisher's biology and his eugenics together. Natural selection is the key to Fisher's evolutionism: he set his face resolutely against theories, such as mutationism or Sewall Wright's 'random drift',[6] that denied the primacy of natural selection. Selection was the central explanation, for Fisher, of the history of human society. And selection – the eugenist's conscious intervention – was the route to the survival of civilisation.

191

Crudely, one can characterise Fisher's quantitative evolutionism as an attempt to show that Bateson had drawn the wrong conclusion from his genetics and that Pearson had failed to grasp the full potential of Mendelism as a support for his Darwinism. Yet simply to say this is not to do full justice to the distinctiveness of Fisher's biology, and it is to fail to tease out how the concept of selection connected this biology to eugenics.

Following Hodge (in Forbes 1978, 448–9), it is important to note the extent to which Fisher's work stood outside the mainstream of evolutionary biology. Fisher's focus on selection meant that in practice he treated evolution as a predictable mass process, working on populations as aggregates of individuals, and homologous to eugenic intervention in human populations. This makes sense if we see his biology as informed by the same goals as Pearson's; but it is also important to note the range of topics this orientation effectively excluded. The *species* was displaced from the centre of attention, and problems of the origin of species, of the fossil record, of evolutionary paths of descent, and so on, became peripheral in the light of Fisher's perspective. As its title tells us, Fisher (1930) is indeed about natural selection, not about the wider range of problems treated by evolutionists. Interestingly, amongst the reasons given by Fisher for his particular approach was its appropriateness for the study of mankind, where it promised 'a more intimate knowledge of the evolutionary processes than is elsewhere possible' (1930, x).

The basis for this promise was the special applicability of Fisher's theory of selection to human beings. Much of the groundwork of this theory was presented in the second chapter of Fisher (1930): 'The Fundamental Theorem of Natural Selection'. Fisher began by defining 'fitness to survive' – initially that of human populations, but by extension that of any particular set of genes. Fitness to survive was measured 'by the objective fact of representation in future generations' (*ibid.*, 34), by the 'Malthusian parameter' – that is, loosely, by the rate of increase or decrease of the population (or sub-population bearing particular genes) concerned.

After showing how one could use the Malthusian parameter to define the 'reproductive value' of people of different ages, and giving a graph of the variation with age of the reproductive value of Australian women, Fisher moved to the next stage of his argument: the examination of the genetic element in the variance of quantitative individual measurements. He had, of course, treated this topic before, in his paper on the 'Correlation between Relatives on the Supposition of Mendelian Inheritance' (1918a). The details of the argument of this paper are extremely complex (see Moran and Smith 1966) but the basic idea is simple: the variance of a quantitative trait, such as human stature, can be partitioned into various components by assuming the trait to be determined by a large number of Mendelian factors, and different percentages of the variance attributed to different causes. This permitted the eugenically important conclusion that it was 'unlikely that more than 5 per cent of the variance of the physical measurements of man is due to non-heritable causes' (Fisher 1918b, 220). Indeed, Norton (1978c) concludes that this paper (Fisher 1918a) has to be seen, 'predominantly', as 'a contribution to the hereditarian social ideology of eugenics'. In particular, argues Norton, Fisher wished to strengthen Pearson's argument (reviewed in chapter 7 above) that nature predominated over nurture in the determination of human characteristics. 'Pearson's "proof" seemed to leave 75 % of the observed phenotypic variance unaccounted for' (Norton 1978c, 488), leaving a gaping hole in the eugenic case, which Fisher was trying to close by showing that only a negligible percentage of the variance was conceivably of environmental origin.[7]

In the *Genetical Theory,* Fisher did not present the whole of this previous analysis. He contented himself with deriving an expression for the contribution of each Mendelian factor to the genetic variance of any quantitative trait in an idealised population 'in which fortuitous fluctuations in genetic composition have been excluded'. Next, he applied this analysis to one very particular quantitative trait: the Malthusian parameter measuring 'fitness'. By a neat mathematical sleight-of-hand, he showed that the genetic variance of fitness exhibited by the population was equal to the rate of increase of fitness due to changes in the ratios of the different genes contributing to fitness. He went on to state 'the fundamental theorem of Natural Selection' (1930, 35; emphasis deleted):

> The rate of increase in fitness of any organism at any time is equal to its genetic variance in fitness at that time.

Why did Fisher choose to build his work round this theorem and to regard it as 'fundamental'? One reason seems to have been that it enabled him to insist on the *predictability* of natural selection. Admittedly, his theorem had been developed for an idealised population, but he could now calculate the standard error of the rate of fitness caused by the fact that actual populations would exhibit

193

'fortuitous fluctuations'. This standard error was small, providing one was dealing with large populations with substantial variabilities in fitness. So, given that selection was seen as a *mass* process, it was not a fortuitous one: the laws of chance operated, but in a 'continuous', 'cumulative' and predictable fashion (1930, 37). As he wrote much later, attacking Sewall Wright, 'the effects of chance are the most accurately calculable, and therefore the least doubtful, of all the factors of an evolutionary situation' (1953, 515).

Fisher was also able to use the idea of 'genetic variance' found in the 'fundamental theorem' to attack the 'saltationist' view that large mutations were the cause of evolution. He did not deny that mutation – even large mutation – was a real phenomenon, but he argued that its role in evolution was secondary to natural selection, and was perfectly predictable: mutation maintained the stock of variation on which selection acted. Drawing on the experimental evidence about mutation produced by the *Drosophila* workers, he claimed that large mutations would be harmful and would be selected against. This deleterious effect would be cancelled out by the improvement resulting (according to the 'fundamental theorem') from the increase in genetic variance caused by mutation:

> ... each mutation of this kind is allowed to contribute exactly as much to the genetic variance of fitness in the species as will provide a rate of improvement equivalent to the rate of deterioration caused by the continual occurrence of the mutation.
> (Fisher 1930, 41)

So the role of mutation in Fisher's theory was merely to contribute to the *raw material* for natural selection. By 'maintaining the stock of genetic variability', mutation could keep up the speed, but not affect the *direction* of evolution (1930, 48). Hence, to quote what Fisher had written six years earlier, 'selection is the only agency by which species can be modified to any appreciable extent' (1924b, 210). And this earlier quotation, like the *Genetical Theory*, indicates the eugenic importance of this, for it continues:

> This conclusion gives a special importance to the study of the nature of the selection actually in progress in civilised man.

So Fisher's approach can in part be seen, like that of Pearson, as an attempt to maintain the idea of evolution as a gradual and predictable process in the face of non-gradualist accounts. Certainly, Fisher was as consistently hostile as Pearson to saltationist theories of evolution, and it is perhaps worth speculating that his bitter opposition to the notion of 'random drift' as an evolutionary mechanism might also be based on his concern to maintain the predictability – and mass character – of evolution. It is, in addition, true that Fisher's evolutionism shared with Pearson's an individualistic, aggregative character. There is no trace in his work of any attribution to biological populations of characteristics, such as tendencies to 'stability' or notions of a 'species type', that were not simply reducible to the aggregate of the characteristics of the individuals and genotypes making up the population.

Another possible indicator of similarity in goals between Fisher and Pearson can perhaps be seen in another reason for Fisher's focus on the 'fundamental theorem'. Like Pearson, Fisher was worried, at least initially, about basing general eugenic policies on the *details* of Mendelian accounts. He liked to draw the analogy between evolutionary biology and statistical mechanics. One could have sure knowledge of the properties of gases without detailed knowledge of the laws governing the behaviour of molecules. Similarly, one could have sure knowledge of evolution without knowing the details of the heredity of all individual characteristics. Such detailed knowledge was 'unnecessary', both 'for a general theory of gases and for a general theory of eugenics' (Fisher and Stock 1915, 61).

Thus the *generality* of the 'fundamental theorem' – its independence of particular assumptions about, for example, dominance or assortative mating – was important to Fisher. Significantly, he returned to his earlier analogy with statistical mechanics. The 'fundamental theorem' was, he claimed, similar to the second law of thermodynamics, with 'fitness' substituted for 'entropy'. And both laws 'are properties of populations, or aggregates, true irrespective of the nature of the units which compose them' (1930, 36). So the 'fundamental theorem' enabled Fisher to escape the uncertainty of detailed Mendelian accounts, not by remaining, like Pearson, at the phenotypic level, but by attaining more complete generality.

This generality of Fisher's genetic model of natural selection stood him in good stead when his attention in the *Genetical Theory* moved to human beings exclusively. His aim in the last five chapters of the book was indeed ambitious: to provide a naturalistic, eugenic account of the rise and decline of human civilisation. Why had all previous great civilisations, for all their economic and organisational strengths, collapsed? Fisher had, in fact, found his answer to this question many years earlier, in part in an article by a fellow eugenist (Cobb 1913); he had stated it in his first published paper on eugenics (Fisher 1914). In our society – and in all the great urban civilisations – 'members of small families enjoy a social advantage over members of large ones'.

> . . . in such a society, the highest social strata, containing the finest representatives of ability, beauty, and taste which the nation can provide, will have, apart from individual inducements, the smallest proportion of descendants . . . civilizations in the past . . . have ultimately collapsed owing to the decay of the ruling classes to which they owed their greatness and brilliance. (Fisher 1914, 312–13)

The reproduction crisis of the professional middle class threatened our civilisation with the same fate. As Fisher put it twenty years later:

> . . . the elimination of professional stocks constitutes the elimination from the race of just those qualities which we recognise as most valuable in the working of a civilised society. (Fisher 1934, 300–1)

In the *Genetical Theory* Fisher presented a new, strengthened argument for his old conclusion. The key to this new argument was his analysis of human fertility. Eugenists were, of course, long familiar with great individual and class differences in fertility, and Karl Pearson had tried to show that fertility was inherited (Pearson, Lee and Bramley-Moore 1899). To this old data Fisher applied his new theoretical apparatus, and estimated that about 40 per cent of the observed variance in fertility was genetic. Reference back to the earlier chapters of the *Genetical Theory* then enabled a striking comparison to be drawn. Taking two groups differing from mean fertility by one standard deviation of 'genetic fertility'[8] in either direction, Fisher showed that average family size for these two groups would be in the ratio 5.7 to 2.2 – corresponding to a 'selective advantage' of over 95 per cent. In general evolutionary theorising a selective advantage of 1 per cent was typically assumed. Hence, Fisher concluded (1930, 199):

> Civilised man, in fact, judging by the fertility statistics of our own time, is apparently subjected to a selective process of an intensity approaching a hundredfold the intensities we can expect to find among wild animals. . . .

And, as Fisher of course went on to add in later chapters, this selection was disastrously anti-eugenic in its impact.

The Genetical Theory of Natural Selection was thus more than just a biological work ; it was simultaneously a political intervention in a crisis. The Great Slump had begun the year before it was published. Under the impact of depression, the eugenists' flagging fortunes were beginning to revive (Searle 1979). After what had happened on Wall Street, to talk of the collapse of civilisation might not necessarily brand one as hysterical, especially when one had a remarkably simple solution to offer. Fisher had. The key to it was family allowances: not flat-rate family allowances as they were finally introduced, but allowances proportional to wages, salaries, or professional fees so as to favour the more prosperous. This was, Fisher felt, the only long-term solution to the declining fertility of superior classes and the threat it posed to civilisation.

Perhaps fearing that not everyone might penetrate the mathematics of the *Genetical Theory* to its political core, Fisher included letters explaining his ideas about family allowances with some of the complimentary copies of the book. A conference of churchmen was organised by one recipient, the Bishop of Birmingham (together with the Bishop of Winchester) to see if Fisher's ideas could be applied to the clergy by varying clergymen's stipends according to their fertility; the idea was also raised at the Headmasters' Conference (Box 1978, 192–5). With the formation during the crisis of the National Government, 'pledged as a first charge upon returning prosperity to restore to a large class of salaried servants, in the teaching and other professions, the deductions or cuts by which their salaries have been reduced' (Fisher 1932, 87), Fisher's hopes were high. But although the Eugenics Society adopted Fisher's ideas as its official policy (Box 1978, 194), nothing came of them. During the Second World War Fisher made another effort to push his ideas (Fisher 1943), but, despite the not entirely unfavourable impression Fisher's ideas made on Sir William Beveridge (1943), the 1945 Family Allowances Act opted firmly for flat-rate rather than differential allowances, and Fisher seems then to have given up.

What of the two men conventionally held to be co-founders with Fisher of modern theoretical population genetics, Sewall Wright and J. B. S. Haldane? Did their work manifest the same goals as that of Fisher? In the case of Wright, the answer seems to be no. In Wright's work notions of 'stability' of various kinds are present in a way that makes his work subtly different from that of Fisher. Thus in his famous 'Evolution in Mendelian Populations' he talks of 'an indefinitely continuing evolutionary process' depending upon a 'state of poise among opposing tendencies' (1931, 158). In a later article he spelt out this idea further:

Evolution depends on the fitting together of a harmonious system of gene effects. There may be a vast number of different, more or less harmonious systems. Natural selection tends to hold the population to one, not in general the best one, that is possible from available genes. For an effective evolutionary process there must be a shifting balance between local random changes in gene frequencies and the local pressures of selection, and also a balance betweeen local inbreeding and cross-breeding, that permits the continual selection among demes through differential population growth and migration. The most effective process either of perfecting an adaptation along a particular line, or of exploiting a major ecological opportunity is thus not, in the long run, the almost deterministic pressure of mass selection acting on recurrent mutations, but rather one of continuous trial and error, made possible by labile balance among all of the factors. (Wright 1964, 108).

I cannot enter here into a discussion of the reasons why Wright's and Fisher's views diverged, but it is interesting to speculate that concern for those characteristics of wholes that are not merely the sum of their parts may have played a part in Wright's work.[9]

On this sort of issue Haldane's work reads more like Fisher's. Hodge (n.d.), in an extremely interesting discussion of differences between the work of the co-founders of modern population genetics, comments:

The primary goal of Haldane's evolutionism . . . remains throughout to vindicate natural selection by providing the mathematical deductions from quantitative experimental determination of genetic differences in fitness, to the probability that natural selection not only could have but has caused evolution in the time available.

Was Haldane's work a *social* evolutionism in the sense that the above evidence has led us to infer that Fisher's was? Certainly Haldane, like Fisher, became a eugenist in his undergraduate days, and advocated the eugenic case in the Oxford Union (Searle 1976, 13). Although he left the Eugenics Society after 1920 (Werskey 1971, 179), and criticised many of its policies in his writings of the 1930s, he retained a considerable sympathy for the most basic social assumptions of eugenics. This emerges in, for example, the following comment from *The Causes of Evolution*:

The classes which are breeding most rapidly in most human societies today are the unskilled labourers. Society depends as much, or perhaps more, on the skilled manual workers, as on the members of the professional and ruling classes. But it could well spare many of the unskilled. (Haldane 1932, 129)

Even Haldane's later membership of the Communist Party did not entail a departure from loyalty to his fellow professionals. In a pamphlet explaining *Why Professional Workers should be Communists* he wrote:

> The answer is that if you are good at your job, you would (in a socialist society) have more power and more responsibility than you have now. The leading commissars in the Soviet Union who direct great socialised industries, compared to which i.c.i. or any of the British railways are small fry, are business executives mostly trained as engineers. The leading scientists, writers and artists are very important people.
> (quoted by Werskey 1978, 269)

As Werskey suggests, this was not mere rhetoric but expressed a consistent position. Like Pearson, Haldane had come to the conclusion that state socialism served the professional better than capitalism. Indeed, his speech on the centennial of Pearson's birth (Haldane 1957) shows the considerable extent of his sympathy for Pearson's politics.

It would, however, be hard to conclude that Haldane's evolutionism and his eugenics were as closely tied as Pearson's or Fisher's. There is not their sense of urgency in passages such as this (Haldane 1932, 167):

> And the usual course taken by an evolving line has been one of degeneration. It seems to me altogether probable that man will take this course unless he takes conscious control of his evolution within the next few thousand years.

Nor do we find in Pearson and Fisher a distancing of biology and politics such as the following (Haldane 1932, 126):

> If, like the authors of mediaeval bestiaries, I were using zoology to impart a moral lesson, I should suppress the paragraph which follows. . . .

Of course, this distancing does not prove that more subtle connections were absent, merely that much more detailed examination of Haldane's work will be needed to settle the question.

It would seem, then, that the almost exclusively 'internal' focus of existing studies of the contribution of population genetics to modern evolutionism, such as Provine (1978), may need to be supplemented. Political and philosophical factors quite possibly played a role in determining the different shapes taken by this contribution: in the case of Fisher's work this seems highly likely. Perhaps the study of Fisher's work in quantitative biology – and indeed that of Wright, Haldane and their less well-known Soviet contemporary, Chetverikov (see Adams 1968 and 1970) – should also begin to employ the wider perspective that is already being used in the study of the work of Galton and Pearson.

The Theory of Statistical Inference

Much statistical theory – especially twentieth-century statistical theory – is concerned with the problem of inference. Put crudely (and here crudeness is an advantage in that precision would be explicitly theory-laden) the problem is one of the nature of the statements that statisticians can make on the basis of their analyses. Typically, they will have data on only a subset of the cases they are interested in, and will wish to say something about all of them. They may want to make a prediction, on the basis of past experience, as to what will happen in the future. They may wish to change their estimates of the plausibility of a hypothesis in the light of an experiment. They may wish to say something about a population on the basis of having examined a sample of it chosen at random. Generally, they want to *infer* from the known and examined to the unknown and unexamined.

In the contemporary world, problems of statistical inference tend to be closely linked with technical prediction and control: for example, in the techniques of quality control. However, the historical roots of statistical inference lie elsewhere. Much of the framework of inference was developed in the context of problems of belief in a general sense, and in particular of theological belief. The problem of inference was this: given our limited knowledge, ought we to believe in God? Or, given our lack of knowledge of God, what is the rational decision to take with regard to Christianity? The concept of probability was used to interpret and give meaning to decisions about religion. By metaphoric extension a concept from games of luck (that of chance, *hasard*) was linked to the old, non-quantitative concept of probability used by the schoolmen of the Middle Ages to discuss particular doctrines of Christianity that were disputed (Hacking 1975).

In Britain, Newtonian natural theology provided much of the framework for the eighteenth-century development of probability theory (Pearson 1924, 1978; Buck 1977, 83–4). The Reverend

Thomas Bayes (for whom see Barnard 1958) worked within this tradition of 'social Newtonianism'. The problem that has made Bayes famous was, in the words of his friend Richard Price, to 'give a clear account of the strength of *analogical* or *inductive reasoning*' (Bayes 1764, 135; Price's emphasis); induction had, of course, been under attack by sceptics. De Moivre and others had not, according to Price, fully achieved the main purpose of the doctrine of chances, namely:

> . . . to shew what reason we have for believing that there are in the constitution of things fixt laws according to which events happen, and that, therefore, the frame of the world must be the effect of the wisdom and power of an intelligent cause; and thus to confirm the argument taken from final causes for the existence of the Deity. (Bayes 1764, 135)

Bayes's detailed analysis is less important for our purposes than the way it was generalised by Laplace (1814, especially 177–8 and 363–401), and became the foundation of nineteenth-century approaches to inference. British writers typically referred to a particular form of the generalised version of Bayes's analysis as 'the method of inverse probability'.[10] It can be presented in brief as follows. Let X be a random variable whose frequency distribution depends on an unknown parameter θ. On the basis of previous knowledge and experience, we ascribe a 'prior' probability distribution, $\pi(\theta)$, to θ. We then perform an experiment, or make certain observations, and obtain a sample of values of X; call these values $\underline{x}$. Let $g(\underline{x}; \theta)$ be the probability of these values occurring for a given value of θ. $g(\underline{x}; \theta)$ tells us how likely our observations are for each value of the unknown θ, while $\pi(\theta)$ is our prior estimate of the probability of the different values of θ. We then combine these together to form a 'posterior' distribution of θ – one that takes into account *both* our prior beliefs about θ *and* the experience provided by our observations, $\underline{x}$. Call this posterior distribution $\pi'(\theta|\underline{x})$. Then the key theorem of this approach tells us that the posterior distribution is proportional to the prior distribution multiplied by $g(\underline{x}; \theta)$:

$$\pi'(\theta|\underline{x}) \propto g(\underline{x}; \theta)\,\pi(\theta)$$

Intuitively, this can be read as saying that multiplication of the prior distribution by $g(\underline{x}; \theta)$ boosts the probability of those values of θ that yield relatively high values of $g(\underline{x}; \theta)$ (i.e. of those that imply high values for the probability of the observed sample), and reduces the probability of those values of θ that imply low values for the probability of the observed sample. Put simply, the Bayesian approach can be summarised as telling us how to modify our prior beliefs in the light of our experiences.

The obvious problem then arises of how to quantify our prior beliefs. Nineteenth-century writers typically made the assumption of 'the equal distribution of ignorance'; they assumed that nothing in our prior experience or knowledge led us to say that one value of θ was any more likely than another. In other words, they assumed $\pi(\theta)$ to be a constant independent of θ.[11] Then the above theorem reduces to:

$$\pi'(\theta|\underline{x}) \propto g(\underline{x}; \theta)$$

So the posterior distribution of θ is a constant multiple of $g(\underline{x}; \theta)$; apart from the constant of proportionality, we can treat $g(\underline{x}; \theta)$ as the posterior distribution of θ. This appears to have been the meaning to nineteenth-century British mathematicians of the 'method of inverse probability' (see, e.g., Todhunter 1865, 584 and 592): using 'inverse probability' meant treating the expression for the (direct) probability of the observations given the value of the unknown parameter as, in fact, the (inverse) probability distribution of the unknown parameter. The assumptions of the method as spelt out above – such as that of the 'equal distribution of ignorance' – were by no means always explicit. Indeed, it may be that many mathematicians might have remembered the method – that $g(\underline{x}; \theta)$ could be treated as the probability distribution of θ – without always being fully conscious of the assumptions on which the method rested.

Those who were conscious of the method's assumptions found themselves in something of a dilemma, given the philosophical climate of nineteenth-century Britain. On the one hand, the promise of Bayesianism to 'give a clear account of the strength of inductive reasoning', to show precisely how our beliefs should be modified in the light of our experience, was an attractive one, especially to those sympathetic to basing knowledge on experience of the world. On the other, the foundations of the method, particularly the principle of the 'equal distribution of ignorance', came under philosophical attack, notably from Venn (1866), as being insufficiently empiricist. Venn, who held that 'experience is our sole guide' (*ibid.*, 26) to probability, argued that the proper objects for analysis by the theory of probability are series of observed events, not gradations of belief. But while Venn was able to propose an alternative concept of probability – he defined the probability of an event as the limiting value of its relative frequency in an infinite series of trials (*ibid.*, 107–8) – he had no replacement to offer for the method of inverse probability itself.

Karl Pearson exemplifies this dilemma perfectly. In *The Grammar of Science* he used Bayesianism to justify induction, a task fully in keeping with the empiricist and positivist thrust of the book. But he was clearly aware of the force of the criticisms that had been made of the method: he attempted, in a rather unconvincing passage, to argue that the principle of the equal distribution of ignorance could be justified on empirical grounds (1892a, 174–5). In a lecture delivered in November 1892 (reprinted as Pearson 1941), he conceded to Venn that 'objective chance' could be based only 'upon the statistics of the actual event in question'. 'Subjective chance', an individual's degree of belief in the event's occurrence, was not to be scorned:

> If we ask what is the relation between subjective chance and objective chance, I think we can safely say, that while the two often differ widely, yet the more deep a man's experience, the more thorough his observation and his knowledge of phenomena, the more closely his subjective statistics will fit the objective statistics. He will never, perhaps, make the two coincide, but in the long run of practical life his mistakes will be few and tend to balance each other. (*ibid.*, 95)

After discussing actual experiments in coin tossing and drawing coloured balls from bags, Pearson concluded that 'it is on experience of this kind, on accurate statistical measurement, not on *a priori* reasoning or subjective opinion, that the data of probability are to be based' (*ibid.*, 100).

Pearson thus wished to retain Bayesianism, but without admitting any subjective, non-empirical elements into his science. It seems, however, that he was not entirely convinced by his own defence of empirical Bayesianism. His major early contribution to the theory of inference (Pearson and Filon 1898) indeed relied on the 'method of inverse probability' – implicitly rather than explicitly (see appendix 6) – in its evaluation of the probable errors and correlations of errors of the parameters of frequency distributions. But when W. F. Sheppard (1898b), privately a follower of Venn in these matters (Sheppard to Galton, 29 February 1896; Galton Papers 315), provided a non-Bayesian method of deriving probable errors, Pearson adopted it rather than his own approach. Where the results of Sheppard's approach and his own differed, Pearson chose to rely on Sheppard's formulae (see Pearson 1914, Fisher 1922a, 329n), although without drawing attention to the divergence.[12]

Yet Pearson never discarded Bayesianism. It would appear that, uneasy as he may have been about it, and ready as he was to adopt non-Bayesian methods such as Sheppard's when these were available, he could see no *general* replacement for Bayesianism. He justified his continued adherence to the traditional view of inference on explicitly pragmatic grounds:

> If science cannot measure the degree of probability involved [in prediction from past to future experience] – so much the worse for science. The practical man will stick to his appreciative methods until it does, or will accept the results of inverse probability of the Bayes/Laplace brand till better are forthcoming. (Pearson 1920a, 3)

To provide these 'better' methods was to form the goal of much of Fisher's statistical theory.[13]

Fisher's Early Work on Statistical Inference

In the preceding section we have seen that empiricism in Britain had come up against something of an obstacle in the late nineteenth century. The Bayesian analysis that appeared to guarantee the reliability of induction from experience had itself been criticised on empirical grounds. Pearson's attempts to defend it had not proved entirely convincing, even, it seems, to himself. The theory of statistical inference was thus something of an 'anomaly' for the empiricist programme.

Much of Fisher's work in the theory of statistical inference can be understood as an attempt to resolve this anomaly by showing that Bayesianism could, in fact, be wholly discarded. It was possible, Fisher claimed, to do statistical inference, and to justify and refine scientific induction, without reliance on Bayesian methods. Whether Fisher succeeded in this is debatable: convinced Bayesians such as Jeffreys (1974) or Savage (1976) argue that his success was only apparent, and that prior distributions of belief are implicit in his methods. Nevertheless, the historically important point is that Fisher's goal was the construction of a general non-Bayesian theory of inference.[14]

His very first article on statistical theory (Fisher 1912c) reflects this. The immediate problem discussed was a practical one: the fitting of frequency curves to observed data. Fisher was not satisfied with pragmatic solutions provided by Pearson's method of moments (Pearson 1895), and sought instead an 'absolute criterion' with a clear theoretical justification. Fisher's method *looked* like the old method of inverse probability, in that it involved maximising the quantity referred to in the previous section as $g(\underline{x}; \theta)$. He seemed to be saying that one should fit frequency curves by using the maxima of the posterior probability distributions of their constants: to put it crudely, that one fit the most highly probable curve. Yet on the very last page of this short paper he showed that the method of inverse probability as usually employed led in this case straight into contradictions. One could equally well characterise a given curve by various different functions of the same parameters (a normal curve, for example, is equally well characterised by its variance σ^2 as by its standard deviation σ). Which set of parameters one uses should not matter, as they all refer to the same curve when given equivalent values (a normal curve with variance 4 is the same as a normal curve with standard deviation 2). Yet applying the method of inverse probability to the different sets of parameters will in general lead to different posterior distributions, since a uniform prior distribution for any given set will usually imply a non-uniform distribution for other sets (Fisher's argument is spelt out in more detail in appendix 7). Hence it was impossible consistently to interpret $g(\underline{x}; \theta)$ as the posterior distribution of θ; it was 'a relative probability only, suitable to compare point for point, but incapable of being interpreted as a probability distribution over a region, or of giving any estimate of absolute probability' (Fisher 1912c, 160).

Nine years later, in part in response to misunderstanding of his own approach, Fisher clarified the divergence between it and the method of inverse probability:

> The attempt made by Bayes, upon which the determination of 'inverse probabilities' rests, admittedly depended upon an arbitrary assumption [the equal distribution of ignorance], so that the whole method has been widely discredited . . . two radically distinct concepts have been confused under the name of 'probability' and only by sharply distinguishing these can we state accurately what information a sample does give us respecting the population from which it is drawn. (1921a, 4–5)

Ordinary direct probability – which Fisher defined in terms of relative frequency (1922a, 312) – was, for example, what one used in describing the probability distribution of a sample correlation coefficient r for a definite value of the correlation, ρ, of the population from which it was drawn. When, however, one discussed the unknown value of ρ on the basis of knowledge of a particular sample with a correlation of r, it was impossible to find a probability distribution of ρ:

> Such a problem is indeterminate without knowing the statistical mechanism under which different values of ρ come into existence; it cannot be solved from the data supplied by a sample, or any number of samples, of the population.
> (1921a, 24)

The best one could do was to find what we referred to above as $g(\underline{x};\theta)$, the quantity Fisher now christened 'likelihood':

> What we can find from a sample is the *likelihood* of any particular value of ρ, if we define the likelihood as a quantity proportional to the probability that, from a population having that particular value of ρ, a sample having the observed value r should be obtained. (*ibid.*, 24)

The concepts of probability and likelihood were, Fisher said, radically different in their nature.

> We may discuss the probability of occurrence of quantities which can be observed or deduced from observations, in relation to any hypotheses which may be suggested to explain these observations. We can know nothing of the probability of hypotheses or hypothetical quantities. On the other hand, we may ascertain the likelihood of hypotheses and hypothetical quantities by calculation from observations: while to speak of the likelihood (as here defined) of an observable quantity has no meaning. (*ibid.*, 25)

Later Fisher was to qualify (with his concept of 'fiducial probability') the radicalism of his denial of the meaningfulness of probability statements about hypotheses. Nonetheless, this paper is of vital importance, constituting as far as I am aware the first clear public rejection by a practising British statistician of Bayesian methods.

If Fisher had merely *rejected* Bayesianism his work would have been of little importance. But he added to his rejection of Bayesianism other ideas, and, when combined, they formed at least what appeared to be a fully-fledged and viable alternative to Bayesianism. The most important of these other ideas was Fisher's focus on the exact distribution of sample statistics. As explained in chapter 5, this was not a topic to which the biometricians had paid much attention. Only Gosset, because of his different practical concerns, saw it as central. Gosset knew Fisher's Cambridge tutor, and read Fisher (1912c) when it was published. He thought Fisher's approach 'unpractical and unserviceable' and wrote to Fisher making some particular criticisms. It appears to have been in pondering these that Fisher came up with the mathematical key to his work on exact distributions: the idea of representing a sample of size n by a point in n-dimensional space. By the end of the Summer of 1912 he had written to Gosset giving, by use of his method, a proof of Gosset's z-distribution.[15] Two years later he had solved by this method an even more difficult problem, that of the sampling distribution of the correlation coefficient. The biometricians had tried unsuccessfully to solve this problem (Soper 1913) and Fisher's solution was accepted for publication in *Biometrika* (Fisher 1915). Fisher was established as a mathematical statistician of note.

It was, however, seven years before Fisher finally published his 'manifesto' on the theory of statistical inference: 'On the Mathematical Foundations of Theoretical Statistics' (1922a). In this paper he claimed that the job of the statistician could be broken down into three parts. The statistician should treat any set of data as a sample from a (possibly hypothetical) population. The first problem faced by the statistician was that of deciding what mathematical form the distribution of the population should be assumed to take. This should initially be done on a pragmatic and empirical basis, and the assumptions made tested later. The second problem was that of the estimation, from the sample data, of the parameters of this population distribution (e.g., of its mean and standard deviation if it were a normal distribution). The third part of the statistician's job Fisher summed up as 'problems of distribution', that is problems of the discovery of the exact sampling distributions of the 'statistics' used to estimate the population parameters. This was of crucial importance, because only through knowledge of these sampling distributions could estimation be changed from a matter of common-sense to one of science:

> . . . the study of the random distribution of different suggested statistics, derived from samples of a given size, must guide us in the choice of which statistic it is most profitable to calculate.
> (Fisher 1922a, 314)

Fisher suggested three 'criteria of estimation' (*ibid.*, 316). The first was 'consistency': 'that when applied to the whole population the derived statistic should be equal to the parameter'. The second was 'efficiency': 'that in large samples, when the distribution of the statistics tend to normality, that statistic is to be chosen which has the least probable error'. The third was that of 'sufficiency': 'that the statistic chosen should summarise the whole of the relevant information supplied by the sample'.

This last criterion had emerged in Fisher's discussion (1920) of different means of estimating the standard deviation of a normal population. Fisher had shown that the formula

$$\sigma_2 = \sqrt{\frac{\Sigma(x - \bar{x})^2}{n}}$$

was more 'efficient' (in the above sense) than its competitor, Bessel's formula,

$$\sigma_1 = \sqrt{\frac{\pi}{2}} \frac{\Sigma|x - \bar{x}|}{n}$$

This result had been known to at least some error theorists. What was new was that Fisher showed that for a given value of σ_2, the distribution of σ_1 was independent of the value of the population standard deviation σ, and thus 'the actual value of σ_1 can give us no further information as to the value of σ' (Fisher 1920, 768).

In the 'Mathematical Foundations of Theoretical Statistics', Fisher then returned to the anti-Bayesian approach of Fisher (1912c), now described as the 'method of maximum likelihood'. He carefully distinguished likelihood from inverse probability, and solved a problem that had not been raised in his previous work: that of providing a general expression for the 'standard error'[16] of statistics obtained by the method of maximum likelihood. Suppose the population distribution of a variable X depends on a single parameter θ: call this distribution $f(x; \theta)$. Let $\hat{\theta}$ be the maximum likelihood estimator of θ. Then $\sigma_{\hat{\theta}}$, the standard error of $\hat{\theta}$, is given, Fisher (1922a, 327–9) showed, by the formula

$$-\frac{1}{\sigma_{\hat{\theta}}^2} = n \left\{ \text{mean value of } \frac{\partial^2 \log f(x; \theta)}{\partial \theta^2} \right\}$$

This result was reached by a process analytically very similar to that of Pearson and Filon (1898), but interpreted in terms of relative frequency, not inverse probability.[17] Fisher went on to argue (incorrectly, as he was later to acknowledge) that maximum likelihood estimators generally satisfy the criterion of sufficiency.[18] The paper ended with an extensive discussion of various practical applications of the new approach: for example, Fisher showed that Pearson's 'methods of moments' was not in general 'efficient'.

Fisher versus Pearson

Fisher's reformulation of statistical theory did not depend *logically* on the work of the previous generation of British statisticians. However, it seems unlikely that without this previous generation Fisher would ever have been able to do this work: without them there would have been precious little to reformulate. Moreover, although it is impossible without more evidence to be certain of the detailed genesis of Fisher's concepts, it seems likely that they arose in part in consideration of particular problems. Consideration of Pearson's method of moments seems to have played an important role in the evolution of the method of maximum likelihood. It is unlikely that Fisher would have focused in the way he did on exact distributions had he not had two partially worked-out exemplars (Gosset 1908a,b) before him. The concept of sufficiency arose from consideration of a long-established problem of error theory. Thus, in a certain sense, the pre-condition for Fisher's 'metastatistics' – a relatively rich body of statistical practice and partially theorised techniques – had been laid down by the work of men like Pearson and Gosset: their work was a vital resource for his.

'Metastatistics' of Fisher's kind had, inevitably, a critical edge. Inadequacies in the statistical practice and crudity in the statistical theory of the previous generation were highlighted by Fisher. They, by and large, had been people concerned with the development of adequate tools for tasks defined largely by their extra-statistical concerns; Fisher, by comparison, studied the tools in themselves and their relations to each other. Part of the dispute that arose between Fisher and Pearson was arguably misunderstanding, as when Pearson interpreted Fisher's application of his 'absolute criterion' to sample estimates of the correlation coefficient as a Bayesian argument involving a uniform prior distribution.[19] More serious in effect was Fisher's direct criticism of some of Pearson's methods, notably the method of moments (see above) and the choice of degrees of freedom for the chi-square test when applied to a two-way table. Pearson had argued (1900c, 164–7) that in cases (of which the two-way table was one) where the parameters of the theoretical frequency distribution were estimated from the data, the chi-square test could be used without alteration. Fisher (1922b) argued that the degrees of freedom of chi square were reduced by one for each parameter estimated from the data. For a two-by-two table, Fisher concluded, the correct number of degrees of freedom was not three, as Pearson had assumed, but one.

The dispute between Pearson and Fisher probably should not be seen (as that between Pearson and Bateson, say, can be) as resulting from fundamentally incompatible scientific goals. One is tempted to say, in the case of the degrees of freedom for chi square, that Pearson was simply mistaken.[20] More generally, it can indeed be said that Pearson and Fisher differed in their approaches to inference (Pearson 1936–38, part 1, 222–3 and part 2, 211–13). Yet it still makes sense to see both approaches as embodying the same goals, as attempting to improve the scientific capacity to generalise from the known to the unknown, while remaining within an empiricist and inductivist framework.

Two consequences flow from this. The first is that to some extent a model of cumulative growth, rather than of incommensurability in the full sense, must be seen as applying to development of statistics from the biometric to the 'Fisherian' paradigm.[21] Acceptance of Fisher's approach did not, in general, entail *discarding* the theoretical work of the biometricians; the practical inferences made with biometric statistics could (perhaps with minor modifications) still be made using Fisher's approach. Thus, Fisher did not say that the method of moments was wrong, merely that it was not always the most efficient; he did not discard the chi-square test, but simply suggested how it could more accurately be used. This is in sharp contrast with the divergence between Pearson and Yule, where acceptance of the approach of one side entailed discarding the techniques of the other side virtually in their entirety and often rejecting the concrete inferences of the other side. The second consequence was that the Pearson/Fisher controversy largely lacked the 'group' structure characteristic of the debates discussed in chapters 6 and 7. Pearson was, in effect, isolated. The older generation of statisticians accepted, albeit with reluctance,[22] that Fisher, in relation to Karl Pearson, was 'right'. Fisher's approach was acknowledged to be more general and more powerful.[23]

Statistics and Agricultural Research:
Fisher at Rothamsted

It would, of course, be grossly misleading to leave an impression of Fisher's work in statistical theory as being solely 'metastatistical' in its nature. In 1919 Fisher was appointed to the newly created post of statistician at the Rothamsted Experimental Station, and some of his most important work was done in the context of the practical demands of agricultural research.

Fisher was not, in fact, the first British statistician to become involved in agricultural research. As pointed out above, the interests of Guinness Brewers included agriculture, as well as brewing. In the period prior to 1914, Gosset was already interested in agricultural research and was in contact with workers in England who, presumably as a result of the resurgence of agricultural research in this period, had already started to apply elementary statistical techniques to the results of agricultural experiments.[24] Interestingly enough, it was through these contacts that Gosset first came to know of the work of Fisher, and it may have been partly through Gosset that Fisher was appointed to Rothamsted.[25]

Fisher worked at Rothamsted from 1919 to 1933, and, even after he left to take up the Galton Chair of Eugenics vacated by Karl Pearson, he continued to live in Harpenden and to play an active role in the life of the research station (Yates and Mather 1963, 94). His publications almost immediately reflected the new environment. A paper on 'the yield of dressed grain from broadbalk' (1921b) shows Fisher getting to grips with the problem that was the immediate cause of his appointment: the existence at Rothamsted of a huge bulk of only partially analysed experimental records (Russell 1966, 325). In this paper Fisher analysed the wheat yields in thirteen plots that had been under continuous observation from 1852 to 1918, developing in the course of the analysis a novel method of curve-fitting using orthogonal polynomials. The long series of papers published by Fisher at Rothamsted (reprinted in Bennett 1971–74, *1* and *2*) gives ample evidence of the highly productive nature of Fisher's response to the practical demands of the research station. This response utilised Fisher's previous practical and theoretical statistical experience: an interesting example being the use of the technique of the analysis of variance, originally developed in eugenic research (Fisher 1918a), as the basis for the design and analysis of agricultural experiments (Fisher and Mac-Kenzie 1923). Fisher himself commented that his '"factorial" method of experimentation derives its structure and its name from the simultaneous inheritance of Mendelian factors' (Fisher 1952, 3).

The most important published product of Fisher's early years at Rothamsted was his *Statistical Methods for Research Workers* (1925). Fisher introduced the book as follows:

For several years the author has been working in somewhat

intimate co-operation with a number of biological research departments; the present book is in every sense the product of this circumstance. Daily contact with the statistical problems which present themselves to the laboratory worker has stimulated the purely mathematical researches upon which are based the methods here presented. Little experience is sufficient to show that the traditional machinery of statistical processes is wholly unsuited to the needs of practical research. Not only does it take a cannon to shoot a sparrow, but it misses the sparrow! The elaborate mechanism built on the theory of infinitely large samples is not accurate enough for simple laboratory data. Only by systematically tackling small sample problems on their merits does it seem possible to apply accurate tests to practical data. (1925, vii).

In part, the book was a presentation of Fisher's approach to the foundations of statistical inference together with his extensive work on exact distributions. But it was also more than that. Fisher drew on his experience to show the usefulness of his methods of inference to practical problems. Thus, he showed the applicability of the method of maximum likelihood to the estimation of genetic linkage in self-fertilised animals and plants (*ibid.*, 24–5). The Poisson distribution was illustrated with Gosset's work on counting yeast cells (*ibid.*, 58–9), and problems of bacterial counting were discussed (*ibid.*, 61–4). Chi square was discussed in the context of breeding experiments (*ibid.*, 77–90). Gosset's practically motivated work on small-sample theory was systematically presented and integrated into Fisher's general approach (*ibid.*, 101–13). Regression was illustrated by analysis of the effect of nitrogenous fertilisers on grain yield and by the comparison of the relative growth rates of two cultures of an alga (*ibid.*, 119–25). The discussion of the correlation coefficient showed how Fisher's work on its exact distribution could be used to test the significance of particular values (*ibid.*, 138–75). The analysis of variance was presented and illustrated from both genetics and experimental field trials (*ibid.*, 188–209). The analysis of field trials was further developed, and it was shown how the analysis of variance, combined with a restricted but randomised experimental design (the famous 'Latin square'), provided a powerful technique for agricultural experimentation (*ibid.*, 224–32).

While this approach does not sound exceptional to the modern reader, *Statistical Methods for Research Workers* was a remarkable innovation. It incorporated Fisher's conviction that a theory of statistical inference could be developed that did not rely on inverse probability and was not restricted to large samples. But, almost more importantly, the book incorporated an effectively new concept of the statistician's role, and therefore a new function for statistical theory. The message was that the statistician should get involved in the practical business of experimentation. This clearly pre-supposed the diffusion of the type of occupational role that Fisher (and Gosset) occupied. It was not even enough that the scientists should hand their results to the statistician for analysis: experiments (especially large-scale applied experiments that were difficult to 'control') had to be designed by those with statistical expertise.

The sales of Fisher's book over the following twenty-five years indicate something of the diffusion of the model of the role of the statistician and of statistical theory contained in it. Seven editions appeared within thirteen years, and by 1950 nearly 20,000 copies in all had been sold (Yates 1951, 31). Within British statistics, Fisher's work exerted tremendous influence, even amongst those closest to Karl Pearson (Pearson 1974). Rothamsted emerged as a centre of statistical research (and even, in an informal sense, teaching, as many came, especially from outside Britain, to learn in an 'apprentice' role) to rival University College. Thus, in 1926, two of Karl Pearson's new staff (Oscar Irwin and John Wishart) left University College 'to gain new experience with R. A. Fisher at Rothamsted' (Pearson 1970b, 456).

By the mid-1920s there were, therefore, clear signs of the beginning of a new era in the development of statistical theory in Britain. The new role for the statistician in agricultural and industrial production, and in scientific research in general, may have been in some ways more modest than the position of central political influence hoped for by Karl Pearson. The new role was, however, one of considerable importance. Its evolution, and the way in which the practical demands associated with it translated themselves into goals of statistical theory, are interesting problems. They fall, however, outside the scope of this book.

9

Conclusion

· · : · ·
    : :
     ·

At the start of this book, the question of the extent and nature of
social influence on science was raised. To what extent, and in what
ways, is scientific knowledge socially constructed? It is now time to
pull together various threads of the discussion of the previous
chapters, and to see what they contribute to an answer to this
question.

Discovery or Invention?

Perhaps the most basic issue is whether it makes any sense to talk of
a mathematical discipline like statistical theory being *constructed*.
For one important account of mathematics, which we can label
Platonism or mathematical realism, denies that the concepts of
mathematical science are the products of human creative activity.
On the Platonist view, the job of mathematics is to describe a
non-physical but nonetheless real world of mathematical objects.
G. H. Hardy (1967) gave a classical summary of this view:

> I believe that mathematical reality lies outside us, that our
> function is to discover or *observe* it, and that the theorems
> which we prove, and which we describe grandiloquently as our
> 'creations', are simply our notes of our observations.
>
> 317 is a prime, not because we think so, or because our minds
> are shaped in one way rather than another, but *because it is so*,
> because mathematical reality is built that way. (*ibid.*, 123–4,
> 130; quoted by Bloor 1973, 176; Hardy's emphasis)

I have not found any writer who takes an explicitly Platonist view
of the concepts of statistical theory. Nevertheless, a version of
Platonism does seem to underlie much writing about statistics. Thus
the idea of the 'discovery' of statistical concepts is often present,
especially in older work such as Walker (1929). The literal implica-

tion of the word – that concepts in some sense existed, waiting to be uncovered – is never spelt out. But the way history is written is affected.

Take Walker's account of the history of correlation theory (1929, 92):

> . . . correlation was the unique discovery of Sir Francis Galton.
> . . . Nevertheless there were others in that century who hovered on the verge of the discovery of correlation. Any one of them might have discovered it. None of them did.

Suppose this actually were true. Then to talk of statistical theory as socially constructed would be largely vacuous, for the differing goals and interests underlying the work of Galton and the others would be essentially irrelevant. At most, they might explain why Galton actually made the 'discovery', while the others only 'hovered on the verge'. They would not play any part in explaining the content of the 'discovery'. And the history of statistics would become like the conventional history of geographical exploration. When and by whom America (or correlation) was 'discovered' might be accountable for sociologically, but the topography of America (or the mathematical content of Galton's statistics) would obviously not be subject to social explanation. So the conclusion would indeed be reached that, in the case of statistical theory, social factors might affect the rate and direction of scientific development, but not the actual content of science – at least of 'good' science that is in accord with Platonic 'reality'.

However, much of the material discussed above is sufficient to throw doubt on the empirical usefulness of a Platonist account of the history of statistics. Thus, in chapter 3, it was shown that the error theorists were not 'on the verge of' the *same* 'discovery' as Galton. They were working in a different tradition, with different goals that caused their work – even when dealing with closely similar mathematical expressions – to take quite a different form. In chapter 7 we saw how researchers with different goals developed the theory of association in quite different, incompatible directions, with no evidence of their work being pulled towards any Platonic endpoint. In chapter 8 we looked at Fisher reformulating the theory of inference in a non-Bayesian direction that is still controversial. There is little evidence that hypothesising a timeless Platonic world of statistical concepts, an ahistorical 'internal logic' of statistical theory guiding the hands of statisticians, would have helped us understand these episodes any better.

Of course, Platonism is not refuted by this, because the Platonist account makes no necessary claims about the empirical world. But what can, I think, be concluded is that we need have no fears about abandoning Platonism and investigating the consequences of studying the history of statistics from an explicitly anti-Platonic viewpoint. We have nothing concrete to lose.[1] The core of this viewpoint is a simple one: it is to see what statisticians do as *invention* rather than *discovery*. That is to say, we should see statistical theory as the result simply of the creative activity of statisticians and of their communal evaluation of the validity of the results of this activity. There is no need to see it as the gradual revelation of timeless truth.

An immediate objection to this approach might be that it would make statistical theory merely arbitrary, the consequence of statisticians' personal whims: in other words, that one cannot on these lines account for the feelings of empirical utility and theoretical correctness that statistics undoubtedly induces. However, nothing in this approach denies connections between statistics and the material world. Indeed, in chapter 3 the role of sets of empirical data as resources in Galton's theorising has been emphasised. Further, to say that the test of validity is communal evaluation, and not correspondence to ultimate Platonic reality, is not to assert that this evaluation is necessarily ill-founded. The *feeling* that things could not have been otherwise than they are – that our statistics is the only possible correct statistics – is also quite accountable for in this perspective. After techniques or theories have passed the test of communal evaluation, they take on within the community of statisticians the status of social institutions: they are taught as correct, work in accord with them is rewarded, and work violating them may well be seen as wrong and subject to sanctions.[2]

Science as Goal-Oriented

One advantage of seeing innovation as invention rather than as discovery is that it permits us to ask the question 'what is invention for?'. It makes it possible to see sciences, even mathematical disciplines, as oriented to secular and definable goals, and not to see them merely abstractly as the pursuit of truth. The material in the previous chapters has, hopefully, shown that this is a perspective that is indeed useful in understanding scientific practice.

To say that science is goal-oriented is, emphatically, not the same as to say that scientists' motivations are pragmatic and utilitarian, or that all science is merely technology. Even in the case of statistical theory, an 'applied' discipline, we have seen that theorising often has little to do with the specifics of particular applications. Thus Fisher's work on the theory of inference, productive though it was of useful techniques, cannot merely be said to have been oriented towards the production of these techniques: Fisher's concerns were of a much higher level of generality.

One way to think of these matters is to follow Jürgen Habermas's *Knowledge and Human Interests* (1972) and to see science as reflecting the goal of the expansion of human capacity to predict and control the world.[3] This instrumental goal is obviously a pervasive one, and much of statistical theory makes sense in terms of it. Statistical inference was (and is) an attempt to predict from a known sample the characteristics of an unknown population. A regression analysis yields a rule for predicting the expected value of one variable from that of another variable or set of variables. Successful statistical procedures enhance the potential for control; this is most obviously the case when statistical theory is used in production ('quality control', yield trials, and so on), but it holds also in other areas (for example, in the relationship between biometric statistical theory and eugenic intervention). And it is not merely statistical theory that can be analysed in this way. As chapter 6 has shown, the notion of a goal of prediction and control can help us make sense of biology as well.

Yet the analytical approach of Habermas's *Knowledge and Human Interests* cannot be adopted straightforwardly as a description of scientific practice (indeed it is clearly not intended as such). Part of Habermas's point is the distinction between 'empirical-analytical sciences' and 'hermeneutic' sciences.[4] The latter are based on techniques such as the interpretation of documents, and are seen by Habermas as oriented around meaningful communication rather than instrumental action. While the analytical distinction may be clear (though Barnes 1977, 12–19, disagrees), the Kuhnian and post-Kuhnian history and sociology of science have taught us that these categories are inextricably intertwined in what scientists actually do. Prediction and control take place within a shared framework of meanings and assumptions, which is sustained by consensus and authority.

This shared framework is not only that internal to the scientific community. Consider Pearson's biometry. The goal of the prediction of the characteristics of future generations of organic populations, and that of the control of those of human populations, were clearly present. But the very instrumentalism of this approach made it into a symbolic statement laden with meaning for human values, as Bateson, in rejecting it, arguably saw. In its context, Pearson's work was not *just* a contribution to a 'general populational genetic engineering'.[5] In its assertion that this form of engineering should be used to improve human societies, it also bore a message about ethics and human purposes.

And Bateson's opposition to biometry brings us to the core of the problem. For Bateson did not merely send out an opposing message about values, he also helped construct a theory that he claimed was *scientifically* superior to biometry. Further, there was no single criterion of predictive power that would enable us to decide the issue. The biometric approach was oriented towards the prediction of the quantitative, observable characteristics of whole populations; the Mendelian approach was initially relatively restricted (to a more limited range of organisms and characteristics, and to controlled rather than natural settings), but was argued to be more powerful within these restrictions. And this was not a unique instance. The two sides in the debate about association might also *both* have claimed a superior predictive potential for their techniques, for they were using different, and incompatible, criteria to assess this.

So, examined in detail, the goal of prediction and control tends to fragment into a multiplicity of differing specific goals. There does not appear to be any general criterion of predictive power or capacity for control. The assessment of the instrumental adequacy of techniques and theories seems typically to be in terms of their particular adequacy for particular types of prediction and control, and this arguably is what *has* to be the case.[6] Furthermore, these different particularisations of the goal of prediction and control seem, at least on occasion, to be associated with different political or ethical stances: that, at least, is what appears to be indicated by the debates over Mendelism and association. Not only is there a multiplicity of predictive goals, but these are connected to different symbolic forms. Scientific practice is constitutively linked both to instrumental action *and* to communicative interaction.

Up to now, I have used the term 'goals' very informally. So it is perhaps worthwhile to clarify this usage in order to spell out a little further how the view of science as goal-oriented may inform historical and sociological accounts of science. First, the term 'goal' is meant to encompass both the production and the evaluation of innovations. In writing about episodes such as those discussed here,

I can see little point in rigorously separating a 'context of justification' from a 'context of discovery'. To take the example of the debates discussed in chapters 6 and 7, there seems to be no essential difference between the goals apparent in each side's production of new knowledge, and the criteria employed in judging the work of the other side. There was no abstract scientific community, over and above the warring groups, applying 'neutral' criteria. Evaluation was thus no more independent of particular goals than was initial innovation.

Secondly, to say that evaluation is goal-oriented does not mean that it is necessarily inadequate, unscientific or biased. Indeed there is little correlation to be found in the episodes I have examined between the narrowness of the goals informing judgement and the correctness, as we would now assess it, of the judgements made. Thus the goals manifest in Gosset's work were perhaps the narrowest – certainly the most utilitarian – of those examined in this book; but we would now say that his judgement was correct. Pearson was the philosophically most aware of the scientists we have examined, and one whose judgements were presented as being in terms of explicit, 'rational' criteria; but he was wrong (in our terms) to reject Mendelism. If the perspective suggested here is correct, then all judgement is in any case goal-oriented. To point to the goals underlying evaluation is not to *expose* it, it is merely to describe it.

Thirdly, I do not intend the term 'goal' to imply a distant objective, the pot of gold at the end of the scientific rainbow. Goals are fully reflected, I would argue, in the day-to-day practice of science, as constitutive features of what scientists do. The biometric school's goal of the prediction of the quantitative characteristics of populations affected, as suggested in chapter 6, even such details as the form in which records should be kept. Results, they argued, should not be lumped into the 'craft-knowledge' categories of the traditional biologist, but detailed quantitative records should be kept if at all possible. Only then could the quantitative predictive apparatus of correlation and regression be brought cleanly to bear on them.

The fourth point is that goals are not *necessarily* motives. The term 'goal' is intended to describe a typically trans-individual feature of the production and evaluation of innovation, which may be, but is not always, translatable into individual motivation. Take, for example, the work of the biometric school on association. I have suggested that the goal of this was to maximise the analogy between association and interval-level correlation, and that this goal was the result of the connection between biometric statistics and the needs of eugenic research. As pointed out in chapter 7, there is no way of telling whether all of the biometricians who worked on the mathematics of association were motivated by eugenics, or that they personally cared whether association and correlation were run together or held apart. Their motives might have been enjoyment of mathematical puzzles, desire for professional advancement, or whatever. Nevertheless, their public judgements – that association should be measured by r_T and not by Q, and so on – are intelligible only in terms of the objective of harmonising correlation and association.

Social Interests

One way of summarising the above discussion of goals would be to say that goals are, typically, institutionalised features of scientific judgement, remembering that the term 'institution' is here being used in a wide sense to mean stable patterns of social behaviour. While we obviously can talk of the goals underlying an individual's work, the term can also be used to describe the criteria that groups of scientists bring to bear on the practice of science. As with social institutions more generally, science done in conformity with group goals generally brings rewards, while judgements at odds with these goals run the risk of being perceived as deviant.

So the individual scientist's decision to work in accord with group goals may well not need special explanation. Nevertheless, this does not tell us what sustains the goals themselves. To draw the analogy with the social institution of marriage, to explain why individuals choose to marry is not the same as to explain the permanence of this way of organising relations between men and women.

What is suggested in this book is that goals are typically sustained by social interests. Often, and probably usually, these interests are to be located within the social structure of science itself. Imagine a group of scientists who have spent a great deal of time and effort acquiring a particular set of skills. Imagine also that the goals exemplified in their science – the way they innovate, their routine judgements – are such that scientific approaches that make full use of their skills are favoured, and those that make their skills redundant are rejected. Then we might quite reasonably postulate that social interests – group 'investment' in particular skills – are sustaining the goals manifest in their science.

There is indeed evidence, notably in the biometrician/Mendelian dispute, of interests of this kind operating. What may be more controversial, however, is the suggestion that sometimes scientific goals were sustained by interests that had their origins outside science. One way I have identified the operation of these is through the connection between statistics and eugenics. Eugenics, I have argued, was ultimately one particular manifestation of the social interests of the British professional middle class. And the further-ance of eugenics (or, more tentatively and in any case much less frequently, opposition to it), was a crucial factor in sustaining particular kinds of work in statistical theory. Connections between eugenics and statistics can be seen both at the organisation level, as discussed in chapter 5, and at the detailed level of the mathematics of regression and association discussed in chapters 3 and 7. Without eugenics, statistical theory would not have developed in the way it did in Britain – and indeed might not have developed at all, at least till much later.[7]

One crucial point is that, in the same way as goals are not necessarily motives, so social interests need not be translated direct-ly into motives. Take Gosset's work as an example. The goal of this work – the extension of existing theory to cope with the small samples used in industrial and agricultural practice – is surely to be explained in terms of the interest of Guinness & Co. in expanding their control over processes of production, and ultimately in terms of their interest in enhanced profits. Yet we need not assume that Gosset's *motive* was pleasure at increased beer production or healthier balance sheets. It is at least equally plausible to imagine him as motivated by a desire to get on in the company, and thus as working for the interests of Guinness – as the best way of achieving promotion – without personal commitment to these interests.

In this case the appeal to 'interests' as an explanatory factor is a very obvious and commonsense one. It becomes less so in the discussions of, for example, the social interests of the professional middle class. I have freely admitted that these interests are not susceptible to easy empirical identification. The postulating of a social interest inevitably involves a move beyond the evidence: it is a step that is in principle contestable, and one that has in practice been contested.

I have no desire to enter here into the difficult theoretical and empirical problems raised by the relationship of individual behavi-our to social interests – these have been touched on several times in the previous chapters. One reaction to the appeal to social interests as an explanatory factor however needs to be anticipated. I am well aware that because this appeal involves a move beyond the evidence it will seem alien to many historians of science. To remain close to the 'documents', to make no inferences not justifiable from them, is a quite understandable desire (indeed, to my mind, one that is much healthier than its obverse, theorising without reference to the concrete). But it is an objective that can never be achieved, at least not if history is to be other than mere documentation.

For consider the question of the relation of the content of science to its social context, as treated by the three main approaches of the contemporary history of science that are represented amongst writers on the period and material discussed here. The first approach we can label the 'descriptive-intellectualist'. This seeks to reconstruct comprehensively and accurately the scientific past. It is an ideal-type, to the extent that few authors can resist the temptation to some kind of explanation as well as description, but nevertheless one can find many examples of work that approximates more or less closely to it: the writing of Froggatt and Nevin (1971a,b) on the biometrician/Mendelian controversy is one. While the information produced by this kind of work is of prime importance, it is clear that it cannot in itself answer such questions as 'was this piece of science conditioned by its social context?'. For this would clearly involve explaining what happened rather than merely describing it. Further, it would be mistaken to conclude that this approach produces theory-free data by which explanations can be tested. After all, description always involves selection of what is important and what is not, and this selection must always be guided by some principles, even if they are implicit ones. Most seriously, the implicit base often involves a decision as to what is science (and therefore relevant) and what is not science (and therefore to be ignored).

The most common means of moving from description to explanation is the use of the second main approach: biography. This involves 'getting inside the head' of the people being studied in order to explain what they did in terms of their past experiences, beliefs, commitments, personalities, and so on. Most of the important historical writings on which I have drawn in this book involve this approach: for example, Cowan (1972a, etc.) on Galton; Norton (1975a,b, 1978a) on Pearson; Coleman (1970) on Bateson; Box (1978) on Fisher. Again, I would not for a moment question the value of this work. The surprising aspect, however, is that its theoretical nature has gone almost unnoticed.

In his spirited defence of biography, Thomas Hankins (1979, 2) comments that the 'recreation of ideas, motives, and perceptions of events in the mind of a single individual is the task confronting every historical biographer'. With the exception of biographies explicitly informed by psychoanalytical theory, this is almost always done in a commonsense fashion. So it does not *appear* to be theoretical. Yet as Shapin and Barnes (1979) point out, it is a highly problematic exercise. The internal mental states of others are not directly accessible to us, and in giving accounts of them we are inevitably moving beyond the evidence. Thus in explaining Pearson's hostility to Mendelism in terms of his philosophical views, Norton (1975a,b) is making an implicit claim about Pearson's state of mind: that Pearson's philosophy was a determinant of other aspects of his thinking. Yet it is perfectly possible to suggest other states of mind that might equally well account for the written record that is all the historian has to go on. Pearson might be seen as actively using his philosophy, rather than being passively determined by it. His philosophical pronouncements, such as his statements that the theories of those he opposed failed to meet the positivist criteria of 'good' science, could then be interpreted as his use of the rhetorical resources of philosophy to justify the rejection of positions he in fact disliked on other grounds. There is no *need* to see these pronouncements as constituting the actual causes of his other beliefs.

This pervasive type of biographical explanation has the following form. One part of an individual's writings is taken as the cause of another part, via the explicit or implicit assumption of an internal psychological state: 'X's science was motivated by his political beliefs', 'Y's experimental results led her to reject this theory', 'Z's philosophical commitments caused him to write this'. It is an extremely important form, because in it resides biography's claim to be able to answer questions about the relation of science to its social context. If the part that is doing the 'influencing' is the individual's writings on social and political matters, then that is a victory for 'externalism' – and so on. The problem is that the claim of causation, or 'influence', or whatever, rests not only on the documents but more crucially on the hypothesised internal psychological state. So the explanation depends on the unobservable. However secure or contestible this step beyond the empirical appears, it remains a step beyond the empirical.

The move from individual to collective biography (head-counting or 'prosopography' as it is sometimes called) may avoid the problems resulting from the postulating of internal psychological states, but even it does not promise a theory-free solution to problems of the relation of science to its social context. A relatively new approach in the history of science, it is the least common of the three major styles of work. Only Farrall (1970) amongst the historians considered here uses collective biography, but his work makes the crucial point amply clear. Farrall, it will be remembered, examined the occupations of the Council of the Eugenics Education Society, and of a random sample of its membership. This is extremely useful information, and certainly evidence relevant to explanations of eugenics, but it is inherently ambiguous. To find a preponderance of people in a particular social position amongst the public adherents of a particular system of belief does not itself tell us the nature of the relation between that position and the belief, even if the numerical preponderance is, as in this case, almost total. To explain the connection is a different matter, and involves going beyond the statistical evidence. Indeed in this case, as has been discussed in chapter 2, historians have done this in very different ways: for example, Farrall himself postulating psychological states, this author social interests.

My point is not that these three methods of doing history should be avoided, nor is it that explanations in terms of motives or other psychological states are necessarily wrong. Quite the reverse: the chapters above have employed intellectual reconstruction, biography and collective biography, and I cannot imagine how this study could have been written without use of them. Where I have felt confident about hypothesising individual motives I have done so. All that is being argued is that would be wrong to reject the explanations in terms of social interests that are used here on the grounds that they are theoretical while biographical explanations (say) are not. All explanation, perhaps even all description, in the history of science is inevitably theoretical, and this is no less so if the theory used is implicit.

Of course, this is not to say that a complacent, 'anything goes', attitude should be adopted. Theory must be used to explain actual events, and in this use lies the hope of refining and testing it. I am fully aware that the approach suggested in this book has hardly begun to be employed, and much work is needed before definitive statements about, say, the relationship of eugenics or biometry to the professional middle class can be made with confidence. It is, however, surely by bold conjecture – and not by keeping our theories in the closet – that the history of science will progress.

Then and Now

The image of science suggested by this study is thus the following. Science is an activity not of passive contemplation and 'discovery' but of invention. It is goal-oriented, and, while its goals may all in a general sense have to do with the enhancement of the human potential to predict and control the world, they represent different particularisations of this overall objective. The pursuit of particular goals is typically sustained by social interests located either in the internal social structure of science or in that of society at large. Scientific knowledge is thus a social construct in two senses. First, in that it is typically the product of interacting groups of scientists. Second, in that social interests affect it not merely at the organisational level but at the most basic level of the development and evaluation of theories and techniques. Because science is goal-oriented, and because its goals are socially sustained, scientific knowledge is constitutively social.

A final note of caution is, however, perhaps in order. To say, following Habermas, that goals and interests are *constitutive* of knowledge is to invite a possible misunderstanding. The German language differentiates between two aspects of the notion of 'knowledge'; *Erkenntis* ('the act, process, form or faculty of knowing') and *Wissen* ('the passive content of what is known'). Habermas's analysis refers to the first, rather than the second (Habermas 1972, 319). So must any similar analysis, if it is to avoid the 'genetic fallacy' of concluding that the origins of knowledge forever determine its status. Knowledge must be analysed as a resource for practice, and knowing must be seen as a process.

The analogy between knowledge as a resource for practice and tools in the everyday sense may make this point clearer. A tool's construction will reflect the tasks for which it was designed, and it will initially be evaluated according to its adequacy in the performance of these tasks. This does not mean, however, that its use is always limited to these tasks: it may well be found helpful for purposes quite different from those for which it was developed. Similarly, the construction and evaluation of knowledge can be structured by particular goals without these determining for all time the fate of this knowledge. Of course, it is true that the initial uses of a tool may well give us a clue as to other possible uses, may suggest the amendments that will be required to achieve different objectives with it, and may indicate in which situations we may have to discard it. All of this, however, is contingent, not necessary.

That eugenic concerns structured Galton's and Pearson's statistical theory does not imply, therefore, that the modern statistician who does not share these concerns need necessarily eschew the use of the concepts developed by them. It is not that the acceptance of a technique by modern statisticians guarantees its context-independent validity. Rather, the construction and evaluation of statistical theory by modern statisticians needs to be studied in its own right before any conclusions can be drawn as to the goals and interests constitutive of present-day statistics.

'Our statistics *is* different', the modern statistician may well claim. To say this is false in one sense, true in another. It is false, in that to claim that 'we' have achieved eternally valid knowledge, or evaluations not structured by context or interest, would be unjustifiable. It is true, to the extent that 'our' statistical theory has emerged in a historical process from 'theirs'. This historical process has largely been one of the generalisation of the scope of statistical theory, as statisticians have come to grips with new situations. 'Their' concepts have been modified, stretched or discarded. So 'our' statistics is in this sense more general than 'theirs', and hence it is relatively easy for us to see the context-bound nature of 'their' thought. It is not that 'our' statistics explains 'theirs' as a special case; rather, 'theirs' helps to explain 'ours', in that 'their' knowledge was used in the construction of 'ours'. It is not, as a Platonist might have it, that Galton and Pearson discovered some of the current stock of truths; rather, it is that they, in solving their problems, produced resources that have been used by later statisticians to solve other problems. 'Our' statistics is different from 'theirs' in that it has evolved from it; but, like 'theirs', it is a social and historical product, and can and should be analysed as such.

Appendixes

. . . . .
. . .
.

1. *Archival Sources*

The following archival sources were consulted in the course of the preparation of this book, and I should like to express my thanks to the relevant individuals and institutions for permission to see them. I was unable to find or obtain access to two sets of papers. The first of these consists of the technical reports, etc., prepared by W. S. Gosset while employed by the Guinness Brewery in Dublin. These were used by E. S. Pearson in writing his biography of Gosset (Pearson 1939), and thus this omission is perhaps not too serious. I should like to thank Mr A. V. Vincent, Head of Management Services, Arthur Guinness Son & Co. (Dublin) Ltd, who attempted to locate these for me. Access to the papers of R. A. Fisher, in the care of the Department of Genetics, University of Adelaide, was refused.

Bateson Papers. Dr Alan Cock kindly allowed me to see parts of his copy of a microfilm of the papers of William Bateson prepared by William Coleman. Sections 10a–c, 13, 14b, 15 and 18 contain material relevant to Bateson's controversy with the biometricians. (In addition, Professor C. D. Darlington showed me some further correspondence of Bateson's not on the microfilm, as did the Librarian of St John's College, Cambridge.)
Black's Notebooks. A set of 23 manuscript notebooks by Arthur Black. These were found for me by Messrs David and Richard Garnett. Mr David Garnett has kindly allowed them to be placed in the Library of University College, London.
Cambridge University Eugenics Society Papers. These were found in the library of the Eugenics Society, Eccleston Square, London SW I, under reference C.1.393. They consist of a set of manuscripts,

typescripts and press-cuttings referring to the activities of the Cambridge University Eugenics Society, and contain important unpublished papers by R. A. Fisher (1911, 1912a,b).

Darwin, Leonard, Papers. Dr Roy MacLeod kindly allowed me to examine a set of the papers of Major Leonard Darwin being catalogued at the University of Sussex and now in Cambridge University Library. Unfortunately, they provided no information on the chief point of interest, the relations between Major Darwin and R. A. Fisher. The few items of correspondence of Major Darwin's in the care of the Royal College of Surgeons at Down House include no letters to or from Fisher.

Davenport Papers. These are in the care of the American Philosophical Society, Philadelphia. They include letters from Francis Galton, Karl Pearson and R. A. Fisher. Although they are of considerable general interest, the Davenport papers do not in general throw much light on the development of statistical theory.

Galton Papers. These are in the Library of University College, London. Along with the Pearson Papers, they form the major archival source on the history of statistical theory in Britain. A handlist compiled by M. Merrington and J. Golden was issued in 1976.

Pearl Papers. These are in the care of the American Philosophical Society, Philadelphia. From the point of view of British statistics, the most interesting part of these papers is the extensive correspondence from Major Greenwood and George Udny Yule, which contains a lot of informal information on the British statistical community.

Pearson Papers. These are in the Library of University College, London. A handlist compiled by M. Merrington was issued in 1974. Material of particular interest includes Pearson's first written reflections on Galton's work (Pearson 1889), and his correspondence with friends such as Robert Parker and colleagues such as Yule.

Royal Statistical Society Minutes. The minutes of the Council and Executive Committee of the Society for the period of the book were examined. In the light of their formal nature (and of the relatively small role of the Society in the development of statistical theory in this period), these proved to be of little interest. The records of the Society for the period after 1930 (such as material on the 'Study Group', on the Industrial and Agricultural Research Section and on the activities of the Society in the Second World War) are of greater interest, but fall outside the scope of this book.

Yule-Greenwood Letters. These consist of a set of letters from George Udny Yule to Major Greenwood, arranged in chronological order and dating from the period 1910 to 1949, in the possession of Mr George B. Greenwood. This series of letters, which appears reasonably complete, is probably the best single manuscript source for the study of Yule.

Yule's Notes. These are five manuscript notebooks by George Udny Yule, and are his notes of Karl Pearson's lectures on statistical theory in the academic years 1894–95 and 1895–96. They were given by Yule to the Department of Statistics, University College, London. These proved useful in elucidating some otherwise opaque published work (in particular, Pearson and Filon 1898). They are now in the Pearson Papers, 84.

Yule Papers. These are the papers of George Udny Yule in the care of the Royal Statistical Society. Of particular interest are letters between Yule and Major Greenwood prior to 1914, including letters from Greenwood to Yule not duplicated in the Yule-Greenwood Letters, and material gathered by Yule in writing his obituary of Karl Pearson.

2. *The Council of the Eugenics Education Society in 1914*

The group of 41 Council members for 1914 is a subset of Farrall's group of 111 Council members for 1908–20. Individuals already identified by Farrall are asterisked.

*President: Major Leonard Darwin, son of Charles Darwin. Retired army engineer. (*Who was Who,* 1929–40)

*Hon. Secretary: Mrs Sybil Gotto. Hon. Secretary 1907–20. Widow of Naval Officer. Effectively worked full-time for eugenics. (*Eugenics Review 47* [1955–56], 149)

Hon. Treasurer: Paul von Fleischl. Treasurer of E.E.S., 1907–22. Occupation unknown.

Mr Crofton Black: Barrister and official of Land Union. (E.E.S., *Sixth Annual Report,* 25, and *Eugenics Review 12* [1920–21], 91)

Sir Edward Brabrook: Barrister, Chief Registrar of Friendly Societies, 1891–1904. Director of Society of Antiquaries and former President of the Anthropological Institute. (*Who's Who,* 1914)

Mrs Theodore Chambers: Wife of Theodore Chambers, civil servant and businessman. (*Who was Who,* 1951–60)

Hon. Sir John Cockburn: Former Minister of Education, South Australia. Doctor. Represented Australia at international conferences on health, eugenics, etc. (*Who was Who,* 1914)

Mr R. Newton Crane: International lawyer. (*Who's Who*, 1914)

Mr A. E. Crawley: Author. Wrote on anthropology, sport, etc. (*Who's Who*, 1914)

Sir H. Cunningham: Former lawyer and judge in India. (*Who's Who*, 1914)

Dr Langdon Down: Physician to National Association for Welfare of Feeble-Minded. (*Medical Directory*, 1914)

*Mr Havelock Ellis: Scientist and author. (*Who's Who*, 1914)

Prof. J. Findlay: Professor of Education, University of Manchester. (*Who's Who*, 1914)

Mr E. G. Wheler Galton: Nephew of Francis Galton. Farmer at Claverdon. Interested in scientific aspects of agriculture. (Pearson 1914–30)

*Dr M. Greenwood: Medical statistician. See chapter 5.

Dr W. Hadley: Lecturer in Medicine, London Hospital. Physician, Chest Hospital, Victoria Park. (*Who's Who*, 1914)

Mrs W. H. Henderson: Wife of Admiral Henderson, who since retirement had served on Metropolitan Asylums Board. (*Who's Who*, 1914)

*Major E. H. Hills, F.R.S.: Director of Durham University Observatory, President of Royal Astronomical Society. Former military engineer. (*Who's Who*, 1914)

Very Rev. W. R. Inge: Dean of St Paul's. Former Professor of Divinity at Cambridge. (*Who's Who*, 1914)

Miss Kirby: Secretary, National Association for Welfare of Feeble-Minded. (*Eugenics Review 1* [1909–10], 85)

Dr Ernest Lane: Senior surgeon, St Mary's Hospital. (*Who's Who*, 1914)

*Prof. E. W. MacBride: Professor of Zoology, Imperial College. (*Who's Who*, 1914)

Lady Owen MacKenzie: Widow of Sir George Sutherland MacKenzie (1844–1910), merchant and geographer. (D.N.B.)

*Mr Robert Mond: Industrial Chemist, Director of Brunner, Mond & Co. (*Who's Who*, 1914)

*Dr F. W. Mott, F.R.S.: Neuropathologist. Physician to Charing Cross Hospital. (*Who's Who*, 1914)

Mr G. P. Mudge: Surgeon, university teacher, and author of biology textbooks. (*University of London Calendar* and *British Museum Catalogue*)

*Mrs G. Pooley: Wife of opthalmic surgeon, G. H. Pooley. (*Who's Who*, 1914)

*Mr W. Rae, M.P.: Liberal M.P. for Scarborough.
(*Who's Who*, 1914)

*Dr Archdall Reid: Physician and author of books on heredity, alcoholism, etc. (*Medical Directory*, 1914)

Mr John Russell: Headmaster of King Alfred's School, Hampstead. (*Alumni Cantabrigienses*, part II)

*Mr F. C. S. Schiller: Philosopher, Oxford University.
(*Who's Who*, 1914)

*Prof. A. Schuster, F.R.S.: Secretary of Royal Society. Formerly Professor of Physics, University of Manchester. (*Who's Who*, 1914)

*Mr Edgar Schuster: Former Galton research fellow in eugenics. In 1914 at Oxford University. (Paton and Phillips 1973)

*Dr C. G. Seligmann: Professor of Ethnology, University of London. Formerly Hunterian Professor at Royal College of Surgeons. (*Who's Who*, 1914)

*Prof. C. Spearman: Grote Professor of Mind and Logic, University of London. (*Who's Who*, 1914)

*Prof. J. A. Thomson: Professor of Natural History, University of Aberdeen. (*Who's Who*, 1914)

Dr A. F. Tredgold: Physician specialising in mental diseases.
(*Who's Who*, 1914)

Mrs Alec Tweedie: Writer and columnist. (*Who's Who*, 1914)

*Mr W. C. D. Whetham, F.R.S.: Senior tutor, Trinity College, Cambridge. Physicist. (*Who's Who*, 1914)

Dr Douglas White: Physician. (*Medical Directory*, 1914)

Dr Florence Willey: Lecturer in midwifery, London School of Medicine for Women. (*Who's Who*, 1914)

3. *Galton and the Bivariate Normal Distribution*

Galton's statement of his problem (Galton 1886, 63) can be presented in modern terminology and notation as follows. Let y represent mid-parental height, and x offspring height, where both y and x are measured from the means of their respective generations. Suppose that y is normally distributed with standard deviation σ_2. Let the probability density of y be $g(y)$. Then

$$g(y)\,dy = \frac{1}{\sigma_2\sqrt{2\pi}}\exp\left\{-\frac{y^2}{2\sigma_2{}^2}\right\}\,dy \qquad (1)$$

Consider now the offspring of those mid-parents with a particular height y. These offspring have mean height $\beta_{12}y$, where β_{12} is Galton's (1877) coefficient of reversion, b. Further, this array of offspring has a standard deviation independent of y; again this is a result originally formulated in 1877. Call this standard deviation $\sigma_{1.2}$. The conditional probability density of x, given y, is thus

$$f(x|y)\,dx = \frac{1}{\sigma_{1.2}\sqrt{2\pi}}\exp\left\{-\frac{(x-\beta_{12}y)^2}{2\sigma_{1.2}^2}\right\}dx \tag{2}$$

To obtain $h(x, y)$, the joint distribution of x and y, all Hamilton Dickson had to do was to multiply the conditional probability density of x, given y, by the probability density of y.

$$h(x, y)\,dx\,dy = f(x|y)\,dx\,g(y)\,dy$$

$$= \frac{1}{2\pi\sigma_{1.2}\sigma_2}\exp\left\{-\frac{(x-\beta_{12}y)^2}{2\sigma_{1.2}^2}\right\}\exp\left\{-\frac{y^2}{2\sigma_2^2}\right\}dx\,dy$$

$$= \frac{1}{2\pi\sigma_{1.2}\sigma_2}\exp\left\{-\frac{1}{2}\left[\frac{(x-\beta_{12}y)^2}{\sigma_{1.2}^2}+\frac{y^2}{\sigma_2^2}\right]\right\}dx\,dy \tag{3}$$

The contours of equal frequency are given by

$$\frac{(x-\beta_{12}y)^2}{\sigma_{1.2}^2}+\frac{y^2}{\sigma_2^2} = \text{constant}$$

and are, as Galton had found empirically, ellipses.

The joint probability density can then be factored differently, so that it represents the conditional probability density of y, given x, multiplied by the probability density of x. An expression for the ratio of β_{21} (the regression of mid-parents on offspring) to β_{12} (the regression of offspring on mid-parents) can then be found:

$$\frac{\beta_{21}}{\beta_{12}} = \frac{\sigma_2^2}{\sigma_1^2}$$

Now σ_2, the standard deviation of the mid-parental generation, is, as shown in chapter 3, $\sigma_1/\sqrt{2}$. So $\beta_{21}/\beta_{12}=\frac{1}{2}$, and if $\beta_{12}=\frac{2}{3}$ then $\beta_{21}=\frac{1}{3}$, precisely as Galton had found empirically. [In the notation used by Hamilton Dickson, $\beta_{12}=\tan\theta$, $\beta_{21}=\tan\phi$, $k\sigma_2=a$, $k\sigma_1=c$, $k\sigma_{1.2}=b$, where $k=0.6745$, the 'conversion factor' from standard deviations to probable errors on the assumption of a normal distribution. In the numerical example (Galton 1886, 63–4), $\tan\theta=\frac{2}{3}$, $a=1.22$ inches, $b=1.50$ inches.]

Galton had thus, with the assistance of Hamilton Dickson, constructed an expression for what would now be called the bivariate normal distribution. The expression is not in its ordinary modern form

$$h(x, y)\, dx\, dy =$$

$$\frac{1}{2\pi\sigma_1\sigma_2\sqrt{(1-r^2)}}\exp\left[-\frac{1}{2(1-r^2)}\left\{\frac{x^2}{\sigma_1^2}-\frac{2rxy}{\sigma_1\sigma_2}+\frac{y^2}{\sigma_2^2}\right\}\right] \quad (4)$$

because Galton had not yet invented the correlation coefficient r. But Galton's formula can easily be derived from the modern form. The expression in square brackets can be factorised as follows:

$$\frac{1}{(1-r^2)}\left\{\frac{x^2}{\sigma_1^2}-\frac{2rxy}{\sigma_1\sigma_2}+\frac{y^2}{\sigma_2^2}\right\}=\frac{[x-r(\sigma_1/\sigma_2)y]^2}{\sigma_1^2(1-r^2)}+\frac{y^2}{\sigma_2^2}$$

So $\quad h(x, y)\, dx\, dy = \dfrac{1}{2\pi\sigma_1\sigma_2\sqrt{(1-r^2)}}$

$$\exp\left\{-\frac{[x-r(\sigma_1/\sigma_2)y]^2}{2\sigma_1^2(1-r^2)}\right\}dx\,\exp\left\{-\frac{y^2}{2\sigma_2^2}\right\}dy$$

$$=\frac{1}{\sqrt{2\pi}\,\sigma_1\sqrt{(1-r^2)}}\exp\left\{-\frac{[x-r(\sigma_1/\sigma_2)y]^2}{2\sigma_1^2(1-r^2)}\right\}dx$$

$$\frac{1}{\sqrt{2\pi}\,\sigma_2}\exp\left\{-\frac{y^2}{2\sigma_2^2}\right\}dy$$

The second part is the unconditional distribution of y. The first part is the distribution of x given y, showing the regression of x on y. Comparing these with equations (1) and (2), we see that they are equivalent, with

$$\beta_{12}=r(\sigma_1/\sigma_2)$$

and $\sigma_{1.2}=\sigma_1\sqrt{(1-r^2)}$

So, with these substitutions, the modern form (equation 4) yields Galton's form (equation 3).

The approach of the error theorists, Bravais and Schols, was quite different.' They too reached expressions formally equivalent to the modern expression for the bivariate normal distribution, but, as argued in the text, the meaning of this formalism for them was quite different. No notion of regression is to be found in it, nor that of correlation beyond the basic sense of non-independence.

Take the case of the measurement of the position of a point in a plane. Let the error in measuring one coordinate be denoted by x, and in measuring the other coordinate by y. Assume that both x and

y each follow the 'law of error', with zero means and probable errors given by $0.6745\sigma_1$ and $0.6745\sigma_2$ respectively. Then error theorists well know that if x and y were independent their joint distribution was just the product of their separate distributions:

$$h(x, y)\, dx\, dy = \frac{1}{2\pi\sigma_1\sigma_2} \exp\left[-\frac{1}{2}\left\{\frac{x^2}{\sigma_1^2} + \frac{y^2}{\sigma_2^2}\right\}\right] dx\, dy \quad (5)$$

Bravais and Schols were both dealing with the case where x and y were not independent, and both deduced that the joint 'law of error' must then contain an extra term apart from those in x^2 and y^2. Bravais explicitly wrote this out, deducing that $h(x, y)$, as I have called it, must have the form

$$\frac{K}{\pi}\exp\left[-(ax^2 + 2exy + by^2)\right]$$

where K, a, b and e were to be determined (Bravais 1846, 268–9). The process of their determination was, however, one that involved no recourse to concepts similar to Galton's.

Schols treated the distribution of error as analogous to the inertia of a rigid body, showing that probable errors corresponded to moments of inertia. He concluded that the distribution of error would have principal axes similar to those of the ellipsoid of inertia, and showed that with respect to these principal axes the law of error would have terms only in x^2, y^2 and z^2 (i.e. would be the three-dimensional equivalent of expression 5).

4. Galton and the Mathematicians

Rev. H. W. Watson, 1827–1903. Watson (for whom see Bryan 1903) studied mathematics at Trinity College, Cambridge, and in 1850 was Second Wrangler. After a brief period as a mathematics teacher he entered the church, where he continued to pursue his interests in mathematics, which were chiefly in the area of mathematical physics (Watson 1876, Watson and Burbury 1879, 1885–89). Galton contacted Watson to help him solve a problem of probability theory that had arisen in his eugenics, that of the probability of the extinction of family names. Watson's partial solution of it (Watson and Galton 1874) is now regarded as the beginning of the theory of branching processes. D. G. Kendall (1966) discusses it, and describes the subsequent history of the theory. At the time, the 'Galton–Watson process' was taken no further. Watson returned to his own concerns, and did no further work in statistics, apart from one paper (Watson 1891) in which he discussed a problem, again submitted to him by Galton, to do with the combination of probable errors (for example, in deducing intra-fraternity variability from population variability and the variability of fraternity means).

Galton's collaboration with Watson fell short of what Galton wanted. Writing to Sheppard, Galton commented: 'Watson is over busy and I think too fastidious and timid' (quoted by Pearson 1914–30, *3B*, 486–7). It is interesting to speculate how much of Watson's failure to do more work on Galton's problems could be attributed to the cautious attitude to hereditarianism shown by his comment on *Hereditary Genius* (Watson to Galton, 7 January 1870; Galton Papers, 120/4):

> . . . you do not allow perhaps sufficient importance to the influence of association and surrounding circumstance on the determination of a man's career up to his time of University degree.

Sir Donald MacAlister, 1854–1934. MacAlister (for whom see Mac-Alister 1935) was another Cambridge-trained mathematician, and Senior Wrangler in 1877. Like Watson, MacAlister spent a short period as a mathematics teacher before turning to one of the more established professions, in his case medicine. From 1881 he practised and taught medicine in Cambridge. In 1907 he was appointed Principal of the University of Glasgow.

Galton approached MacAlister, whom he first met socially, and set him the problem of finding a 'law of error' for those cases (such as those covered by Fechner's Law) in which the geometric mean was the best measure of central tendency: Galton wanted something corresponding to the normal curve in its relation to the arithmetic mean. In response, MacAlister produced what has become known as the log-normal distribution (Galton 1879, MacAlister 1879). That was, however, his only contribution to statistical theory. Galton retained a high opinion of him:

> He is very favourably disposed towards Eugenics and is, as you know, a vigorous mathematician. (Galton to Pearson, 18 August 1910; quoted in Pearson 1914–30, *3A*, 430)

MacAlister did help Weldon with his first biometric paper, 'explaining . . . many points connected with the law of error' (Weldon 1890, 445). In general, though, MacAlister's medical career seems to have prevented him from doing as much in the field as he might have wanted. Writing to Galton he commented:

Heredity in your hands is becoming fast an exact study. I only wish that my pressing avocations had allowed me to help you more. (2 March 1889; Galton Papers, 279/3)

J. D. Hamilton Dickson, 1849–1931. Hamilton Dickson (for whom see M. McC. F[airgrieve] 1931) was educated at Glasgow and Cambridge Universities, and was placed Fifth Wrangler in the 1874 Mathematical Tripos. In 1877 he was appointed a tutor of Peterhouse, and he spent most of the remainder of his life in mathematical teaching and research at Cambridge. Hamilton Dickson's famous collaboration with Galton is described in chapter 3 and appendix 3.

In his autobiography Galton (1908, 305) mentioned one mathematical collaborator with whom he had particular difficulties of communication because of the divergence between the goals embodied in his approach and that of error theory. There is some reason to believe that that mathematician was in fact Hamilton Dickson. A letter to Galton, dated Christmas Day 1890 (Galton Papers, 236/4), shows Hamilton Dickson struggling unsuccessfully with the problem of the combination of probable errors solved for Galton by Watson (1891). Hamilton Dickson appears to have been attempting to apply a simple error theory model to a situation in which, as Watson showed, it was inapplicable. Despite the importance of its first product, Galton's collaboration with Hamilton Dickson thus did not bear further fruit.

John Venn, 1834–1923. Venn, a member of one of the leading families of the 'intellectual aristocracy' (Annan 1955, 276), was educated at Cambridge, being placed Sixth Wrangler in the 1857 Mathematical Tripos. He then entered the Church, but returned to Cambridge in 1862 to become lecturer in moral science at Gonville and Caius College. He remained in Cambridge for the rest of his life, becoming President of his College in 1903.

Venn was, of course, primarily a philosopher, not a mathematician, and his best known work was on symbolic logic and the foundations of the theory of probability. In the 1880s he developed an interest in anthropometry. Little is known of the origins of this interest, but the immediate stimulus to Venn appears to have been a lecture Galton gave in Cambridge in 1884 (see Pearson 1914–30, 2, 268 and Venn 1888, 140–1). Following Galton's lecture a small committee was established to obtain measurements of Cambridge undergraduates similar to those already obtained by Galton in his Anthropometric Laboratory in London. Venn analysed the data gathered on the undergraduates, comparing the physical characteristics of three groups classified according to the class of degree they obtained. Venn adapted well-known error theory techniques in a way that was then somewhat unusual to test the significance, as we would now put it, of the differences found.

Venn did do some further statistical work: Venn (1891) discusses non-Gaussian error curves. He did not, however, go beyond these beginnings to make any major contributions to statistical theory.

S. H. Burbury, 1831–1911. Burbury (for whom see Bryan 1911, 1913) was trained at Cambridge in both classics and mathematics. For twenty years after leaving Cambridge he did no scientific work, pursuing instead a legal career. H. W. Watson, who was a close friend of his, reawakened his scientific interests, and together they worked on electromagnetic theory and the kinetic theory of gases (Watson and Burbury 1879, 1885–89).

At the end of the 1880s Burbury became interested in problems of the foundations of the kinetic theory. He came to doubt whether the molecules of a gas could be treated as independent from each other in their relative motion. Burbury felt that Galton's theory of correlation provided a possible route to a generalisation of the assumptions underlying the derivation of theorems of the kinetic theory. This seems to have been his primary motive for work on correlation, although his letters to Galton (Galton Papers, 212) and membership of the Royal Society's Evolution Committee (Pearson 1906, 289) indicate a certain interest in biometry.

The Maxwell-Boltzmann distribution, derived on the assumption of the mutual independence of velocities, was, Burbury argued, analogous to the distribution of independent normal variables. Burbury (1894, 1895) modified this distribution by the introduction of product terms, making it analogous to the distribution of correlated normal variables. In doing this he derived, apparently independently of Edgeworth and Pearson, a multivariate generalisation of Galton's bivariate normal surface.

Burbury's approach was sophisticated. In modern terminology we would describe him as having used characteristic functions to obtain a multivariate version of the central limit theorem. The statistician of today would undoubtedly prefer his approach to the problem to that of either Edgeworth or Pearson. Burbury's work was, however, relatively sterile. He attempted to apply his refined model to the problem of the liquefaction of a gas (Burbury 1899), but was unable to obtain specific quantitative predictions. He did no further work of relevance to statistical theory.

W. F. Sheppard, 1863–1936. William Fleetwood Sheppard (for whom see Sheppard 1938, Aitken 1938, Fisher 1938) was born in Australia but sent to England to complete his education. He won a scholarship to Trinity College, Cambridge and in 1884 was placed Senior Wrangler, ahead of William Bragg. He became a Fellow of Trinity, and published a paper dealing with Bessel functions (Sheppard 1889). He soon left Cambridge, however, and took up a legal career; in 1896 he joined the Education Department (later Department of Education and Science), where he worked until his retirement in 1921.

In his Cambridge days he became interested in Galton's work, and visited Galton's Anthropometric Laboratory several times (Sheppard 1938, 3). In the early 1890s he entered into correspondence with Galton (Galton Papers, 245/22 and 315). Galton strongly encouraged him to take up statistical work. Sheppard does not appear to have done so immediately, but in the summer of 1895 he began work on the paper that was to become Sheppard (1898b); by October 1895 he had already reached the main results of that paper (Sheppard to Galton, 8 October 1895; Galton Papers, 315). Galton gave Sheppard considerable help and encouragement, paying for his paper to be typed and negotiating its acceptance by the Royal Society (see the letters between Sheppard and Galton in 1896; Galton Papers, 245/22, 315). By the Autumn of 1896 Sheppard seems to have developed the basic ideas of 'Sheppard's corrections'. A summary of these appeared as Sheppard (1897b), and they were fully presented in Sheppard (1898c). The first reference to this work is in a letter to Galton of 26 September 1896 (Galton Papers, 315).

Towards the end of the 1890s the full range of Sheppard's mathematical concerns became clear, with the appearance of a series of papers ranging from pure mathematics (Sheppard 1898a) to statistical theory (1899a, 1900) and numerical analysis (1899b,c).

It is not entirely clear why Sheppard took up statistical work. He had fairly wide-ranging interests in politics – Sheppard (1938, 3) quotes a description of him as 'a genuine Liberal . . . a social reformer of the Toynbee Hall type' – and in culture – Sheppard (1897a) indicates his passion for Wagner. It is possible that the eugenic aspects of Galton's work interested him:

> It happens that I have always been interested in 'probabilities', particularly from the logical point of view, and that is the reason why your books have especially interested me as showing their bearing on one branch of the still unsolved mystery of human evolution. (Sheppard to Galton, 30 October 1892; Galton Papers, 315)

Sheppard's statistical work does not, however, reveal any close connections to eugenic applications.

5. *The Tetrachoric Expansion*
of the Bivariate Normal Distribution

In this account I have stayed as close as possible to Pearson's original presentation, while removing some of the more detailed steps of the argument. The modern statistician would of course want to improve this account by systematically distinguishing between sample statistics and population parameters. The derivation of the tetrachoric expansion can also be made neater by the use of characteristic functions and Hermite polynomials. [See Kendall 1943, *1*, 354–6. Note that Kendall's 'Tchebycheff-Hermite Polynomials' (*ibid.*, 145–7) are somewhat differently defined from the Hermite polynomials commonly used in applied mathematics (e.g. Arfken 1968, 477–81).]

Consider a bivariate normal frequency surface

$$z = \frac{N}{2\pi\sigma_1\sigma_2\sqrt{(1-r^2)}} \exp\left\{ -\frac{1}{2(1-r^2)} \left[\frac{x^2}{\sigma_1^2} + \frac{y^2}{\sigma_2^2} - \frac{2rxy}{\sigma_1\sigma_2} \right] \right\}$$

where N is the total number of observations, σ_1 and σ_2 are the standard deviations of x and y (both of which are measured in terms of deviations from their respective means), and r is the correlation of x and y. Let this surface be divided into four parts by planes at right angles to the axes of x and y, at distances h' and k' from the origin, as in figure 3.

Let $h = h'/\sigma_1$ and $k = k'/\sigma_2$. Then h and k can easily be evaluated in terms of the frequencies in the four quadrants formed by the two planes. Let these frequencies be a, b, c, d. Then

$$b + d = \int_{h'}^{\infty} \int_{-\infty}^{\infty} z\, dx\, dy = \int_{h'}^{\infty} \left[\int_{-\infty}^{\infty} z\, dy \right] dx$$

$$\text{Now} \int_{-\infty}^{\infty} z\, dy = \frac{N}{\sigma_1\sqrt{2\pi}} \exp\left\{ -\frac{x^2}{2\sigma_1^2} \right\}$$

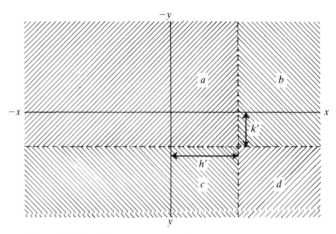

Figure 3. (This figure corresponds to
the horizontal plane of figure 2)

as this is the unconditional distribution of x. So

$$b + d = \frac{N}{\sigma_1 \sqrt{2\pi}} \int_{h'}^{\infty} \exp\left\{ -\frac{x^2}{2\sigma_1^2} \right\} dx$$

$$= \frac{N}{\sqrt{2\pi}} \int_{h}^{\infty} \exp\left\{ -\frac{x^2}{2} \right\} dx$$

and h can be evaluated in terms of $b + d$ by use of tables of the
normal distribution. Similarly

$$c + d = \frac{N}{\sqrt{2\pi}} \int_{k}^{\infty} \exp\left\{ -\frac{y^2}{2} \right\} dy$$

and k can be evaluated in terms of $c + d$. Now

$$d = \int_{h'}^{\infty} \int_{k'}^{\infty} z \, dx \, dy$$

$$= \frac{N}{2\pi \sigma_1 \sigma_2 \sqrt{(1 - r^2)}}$$

$$\int_{h'}^{\infty} \int_{k'}^{\infty} \exp\left\{ -\frac{1}{2(1 - r^2)} \left[\frac{x^2}{\sigma_1^2} + \frac{y^2}{\sigma_2^2} - \frac{2rxy}{\sigma_1 \sigma_2} \right] \right\} dx \, dy$$

$$= \frac{N}{2\pi \sqrt{(1 - r^2)}} \int_{h}^{\infty} \int_{k}^{\infty} \exp\left\{ -\frac{(x^2 + y^2 - 2rxy)}{2(1 - r^2)} \right\} dx \, dy$$

This equation relates r to d, N, h and k (the last two of which we have already evaluated in terms of a, b, c, d), and can be solved for r. If the right-hand side is expanded in a series in r, after some manipulation the following result is obtained:

$$\frac{ad-bc}{N^2 hk} = r + \frac{r^2}{2!}hk + \frac{r^3}{3!}(h^2-1)(k^2-1) + \frac{r^4}{4!}h(h^2-3)k(k^2-3)$$

$$+ \frac{r^5}{5!}(h^4-6h^2+3)(k^4-6k^2+3)$$

$$+ \frac{r^6}{6!}h(h^4-10h^2+15)k(k^4-10k^2+15)$$

$$+ \frac{r^7}{7!}(h^6-15h^4+45h^2-15)(k^6-15k^4+45k^2-15)$$

$$+ \frac{r^8}{8!}h(h^6-21h^4+105h^2-105)k(k^6-21k^4+105k^2-105)$$

$$+ \text{etc.},$$

where

$$H = \frac{1}{\sqrt{2\pi}}\exp(-h^2/2) \text{ and } K = \frac{1}{\sqrt{2\pi}}\exp(-k^2/2)$$

With $|r| > 1$, the series converges rapidly, and terms of orders higher than r^8 can normally be neglected, leaving a polynomial equation for r that can be solved numerically. Thus, given observed frequencies a, b, c, d, it is always possible to fit the model of an underlying bivariate normal distribution to the observations, and to deduce a value for its correlation.

6. An Example of the Bayesian Argument of Pearson and Filon (1898)

Pearson and Filon (1898) is, taken by itself, a rather obscure piece of work (see Pearson 1967, 345), though Welch (1958, 780) seems to me to have shown how it should be interpreted. The nature of the argument Pearson and Filon used is best seen in a simple example given by Pearson in his lectures on statistical theory in the Autumn of 1894. His treatment of it is described in Yule's Notes (*1*, 89–92). From Yule's Notes alone it is not entirely clear what Pearson was doing; but when the relevant passage is interpreted in the light of the nineteenth-century understanding of the 'method of inverse probability' (see pp. 201–2 above) the basis of the analysis becomes clear. The continuity between this particular example and the general theorem of Pearson and Filon (1898) is apparent: for example, a one-dimensional version of the general theorem is given in Yule's Notes (5, 41–2), in a passage dating from January 1896. [In what follows I have altered Pearson's terminology and notation somewhat so that the argument will be clear to the modern reader, but I have not, I hope, violated the spirit of the argument in so doing.]

Consider a simple random sample of size n drawn from a normally distributed population with mean zero and unknown standard deviation θ: denote this sample $x_1, x_2, \ldots, x_n$, or, collectively, $\underline{x}$. The probability of the occurrence of this sample, for a given value of θ, is given by

$$g(\underline{x}; \theta) = \frac{1}{(2\pi)^{n/2}\theta^n} \exp\left\{-\frac{(x_1^2 + x_2^2 + \ldots + x_n^2)}{2\theta^2}\right\}$$

Pearson argued that the best value to give θ is that which maximises $g(\underline{x}; \theta)$. He showed that this value was θ_0, where $\theta_0^2 = (\Sigma x^2)/n$. He then proceeded to evaluate the probable error of the standard deviation as estimated by this method.

Pearson's procedure makes sense only if it is interpreted as an application of the traditional 'method of inverse probability'. It rested on the (implicit) treatment of $g(\underline{x}; \theta)$ as the posterior distribution of θ: his manipulation of $g(\underline{x}; \theta)$ is meaningless if $g(\underline{x};\theta)$ is interpreted as a direct, rather than an inverse, probability. Because θ_0 is the value of θ that maximises $g(\underline{x}; \theta)$, it is the mode of the posterior distribution of θ. Write θ as $\theta_0 + z$. Then

$$g(\underline{x}; \theta) = \frac{1}{(2\pi)^{n/2}(\theta_0 + z)^n} \exp\left\{-\frac{(\Sigma x^2)}{2(\theta_0 + z)^2}\right\}$$

Now $g(\underline{x}; \theta_0) = \dfrac{1}{(2\pi)^{n/2}\theta_0^n} \exp\left\{-\dfrac{(\Sigma x^2)}{2\theta_0^2}\right\}$

So $\dfrac{g(\underline{x}; \theta)}{g(\underline{x}; \theta_0)} = \left[1 + \dfrac{z}{\theta_0}\right]^{-n} \exp\left\{-\dfrac{n}{2}\left[1 + \dfrac{z}{\theta_0}\right]^{-2} + \dfrac{n}{2}\right\}$

since $\Sigma x^2 = n\theta_0^2$. This is the posterior distribution of θ about its mode. It is clearly not normal. However, if we assume that the errors under consideration are small (i.e. that z is small by comparison with θ_0), the distribution can be shown to be approximately normal. For $(z/\theta_0) \ll 1$, we have

$$\left[1 + \frac{z}{\theta_0}\right]^{-n} = \exp\left\{-n \log\left[1 + \frac{z}{\theta_0}\right]\right\}$$

$$= \exp\left\{-n\left[\frac{z}{\theta_0} - \frac{z^2}{2\theta_0^2} + \frac{z^3}{3\theta_0^3} - \cdots\right]\right\}$$

and $\exp\left\{-\dfrac{n}{2}\left[1 + \dfrac{z}{\theta_0}\right]^{-2} + \dfrac{n}{2}\right\} =$

$$\exp\left\{-n\left[-\frac{z}{\theta_0} + \frac{3z^2}{2\theta_0^2} - \frac{2z^3}{\theta_0^3} + \cdots\right]\right\}$$

Neglecting terms in $(z/\theta_0)^3$ and higher powers, we have, therefore,

$$\frac{g(\underline{x};\theta)}{g(\underline{x};\theta_0)} = \exp\left\{-\frac{nz^2}{\theta_0^2}\right\}$$

So the posterior distribution of θ is given by

$$\pi'(\underline{x}|\theta) = Cg(\underline{x};\theta) = \text{constant} \times \exp\left\{-\frac{n(\theta - \theta_0)^2}{\theta_0^2}\right\}$$

since $g(\underline{x}|\theta_0)$ is independent of θ and $z = \theta - \theta_0$. This is a normal curve with mean θ_0 and standard deviation $\theta_0/\sqrt{2n}$. The probable error of θ_0 is thus $0.6745\theta_0/\sqrt{2n}$: that is to say, the posterior probability that the true value of θ lies in the interval $\theta_0 \pm 0.6745\theta_0/\sqrt{2n}$ is 0.5.

The approach to finding the probable errors of frequency constants presented in Pearson and Filon (1898) was a generalisation of that employed in this example. They treated what Fisher called the 'likelihood function' as the joint posterior distribution of the frequency constants in question; they were, therefore, following the 'method of inverse probability' and making the implicit assumption of a uniform joint prior distribution of the frequency constants. From this they showed that – on the assumption of 'small' errors – the joint posterior distribution was multivariate normal, and they gave an expression for what would now be called its covariance matrix, which enabled the probable errors and correlation of errors of frequency constants to be calculated.

7. *The Argument of Fisher (1912c)*

At first sight, Fisher's method looked like the old 'method of inverse probability'. Suppose we are trying to fit a curve of the form $f(x, \theta_1, \ldots, \theta_r)$ to a set of data $(x_1, \ldots, x_n)$, where $\theta_1, \ldots, \theta_r$ are parameters whose best values we are seeking. Fisher suggested that the best values of $\theta_1, \ldots, \theta_r$ were those that maximised P, where

$$\log P = \sum_{i=1}^{n} \log f(x_i, \theta_1, \ldots, \theta_r)$$

On the 'method of inverse probability' P is simply the posterior probability of $\theta_1, \ldots, \theta_r$ (on the assumption of a uniform joint prior distribution of these parameters). Indeed, Fisher wrote 'the probability of any particular set of θ's is proportional to P' (1912c, 157). On the last page of his paper, however, there was to be found a striking passage which showed clearly his divergence from the 'method of inverse probability':

> We have now obtained an absolute criterion for finding the relative probabilities of different sets of values for the elements of a probability system of known form. It would now seem natural to obtain an expression for the probability that the true values of the elements should lie within any given range. Unfortunately we cannot do so. The quantity P must be considered as the relative probability of the set of values $\theta_1, \theta_2, \ldots, \theta_r$; but it would be illegitimate to multiply this quantity by the variations $d\theta_1, d\theta_2, \ldots, d\theta_r$, and integrate through a region, and to compare the integral over this region with the integral over all possible values of the θ's. P is a relative probability only, suitable to compare point with point, but incapable of being interpreted as a probability distribution over a region, or of giving any estimate of absolute probability.
>
> This may be easily seen, since the same frequency curve might equally be specified by any r independent functions of the θ's, say $\phi_1, \phi_2, \ldots, \phi_r$, and the relative values of P would be unchanged by such a transformation; but the probability that the true values lie within a region must be the same whether it is expressed in terms of θ or ϕ, so that we should have for all values
>
> $$\frac{\partial(\theta_1, \theta_2, \ldots, \theta_r)}{\partial(\phi_1, \phi_2, \ldots, \phi_r)} = 1$$
>
> a condition which is manifestly not satisfied by the general transformation. (1912c, 160)

What Fisher was pointing out was that, used in different ways, the standard method of inverse probability (which he described in the first paragraph above) gave different results. Let Ω be a section of the parameter space of the θ's, and Ω' the corresponding section of the parameter space of the ϕ's, and let

$$J = \frac{\partial(\theta_1, \theta_2, \ldots, \theta_r)}{\partial(\phi_1, \phi_2, \ldots, \phi_r)}$$

be the Jacobian of the transformation from the θ's to the ϕ's. Then, by a standard formula of the integral calculus,

$$_\Omega\!\int P \, d\theta_1 \ldots d\theta_r = {}_{\Omega}\!\int P J \, d\phi_1 \ldots d\phi_r$$

and thus the possibility that the value of the ϕ's lies in Ω' is given by

$$_{\Omega'}\!\int P J \, d\phi_1 \ldots d\phi_r$$

However, applying the method of inverse probability directly to the ϕ's, that probability is given simply by

$$_{\Omega'}\!\int P \, d\phi_1 \ldots d\phi_r$$

The two results are thus compatible only if $J = 1$, which, as Fisher pointed out, would not in general be the case.

The paradox arises because the two different applications of the method of inverse probability involve two contradictory assumptions: in the first case of a uniform joint prior distribution of the θ's, in the second of a uniform joint prior distribution of the ϕ's. Phrased in this way, Fisher's result is hardly surprising, but we must remember that assumptions of uniform prior distributions were at the time often made as a matter of course, and non-uniform priors were seldom considered. Fisher was pointing out that the method of inverse probability as it was in fact used (with a more or less automatic assumption of uniform priors), could not provide consistent results. One way of resolving this problem would have been to advocate much more careful consideration of prior distributions (including the use of non-uniform priors). Fisher, however, was to choose a different way: that of attempting to avoid completely the assumption of prior distributions.

8. *A Glossary of some Basic Statistical Terms*

The descriptions below are not intended as formal definitions. They are merely to give the reader without training in statistical theory an intuitive sense of the meaning of some of the concepts used repeatedly in the text.

Mean. The mean of a series of figures is their arithmetic average, formed by adding them up and dividing by the number of figures. So the mean of 3, 5, 7, 9, 16 is $(3+5+7+9+16)/5 = 40/5 = 8$.

Median. The median of a series of figures is the 'middle' figure of the series (if the series is arranged in ascending order). So the median of 3, 5, 7, 9, 16 is 7.

Standard Deviation (and Probable Error). The standard deviation of a series of figures is a number that measures how much the figures taken as a whole deviate from their mean, in other words how variable the figures are. The procedure for working it out is slightly complicated and need not be gone into here.

The standard deviation of 3, 5, 7, 9, 16 is 4.5. If we then increase the variability by altering the 3 to 1, and the 16 to 18, the mean is not altered (as can easily be checked), but the standard deviation rises to 5.7.

Error theorists used the closely related concept of the probable error (see chapter 3). For data that follows a normal distribution (see below), the probable error is 0.6745 of the standard deviation.

Coefficient of Correlation. This is a number measuring the extent to which two sets of measurements (two 'variables') are related to each other. The coefficient of correlation ranges between +1 and −1. It is +1 if a high value for one variable implies a proportionately high value for the other, and similarly for low values (perfect correlation). It is −1 if a high value for one variable implies a proportionately low value for the other (perfect inverse correlation). It is zero if the two variables are unrelated (independent).

Regression. Regression is the name for the statistical procedure of predicting the value of one variable from that of one or more other variables. See pp. 60–2 for a simple example.

The Normal Distribution. This was also known as the Gaussian Law, Law of Frequency of Error, Error Curve, etc. It is a mathematical curve of known proportions, shaped rather like a bell, describing to a reasonably good degree of approximation the distribution of characteristics such as height. Most adult males, say, are of about average height, with relatively few dwarfs and giants, and a symmetrical tapering off of numbers in between. We can show the normal curve graphically by plotting height along the horizontal axis and frequency along the vertical axis as in figure 4. This shows that heights around the average are found relatively often (with high frequency) and that extreme heights (both tall and short) are less frequent.

The normal distribution is used in other contexts apart from the measurement of human characteristics. The error theorists used it

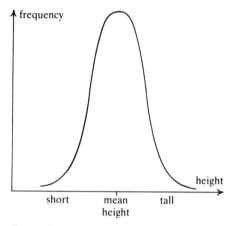

Figure 4

to describe errors in measurement: most measurements falling around the 'true' central value, extreme errors being less frequent. It is also of great importance in the mathematical theory of statistics.

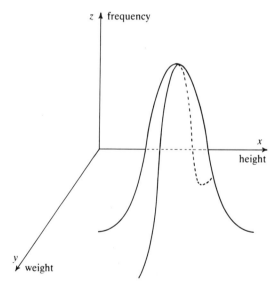

Figure 5

The Bivariate Normal Distribution. This is the equivalent of the normal distribution used to describe the simultaneous distribution of two variables. So we need three dimensions to illustrate it graphically, rather than the two used above. In figure 5, imagine the axes marked x and y to be lying flat in a plane, with the axis marked z rising vertically above the plane; and suppose that the x-axis measures height, the y-axis weight, and the z axis the frequency with which different combinations of height and weight are found. Then we can think of the bivariate normal distribution as rising in a bell shape above the plane of the x-axis and y-axis, remembering that this is a now a three-dimensional bell (though its cross-sections will not usually be round but elliptical), rather than the two-dimensional curve of the single variable normal distribution. Equivalents of the bivariate normal distribution exist for more than two variables. The general case is usually known as the multivariate normal distribution or n-dimensional normal surface.

Notes

. . . . .
. . .
.

Notes to Chapter 1

1. The philosophical work of Imre Lakatos, who argued that 'external history' explained only those intellectual developments not accountable for in terms of a 'rationally reconstructed' internal history (Lakatos 1974), can be seen as broadly parallel to this first position.
2. This journal is obtainable from 9 Poland Street, London W IV 3 DG.
3. For general discussion of these see Child (1941, 1944) and Barnes (1977).
4. This point seems, however, to have been overlooked in the theoretical presentation by Lukács (1971).
5. The main source here is Cullen (1975), but see also Abrams (1968), Elesh (1972), Cole (1972), Hilts (1978) and Young (1960, especially 32-3). More generally, see Oberschall (1972, 187-251), Stephen (1948), Lazarsfeld (1961), Lécuyer and Oberschall (1968). Baines (1970) describes the general features of the nineteenth-century British system of official statistics, while Royal Statistical Society (1934) describes the development of that Society. For medical statistics see Greenwood (1936, 1948), Hodgkinson (1968), Hilts (1970) and Eyler (1973, 1976).
6. Medical statistics was somewhat more advanced in terms of methods than social statistics, but even here techniques were generally crude. Hodgkinson (1968, 185) comments:

    Not even Farr was a good mathematician. People worked with figures using totals and bare averages. Producing the raw materials was sufficient to obtain results.

7. A partial exception to this was actuarial work, where probability theory was linked to the data collected by vital statisticians in an enterprise of commercial importance. Actuarial work provided at least temporary employment for several important British mathematicians in the nineteenth century. Actuarial science

    . . . consists of the application of the laws of probability to insurance, and especially to life insurance. And we shall find that, first of all, there needed to be something for the law of probability to act upon, viz., a mortality table, and also a handmaiden, in the form of a developed law of compound interest and discount and of annuities certain. (Dawson 1914, 95)

As Dawson's review shows, the nineteenth century saw many advances in actuarial science. It would seem, however, that by this period the major technical instruments of actuarial work, such as the life table, had been developed. There was, of course, much theoretical and empirical work to be done to improve them, but this had become a fairly specialised line of work. Actuarial work was thus rather insulated from developments in statistical theory generally during this period.

Works on the social relations of probability theory and actuarial work are Gillispie (1972), Maistrov (1974), Hacking (1975), Baker (1975) and Buck (1977). The work of David (1969) is more 'internally' oriented, as, in general, is that of the most systematic student of this field, the Soviet historian Oscar Sheynin (1966, 1970, 1971a,b, 1972a,b, 1973a,b, 1974, 1976, 1978, 1979). Despite being based on lectures delivered fifty years ago, Pearson (1978) is still a very useful source, and both it and the work of Sheynin throw light on statistics as well as probability theory.

8. See, for example, the Cambridge University Mathematical Tripos examination questions in Gantillon (1852).

9. A partial exception to this is work in error theory, which is discussed below in chapter 3.

10. Gillispie (1963) suggests that the impact of Quetelet's work was, para-doxically, most immediate in British physics (though see also the comments by Hesse, 1963). In any case, it seems established that James Clerk Maxwell read the review of Quetelet (1849) by Herschel (1850), and may have been encouraged by the example of Quetelet's work to use the theory of probability to construct models of physical pheno-mena: that is, to develop a statistical mechanics. See Brush (1967, 152) and Garber (1973, 19-29). Statistical mechanics became an important area of study for British mathematical physicists in the later part of the nineteenth century. This initial episode apart, statistical mechanics and statistical theory proper seem, however, to have developed more or less independently in the period discussed here. Perhaps this was because statistical theorists were attempting to devise tools for drawing inferences from data, while the physicists were attempting to construct deductive models that would explain the observed behaviour of gases. Whatever the explanation, British statisticians seem to have found few intellectual resources to exploit within statistical mechanics.

11. No single work contains an adequate description of this development, but there is a wide range of useful sources. Kendall and Doig's biblio-graphy (1968) together with Lancaster's list of bibliographies of indi-vidual statisticians (Lancaster 1968; the list is annually updated in the *Review of the International Statistical Institute*) are invaluable aids to research. General histories of statistics (Walker 1929, Westergaard 1932) are of only limited usefulness, and the historical works written by British statisticians themselves are much more relevant (K. Pearson 1914-30, E. S. Pearson 1936-38, 1939, 1965, 1967, 1968). The collec-tions edited by Pearson and Kendall (1970) and by Kendall and Plack-

ett (1977) contain many of the most important articles on British statistics. Apart from these other sources worth consulting are Cowan (1972a,b, 1977), Hilts (1967, 1970, 1973), Farrall (1970), Norton (1971, 1975a,b, 1978a,b,c), Weiling (1969), Wei-Ching Chang (1973), Ben-David (1971, 147-52), Eisenhart (1974) and Box (1978).

Notes to Chapter 2

1. Galton's original definition of 'eugenics' was as follows:
   ... the science of improving stock, which is by no means confined to questions of judicious mating, but which, especially in the case of man, takes cognisance of all influences that tend in however remote a degree to give to the more suitable races or strains of blood a better chance of prevailing speedily over the less suitable than they otherwise would have had. (Galton 1883, 25)
2. It should not be thought, however, that there was any tight logical connection between eugenics and the rejection in biology of the Lamarckian theories of the inheritance of acquired characteristics. Thus E. W. MacBride, Professor of Zoology at Imperial College, was both a leading neo-Lamarckian and a virulent eugenist (see MacBride 1924). MacBride's position seems to have been that Lamarckian mechanisms were too slow to be relied on to improve human populations. See also Darwin (1926, 94-111).
3. Certain physical conditions, notably tuberculosis and epilepsy, also rendered individuals eugenically suspect.
4. Several of the doctors held university or medical school teaching posts.
5. One, Cockburn, was a doctor by training.
6. One was Havelock Ellis, the pioneer sexologist. The other, Robert Mond, came from the dynasty that founded Imperial Chemical Industries; however, a perusal of Reader (1970-75) indicates that his role in the firm was relatively slight. In view of this, and in the light of his work in chemistry and archaeology (see the *Dictionary of National Biography*), I have classed him as a scientist rather than as a businessman.
7. One official of the National Association for the Welfare of the Feeble-Minded, one farmer (and amateur agricultural scientist), a retired army engineer, and five wives or widows (of a naval lieutenant, an admiral, a civil servant and businessman, a merchant and geographer, and a surgeon) for whom no other occupational data could be found.
8. As Farrall (1970) did not list the members of his random sample that he failed to identify, a similar test was not carried out on them. But other evidence – for example an undated (circa 1927) note found in the press-cutting files of the Eugenics Society lamenting its failure to recruit amongst businessmen – gives us no reason to suspect that such a test would endanger Farrall's conclusion.
9. Such evidence as we have for other historical periods, notably Searle (1979) on the 1930s, indicates continuing professional dominance of the Society beyond the period discussed here.
   What we know of eugenics movements other than the British suggests that they too had similar social compositions: see, for example, Ludmerer (1972, 92). Nevertheless I would be cautious about genera-

lising the analysis put forward in this chapter to other movements. The eugenics movement in the United States, say, was significantly different from that in Britain: see Haller (1963), Ludmerer (1972), Pickens (1968), Allen (1975b, 1976), Gordon (1977) and Kevles (1979).

10. Searle (1978, 19) makes this point.

11. See, for example, B. and J. Ehrenreich (1976), Carchedi (1975a,b, 1976) and Johnson (1977).

12. It is true that Gouldner, with his attention to the new class's 'project', escapes this stricture.

13. That the divide between mental and manual labour is a social and negotiated one, not an absolute one, can be seen in the fact that we do not classify surgeons as manual labourers.

14. Mitchell and Deane (1962, 60) give a table of figures for the period 1841-1921 suggesting that the percentage of occupied males who were in 'professional occupations and their subordinate services' rose from about 2% in 1841 to 3% in 1921, while the corresponding figures for females were 3% in 1841 and 8% in 1921. These bald figures are, however, misleading. For example, 'professional entertainers and sportsmen' are included, but veterinary surgeons excluded. Even more seriously, the rapid change in the position of particular occupations in this period means that the social content of particular occupational labels completely altered in many cases.

15. Its career as a sociological theory in the academic sense can be followed in Abrams (1968): eugenics was of extreme importance in the early development of British sociology.

16. Keynes was treasurer of the Cambridge University Eugenics Society. For Beveridge's at least muted support, see Beveridge (1943).

17. See Webb (1907), the preface to Shaw (1972), Hyde (1956), McLaren (1978, 186-93), Kevles (1979, 13).

18. See also Semmel (1960) and Searle (1971, 1976).

19. The major contemporary discussion of this – which stopped short of full-blown eugenic analysis – is to be found in the report of the National Birth-Rate Commission (1916). Banks (1965) points out the connections between the falling middle-class birthrate and problems of class reproduction in the more general sense, for example the growing relative cost of education for a professional career.

20. This possibility was being discussed in the 1880s in the 'Men's and Women's Club' (see chapter 4). The combination of birth control, feminism and eugenics is to be found in published form as early as 1885 in the work of Jane Hume Clapperton. Gordon (1977, 126-35) discusses feminist eugenics in America.

21. Perhaps the person who perceived it most clearly was the communist feminist Stella Browne, who has recently been discussed by Rowbotham (1977). Browne, who became one of the founders of the Abortion Law Reform Association, is one of the most interesting thinkers of this period. The following passage from her 1935 essay on 'The Right to Abortion' indicates her position:

> Abortion must be the key to a new world for women, not a bulwark for things as they are, economically nor biologically.

> Abortion should not be either a prerequisite of the legal wife only, nor merely a last resort against illegitimacy. It should be available for any woman, without insolent inquisitions, nor ruinous financial charges, nor tangles of red tape. For our bodies are our own. (Rowbotham 1977, 114)

22. For this article, and *Nature*'s policy on eugenics generally, see Werskey (1969). The attribution of the unsigned editorial to F. A. E. Crew follows Werskey.
23. Gordon (1977) discusses some of the policies of 'crypto-eugenics' pursued by American eugenists.
24. It includes over fifty professors and some quite well-known names, e.g. Lord Goodman, Sir Peter Medawar and Naomi Mitchison.
25. I have found Searle (1978) particularly thought-provoking on the theoretical significance of opposition to eugenics.
26. Another follower of Henry George who can be counted an opponent at least of mainstream eugenics was Alfred Russel Wallace (see Wallace 1890).
27. See Searle (1979, 169).
28. By use of the term 'mainstream' environmentalism I wish to exclude radical and Marxist positions that happen to draw on environmentalism.
29. Even at this level eugenics and environmentalism are by no means polar opposites. It is clearly possible to employ both strategies together, to seek to integrate some groups while excluding and segregating others.
30. I must re-emphasise the tentative nature of my discussion of environmentalism. The obvious attractiveness of eugenics as a topic for recent historians has led to a strange neglect of environmentalism, and in the absence of any major study of environmentalist thought any conclusions about it are precarious. But in the long run we obviously cannot hope to understand eugenics without understanding environmentalism (and *vice versa*).

Notes to Chapter 3

1. The other source Galton mentions was his ethnological work on 'the mental peculiarities of different races' (Galton 1869, v).
2. This was never published in Galton's lifetime. The surviving fragments are reproduced in Karl Pearson (1914-30, *3A*, 411-25).
3. Buss (1976) interprets the origins of Galton's eugenics differently. He argues that it arose from the contradictions between the liberal individualist emphasis on the existence of equality of opportunity and the facts of the hierarchical division of labour: a hereditarian interpretation of mental ability being necessary to explain why, given equal opportunities, such grossly unequal outcomes could result.

   It seems to me that while this view is useful in understanding eugenics in general, there is little evidence that it throws much light on Galton's eugenics in particular. Further, Buss's account of 'democratic-liberal-capitalistic-individualism' seems idealised, as when he claims:

   > We see in *Kantsaywhere* an ideological doctrine of eugenics that

was a distortion of reality vis-à-vis British nineteenth century liberal individualism. . . . In *Kantsaywhere* the political system would seem to be totalitarian. . . (Buss 1976, 56)

4. Perhaps the most important of these was the Cambridge mathematician and astronomer, J. W. L. Glaisher (see especially Glaisher 1872); for Glaisher's life and work see Forsyth (1929). The most important British textbook seems to have been Airy (1861).

5. For Quetelet's work see, for example, Quetelet (1849). The review of this by Herschel (1850) played a major part in making Quetelet's work known in Britain. Galton learnt of the law of error from his friend William Spottiswoode, the geographer. See Galton (1908, 304), also Cowan (1972a, 512) and Spottiswoode (1861).

6. The argument of this paragraph is largely that of Hilts (1973).

7. Fechner (1874) also developed the concept of the median value, *der Centralwerth*. (I owe the reference to Walker (1929, 184).) Galton's work appears to have been independent of Fechner's (though see Singer 1979, 7).

8. Of course, for a normally distributed population the median and half the inter-quartile distance are equal to the mean and probable error respectively. Galton presumably continued to use the old terms so as to be understood by those trained in error theory.

9. For the history of these terms, see Walker (1929, 185 and 188).

10. For exceptions to this generalisation, see pp.68-72 below.

11. K. Pearson (1914-30, *2*, 156-66), Cowan (1977, 173-9). Darwin responded to Galton's experiments by claiming that it was not an essential part of the theory of pangenesis that the 'gemmules' in fact circulated in the blood and that they could travel through the body in other ways.

12. For Galton's attitude to the theory of the inheritance of acquired characteristics see Cowan (1968, 1977).

13. Galton (1885c, 258-60) discussed the relationship between the *diameters* of parent and offspring seeds and gave a table of figures for this. The original records of the sweetpea experiment have not been found in the Galton papers.

14. Galton used r, not b. I have changed his notation to make it clear that, to use Galton's later terminology, the constant is a coefficient of regression, not of correlation.

15. K. Pearson (1914-30, *3A*, 4) has reconstructed from Galton's seed diameter data a diagram that shows the relatively poor approximation of this data to the simple 'law of reversion'.

16. Cowan (1972a, 520) argues that Galton changed his terminology because he now realised the greater generality of the relationship he had found.

17. Galton's copy is in the library of the Galton Laboratory. Ruth Cowan notes the underlining (1972a, 526).

18. Galton did not consider in this paper the possibility of negative values of r.

19. Robert Adrain appears to have been the first mathematician to consider the simultaneous occurrence of two errors (Walker 1928, 467-8). Gauss (K. Pearson 1920b, Seal 1967) and Giovanni Plana (Walker

1928, 470-6) dealt with simultaneous errors; neither, however, approached the problem of dependent variables as clearly as Bravais and Schols. Bravais's work probably became known to Karl Pearson through the references to it in Czuber (1891); Seal (1967) drew attention to the work of Schols.

For biographical details of Bravais see Walker (1928) and the *Index Biographique des Membres et Correspondants de l'Académie des Sciences*; for those of Schols see Poggendorf's *Biographisch-Literarisches Handwörterbuch*.

Notes to Chapter 4

1. This idea is clearly linked with Lukács's defence of 'realism' as against 'naturalism' in literature. For an account of this, see for example, Eagleton (1976, 27-31).
2. The example of class structure as the overall structure does not imply that this approach is limited to social theories which see class structure as primary. The approach could equally well be employed in theories such as radical feminism, which takes gender differences as the overall structure and class as an aspect of fine structure.
3. The Pearson Papers, CII D1, contain some interesting letters from Karl Pearson to his family. Pearson gives a portrayal of his father in Pearson (1914-30, *3A*, 327-8). I found the following works on Pearson particularly useful in developing my view of him: E. S. Pearson (1936-38), Norton (1978a) and Eisenhart (1974).
4. See the correspondence in the Pearson Papers, CII D1J.
5. For example Pearson (1877). Pearson (1881a) gives some evidence of his criticisms of Cambridge.
6. See Norton (1978a, 22-24) and Pearson's letters to Robert Parker in the Pearson Papers, CII D1.
7. For the *Katheder-Socialisten*, see Schumpeter (1954, 800-20). For Pearson's contact with their ideas, see Pearson (1880 and 1881-82).
8. Apart, that is, from in his very early political thinking. See his letter to Parker of 28 December 1879, Pearson Papers, CII D1.
9. Pearson Papers CII D1 and CV D2.
10. Pearson's approach to matter theory exemplifies well his theory of knowledge. He vigorously defended himself against the charge (Mivart 1895) that he was basically a materialist. 'Matter', for Pearson, was an idea that had 'no place in the field of knowledge, and ought to be excluded from all scientific treatises' (1897, *1*, 382). For we cannot *know* what 'lies behind the perceptual veil', be it 'matter', 'spirit', or whatever. So while Pearson was no materialist – as Lenin (1970) was quick to perceive – neither did he embrace the kind of spiritualist idealism that was becoming influential amongst late Victorian British physicists (Wynne 1979). Like them he was interested in theories of the ether, and even in ethereal models of the atom, but, to quote Wilson (1977, 215), 'Pearson's ether was a construct of the mind employed to describe sense impressions in an economical manner'. He disdained the 'ultimate realities in a shadowy unknown' (Wynne 1979, 172) that were being appealed to in the attempt to re-unify science and religion.

11. See his letter to the editor of the *Manchester Guardian*, 15 February 1901, quoted by Norton (1978a, 20-21).
12. The fullest statement of Pearson's views on this is his essay 'Socialism and Natural Selection' (1897, *1*, 103-39).
13. Hofstader (1968) notes a similarly-based transition in American social Darwinism at about this time.
14. The quotation is from an unpublished paper circulated by Pearson to the members of the Men's and Women's Club entitled 'Emancipation?' (Pearson Papers, C V D6A). It appears to have been written late in 1888.
15. In arguing this I am opposing the view of Pastore (1949, 29-41), who sees Pearson as a socialist environmentalist prior to 1900 and a conservative hereditarian after that date. I can see no such radical break in Pearson's thought.
16. The controversy over alcoholism is discussed by Farrall (1970, 250-82).
17. Note, for example, Pearson's comment on his opponents in the controversy over tuberculosis (1911, 12):

    . . . quite recently and solemnly assembled in conclave, the wise men of medicine agreed that the constitution *was* an important factor in tuberculosis, but that it was not desirable to lay stress on it at the present time, for it would check the flow of public money into the fight against the tubercle bacillus. But what if the tubercle bacillus is actually committing suicide, or what if immunity be surviving without the aid of the expenditure of thousands of pounds of public money? Well, to say that, means that you will cut off the present or prospective occupation of a certain number of gentlemen who are fighting in one special manner the tubercle bacillus, and therefore, even if true, it must not be rashly said in public.

18. Pearson's opponents are not being accused of *logical* inconsistency. Thus, it was perfectly logical to hold to a generalised hereditarianism but to argue that particular environmental 'race poisons' such as alcohol might have a direct chemical effect on the germ plasm. See, for example, Herbert (1910, 115).
19. This is one of the key arguments of Norton (1978a).

Notes to Chapter 5

1. For example, Ben-David (1960), Ben-David and Collins (1966), Hagstrom (1965, 159-253), Fisher (1967), Clark (1972, 1973), Cole (1972), Oberschall (1972, 187-251), Mulkay (1972, 1974, 1975, 1976a,b), Mulkay and Edge (1973), Edge and Mulkay (1975, 1976), Mulkay, Gilbert and Woolgar (1975), Mullins (1972, 1973a,b, 1975), Griffith and Mullins (1972), Law (1973), Law and Barnes (1976), Whitley (1974, 1975), Stehr (1975), Krohn and Schäfer (1976), Dolby (1976), Worboys (1976), Van der Daele and Weingart (1976), Chubin (1976), Johnston and Robbins (1977).
2. For biographical studies of Edgeworth see Keynes (1926), Bowley (1934), Kendall (1968) and, most recently, Stigler (1978). The best available bibliography of Edgeworth's writings is Johnson (n.d.).

A. L. Bowley (1972; first published in 1928) is a useful guide to parts of Edgeworth's difficult work in mathematical statistics. Edgeworth's work on inference is discussed in Pratt (1976).

3. Welch (1958) points out that Edgeworth (1883b) provided a Bayesian solution to the problem, later made famous by Gosset, of making inferences about means from small samples. For Edgeworth this was, however, a completely theoretical problem, devoid of the practical context that was to give Gosset's work its force.

4. From Kendall and Doig (1968) I produced a list of papers published in Britain in the 1880s in the fields of statistical theory, error theory and actuarial theory (papers on narrow areas of probability theory, such as solutions to problems posed in Whitworth's *Educational Times,* were excluded). Edgeworth and Galton together accounted for a majority of these papers (40 out of 78).

5. See the Edgeworth-Galton correspondence in the Galton Papers (189 and 237).

6. This work has been the subject of some disagreement. Pearson (1920b) doubted whether Edgeworth should really be said to have solved the problem; Seal (1967) disagrees, arguing that Edgeworth showed in principle how to obtain the result. Once Edgeworth's determinantal notation is understood (it follows Salmon 1859), what he was doing becomes clear; and Edgeworth (1893d), which was apparently over-looked by both Pearson and Seal, states explicitly how to construct an expression for the multivariate normal distribution.

7. I am indebted to Messrs David and Richard Garnett for providing me with information about Arthur Black, and for locating the surviving notebooks. Professor Egon Pearson, with the assistance of Miss Peek, Keeper of the Archives at Cambridge University, succeeded in discovering information on the abortive efforts to publish Black's *Algebra.* For Black's family background, see Garnett (1953, 4-6).

8. For discussion of other early work on chi square, see Pearson (1931), Lancaster (1966), Sheynin (1966, 1971a) and Kendall (1971).

9. See pp.95-6 above.

10. Karl Pearson himself (1906; 1914-30, *3A*), E. S. Pearson (especially 1936-38) and Lyndsay Farrall (1970, 54-202 and 318-25) have all discussed in some detail the development of the biometric school.

11. A list of these papers, produced from Kendall and Doig (1968) in the same way as that referred to in note 4, contained 122 items. Of these Galton, Pearson and their associates were responsible for 64; the next most important source was Edgeworth, who produced 13.

12. In terms of the overall development of biology, the most significant new approach was Roux's work in what he called *Entwicklungsmechanik,* the first parts of which were published in 1888 (Allen 1975a, 21-8).

13. See Norton (1973) for a discussion of this paper and of the reaction to it.

14. See, for example, Warren (1902), Darbishire (1902-4), Schuster (n.d.).

15. These last two factors are discussed in chapter 6.

16. See Farrall (1970, 186-9).

17. Thus, from 1903 onwards he received through the University College authorities a grant of £500 per annum from the Worshipful Company of Drapers (Farrall 1970, 129-31).

18. Calculated from the official subscription list in the Pearson Papers (247).

19. The Hon. Rupert Guinness and Lord Northcliffe both contributed, but only relatively small sums (£100 and £25).

20. Pearson Papers (239). The money was passed to University College through the leading 'Liberal Imperialist', Lord Roseberry. Roseberry seems to have been sympathetic to eugenics, having previously promised £100 to the appeal fund (Pearson Papers, 238), and may have been responsible for 'steering' the money towards the Eugenics Laboratory.

21. For the sake of completeness, it is perhaps worth mentioning some individual statisticians who were *not* members of the biometric school. Perhaps the most significant point about them was that they were indeed individuals. There was no other coherent group of workers in Britain to rival the biometric school. Edgeworth, the most distinguished statistician of the older generation not trained in or associated with the biometric school, remained an effective isolate. His sole statistical follower, Arthur Lyon Bowley (1869-1957), lectured on statistics at the London School of Economics, and in 1915 was appointed Professor of Statistics there (A. H. Bowley 1972, Allen and George 1957). Important though Bowley's work in social statistics and econometrics was, he did not develop a school of statistical theory. Within psychology, a number of workers turned to 'psychometrics', notably Charles Spearman, Cyril Burt and Godfrey Thomson. Again, their work, while important within psychology, was not productive of much innovation within statistical theory: from the statistical point of view it can indeed be seen as largely derivative of that of Galton and Pearson. A number of other individuals became interested in statistical theory from a wide variety of viewpoints, such as John Brownlee (medical statistics and perhaps eugenics) and John Maynard Keynes (probability in relation to philosophy and logic).

22. The following list, which does not claim to be exhaustive, was compiled from the employees of the Laboratories as listed by Farrall (1970, 320-1), together with those who collaborated with Pearson in published work: Ethel Elderton, W. P. Elderton, P. F. Everitt, David Heron, W. S. Gosset, J. A. Harris, C. B. Goring, John Blakeman, W. R. MacDonnell, Raymond Pearl, Leon Isserlis, E. C. Snow, H. E. Soper and Major Greenwood, all of whom did work requiring considerable knowledge of statistical theory; and A. Fry, A. O. Powys, M. Lewenz, F. E. Cave-Browne-Cave, S. Jacob, M. Radford, A. Barrington, G. Uchida, A. Wright, E. Pope, Julia Bell, E. Y. Thomson, H. G. Jones, E. H. Nettleship, C. H. Usher, W. Gilby, R. Crewdson Bennington, E. Lea-Smith, M. Crawford, H. Rishbieth, Edith M. M. de G. Lamotte, H. J. Laski, G. McMullan, K. V. Ryley, M. H. Williams, B. Cave, G. Jaederholm and A. Davin, all of whom contributed to other aspects of the work of the Laboratories.

23. Martin (1953, 14-16), K. Pearson (1914-30, *3B,* 606-9), H. J. Laski (1912).
24. The following draws chiefly on E. S. Pearson (1939) and on the fascinating unpublished material quoted therein. Biographical information on Gosset is contained also in McMullen (1939) and Fisher (1939).
25. The case of Gosset could well be taken as evidence for the claim by Barnes (1971) – as against that of Kornhauser (1962) – that individuals do not necessarily experience conflict between the demands of an industrial organisation and the 'norms of pure science'.
26. E. S. Pearson suggests that 'given a little more time . . . Gosset would have found for himself Galton's correlation coefficient' (1939, 366). This seems to me unlikely. In one sense, Galton and Gosset shared a common problem: the inapplicability of the standard error theory techniques when dealing with dependent variables. But Galton's thought was informed by his work on heredity, and it was from this that he drew the key notion of reversion. Gosset does not seem to have had available to him a comparable intellectual resource, and so he approached the problem differently: unlike Galton, he worked directly from the 'anomaly' that arose in the application of error theory to brewery data. He deduced from this a criterion to help him judge whether or not two variables were independent, but apparently did not go on to seek a measure of the degree of their dependence. See the passage 'What is the right way to establish a relationship between sets of observations?', quoted by Pearson (1939, 366).
27. In fact a third paper came out of his year's work, again a solution to a practical problem of the brewery. Gosset independently reinvented the Poisson distribution in studying the error involved in counting yeast cells with a haemacytometer (1907).
28. If the ratio of sample mean to sample standard deviation is called (following Gosset's notation in this paper) z, then the distribution of z is a constant multiple of $(1+z^2)^{-\frac{1}{2}n}dz$ where n is the sample size (Gosset 1908a, 18).
   [This yields the *t*-distribution if we put $t = z(n-1)^{\frac{1}{2}}$.]
29. Gosset's expression was $y_0(1-r^2)^{(n-4)/2}dr$, where y_0 is a constant (Gosset 1908b, 39; substituting r for his x).

Notes to Chapter 6

1. See Froggatt and Nevin (1971a,b), Provine (1971), Cock (1973), Norton (1973; 1975a; 1978b, 155-200), de Marrais (1974), Farrall (1975) and Kevles (1978). My indebtedness to the work of these historians is considerable, even if the interpretation of the controversy put forward here differs markedly in some respects from theirs. With the exception of Kevles, they all seek explanations of the controversy almost exclusively in the realms of ideas or individual psychology. For the difference between that strategy and one of sociological explanation, see Mac-Kenzie and Barnes (1975), in which the account of the controversy developed here was first put forward.
2. I place the word 'rediscovered' in inverted commas because of the extremely interesting suggestion by Olby (1979) that twentieth-century

geneticists read into Mendel's work what was not in fact there: a theory of genetic determinants in the modern sense.

3. See below, note 8, for some of the complexities that have been revealed by unpublished documents in the Galton and Pearson Papers.

4. As Provine points out, Punnett's memory was not quite accurate: Weldon had in fact spoken before lunch.

5. K. Pearson (1906, 311). Again, Pearson's account is not exact: the last speaker was in fact Professor Hickson.

6. An undated manuscript entitled 'Mendel's Law', a copy of which was kindly sent to me by Dr Maxine Merrington of University College, London.

7. If Olby's view of Mendel's papers (Olby 1979) is justified, then Pearson, in considering Mendelism a theory of phenotypic resemblances and not of genetic determinants, was reading them correctly, and the early Mendelians were reading them incorrectly!

8. In seeking to characterise briefly the salient points of divergence between the two sides I have undoubtedly engaged in oversimplification. For example, Karl Pearson and W. F. R. Weldon were not in complete agreement on the strategy for a science of heredity. Weldon, it appears, placed more importance on the construction of a theoretical model of the process of inheritance than did Pearson. His work on this was never published in his lifetime, though shortly after his death Pearson (1908) summarised and developed some of the main themes of his thinking. Particularly important surviving documents are Weldon's manuscript *Theory of Inheritance* (Pearson Papers 266) and his correspondence with Pearson (Pearson Papers 624 and 625) and Galton (Galton Papers 340 G-J). To summarise this large body of tentative and partly worked-out ideas is difficult, but there appears to be one consistent theme: Weldon's belief that the Mendelian model was too narrow and his search for a more general and flexible theory that might include 'pure' Mendelism as a special case but was also capable of accounting adequately for the much more complex situations studied by the biometricians. As Norton (1978b, 183-94 and 190-93) points out, Weldon sought at least in part to return to Galton's 'stirp' model of inheritance. Weldon wrote in the *Theory of Inheritance* (chapter 2, 20):

Galton's theory of hereditary transmission has at least this advantage over Mendel's, that it takes all the known phenomena of inheritance into account, and endeavours to describe them all in terms of a single process.

Weldon, then, appears to have been more prepared than Pearson to theorise about heredity, but it would seem that his theorising remained subordinate to the description of phenotypic resemblance. As he put it at the very start of the *Theory of Inheritance* (chapter 1, version A, 2), his interest was in

the bearing of what we actually know concerning the relation between the visible characters of parents and those of their offspring upon the possible interpretation of structural changes revealed by minute study of the germ-cells and of embryonic processes in general.

9. The colour plate illustrating Weldon's article caused much concern because, through technical difficulties in colour reproduction, it at first showed half the pea seeds green, and half yellow, instead of the continuous gradation of colour that Pearson and Weldon felt undermined Mendel's approach. (Pearson to Galton, 28 January 1902; Galton Papers, 293E).

10. Bateson's position should not be overdrawn. He was quite prepared to use elementary statistical techniques in his own work. What he objected to was the subordination of the biological to the mathematical that he perceived in biometry.

11. This view of the relationship of socialisation and future behaviour is largely taken from Becker (1960, 1964).

    Just how competitive the market for knowledge was in Britain is emphasised by Kevles (1978), who suggests that the greater degree of institutional support for genetics research in the United States led scientists there to take a much more tolerant attitude to different approaches. The scarcity of money and jobs in Britain led, he argues, to a conviction that 'satisfactory professional survival' (*ibid.*, 12) was possible for only one approach.

12. For an interesting account of the reasons for Bateson's favourable assessment of Mendelism see Darden (1977).

13. For biographical details of Davenport, see MacDowell (1946) and Rosenberg (1961).

14. The split can be followed in their correspondence in the Davenport Papers (Pearson File).

15. For the debate about Darwin, see Shapin and Barnes (1979). For one of many examples of this social use of biology, see Durant (1979).

16. Thus they rejected the notion of a fixed species 'centre of regression', arguing that regression took place only to the shifting mean of individual characteristics (see pp.90-1 above). Had they accepted the notion of the fixed 'centre of regression', their predictions about individual organisms would then have been based on a characteristic of the species, rather than *vice versa*. As Provine (1971) points out, the clash of these two different interpretations of regression was an important aspect of the debate.

17. The proviso relating to concern with the planned improvement of whole populations is important. Eugenists without this concern – say those who wished to restrict eugenic attention to sub-populations identified on the basis of qualitatively distinct traits – might well have found Mendelism a more useful approach. It is interesting to speculate whether this may throw some light on the phenomenon of 'Mendelian eugenics' in, for example, Davenport (1910 and 1911).

18. Galton is a complex figure as far as this controversy is concerned. On the one hand he was the originator of the biometric method, and, as argued in chapter 3, the connection suggested here between biometry and eugenics clearly holds for this aspect of his thought. On the other hand, there are facets of Galton's substantive theorising, particularly his emphasis on the idea of 'stability' and the related notion that evolution consists of jerks from one position of stability to another,

that are much closer to Bateson's thought (see Cowan 1977, 179-97, for a good account of Galton's thought on these matters). One is almost tempted to posit two Galtons: a $Galton_1$ who was a eugenist and biometrician, and a $Galton_2$ whose biology might be understood in the light of the analysis suggested below for Bateson's. Certainly both sides in the controversy found resources to draw on in Galton's rich and contradictory thinking.

19. Norton suggests another possible cause of Pearson's opposition to Mendelism: his upholding of a *Weltbild* in which it was denied that any two objects were totally alike (as Mendelian factors in a sense were). It seems to me that, to the extent that Pearson held to this, it can best be seen as a generalisation from his biological beliefs and experience, rather than as a determinant of them. That is how I would interpret the following, which is perhaps his most explicit statement on the matter (Pearson 1914-30, *3A*, 84n):

> I must confess to feeling it extremely difficult to accept the view that the population of germ cells belonging to an individual organism are like atoms, identical in character, and have a germinal capacity defined by absolutely the same formula. Such a population of germ cells is, if parasitical, still an organic population, and one continually in a state of reproduction and change. No other organic population that we know of is without variation among its members . . .

This interpretation is, I think, supported by Norton's account (Norton 1975a) of the origins of Pearson's belief in biological variability.

20. Weldon's actual *motives* for opposing Mendelism seem to me most likely to be accountable for in terms of his personal investment in mathematical and statistical method. He wrote to Pearson on 23 June 1902 (Pearson Papers 625):

> It seems to me, quite apart from my own share in the matter, that the present is a rather interesting and important moment. There is a 'boom' in a quite unstatistical theory of inheritance, which is so simple that everyone can understand it, and is stated so confidently that all sorts of people are getting interested in it. We can make it ridiculous, and I think we must. It is really the first time the unstatistical folk have fairly recognised that there is a fundamental antithesis, and have accepted battle on that issue. The side which can now get a vulgarly dramatic 'score' will have a better hearing presently.

In addition, it is interesting to note that Weldon's (1894) criticism of Bateson (1894) – the opening skirmish of the whole controversy – was largely methodological, and based on Bateson's reliance on 'museum preparations' and 'printed records', rather than on statistical surveys of variation.

21. An account of these is to be found in Pearson (1914-30, *3A*, 405-9).

22. In this chapter, only Bateson's own writings are drawn upon. Other evidence could be adduced from the work of his collaborators. Thus the most important of these, R. C. Punnett, seems to have shared both Bateson's biological views and many of his social and political atti-

tudes: for example, he too was a leader of the campaign for the retention of compulsory Greek. See the material cited below in note 4 to chapter 8 (p.267), where Punnett's controversy with R. A. Fisher is briefly discussed.

23. Dr Alan Cock believes some of Coleman's argument to be wrong. Judgement on these points must await the publication of Cock's full study. In the text, I have restricted myself to assertions about Bateson's work that seem capable of independent justification.

24. Bateson (1894), and Bateson (1928, 39-43).

25. Coleman does, however, suggest that for Bateson, 'Darwinism hued all too closely to the blighted atomistic individualism of the utilitarians' (Coleman 1970, 295).

26. Apparently on this basis, Crowther (1952, especially 256 and 289) suggests that Bateson should be placed among the class of *rentiers*. He puts forward an interesting but quite unsupported hypothesis that Bateson's early break with evolutionary embryology is connected with his *rentier* background and with the association of comparative embryology with the landed class through the person of F. M. Balfour and through the aristocratic nature of Balfour's College, Trinity.

27. On one issue Bateson was a 'progressive' – indeed on the same side as Pearson. He was in favour of the admission of women to Cambridge degrees. Why he should have felt that this did not violate the Cambridge ethos, I do not know: it may be connected to the fact that his family contained several highly talented women.

28. Of course, had we more information about his early life, psychological makeup and so on, we might no longer see this choice as free. The point, however, is that it would be mistaken to see it as constrained simply by his social background. I found the discussion of Bateson in Norton (1978b) extremely helpful on this point.

29. See also Rothblatt (1968). It is interesting to contrast this conservative response with Pearson's call for Cambridge University to become more relevant and technologically-oriented (Pearson 1886a).

30. It is difficult to find a *scientist* of this time who unequivocally opposed the sociobiological strategy. Huxley's *Evolution and Ethics* (1893), commonly taken as the classic instance of such opposition, has recently been reinterpreted by Helfand (1977) as a contribution to sociobiological argument, rather than as a complete rejection of it.

31. This latter is an idea with which Bateson toyed. See Bateson (1928, 212 and 285-96).

32. It is interesting that a recent study by Robert McAulay (1978) of the Velikovsky controversy has suggested broadly similar connections. Velikovsky and his followers are portrayed by McAulay as romantic-conservative catastrophists, and their opponents within the scientific community as progressive uniformitarians of a type similar to Pearson.

Notes to Chapter 7

1. Two useful sources of information about work on statistical association are Walker (1929, 130-41) and Goodman and Kruskal (1954-59). Professor Nancy C. Thomson, of the State University of New York at Far-

mingdale, has completed a dissertation, which unfortunately I have not seen, on the history of the development of measures of association.

2. The use of terms such as 'interval' and 'nominal' here is anachronistic, but their use clarifies the issue at stake. For these terms see Stevens (1946).

3. This disagreement is discussed below in note 8.

4. In the following I have been forced, for the sake of clarity, to use a standard form of notation. This is to be regretted, as Yule's and Pearson's notations did to some extent reflect their differing approaches. Yule used a notation drawn from symbolic logic. For A_1 and A_2 he wrote A and α, where α signified not-A, and for B_1 and B_2 he wrote B and β, with β signifying not-B. His notation for the frequency I label a was (AB); for b, $(A\beta)$; etc.

5. Pearson also proposed a second coefficient of contingency, based on a different function of the divergence between observed and expected frequencies. This was easier to calculate but did not have any similar clear relationship to r, and was less used.

6. The product-sum coefficient was first introduced by Yule (1911, 212-13). This coefficient had previously and independently been suggested by the geneticist W. Johannsen (1909, 272-9) and by the anthropologist F. Boas (1909). It had even been used by Pearson (1904a) quite without comment, but in a very different situation, that of theoretical Mendelian inheritance (for which see p.163 below).

7. For examples of this process of evaluation see Pearson (1900b, 15-18) and Pearson and Heron (1913, 193-202). Pearson's use of it can be found from the very beginning of his work on association. Thus, on 6 May 1899, before the appearance of the first published papers on the topic, he wrote to Yule pointing out to him that Q failed this test (Pearson Papers, CI D6).

8. Pearson felt that an approach to the correlation of non-normal variables must be built on knowledge of the particular form of their joint distribution, for only if this was known would it be possible to know how best to predict values of one variable from that of the other (Pearson 1896, 274; Pearson 1920b). Yule, by comparison, claimed that the ordinary product-moment coefficient could be used for these non-normal variables as it had an interpretation as the slope of the best-fitting line (in the least-squares sense) through their joint distribution, irrespective of the particular form of this distribution (Yule 1897a). This difference of opinion can be seen in the letters of 1896 between Pearson and Yule in the Pearson Papers (CI D1).

9. Indeed Yule was to come to doubt whether a coefficient of association was always what was needed. He wrote to Major Greenwood on 2 March 1915 (Yule-Greenwood Letters):

> Here are the cholera arithmetic and diagrams. I have also enclosed a couple of sheets of lucubration on the measure of the advantage, and efficiency or effectiveness, of immunisation or similar processes. I cannot see my way to a measure of association, for I cannot get clear in my mind to begin with what we want to measure by the association coefficient: I seem to get more muddle headed when-

ever I try to think it out. In fact I don't seem really to want a measure of association at all. The 'advantage' or 'effectiveness' give what I want and neither is of the nature of an association coefficient, but the first is a regression and the second G O D knows what.

10. This issue is discussed in Barnes and MacKenzie (1979).
11. See Yule (1912, especially 145-6 and 159-63), Pearson and Heron (1913, especially 171-83 and 193-202), Pearson (1904b, 8-9), Pearson (1913a).
12. Later Pearson attempted to demonstrate the small role of environment by comparing 'coefficients of heredity' with correlations between the characteristics of children and particular aspects of their home environment; however, this was for him a subsidiary problem, as he believed that home environment was in any case largely a reflection of the innate characteristics of a child's parents. See, for example, Pearson (1910b).
13. See Pearson (1914-30, *3A*, 332).
14. Sibling correlations and parent-child correlations were of course connected by the Galton/Pearson 'Law of Ancestral Heredity': see Pearson (1898, 404-7).
15. Three crucial differences between Pearson's work and later studies are the introduction of a numerical scale of 'intelligence', the use of twins as well as siblings in general, and the application of multi-factorial Mendelian models (in addition to simple measures of resemblance) to gain estimates of 'heritability'. Important though these differences are, this later work can be seen as elaborating Pearson's basic approach, rather than diverging radically from it.

    For an interesting point of view on Pearson's Huxley Lecture, see Welch (1970); see also the comments by E. S. Pearson (1972).
16. From the letters of Yule to Greenwood of 3 April 1912, 8 August 1912, 8 November 1912 and 17 August 1920 (Yule-Greenwood Letters).
17. I am not clear whether Yule's attacks on the biometric school's work were at any point motivated by hostility to eugenics as such. Certainly Yule (1910, 551) made such basic critical points as that 'a correlation between parent and child does not necessarily imply heredity'. It is, however, unnecessary for the argument of this chapter that Yule's work have been motivated in this way. All that is asserted is that no positive commitment to eugenics is manifested in it.
18. Biographical details for Yule are to be found in F. Yates (1952) and M. G. Kendall (1952).
19. For these debates see MacLeod (1967b).
20. In measuring the association of vaccination and survival it is obviously desirable for comparative purposes to have a measure which is independent of both the virulence of the epidemic (of the overall proportion of cases falling into the 'survived' and 'died' columns) and of the degree of activity of the medical authorities (proportions vaccinated and unvaccinated). Yule thus sought to construct coefficients which were unaltered by multiplication of any row or column by a constant. See Yule (1912, 113-23).
21. See K. Pearson (1900b, 43-5), Yule (1912) and Yule (1906a).

22. The list omits those who wrote only one paper in the field and who did not, therefore, seem to have had an ongoing active interest in it. The most obvious problem of inclusion/exclusion is the decision as to whether a piece of work contains a development of statistical theory and method or simply an application of existing methods. Thus, for example, Charles Spearman is included but Cyril Burt excluded, and while this does indicate real differences in the type of work they did, it shows that there is no absolute division between those included and those excluded.

23. I would class the following as members of the biometric school: J. Blakeman, E. M. Elderton, W. P. Elderton, P. F. Everitt, F. Galton, D. Heron, L. Isserlis, A. Lee, K. Pearson, E. H. J. Schuster, E. C. Snow, H. E. Soper. The 'others' are A. L. Bowley, J. Brownlee, F. Y. Edgeworth, R. A. Fisher, W. S. Gosset, M. Greenwood, R. H. Hooker, J. M. Keynes, G. J. Lidstone, A. G. McKendrick, W. F. Sheppard, C. Spearman, G. H. Thomson, G. U. Yule.

24. See his letters to Yule in this period in the Yule Papers (box 1) and Greenwood and Yule (1915).

25. See Eugenics Education Society (1911, 1912). Brownlee even used r_T in the case of theoretical Mendelism, where the biometricians denied its applicability: see Brownlee (1910) and Snow (1912).

26. Edgeworth's one flirtation with hereditarianism is described in chapter 5. I have not been able to find any writings by Hooker dealing with eugenics.

27. This was the account given by Yule to Greenwood in his letters of 18 May and 26 May 1936 (Yule Papers, box 2). The Yule-Pearson correspondence (Pearson Papers, CI D3 and C1 D6) bears this out, as it continues on an amicable basis up to Yule's first criticism of Pearson in 1905 and is then abruptly terminated (apart from three letters of 1910, dealing with a personal matter).

28. In the light of the biographical information on Yule, Edgeworth, Hooker and Bateson, it is interesting that Levitas (1976, 547) suggests that Christian Socialism – a paternalist, anti-bourgeois movement – was largely composed of individuals downwardly mobile from the pre-industrial élite.

Notes to Chapter 8

1. Another useful source is Mahalanobis (1938), which according to Frank Yates (personal communication) was based on information given to Mahalanobis by Fisher. Subsequent biographies, with the exception of that by Box, appear to rely primarily on Mahalanobis for the period before 1920, and it should be noted that E. S. Pearson (1968) has shown this account to contain some inaccuracies. In what follows, biographical information is taken from Box (1978), unless otherwise indicated.

   Fisher's papers are in the care of the Genetics Department, University of Adelaide; I was unable to obtain permission to consult them. However, several colleagues and students of Fisher kindly allowed me to interview them: F. Yates, D. Finney, W. Federer, G. Wilkinson and

D. Hayman. Joan Fisher Box helped me by answering some written questions.

2. Perhaps the most likely academic influence is Fisher's tutor, F. J. M. Stratton (1881-1960). Stratton is best-known as an astronomer (Chadwick 1961), but he also worked on the theory of errors (Edwards 1974, 14, informs us that Brunt 1917 was based largely on Stratton's lectures), on the use of error theory in agricultural research (Wood and Stratton 1910) and on the genetics of left- and right-handedness (Stratton and Compton 1910). After Fisher's graduation in 1912 he spent a further year at Cambridge studying error theory with Stratton (and statistical mechanics with James Jeans). So it is possible that Stratton may have turned Fisher towards genetics and statistical theory, but in the absence of more detailed evidence this cannot be accounted as more than simply a possibility.

3. In 1974 I was fortunate enough to find the records of this Society at the Eugenics Society in London. Part of these records (Fisher 1911) has now been published by Norton and Pearson (1976), while Box (1978) has used what appears to be parallel material in the Fisher papers in Adelaide.

4. Evidence, additional to that in the text, for this point of view can be found in the reaction of R. C. Punnett to Fisher's work. See Norton and Pearson (1976), Norton (1978c), Punnett (1915, 1917, 1930), and Fisher (1924a, 1927 and 1930, 146-69). The debate between Fisher and Punnett centred on such issues as whether mimicry in butterflies had evolved gradually, as Fisher said, or by saltation, as Punnett implied; they also disagreed on the efficacy of eugenic intervention, Fisher (1924a) claiming that Punnett had, albeit 'inadvertently', 'supplied material for anti-eugenic propaganda'. In general, Punnett (for whom see Crew 1967) seems to have had very similar social and biological views to his mentor, William Bateson (see Punnett 1925, 1926), and the Punnett/Fisher debate recapitulated many of the issues of the Bateson/Pearson controversy.

One possible objection to the view suggested in the text might be Pearson's failure to welcome Fisher's work, most importantly his often noted unenthusiastic refereeing of Fisher (1918a) for the Royal Society of London. However, the publication of Karl Pearson's report by Norton and Pearson (1976) shows that Karl Pearson did not, in fact, recommend rejection of this paper. Admitting that he had not 'examined in detail' Fisher's work, Pearson concluded:

> Whether the paper be published or not should depend on Mendelian opinion as to the correspondence of the author's hypothesis with observation, and the probability that Mendelians will accept in the near future a multiplicity of independent units not exhibiting dominance or coupling.

So, while it is clearly true that Pearson failed to grasp the potential importance of Fisher's work, it is possible that this may have resulted not from deep-seated hostility but from his being 'overfussed with other work' and from Fisher's very poor presentation of his analysis.

5. Bateson's 'influence upon evolutionary theory was . . . chiefly retrogressive', while his early writings included 'rash polemics' (Fisher 1930, ix-x).

6. That is, the theory that a crucial evolutionary mechanism was the purely random fluctuation of gene frequencies in small, partially isolated populations.

7. If the correlation of two variables is r, then one is said to 'explain' a proportion of r^2 of the variance of the other. So Pearson's typical parent-child correlation of 0.5 meant that parental characteristics explained a proportion of 0.25, or 25 per cent, of the variance in offspring characteristics. Put crudely, Fisher's method was to show that because of factors such as dominance this was a gross underestimate of the total genetic contribution to the explanation of offspring variance. Hodge (in Forbes 1978, 448) has pointed out the crucial role of Fisher's analysis of dominance in his attempt to claim the vast bulk of variance for eugenics, and suggests that this may partly explain Fisher's 'lifelong preoccupation with dominance'.

8. That is, by the square root of the genetic variance in fertility.

9. An extremely interesting passage in Wright's 'Evolution in Mendelian Populations' (1931, 154-55) indicates his sympathy for non-mechanistic and non-deterministic views of 'creative' or 'emergent' evolution, though he denies that 'subjective' interpretation has a place in the 'objective scientific analysis of the problem'. Hodge (n.d.) discusses the possible influence of 'holism' on Wright's work.

10. In 'direct' probability we work from a model or description of a situation to deduce consequences: this urn contains five white balls and five black balls, therefore the probability of drawing a white ball is 0.5. 'Inverse' probability arguments occur when, for example, we work backwards from observation of the outcome of drawing balls to reach probabilistic conclusions about the proportion of white and black balls in an urn.

11. For what happens if the range of possible values of θ is infinite, see D. V. Lindley (1965, 2, 18-19). Full consideration of this issue, which involves some difficult and contentious points, would lead us too far away from the historical material to be discussed.

12. Pearson might reasonably have argued – although I have no evidence that he did – that the general theorem of Pearson and Filon (1898) was correct, even if it had been incorrectly applied to estimates that were not maxima of the posterior probability distribution.

13. The other major practising statistician of this period who was concerned with the theory of inference, F. Y. Edgeworth, was much happier with Bayesianism than either Pearson or Sheppard. He defended it on philosophical grounds (Edgeworth 1884), and his major work on inference was built on it (Edgeworth 1908-9). He did, however, attempt a 'direct probability' justification of his procedure in this latter work (see 1908-9, addendum, and Pratt 1976). It is interesting to note that 'Student' too used a Bayesian approach in his early work (see Gosset 1908b, 35).

14. Precisely why he adopted this goal I do not know. John Venn was President of Gonville and Caius College when Fisher was an undergraduate there, but in view of Venn's advanced age, and the fact that he had long since ceased to do work in this field, I would not be inclined to place much importance on this. Nevertheless, Fisher would presumably have been led to read the *Logic of Chance* at an early stage, and perhaps it was from it that he learnt of the empiricist objections to Bayesianism.
15. Gosset described his early contacts with Fisher in a letter to Karl Pearson of 12 September 1912 (see E. S. Pearson 1968, 406).
16. In this period 'standard error' (standard deviation of the sampling distribution) was gradually supplanting the older 'probable error'. The first use of the former term was apparently by Yule (1897a, 483; see Walker 1929, 188). In part the change reflected the general prominence the biometricians gave to the standard deviation; in part, the increasing tendency to think of the 'error' as an interval of a sampling distribution, not of a posterior probability distribution.
17. Fisher held (1922a, 329n) that the Pearson/Filon approach was correct so long as it was interpreted as giving the standard errors of maximum likelihood estimators.
18. In fact, Fisher proved the converse, that sufficient statistics, when they exist, are maximum likelihood estimators (1922a, 330-1).
19. Fisher (1915, 520-1), Soper *et al.* (1917), Fisher (1921a). It is interesting that the connection between biometric statistics and eugenics may have led the biometricians to feel that the assumption of a uniform prior distribution in the case of the coefficient of correlation was unjustified. They gave a practical example of how Bayesian inference might be used in the case of a researcher confronted with a parent-child correlation of 0.6 based on a sample of 25. They argued that, from their considerable experience of such correlations, a suitable prior distribution would be one which had a mean of 0.46 and a standard deviation of 0.02. The 'most likely value' of the correlation coefficient of the population from which the sample was drawn they found using Bayes's theorem to be 0.46225. 'We see that our new experience scarcely modifies the old and this is what we should naturally conjecture would be the case' (Soper *et al.* 1917, 359). In view of the analysis in chapter 7, this conclusion is interesting as representing formal evidence of the biometricians' degree of belief in the clustering of the values of parent-child correlations.

    Gosset had also found that the use of non-uniform prior distributions for the correlation coefficient 'made a fool of the actual sample'. For him, however, this was an argument *against* their use, and in favour of Fisher's approach. See Gosset's letter to Fisher of 3 April 1922, in McMullen (n.d.).
20. E. S. Pearson (1936-38, part 1, 222) has pointed to the precise lacuna in Pearson's analysis. Yule had already seen it in 1916: see his letter to Greenwood of 12 March 1916 (Yule-Greenwood Letters).
21. Except in so far as the biometric approach was Bayesian, in which case one can talk of incommensurability; but the biometricians were only half-heartedly Bayesian.

22. Thus, Yule wrote to M. G. Kendall following the death of Karl Pearson: 'I feel as though the Karlovingian era has come to an end, and the Piscatorial era which succeeds it is one in which I can play no part' (quoted by M. G. Kendall 1952, 2).

23. For example, it incorporated not only Pearson's techniques but also Gosset's. Of course, Fisher's approach was soon to be challenged by others (the E. S. Pearson/J. Neyman theory of inference, and a revitalised Bayesianism) of equal generality and power.

24. Wood and Stratton (1910); Mercer and Hall (1911). The revival of agricultural research was probably due to the recovery from the late nineteenth-century agricultural depression and the start of large-scale state funding, perhaps occasioned in part by the threat of war. In 1902 its new director, Daniel Hall, found the long-established Rothamsted Experimental Station 'more like a museum than a laboratory' (Russell 1966, 233), but under the energetic direction of Hall and his successor, E. J. Russell, it began to revive. The Liberal government set up a £2.5 million development fund for agriculture, and by the outbreak of war in 1914 there were twelve institutes and two minor centres of agricultural research in Britain (Russell 1966, 272).

25. Gosset to Karl Pearson, 12 September 1912, in E. S. Pearson (1968, 406); Gosset to Fisher, 30 December 1918, in McMullen (n.d.).

Notes to Chapter 9

1. In the text, discussion is limited to statistical theory. But I feel that even so-called 'pure' mathematics should not be regarded by historians in a Platonic light. See Bloor (1973) for a discussion of this.

2. Bloor (1976, especially chapter 5) puts forward a sociological account of mathematics that is useful here. He suggests that mathematics is tied by a kind of metaphoric link to the real world (either directly, as in elementary mathematics, or indirectly, to the extent that higher mathematics is itself built by metaphoric extension from elementary mathematics) but is also a social institution, possessing therefore intersubjective validity. Not all patterns in the empirical world become institutionalised as mathematical truths: that one raindrop plus one raindrop makes one raindrop does not lead us to an arithmetic in which $1 + 1 = 1$. So what is institutionalised is initially open for negotiation and is presumably the result of goals and interests of different kinds. Of course, after its institutionalisation mathematics has the 'feel' of unalterable, timeless, Platonic truth, but this, Bloor suggests, is characteristic of any set of ideas (e.g. moral precepts) that has been institutionalised rigidly.

3. I should emphasise that the term 'goal' as I use it is not translatable into Habermas's notion of a 'cognitive interest'. Habermas's enterprise is philosophical: he is investigating 'the conditions of possible knowledge' (1972, 5) and their connections to the natural history of humanity. My aim is not only more modest, but also different in kind. It is descriptive rather than analytic-conceptual. For this different task, Habermas's concepts obviously require a transformation so thoroughgoing that retention of the same words becomes misleading.

4. He distinguishes also between both of these and what he refers to as 'critical' sciences, such as psychoanalysis, that are characterised by the goal of emancipation.
5. The phrase is Hodge's (in Forbes 1978, 447). He is referring to the work of Fisher, but the point is of relevance to Pearson as well.
6. At the very least, philosophers of science have – despite much effort – failed to provide us with any criterion that could be used to test theories in terms of their power in all possible types of prediction, or techniques for their success in all possible types of control. Some narrowing of focus seems to be necessary for science to proceed, as Kuhn (1970) emphasises.
7. A way of approaching this question that has not been employed here, but that would be helpful, would be a detailed comparison between the situation of statistical theory in Britain and that in other countries, where the influence of eugenics on statistics seems to have been much weaker. Some secondary historical material is available, though it is very patchy. Koren (1970) has an international perspective, but deals primarily with official statistics, not statistical theory; for the former, Westergaard (1932) remains the best source for the period up to 1900. There are a number of useful works referring to specific countries. For France, see Clark (1967; 1973, especially 122-46). For Italy, see Gini (1926). For Germany, see Lexis (1893) and Oberschall (1965). For Russia, see Zarkovich (1956, 1962), Maistrov (1974, 161-224) and Adams (1974, 69-98). For Scandinavia, see Särndal (1971). For the United States, see Owen (1976) and Ben-David (1971, 149-50). It certainly appears from this literature that the concerns typical of British statistical theory in this period are not to be found elsewhere.

Bibliography

. . . . .
 . . .
  .

The following abbreviations of journal titles have been used:

J.R.S.S. *Journal of the Royal Statistical Society*
Phil. Mag. *The London, Edinburgh and Dublin Philosophical Magazine and Journal of Science*
Phil. Trans. *Philosophical Transactions of the Royal Society of London*
Proc. Roy. Soc. *Proceedings of the Royal Society of London*

Certain collections of articles have been much cited:
E. S. Pearson and J. Wishart, eds (1958);
E. S. Pearson and M. G. Kendall, eds (1970);
A. Stuart and M. G. Kendall, eds (1971);
M. G. Kendall and R. L. Plackett, eds (1977).
Citations of articles in these collections are by author and year of original publication, but page references are to the above collections.

Abrams, P. (1968). *The Origins of British Sociology: 1834-1914.* Chicago: University of Chicago Press.

Adams, M. B. (1968). 'The Founding of Population Genetics: the Contributions of the Chetverikov School'. *Journal of the History of Biology, 1,* 23-39.

Adams, M. B. (1970). 'Towards a Synthesis: Population Concepts in Russian Evolutionary Thought, 1925-1935'. *Journal of the History of Biology, 3,* 107-29.

Adams, W. J. (1974). *The Life and Times of the Central Limit Theorem.* New York: Kaedmon.

Airy, G. B. (1861). *On the Algebraical and Numerical Theory of Errors of Observations and the Combination of Observations.* Cambridge and London: Macmillan.

Aitken, A. C. (1938). 'A Note on Sheppard's Contribution to Mathematics and Mathematical Statistics'. *Annals of Eugenics, 8,* 9-11.

Allen, G. E. (1968). 'Thomas Hunt Morgan and the Problem of Natural Selection'. *Journal of the History of Biology, 1,* 113-39.

Allen, G. E. (1969). 'Hugo de Vries and the Reception of the *Mutation Theory*'. *Journal of the History of Biology, 2,* 55-87.

Allen, G. E. (1975a). *Life Science in the Twentieth Century*. New York: Wiley.

Allen, G. E. (1975b). 'Genetics, Eugenics and Class Struggle'. *Genetics, 79*, 29-45.

Allen, G. E. (1976). 'Genetics, Eugenics and Society: Internalists and Externalists in Contemporary History of Science'. *Social Studies of Science, 6*, 105-22.

Allen, G. E. (1978). *Thomas Hunt Morgan: The Man and his Science*. Princeton, N.J.: Princeton University Press.

Allen, R. G. D. and George, R. F. (1957). 'Professor Sir Arthur Lyon Bowley'. *J.R.S.S., 120*, 236-41.

Althusser, L. (1969). *For Marx*. Harmondsworth: Penguin.

Annan, N. G. (1955). 'The Intellectual Aristocracy'. In J. H. Plumb (ed.), *Studies in Social History: A Tribute to G. M. Trevelyan*, 241-87. London: Longmans, Green.

Arbuthnott, J. (1710). 'The Argument for Divine Providence, taken from the Constant Regularity observ'd in the Births of both Sexes'. *Phil. Trans., 27*. Reprinted in M. G. Kendall and R. L. Plackett (eds) (1977, 30-4).

Arfken, G. (1968). *Mathematical Methods for Physicists*. New York: Academic Press.

Arnauld, A. and Nicole, P. (1965). *La Logique, ou l'Art de Penser*. Paris: Presses Universitaires de France.

Baines, A. (1970). 'The History and Development of Statistics in Great Britain and Ireland'. In Koren (ed.) (1970, 365-89).

Baker, K. M. (1975). *Condorcet: from Natural Philosophy to Social Mathematics*. Chicago: University of Chicago Press.

Ball, W. P. (1890). *Are the Effects of Use and Disuse Inherited?* London: Macmillan.

Banks, J. A. (1965). *Prosperity and Parenthood: A Study of Family Planning among the Victorian Middle Classes*. London: Routledge and Kegan Paul.

Barnard, G.A. (1958). 'Thomas Bayes – a Biographical Note'. *Biometrika, 45*. Reprinted in E. S. Pearson and M. G. Kendall (eds) (1970, 131-3).

Barnes, B. (1971). 'Making Out in Industrial Research'. *Science Studies, 1*, 157-75.

Barnes, B. (1974). *Scientific Knowledge and Sociological Theory*. London: Routledge and Kegan Paul.

Barnes, B. (1977). *Interests and the Growth of Knowledge*. London and Henley: Routledge and Kegan Paul.

Barnes, B. and MacKenzie, D. (1979). 'On the Role of Interests in Scientific Change'. In R. Wallis (ed.), *On the Margins of Science: the Social Construction of Rejected Knowledge (Sociological Review Monograph 27)*, 49-66. Keele: University of Keele.

Barnes, B. and Shapin, S. (eds) (1979). *Natural Order: Historical Studies of Scientific Culture*. Beverly Hills and London: SAGE.

Bateson, B. (ed.) (1928). *William Bateson, F.R.S., Naturalist. His Essays and Addresses together with a short Account of his Life*. Cambridge: Cambridge University Press.

Bateson, G. (1973). *Steps to an Ecology of Mind*. St. Albans: Paladin.

Bateson, W. (1894). *Materials for the Study of Variation*. London: Macmillan.

Bateson, W. (1901). 'Heredity, Differentiation, and other Conceptions of Biology: a Consideration of Professor Karl Pearson's paper "On the Principle of Homotyposis"'. *Proc. Roy. Soc.*, *69*, 193-205.

Bateson, W. (1902). *Mendel's Principles of Heredity: a Defence*. Cambridge: Cambridge University Press.

Bateson, W. and Saunders, E. R. (1902). 'Experimental Studies in the Physiology of Heredity'. *Reports to the Evolution Committee of the Royal Society*. London: Royal Society of London.

Bayes, T. (1764). 'An Essay towards solving a problem in the Doctrine of Chances'. *Phil. Trans.*, *53*. Reprinted in E. S. Pearson and M. G. Kendall (eds) (1970, 134-53).

Becker, H. S. (1960). 'Notes on the Concept of Commitment'. *American Journal of Sociology*, *66*, 32-40.

Becker, H. S. (1964). 'Personal Change in Adult Life'. *Sociometry*, *27*, 40-53.

Ben-David, J. (1960). 'Roles and Innovation in Medicine'. *American Journal of Sociology*, *65*, 557-68.

Ben-David, J. (1971). *The Scientist's Role in Society: a Comparative Study*. Englewood Cliffs, N.J.: Prentice Hall.

Ben-David, J. and Collins, R. (1966). 'Social Factors in a New Science: the Case of Psychology'. *American Sociological Review*, *31*, 451-65.

Bennett, J. H. (ed.) (1971-74). *Collected Papers of R. A. Fisher*. Adelaide: the University of Adelaide.

Berger, P. L. and Luckmann, T. (1971). *The Social Construction of Reality*. Harmondsworth: Penguin.

Beveridge, W. (1943). 'Eugenic Aspects of Children's Allowances'. *Eugenics Review*, *34*, 117-23.

Black, A. (1898). 'Reduction of a certain Multiple Integral'. *Transactions of the Cambridge Philosophical Society*, *16*, 219-25.

Blacker, C. P. (1952). *Eugenics: Galton and after*. London: Duckworth.

Bloor, D. (1973). 'Wittgenstein and Mannheim on the Sociology of Mathematics'. *Studies in the History and Philosophy of Science*, *4*, 173-91.

Bloor, D. (1976). *Knowledge and Social Imagery*. London, Henley and Boston: Routledge and Kegan Paul.

Boas, F. (1909). 'Determination of the Coefficient of Correlation'. *Science*, n.s. *29*, 823-4.

Bowles, S. and Gintis, H. (1976). *Schooling in Capitalist America*. London and Henley: Routledge and Kegan Paul.

Bowley, A. H. (1972). *A Memoir of Professor Sir Arthur Bowley (1869-1957) and his Family*. Privately printed.

Bowley, A. L. (1934). 'Francis Ysidro Edgeworth'. *Econometrica*, *2*, 113-24.

Bowley, A. L. (1972). *F. Y. Edgeworth's Contributions to Mathematical Statistics*. Clifton, N.J.: Kelley.

Bowley, A. L. and Burnett-Hurst, A. R. (1915). *Livelihood and Poverty*. London: Bell.

Box, J. F. (1978). *R. A. Fisher: the Life of a Scientist*. New York: Wiley.

Boyer, C. B. (1968). *A History of Mathematics*. New York: Wiley.

Bravais, A. (1846). 'Analyse Mathématique sur les Probabilités des Erreurs de Situation d'un Point'. *Mémoires présentés par divers Savants à l'Académie Royale des Sciences de l'Institut de France, 9,* 255-332.

Browne, H. (1974). *Joseph Chamberlain, Radical and Imperialist*. London: Longman.

Brownlee, J. (1910). 'The Significance of the Correlation Coefficient when applied to Mendelian Distributions'. *Proceedings of the Royal Society of Edinburgh, 30,* 473-507.

Brunt, D. (1917). *The Combination of Observations*. Cambridge: Cambridge University Press.

Brush, S. (1967). 'Foundations of Statistical Mechanics, 1845-1915'. *Archive for History of Exact Sciences, 4,* 145-183.

Bryan, G. H. (1903). 'Rev. Dr. H. W. Watson, F.R.S.' *Nature, 67,* 274-5.

Bryan, G. H. (1911). 'S. H. Burbury, F.R.S.' *Nature, 87,* 281-2.

B[ryan], G. H. (1913). 'Samuel Hawksley Burbury, 1831-1911'. *Proc. Roy. Soc.,* A, *88,* i-iv.

Buck, P. S. (1977). 'Seventeenth-Century Political Arithmetic: Civil Strife and Vital Statistics'. *Isis, 68,* 67-84.

Burbury, S. H. (1894). 'On the Law of Distribution of Energy'. *Phil. Mag.,* series 5, *37,* 143-158.

Burbury, S. H. (1895). 'On the Law of Error in the Case of Correlated Variations'. *British Association Report,* 621-4.

Burbury, S. H. (1899). *A Treatise on the Kinetic Theory of Gases*. Cambridge: Cambridge University Press.

Burnham, J. C. (1972). 'Instinct Theory and the German Reaction to Weismannism'. *Journal of the History of Biology, 5,* 321-6.

Buss, A. R. (1976). 'Galton and the Birth of Differential Psychology and Eugenics: Social, Political, and Economic Forces'. *Journal of the History of the Behavioral Sciences, 12,* 47-58.

Carchedi, G. (1975a). 'On the Economic Identification of the New Middle Class'. *Economy and Society, 4,* 1-86.

Carchedi, G. (1975b). 'Reproduction of Social Classes at the Level of Production Relations'. *Economy and Society, 4,* 361-417.

Carchedi, G. (1976). 'The Economic Identification of the State Employees'. *Social Praxis, 3,* 93-120.

Carr-Saunders, A. M. and Wilson, P. A. (1933). *The Professions*. Oxford: Clarendon.

Castellon, N. J., Jr. (1966). 'On the Estimation of the Tetrachoric Correlation Coefficient'. *Psychometrika, 31,* 67-73.

Chadwick, J. (1961). 'Frederick John Marrian Stratton 1881-1960'. *Biographical Memoirs of Fellows of the Royal Society, 7,* 281-93.

Chang, W-C. (1973). *A History of the Chi-Square Goodness-of-Fit Test*. Ph.D. thesis: University of Toronto.

Chesterton, G. K. (1922). *Eugenics and other Evils*. London: Cassell.

Child, A. (1941). 'The Problem of Imputation in the Sociology of Knowledge'. *Ethics, 51*, 200-19.

Child, A. (1944). 'The Problem of Imputation Resolved'. *Ethics, 54*, 96-109.

Chubin, D. E. (1976). 'State of the Field: the Conceptualization of Scientific Specialties'. *Sociological Quarterly, 17*, 448-76.

Cicourel, A. V. (1964). *Method and Measurement in Sociology.* New York: Free Press of Glencoe.

Clapperton, J. H. (1885). *Scientific Meliorism and the Evolution of Happiness.* London: Kegan Paul.

Clark, T. N. (1967). 'Discontinuities in Social Research: The Case of the *Cours Elémentaire de Statistique Administrative'. Journal of the History of the Behavioral Sciences, 3*, 3-16.

Clark, T. N. (1972). 'The Stages of Scientific Institutionalization'. *International Social Science Journal, 24*, 658-71.

Clark, T. N. (1973). *Prophets and Patrons: The French University and the Emergence of the Social Sciences.* Cambridge, Mass.: Harvard University Press.

Cobb, J. A. (1913). 'Human Fertility'. *Eugenics Review, 4*, 379-82.

Cock, A. G. (1973). 'William Bateson, Mendelism and Biometry'. *Journal of the History of Biology, 6*, 1-36.

Cock, A. G. (1979). 'Anna Bateson of Bashley: Britain's First Professional Woman Gardener'. *Hampshire: the County Magazine, 19*, 59-62.

Cole, S. (1972). 'Continuity and Institutionalization in Science: A Case Study of Failure'. In Oberschall (ed.) (1972, 73-129).

Coleman, W. (1970). 'Bateson and Chromosomes: Conservative Thought in Science'. *Centaurus, 15*, 228-314.

Cowan, R. S. (1968). 'Sir Francis Galton and the Continuity of the Germ-Plasm: a Biological Idea with Political Roots'. *Actes du XIIe Congrès International d'Histoire des Sciences, 8*, 181-6.

Cowan, R. S. (1972a). 'Francis Galton's Statistical Ideas: the Influence of Eugenics'. *Isis, 63*, 509-28.

Cowan, R. S. (1972b). 'Francis Galton's Contribution to Genetics'. *Journal of the History of Biology, 5*, 389-412.

Cowan, R. S. (1977). 'Nature and Nurture: the Interplay of Biology and Politics in the Work of Francis Galton'. *Studies in the History of Biology, 1*, 133-208.

[Crew, F. A. E.] (1933). 'State Policies of Eugenic Sterilisation'. *Nature, 132*, 221-22.

Crew, F. A. E. (1967). 'Reginald Crundall Punnett 1875-1967'. *Biographical Memoirs of Fellows of the Royal Society, 13*, 309-26.

Crombie, A. C. (ed.) (1963). *Scientific Change.* London: Heinemann.

Cronwright-Schreiner, S. C. (ed.) (1924). *The Letters of Olive Schreiner.* London: Unwin.

Crowther, J. G. (1952). *British Scientists of the Twentieth Century.* London: Routledge and Kegan Paul.

Cullen, M. J. (1975). *The Statistical Movement in Early Victorian Britain.* Hassocks, Sussex: Harvester.

Czuber, E. (1891). *Theorie der Beobachtungsfehler.* Leipzig: Teubner.

Darbishire, A. (1902-4). 'On the Result of Crossing Japanese Waltzing Mice with European Albino Races'. *Biometrika, 2,* 101-4, 165-73, 282-5 and *3,* 1-51.

Darden, L. (1976). 'Reasoning in Scientific Change: Charles Darwin, Hugo de Vries and the Discovery of Segregation'. *Studies in the History and Philosophy of Science, 7,* 127-69.

Darden, L. (1977). 'William Bateson and the Promise of Mendelism'. *Journal of the History of Biology, 10,* 87-106.

Darwin, C. (1859). *On the Origin of Species.* London: John Murray.

Darwin, C. (1868). *The Variation of Animals and Plants under Domestication.* London: John Murray.

Darwin, L. (1926). *The Need for Eugenic Reform.* London: John Murray.

Davenport, C. D. (1903). '[Report of the] Committee on Variation'. *Science,* n.s. *17,* 46.

Davenport, C. D. (1905). 'Species and Varieties, their Origin by Mutation. By Hugo de Vries'. *Science,* n.s. *22,* 369-72.

Davenport, C. D. (1910). *Eugenics.* New York: Holt.

Davenport, C. D. (1911). *Heredity in Relation to Eugenics.* New York: Holt.

David, F. N. (1969). *Games, Gods and Gambling: A History of Probability and Statistical Ideas.* London: Griffin.

Davin, A. (1978). 'Imperialism and Motherhood'. *History Workshop,* issue 5, 9-65.

Davis, J. A. (1971). *Elementary Survey Analysis.* Englewood Cliffs, N.J.: Prentice Hall.

Dawson, M. M. (1914). 'The Development of Insurance Mathematics'. In L. W. Zartman and W. H. Price, *Yale Readings in Insurance: Life Insurance,* 95-119. New Haven, Conn.: Yale University Press.

De Marrais, R. (1974). 'The Double-Edged Effect of Sir Francis Galton: a Search for the Motives in the Biometrician-Mendelian Debate'. *Journal of the History of Biology, 7,* 141-74.

De Moivre, A. (1738). *The Doctrine of Chances.* Second edition. London: Woodfall.

De Vries, H. (1901-3). *Die Mutationstheorie.* Leipzig: Von Veit.

Dickson, D. (1974). *Alternative Technology and the Politics of Technical Change.* London: Fontana.

Dolby, R. G. A. (1976). 'The Case of Physical Chemistry'. In Lemaine *et al.* (eds) (1976, 63-73).

Durant, J. R. (1979). 'Scientific Naturalism and Social Reform in the Thought of Alfred Russel Wallace'. *British Journal for the History of Science, 12,* 31-58.

Eagleton, T. (1976). *Marxism and Literary Criticism.* London: Methuen.

Eder, M. D. (1908). 'Good Breeding or Eugenics?' *The New Age,* 23 May, 13 June, 18 July, 25 July.

Edge, D. and Mulkay, M. (1975). 'Fallstudien zu wissenschaftlichen Spezialgebieten'. *Kölner Zeitschrift für Soziologie und Sozial-psychologie,* Sonderheft 18 *(Wissenschaftssoziologie),* 197-229.

Edge, D. and Mulkay, M. (1976). *Astronomy Transformed: the Emergence of Radio Astronomy in Britain.* New York: Wiley.

Edgeworth, F. Y. (1877). *New and Old Methods of Ethics*. Oxford: Parker.

Edgeworth, F. Y. (1881). *Mathematical Psychics*. London: Kegan Paul.

Edgeworth, F. Y. (1883a). 'The Law of Error'. *Phil. Mag.*,
series 5, *16*, 300-9.

Edgeworth, F. Y. (1883b). 'The Method of Least Squares'.
Phil. Mag., series 5, *16*, 360-75.

Edgeworth, F. Y. (1884). 'The Philosophy of Chance'. *Mind, 9*, 223-35.

Edgeworth, F. Y. (1885). 'Methods of Statistics'. *J.R.S.S.*,
Jubilee Volume, 181-217.

Edgeworth, F. Y. (1887). *Metretike: or the Method of Measuring
Probability and Utility*. London: Temple.

Edgeworth, F. Y. (1892a). 'Correlated Averages'. *Phil. Mag.*,
series 5, *34*, 190-204.

Edgeworth, F. Y. (1892b). 'The Law of Error and Correlated Averages'.
Phil. Mag., series 5, *34*, 429-38 and 518-26.

Edgeworth, F. Y. (1893a). 'Statistical Correlation between Social
Phenomena'. *J.R.S.S., 56*, 670-5.

Edgeworth, F. Y. (1893b). 'A New Method of treating Correlated
Averages'. *Phil. Mag.*, series 5, *35*, 63-4.

Edgeworth, F. Y. (1893c). 'Exercises in the Calculation of Errors'.
Phil. Mag., series 5, *36*, 98-111.

Edgeworth, F. Y. (1893d). 'Note on the Calculation of Correlation
between Organs'. *Phil. Mag.*, series 5, *36*, 350-1.

Edgeworth, F. Y. (1908-9). 'On the Probable Errors of Frequency-
Constants'. *J.R.S.S., 71*, 381-97, 499-512, 651-78. Addendum,
J.R.S.S., 72, 81-90.

Edgeworth, F. Y. (1912). [Contribution to discussion of Yule (1912).]
J.R.S.S., 75, 643-4.

Edwards, A. W. F. (1974). 'The History of Likelihood'. *International
Statistical Review, 42*, 9-15.

Ehrenreich, B. and J. (1976). 'The Professional-Managerial Class'.
Radical America, 11, 7-31.

Eisenhart, C. (1974). 'Pearson, Karl'. In C. C. Gillispie (ed.), *Dictionary of
Scientific Biography, 10*, 447-73. New York: Charles Scribner's Sons.

Elesh, D. (1972). 'The Manchester Statistical Society: a Case Study of
a Discontinuity in the History of Empirical Social Research'.
Journal of the History of the Behavioral Sciences, 8, 280-301, 407-417.

Eugenics Education Society (1911, 1912, 1914, 1915). *Annual Reports*.
London: E.E.S.

Eugenics Society (1977a). *List of Fellows and Members*.
London: Eugenics Society.

Eugenics Society (1977b). *Annual Report*. London: Eugenics Society.

Eyler, J. M. (1973). 'William Farr on the Cholera: the Sanitarian's Disease
Theory and the Statistician's Method'. *Journal of the History of
Medicine and Allied Sciences, 28*, 79-100.

Eyler, J. M. (1976). 'Mortality Statistics and Victorian Health Policy:
Program and Criticism'. *Bulletin of the History of Medicine, 50*, 335-55.

F[airgrieve], M. M'C. (1931). 'J. D. Hamilton Dickson, M.A.'
Proceedings of the Royal Society of Edinburgh, 51, 205-6.

Farrall, L. A. (1970). *The Origins and Growth of the English Eugenics Movement 1865-1925*. Ph.D. thesis: Indiana University, Bloomington.

Farrall, L. A. (1975). 'Controversy and Conflict in Science: a Case Study – the English Biometric School and Mendel's Laws'. *Social Studies of Science, 5*, 269-301.

Fechner, G. T. (1874). 'Ueber den Ausgangswerth der kleinsten Abweichungssumme, dessen Bestimmung, Verwendung und Verall-gemeinerung'. *Abhandlungen der Mathematisch-Physischen Classe der Königlich Sächsischen Gesellschaft der Wissenschaften, 18*, 1-76.

Fee, E. (n.d.). 'Women and their Skulls'. Unpublished paper.

Feuer, L. S. (1971). 'The Social Roots of Einstein's Theory of Relativity'. *Annals of Science, 27*, 277-98, 313-44.

Feyerabend, P. K. (1962). 'Explanation, Reduction and Empiricism'. In H. Feigl and G. Maxwell (eds), *Scientific Explanation, Space and Time (Minnesota Studies in the Philosophy of Science, 3)*, 28-97. Minneapolis: University of Minnesota Press.

Fisher, C. S. (1967). 'The Last Invariant Theorists'. *Archives Européennes de Sociologie, 8*, 216-44.

Fisher, R. A. (1911). 'Heredity, comparing the Methods of Biometry and Mendelism'. Paper read to Cambridge University Eugenics Society. Reprinted in B. Norton and E. S. Pearson (1976, 155-62).

Fisher, R. A. (1912a). 'Evolution and Society'. Paper read to Cambridge University Eugenics Society.

Fisher, R. A. (1912b). 'Some Hopes of a Eugenist'. Paper read to Cambridge University Eugenics Society. Revised version published as Fisher (1914).

Fisher, R. A. (1912c). 'On an Absolute Criterion for fitting Frequency Curves'. *Messenger of Mathematics, 41*, 155-60.

Fisher, R. A. (1914). 'Some Hopes of a Eugenist'. *Eugenics Review, 5*, 309-15.

Fisher, R. A. (1915). 'Frequency Distribution of the Values of the Correlation Coefficient in Samples from an Indefinitely Large Population'. *Biometrika, 10*, 507-21.

Fisher, R. A. (1917). 'Positive Eugenics'. *Eugenics Review, 9*, 206-12.

Fisher, R. A. (1918a). 'The Correlation between Relatives on the Supposition of Mendelian Inheritance'. *Transactions of the Royal Society of Edinburgh, 52*, 399-433.

Fisher, R. A. (1918b). 'The Causes of Human Variability'. *Eugenics Review, 10*, 213-20.

Fisher, R. A. (1920). 'A Mathematical Examination of the Methods of Determining the Accuracy of an Observation by the Mean Error, and by the Mean Square Error'. *Monthly Notices of the Royal Astronomical Society, 80*, 758-70.

Fisher, R. A. (1921a). 'On the "Probable Error" of a Coefficient of Correlation deduced from a Small Sample'. *Metron, 1*, 3-32.

Fisher, R. A. (1921b). 'Studies in Crop Variation. I. An Examination of the Yield of Dressed Grain from Broadbalk'. *Journal of Agricultural Science, 11*, 107-35.

Fisher, R. A. (1922a). 'On the Mathematical Foundations of Theoretical Statistics'. *Phil. Trans.*, A, *222*, 309-68.

Fisher, R. A. (1922b). 'On the Interpretation of χ^2 from Contingency Tables, and the Calculation of P'. *J.R.S.S.*, *85*, 87-94.

Fisher, R. A. (1924a). 'The Elimination of Mental Defect'. *Eugenics Review*, *16*, 114-16.

Fisher, R. A. (1924b). 'The Biometrical Study of Heredity'. *Eugenics Review*, *16*, 189-210.

Fisher, R. A. (1925). *Statistical Methods for Research Workers.* Edinburgh: Oliver and Boyd.

Fisher, R. A. (1927). 'On some Objections to Mimicry Theory: Statistical and Genetic'. *Proceedings of the Royal Entomological Society of London*, *75*, 269-78.

Fisher, R. A. (1930). *The Genetical Theory of Natural Selection.* Oxford: Clarendon.

Fisher, R. A. (1932). 'Family Allowances in the Contemporary Economic Situation'. *Eugenics Review*, *24*, 87-95.

Fisher, R. A. (1934). 'Adaptations and Mutations'. *School Science Review*, *15*, 294-301.

Fisher, R. A. (1935). *The Design of Experiments.* Edinburgh and London: Oliver and Boyd.

Fisher, R. A. (1938). 'The Character of Sheppard's Work'. *Annals of Eugenics*, *8*, 11-12.

Fisher, R. A. (1939). '"Student"'. *Annals of Eugenics*, *9*, 1-9.

Fisher, R. A. (1943). 'The Birthrate and Family Allowances'. *Agenda*, *2*, 124-33.

Fisher, R. A. (1948). 'Biometry'. *Biometrics*, *4*, 217-19.

Fisher, R. A. (1952). 'Statistical Methods in Genetics'. *Heredity*, *6*, 1-12.

Fisher, R. A. (1953). 'Croonian Lecture. Population Genetics'. *Proc. Roy. Soc.*, B, *141*, 510-53.

Fisher, R. A. and MacKenzie, W. A. (1923). 'Studies in Crop Variation. II. The Manurial Response of Different Potato Varieties'. *Journal of Agricultural Science*, *13*, 311-20.

Fisher, R. A. and Stock, C. S. (1915). 'Cuénot on Pre-adaptation. A Criticism'. *Eugenics Review*, *7*, 46-61.

Forbes, E. G. (ed.) (1978). *Human Implications of Scientific Advance. Proceedings of the XVth International Congress of the History of Science.* Edinburgh: Edinburgh University Press.

Forman, P. (1971). 'Weimar Culture, Causality, and Quantum Theory, 1912-1927: Adaptation by German Physicists and Mathematicians to a Hostile Intellectual Environment'. *Historical Studies in the Physical Sciences*, *3*, 1-115.

Forrest, D. W. (1974). *Francis Galton: the Life and Work of a Victorian Genius.* London: Elek.

Forsyth, A. R. (1929). 'J. W. L. Glaisher'. *Journal of the London Mathematical Society*, *4*, 101-12.

Froggatt, P. and Nevin, N. C. (1971a). 'Galton's "Law of Ancestral Heredity": its Influence on the Early Development of Human Genetics'. *History of Science*, *10*, 1-27.

Froggatt, P. and Nevin, N. C. (1971b). 'The "Law of Ancestral Heredity" and the Mendelian-Ancestrian Controversy in England, 1889-1906'. *Journal of Medical Genetics, 8,* 1-36.

Galton, F. (1865). 'Hereditary Talent and Character'. *Macmillan's Magazine, 12,* 157-66 and 318-27.

Galton, F. (1869). *Hereditary Genius.* London: Macmillan.

Galton, F. (1874). *English Men of Science: their Nature and Nurture.* London: Macmillan.

Galton, F. (1875a). 'Statistics by Intercomparison, with Remarks on the Law of Frequency of Error'. *Phil. Mag.,* series 4, *49,* 33-46.

Galton, F. (1875b). 'A Theory of Heredity'. *Contemporary Review, 27,* 80-95.

Galton, F. (1877). 'Typical Laws of Heredity'. *Proceedings of the Royal Institution, 8,* 282-301.

Galton, F. (1879). 'The Geometric Mean, in Vital and Social Statistics'. *Proc. Roy. Soc., 29,* 365-7.

Galton, F. (1882). 'The Anthropometric Laboratory'. *Fortnightly Review,* n.s. *31,* 332-8.

Galton, F. (1883). *Inquiries into Human Faculty and its Development.* London: Macmillan.

Galton, F. (1885a). [Address to Anthropological Section of the British Association.] *Nature, 32,* 507-10.

Galton, F. (1885b). 'On the Anthropometric Laboratory at the Late International Health Exhibition'. *Journal of the Anthropological Institute, 14,* 205-19.

Galton, F. (1885c). 'Regression towards Mediocrity in Hereditary Stature'. *Journal of the Anthropological Institute, 15,* 246-63.

Galton, F. (1886). 'Family Likeness in Stature'. *Proc. Roy. Soc., 40,* 42-73. Includes appendix by J. D. Hamilton Dickson, *ibid.,* 63-6.

Galton, F. (1888a). 'Personal Identification and Description [Substance of Lecture at Royal Institution, 25 May 1888]'. *Nature, 38,* 173-7, 201-2.

Galton, F. (1888b). 'Co-relations and their Measurement, chiefly from Anthropometric Data'. *Proc. Roy. Soc., 45,* 135-45.

Galton, F. (1889a). [President's Address.] *Journal of the Anthropological Institute, 18,* 401-19.

Galton, F. (1889b). *Natural Inheritance.* London: Macmillan.

Galton, F. (1889c). 'On the Principle and Methods of Assigning Marks for Bodily Efficiency'. *British Association Report,* 474-7.

Galton, F. (1908). *Memories of my Life.* Second edition. London: Methuen.

Galton, F. (1909). *Essays in Eugenics.* London: Eugenics Education Society.

Gantillon, P. J. F. (ed.) (1852). *A Collection of Cambridge Examination Papers in Arithmetic, Algebra and Plane Trigonometry.* Cambridge: Hall.

Garber, E. (1973). 'Aspects of the Introduction of Probability into Physics'. *Centaurus, 17,* 11-39.

Garnett, D. (1953). *The Golden Echo.* London: Chatto and Windus.

Gilbert, B. (1966). *The Evolution of National Insurance in Great Britain. The Origins of the Welfare State*. London: Michael Joseph.

Gillispie, C. C. (1963). 'Intellectual Factors in the Background of Analysis by Probabilities'. In A. C. Crombie (ed.) (1963, 431-53).

Gillispie, C. C. (1972). 'Probability and Politics: Laplace, Condorcet, and Turgot'. *Proceedings of the American Philosophical Society, 116*, 1-20.

Gini, C. (1926). 'The Contributions of Italy to Modern Statistical Methods'. *J.R.S.S., 89*, 703-24.

Gini, C. (1927). 'The Scientific Basis of Fascism'. *Political Science Quarterly, 42*, 99-115.

Gini, C. (1930). 'The Italian Demographic Problem and the Fascist Policy on Population'. *Journal of Political Economy, 38*, 682-97.

Glaisher, J. W. L. (1872). 'On the Law of Facility of Errors of Observations, and on the Method of Least Squares'. *Memoirs of the Royal Astronomical Society, 39*, 75-124.

Goldmann, L. (1964). *The Hidden God: A Study of Tragic Vision in the Pensées of Pascal and the Tragedies of Racine*. London: Routledge and Kegan Paul.

Gollwitzer, H. (1969). *Europe in the Age of Imperialism: 1880-1914*. London: Thames and Hudson.

Goodman, L. A. and Kruskal, W. H. (1954-59). 'Measures of Association for Cross Classifications'. *Journal of the American Statistical Association, 49*, 732-64, and *54*, 123-63.

Gordon, L. (1977). *Woman's Body, Woman's Right: A Social History of Birth Control in America*. Harmondsworth: Penguin.

Gosset, W. S. ['Student'] (1907). 'On the Error of Counting with a Haemacytometer'. *Biometrika, 5*. Reprinted in E. S. Pearson and J. Wishart (eds) (1958, 1-10).

Gosset, W. S. ['Student'] (1908a). 'The Probable Error of a Mean'. *Biometrika, 6*. Reprinted in E. S. Pearson and J. Wishart (eds) (1958, 11-34).

Gosset, W. S. ['Student'] (1908b). 'Probable Error of a Correlation Coefficient'. *Biometrika, 6*. Reprinted in E. S. Pearson and J. Wishart (eds) (1958, 35-42).

Gouldner, A. W. (1978). 'The New Class Project'. *Theory and Society, 6*, 153-203 and 343-89.

Gramsci, A. (1971). *Selections from the Prison Notebooks*. London: Lawrence and Wishart.

Greenwood, M. (1904). 'A First Study of the Weight, Variability, and Correlation of the Human Viscera, with special reference to the Healthy and Diseased Heart'. *Biometrika, 3*, 63-83.

Greenwood, M. (1909). 'The Problem of Marital Infection in Pulmonary Tuberculosis'. *Proceedings of the Royal Society of Medicine, 2*, Epidemiological Section, 259-68.

Greenwood, M. (1912). 'Infant Mortality and its Administrative Control'. *Eugenics Review, 4*, 284-304.

Greenwood, M. (1913). 'On Errors of Random Sampling in certain cases not suitable for the application of a "Normal" Curve of Frequency'. *Biometrika, 9*, 69-90.

Greenwood, M. (1936). *The Medical Dictator and other Biographical Studies*. London: Williams and Norgate.

Greenwood, M. (1948). *Medical Statistics from Graunt to Farr*. Cambridge: Cambridge University Press.

Greenwood, M. and Yule, G. U. (1914). 'On the Determination of Size of Family and of the Distribution of Characters in Order of Birth from Samples taken through Members of the Sibships'. *J.R.S.S.*, *77*, 179-97.

Greenwood, M. and Yule, G. U. (1915). 'The Statistics of Anti-typhoid and Anti-cholera Inoculations, and the Interpretation of such Statistics in general'. *Proceedings of the Royal Society of Medicine, 8*, Epidemiological Section. Reprinted in A. Stuart and M. G. Kendall (eds) (1971, 171-248).

Griffith, B. C. and Mullins, N. C. (1972). 'Coherent Social Groups in Scientific Change'. *Science, 177*, 959-64.

Habermas, J. (1971). 'Technology and Science as "Ideology"'. In Habermas, *Toward a Rational Society: Student Protest, Science and Politics*. London: Heinemann.

Habermas, J. (1972). *Knowledge and Human Interests*. London: Heinemann.

Hacking, I. (1971a). 'Jacques Bernoulli's *Art of Conjecturing*'. *British Journal for the Philosophy of Science, 22*, 209-29.

Hacking, I. (1971b). 'Equipossibility Theories of Probability'. *British Journal for the Philosophy of Science, 22*, 339-55.

Hacking, I. (1972). 'The Logic of Pascal's Wager'. *American Philosophical Quarterly, 9*, 186-92.

Hacking, I. (1975). *The Emergence of Probability*. London: Cambridge University Press.

Hagstrom, W. O. (1965). *The Scientific Community*. New York: Basic Books.

Haldane, J. B. S. (1932). *The Causes of Evolution*. London, New York and Toronto: Longmans, Green.

Haldane, J. B. S. (1957). 'Karl Pearson, 1857 (1957). A Centenary Lecture delivered at University College London'. *Biometrika, 44*. Reprinted in E. S. Pearson and M. G. Kendall (eds) (1970, 427-37).

Haller, M. H. (1963). *Eugenics: Hereditarian Attitudes in American Thought*. New Brunswick, N.J.: Rutgers University Press.

Halliday, R. J. (1971). 'Social Darwinism: a Definition'. *Victorian Studies, 14*, 389-405.

Hankins, T. L. (1979). 'In Defence of Biography: the Use of Biography in the History of Science'. *History of Science, 17*, 1-16.

Hardy, G. H. (1967). *A Mathematician's Apology*. Cambridge: Cambridge University Press.

Harwood, J. (1979). 'Heredity, Environment, and the Legitimation of Social Policy'. In Barnes and Shapin (eds) (1979, 231-48).

Halfand, M. S. (1977). 'T. H. Huxley's *Evolution and Ethics*: The Politics of Evolution and the Evolution of Politics'. *Victorian Studies, 20*, 159-77.

Henderson, P. (1976). 'Class Structure and the Concept of Intelligence'.
In R. Dale *et al.* (eds), *Schooling and Capitalism*, 142-51.
London and Henley: Routledge and Kegan Paul.

Herbert, S. (1910). *The First Principles of Heredity*. London: Black.

Heron, D. (1906). 'On the Relations of Fertility in Man to Social Status'.
Studies in National Deterioration, I. London: Dulau.

Heron, D. (1910). 'The Influence of Defective Physique and Unfavourable
Home Environment on the Intelligence of School Children'. *Eugenics
Laboratory Memoirs*, VII. London: Dulau.

Heron, D. (1911). 'The Danger of Certain Formulae Suggested as
Substitutes for the Correlation Coefficient'. *Biometrika, 8,* 109-22.

Heron, D. (1913). 'Mendelism and the Problem of Mental Defect.
I. A Criticism of Recent American Work'. *Questions of the Day
and the Fray*, VII. London: Dulau.

Heron, D. (1919). [Contribution to discussion of paper by L. Darwin.]
J.R.S.S., 82, 27-9.

Herschel, J. (1850). [Review of Quetelet (1849).] *Edinburgh Review,
92,* 1-57.

Hesse, M. B. (1963). 'Commentary [on Gillispie (1963)]'.
In A. C. Crombie (ed.) (1963, 471-6).

Hilts, V. (1967). *Statist and Statistician: Three Studies in the History of
Nineteenth-Century English Statistical Thought*. Ph.D. thesis:
Harvard University.

Hilts, V. (1970). 'William Farr (1807-1883) and the "Human Unit"'.
Victorian Studies, 14, 143-50.

Hilts, V. (1973). 'Statistics and Social Science'. In R. N. Giere and
R. S. Westfall (eds), *Foundations of the Scientific Method: the Nineteenth Century*, 206-33. Bloomington: University of Indiana Press.

Hilts, V. (1978). 'Aliis Exterendum, or the Origins of the Statistical
Society of London'. *Isis, 69,* 21-43.

Hobhouse, L. T. (1911). *Social Evolution and Political Theory*.
New York: Columbia University Press.

Hobsbawm, E. J. (1968). 'The Fabians Reconsidered'.
In Hobsbawm, *Labouring Men: Studies in the History of Labour*,
250-71. London: Weidenfeld and Nicolson.

Hobson, J. A. (1905). *Imperialism: A Study*. London: Constable.

Hodgkinson, R. G. (1968). 'Social Medicine and the Growth of Statistical
Information'. In F. N. L. Poynter (ed.) *Medicine and Science in the
1860s*, 183-98. London: Wellcome Institute of the History of Medicine.

Hofstader, R. (1968). *Social Darwinism in American Thought*.
Boston: Beacon.

Hogben, L. (1919a). 'The Russian Novel and the New Age'.
Socialist Review, 16, 56-60.

Hogben, L. (1919b). 'Modern Heredity and Social Science'.
Socialist Review, 16, 147-56.

Hogben, L. (1950). 'Major Greenwood, 1880-1949'. *Obituary Notices
of Fellows of the Royal Society, 7,* 139-54.

Hooker, R. H. (1912). [Contribution to discussion of Yule (1912).]
J.R.S.S., 75, 646-7.

Huxley, T. H. (1893). *Evolution and Ethics*. London: Macmillan.
Hyde, W. J. (1956). 'The Socialism of H. G. Wells in the early Twentieth Century'. *Journal of the History of Ideas, 17*, 217-34.
Inge, W. R. (1909). 'Some Moral Aspects of Eugenics'. *Eugenics Review, 1*, 26-36.
Inge, W. R. (1921). 'Eugenics and Religion'. *Eugenics Review, 12*, 257-65.
Inter-Departmental Committee on Physical Deterioration (1904). *Report, 1 (Report and Appendix)*. London: H.M.S.O. Cd. 2175.
Irwin, J. O. (1966). 'Leon Isserlis, M.A., D.Sc. (1881-1966)'. *J.R.S.S.*, A, *129*, 612-6.
Jacyna, L. S. (1980). 'Science and Social Order in the Thought of A. J. Balfour'. *Isis, 71*, 11-34.
Jeffreys, H. (1974). 'Fisher and Inverse Probability'. *International Statistical Review, 42*, 1-3.
Johannsen, W. (1909). *Elemente der exakten Erblichkeitslehre*. Jena: Fischer.
Johnson, H. G. (n.d.). *F. Y. Edgeworth: A Bibliography*. Unpublished. Copies in libraries of British Museum, Royal Statistical Society, London School of Economics, All Souls, Oxford, the Bodleian and the University Library, Cambridge.
Johnson, T. (1977). 'The Professions in the Class Structure'. In R. Sease (ed.) *Industrial Society: Class Cleavage and Control*, 93-110. London: Allen and Unwin.
Johnston, R. and Robbins, D. (1977). 'The Development of Specialties in Industrialised Science'. *Sociological Review, 25*, 87-108.
Jones, G. S. (1971). *Outcast London*. Oxford: Clarendon.
Kendall, D. G. (1966). 'Branching Processes since 1873'. *Journal of the London Mathematical Society, 41*. Reprinted in M. G. Kendall and R. L. Plackett (eds) (1977, 383-404).
Kendall, M. G. (1943). *The Advanced Theory of Statistics*. London: Griffin.
Kendall, M. G. (1952). 'George Udny Yule, 1871-1951'. *J.R.S.S.*, A, 115. Reprinted in A. Stuart and M. G. Kendall (eds) (1971, 1-5).
Kendall, M. G. (1968). 'Francis Ysidro Edgeworth, 1845-1926'. *Biometrika, 55*. Reprinted in E. S. Pearson and M. G. Kendall (eds) (1970, 257-63).
Kendall, M. G. (1971). 'The Work of Ernst Abbe'. *Biometrika, 58*, 369-73.
Kendall, M. G. and Doig, A. G. (1968). *Bibliography of Statistical Literature Pre-1940*. Edinburgh: Oliver and Boyd.
Kendall, M. G. and Plackett, R. L. (eds) (1977). *Studies in the History of Statistics and Probability, 2*. London: Griffin.
Kevles, D. J. (1978). 'Genetics in the United States and Great Britain, 1890 to 1930: Queries and Speculations'. *Humanities Working Paper* 15. Pasadena: California Institute of Technology, Division of the Humanities and Social Sciences.
Kevles, D. J. (1979). 'Eugenics in the United States and Britain, 1890 to 1930: a Comparative Analysis'. *Humanities Working Paper* 19. Pasadena: California Institute of Technology, Division of the Humanities and Social Sciences.

Keynes, J. M. (1926). 'Francis Ysidro Edgeworth 1845-1926'. *Economic Journal, 36*, 140-53.

Kidd, B. (1895). *Social Evolution*. London: Macmillan.

Knorr, K. *et al.* (eds) (1975). *Determinants and Controls of Scientific Development*. Dordrecht: Reidel.

Koren, J. (ed.) (1970). *The History of Statistics: their Development and Progress in Many Countries*. New York: Franklin. First published in 1918.

Kornhauser, W. (1962). *Scientists in Industry: Conflict and Accommodation*. Berkeley and Los Angeles: University of California Press.

Krohn, W. and Schäfer, W. (1976). 'The Origins and Structure of Agricultural Chemistry'. In Lemaine *et al.* (eds) (1976, 27-52).

Kuhn, T. S. (1970). *The Structure of Scientific Revolutions*. Chicago: University of Chicago Press.

Lakatos, I. (1974). 'History of Science and its Rational Reconstructions'. In Y. Elkana (ed.) *The Interaction between Science and Philosophy*, 195-241. Atlantic Highlands: Humanities Press.

Lancaster, H. O. (1966). 'Forerunners of the Pearson χ^2'. *Australian Journal of Statistics, 8*, 117-26.

Lancaster, H. O. (1968). *Bibliography of Statistical Bibliographies*. Edinburgh: Oliver and Boyd.

Lancaster, H. O. (1969). *The Chi Squared Distribution*. New York: Wiley.

Lancaster, H. O. (1972). 'Development of the Notion of Statistical Dependence'. *Mathematics Chronicle, 2*. Reprinted in M. G. Kendall and R. L. Plackett (eds) (1977, 293-308).

Lankester, E. R. (1896). 'The Utility of Specific Characters'. *Nature, 54*, 365-6.

Laplace, P-S., Marquis de (1814). *Théorie Analytique des Probabilités*. Second edition. Paris: Courcier.

Laski, H. J. (1912). 'A Mendelian View of Racial Heredity'. *Biometrika, 8*, 424-30.

Laudan, L. (1973). 'Induction and Probability in the Nineteenth Century'. In P. Suppes (ed.), *Proceedings of the Fourth International Congress for Logic, Methodology and Philosophy of Science*, 429-38. Amsterdam: North-Holland.

Laudan, L. (1977). *Progress and its Problems: towards a Theory of Scientific Growth*. London and Henley: Routledge and Kegan Paul.

Law, J. (1973). 'The Development of Specialties in Science: the Case of X-Ray Protein Crystallography'. *Science Studies, 3*, 275-303.

Law, J. and Barnes, B. (1976). 'Research Note: Areas of Ignorance in Normal Science: a Note on Mulkay's "Three Models of Scientific Development"'. *Sociological Review, 24*, 115-24.

Lazarsfeld, P. F. (1961). 'Notes on the History of Quantification in Sociology – Trends, Sources and Problems'. *Isis, 52*, 277-333.

Lécuyer, B. and Oberschall, A. R. (1968). 'The Early History of Social Research'. *International Encyclopedia of the Social Sciences, 15*, 36-53.

Lemaine, G. *et al.* (eds) (1976). *Perspectives on the Emergence of Scientific Disciplines*. The Hague and Paris: Mouton.

Lenin, V. I. (1947). *What is to be done?* Moscow: Progress.

Lenin, V. I. (1970) *Materialism and Empirio-Criticism: Critical Comments on a Reactionary Philosophy*. Moscow: Progress.

Levidow, L. (1978). 'A Marxist Critique of the IQ Debate'. *Radical Science Journal*, number 6/7, 12-79.

Levitas, R. A. (1976). 'The Social Location of Ideas'. *Sociological Review*, 24, 545-57.

Lexis, W. (1893). 'Statistik'. In W. Lexis (ed.), *Die Deutschen Universitäten: für die Universitätsausstellung in Chicago*, 1, 598-603. Berlin: Asher.

Lindley, D. V. (1965). *Introduction to Probability and Statistics from a Bayesian Viewpoint*. Cambridge: Cambridge University Press.

Love, R. (1979). '"Alice in Eugenics-Land": Feminism and Eugenics in the Scientific Careers of Alice Lee and Ethel Elderton'. *Annals of Science*, 36, 145-58.

Ludmerer, K. M. (1972). *Genetics and American Society: A Historical Appraisal*. Baltimore: Johns Hopkins University Press.

Lukács, G. (1971). *History and Class Consciousness*. London: Merlin.

Lupton, S. (1898). *Notes on Observations*. London: Macmillan.

Lynch, P. and Vaizey, J. (1960). *Guinness's Brewery in the Irish Economy 1759-1876*. Cambridge: Cambridge University Press.

MacAlister, D. (1879). 'The Law of the Geometric Mean'. *Proc. Roy. Soc.*, 29, 367-76.

MacAlister, E. F. B. (1935). *Sir Donald MacAlister of Tarbet*. London: Macmillan.

McAulay, R. (1978). 'Velikovsky and the Infrastructure of Science: the Metaphysics of a Close Encounter'. *Theory and Society*, 6, 313-42.

MacBride, E. W. (1924). *An Introduction to the Study of Heredity*. London: Thornton Butterworth.

MacDowell, E. C. (1946). 'Charles Benedict Davenport, 1866-1944. A Study of Conflicting Influences'. *Bios*, 17, 3-50.

MacKenzie, D. (1976). 'Eugenics in Britain'. *Social Studies of Science*, 6, 499-532.

MacKenzie, D. and Barnes, B. (1975). 'Biometriker versus Mendelianer. Eine Kontroverse und ihre Erklärung'. *Kölner Zeitschrift für Soziologie und Sozialpsychologie*, Sonderheft 18 *(Wissenschafts-soziologie)*, 165-96.

McLaren, A. (1978). *Birth Control in Nineteenth-Century England*. London: Croom Helm.

MacLeod, R. M. (1967a). 'The Edge of Hope: Social Policy and Chronic Alcoholism 1870-1900'. *Journal of the History of Medicine and Allied Sciences*, 22, 215-45.

MacLeod, R. M. (1967b). 'Law, Medicine and Public Opinion: the Resistance to Compulsory Health Legislation, 1870-1907'. *Public Law*, Summer 1967, 107-28 and Autumn 1967, 189-211.

McMullen, L. (1939). '"Student" as a Man'. *Biometrika, 30*. Reprinted in E. S. Pearson and M. G. Kendall (eds) (1970, 355-60).

McMullen, L. (ed.) (n.d.). *Letters from W. S. Gosset to R. A. Fisher, 1915-1936*. Privately printed by Arthur Guinness Son & Co. (Dublin) Ltd.

MacPherson, G. S. (1973). 'Aspects of the Italian Eugenics Movement'. Unpublished paper. Department of the History and Sociology of Science, University of Pennsylvania.

Mahalanobis, P. C. (1938). 'Professor Ronald Aylmer Fisher'. *Sankhyā, 4.* Reprinted in *Biometrics, 20* (1964), 238-50.

Maistrov, L. E. (1974). *Probability Theory: A Historical Sketch.* New York: Academic Press.

Mannheim, K. (1953). 'Conservative Thought'. In Mannheim, *Essays in Sociology and Social Psychology*, 74-164. London: Routledge and Kegan Paul.

Martin, K. (1953). *Harold Laski*. London: Gollancz.

Marwick, A. (1967). *The Deluge: British Society and the First World War.* Harmondsworth: Penguin.

Marx, K. (1968). 'The Eighteenth Brumaire of Louis Bonaparte'. In Marx and Engels, *Selected Works in One Volume*, 97-180. London: Lawrence and Wishart.

Marx, K. (1976). *Capital: a Critique of Political Economy, 1.* Harmondsworth: Penguin.

Mayr, E. (1973). 'Essay Review. The Recent Historiography of Genetics'. *Journal of the History of Biology, 6*, 125-54.

Mendel, G. (1865). 'Versuche über Pflanzen-Hybriden'. English translation in W. Bateson (1902, 40-95).

Menzler, F. A. A. (1962). 'Sir William Palin Elderton, 1877-1962'. *J.R.S.S.*, A, *125*, 669-72.

Mercer, W. B. and Hall, A. D. (1911). 'The Experimental Error of Field Trials'. *Journal of Agricultural Science, 4*, 107-32.

Merriman, M. (1877). 'A List of Writings Relating to the Method of Least Squares, with Historical and Critical Notes'. *Transactions of the Connecticut Academy of Arts and Sciences, 4*, 151-232.

Merriman, M. (1901). *A Text-book on the Method of Least Squares.* Eighth edition. New York: Wiley.

Mitchell, B. R. and Deane, P. (1962). *Abstract of British Historical Statistics.* Cambridge: Cambridge University Press.

Mivart, St.G. (1895). 'Denominational Science'. *Fortnightly Review*, n.s. *58*, 423-38.

Moore, B. (1967). *Social Origins of Dictatorship and Democracy: Lord and Peasant in the Making of the Modern World.* Boston: Beacon.

Moran, P. A. P. and Smith, C. A. B. (1966). 'Commentary on R. A. Fisher's Paper on "The Correlation between Relatives on the Supposition of Mendelian Inheritance"'. *Eugenics Laboratory Memoirs*, XLI. London: Cambridge University Press.

Morant, G. M. (1939). *A Bibliography of the Statistical and other Writings of Karl Pearson.* Cambridge: Cambridge University Press.

Mulkay, M. (1972). *The Social Process of Innovation: a Study in the Sociology of Science.* London: Macmillan.

Mulkay, M. (1974). 'Conceptual Displacement and Migration in Science: a Prefatory Paper'. *Science Studies, 4*, 205-34.

Mulkay, M. (1975). 'Three Models of Scientific Development'. *Sociological Review, 23*, 509-26.

Mulkay, M. (1976a). 'Methodology in the Sociology of Science: Some Reflections on the Study of Radio Astronomy'. In Lemaine *et al.* (eds) (1976, 207-20).

Mulkay, M. (1976b). 'The Model of Branching'. *Sociological Review, 24,* 125-33.

Mulkay, M. and Edge, D. (1973). 'Cognitive, Technical and Social Factors in the Growth of Radio Astronomy'. *Social Science Information, 12,* 25-61.

Mulkay, M., Gilbert, G. N. and Woolgar, S. (1975). 'Problem Areas and Research Networks in Science'. *Sociology, 9,* 187-203.

Mullins, N. C. (1972). 'The Development of a Scientific Specialty: The Phage Group and the Origins of Molecular Biology'. *Minerva, 10,* 51-82.

Mullins, N. C. (1973a). 'The Development of Specialties in Social Science: the Case of Ethnomethodology'. *Science Studies, 3,* 245-73.

Mullins, N. C. (1973b). *Theories and Theory Groups in Contemporary American Sociology.* New York: Harper and Row.

Mullins, N. C. (1975). 'A Sociological Theory of Scientific Revolution'. In Knorr *et al.* (eds) (1975, 185-203).

National Birth-Rate Commission (1916). *The Declining Birth-Rate: its Causes and Effects.* London: Chapman and Hall.

Nature (1904). 'Zoology at the British Association'. *Nature, 70,* 538-41.

Norton, B. J. (1971). *Theories of Evolution of the Biometric School.* M.Sc Thesis: University of London.

Norton, B. J. (1973). 'The Biometric Defense of Darwinism'. *Journal of the History of Biology, 6,* 283-316.

Norton, B. J. (1975a). 'Biology and Philosophy: the Methodological Foundations of Biometry'. *Journal of the History of Biology, 8,* 85-93.

Norton, B. J. (1975b). 'Metaphysics and Population Genetics: Karl Pearson and the Background to Fisher's Multi-factorial Theory of Inheritance'. *Annals of Science, 32,* 537-53.

Norton, B. J. (1978a). 'Karl Pearson and Statistics: the Social Origins of Scientific Innovation'. *Social Studies of Science, 8,* 3-34.

Norton, B. J. (1978b). *Karl Pearson and the Galtonian Tradition: Studies in the Rise of Quantitative Social Biology.* Ph.D. thesis: London University.

Norton, B. J. (1978c). 'Fisher and the Neo-Darwinian Synthesis'. In Forbes (ed.) (1978, 481-94).

Norton, B. J. (1978d). 'Psychologists and Social Class'. In *The Roots of Sociobiology* (Past and Present Society/British Society for the History of Science Conference Papers). Oxford: Past and Present Society.

Norton, B. J. and Pearson, E. S. (1976). 'A Note on the Background to, and Refereeing of, R. A. Fisher's 1918 Paper "On the Correlation of Relatives on the Supposition of Mendelian Inheritance"'. *Notes and Records of the Royal Society, 31,* 151-62.

Oberschall, A. (1965). *Empirical Social Research in Germany 1848-1914.* Paris and The Hague: Mouton.

Oberschall, A. (ed.) (1972). *The Establishment of Empirical Sociology.* New York: Harper and Row.

Olby, R. (1979). 'Mendel no Mendelian?'. *History of Science, 17*, 53-72.

Owen, D. B. (ed.) (1976). *On the History of Statistics and Probability.* New York: Dekker.

Parkin, F. (1968). *Middle Class Radicalism.* Manchester: Manchester University Press.

Pastore, N. (1949). *The Nature-Nurture Controversy.* New York: King's Crown Press.

Paton, W. D. M. and Phillips, C. G. (1973). 'E. H. J. Schuster (1897[*sic*]-1969)'. *Notes and Records of the Royal Society, 28*, 111-17.

Pearson, E. S. (1936-38). 'Karl Pearson. An Appreciation of some Aspects of his Life and Work'. Part 1, *Biometrika, 28*, 193-257; part 2, *Biometrika, 29*, 161-248.

Pearson, E. S. (1939). '"Student" as a Statistician'. *Biometrika, 30.* Reprinted in E. S. Pearson and M. G. Kendall (eds) (1970, 360-403).

Pearson, E. S. (1965). 'Some Incidents in the Early History of Biometry and Statistics, 1890-94'. *Biometrika, 52.* Reprinted in E. S. Pearson and M. G. Kendall (eds) (1970, 323-38).

Pearson, E. S. (1967). 'Some Reflections on Continuity in the Development of Mathematical Statistics, 1885-1920'. *Biometrika, 54.* Reprinted in E. S. Pearson and M. G. Kendall (eds) (1970, 339-53).

Pearson, E. S. (1968). 'Some Early Correspondence between W. S. Gosset, R. A. Fisher and Karl Pearson, with Notes and Comments'. *Biometrika, 55.* Reprinted in E. S. Pearson and M. G. Kendall (eds) (1970, 405-17).

Pearson, E. S. (1970a). 'David Heron, 1881-1969'. *J.R.S.S.,* A, *133*, 287-91.

Pearson, E. S. (1970b). 'The Neyman-Pearson Story: 1926-34'. In E. S. Pearson and M. G. Kendall (eds) (1970, 455-77).

Pearson, E. S. (1972). '"Statistics – a Vocational or a Cultural Study?". Some Comments on B. L. Welch's Paper and the Discussion which followed'. *J.R.S.S.,* A, *135*, 143-6.

Pearson, E. S. (1974). 'Memories of the Impact of Fisher's Work in the 1920's'. *International Statistical Review, 42*, 5-8.

Pearson, E. S. and Kendall, M. G. (eds) (1970). *Studies in the History of Statistics and Probability.* London: Griffin.

Pearson, E. S. and Wishart, J. (eds) (1958). *'Student's' Collected Papers.* Cambridge: Cambridge University Press.

Pearson, K. (1877). '[First] Common-Place Book'. Pearson Papers, CII D1B.

Pearson, K. ['Loki'] (1880). *The New Werther.* London: Kegan Paul.

Pearson, K. ['Loki'] (1881a). 'A Farewell to Cambridge'. *The Cambridge Review, 2*, 190-1.

Pearson, K. (1881b). 'Anarchy'. *The Cambridge Review, 2*, 268-70.

Pearson, K. (1881c). 'Political Economy for the Proletariat'. *The Cambridge Review, 3*, 123-6.

Pearson, K. (1881-82). 'Social Democracy in Germany'. Pearson Papers, CII D2J.

Pearson, K. (1886a). 'A Plea for the Establishment of a Technical Laboratory at Cambridge'. *The Cambridge University Magazine,* no. 15, 173-4.

Pearson, K. (1886b). 'The Russian Storm-Cloud'. *Cambridge Review, 8,* 406-07.

Pearson, K. (1888). *The Ethic of Freethought.* London: Unwin.

Pearson, K. (1889). 'On the Laws of Inheritance according to Galton'. Pearson Papers, C V D6.

Pearson, K. (1890). '[Review of] Fabian Essays in Socialism. Edited by G. Bernard Shaw'. *The Academy, 37,* 197-9.

Pearson, K. (1892a). *The Grammar of Science.* London: Scott.

Pearson, K. (1892b). *The New University for London. A Guide to its History and a Criticism of its Defects.* London: Unwin.

Pearson, K. (1894). 'Contributions to the Mathematical Theory of Evolution'. *Phil. Trans.,* A, *185,* 71-110.

Pearson, K. (1895). 'Contributions to the Mathematical Theory of Evolution. II. Skew Variation in Homogeneous Material'. *Phil. Trans.,* A, *186,* 343-414.

Pearson, K. (1896). 'Mathematical Contributions to the Theory of Evolution. III. Regression, Heredity and Panmixia'. *Phil. Trans.,* A, *187,* 253-318.

Pearson, K. (1897). *The Chances of Death and other Studies in Evolution.* London: Arnold.

Pearson, K. (1898). 'Mathematical Contributions to the Theory of Evolution. On the Law of Ancestral Heredity'. *Proc. Roy. Soc., 62,* 386-412.

Pearson, K. (1900a). *The Grammar of Science.* Second edition. London: Black.

Pearson, K. (1900b). 'Mathematical Contributions to the Theory of Evolution. VII. On the Correlation of Characters not Quantitatively Measurable'. *Phil. Trans.,* A, *195,* 1-47.

Pearson, K. (1900c). 'On the Criterion that a given system of Deviations from the Probable in the case of a Correlated System of Variables is such that it can be reasonably supposed to have arisen from Random Sampling'. *Phil. Mag.,* series 5, *50,* 157-75.

Pearson, K. (1901a). *National Life from the Standpoint of Science.* London: Black.

Pearson, K. (1901b). 'On the Inheritance of the Mental Characters in Man'. *Proc. Roy. Soc., 69,* 153-5.

Pearson, K. (1901c). *The Ethic of Freethought.* Second edition. London: Black.

Pearson, K. (1902a). 'On the Fundamental Conceptions of Biology'. *Biometrika, 1,* 320-44.

Pearson, K. (1902b). 'Prefatory Essay. The Function of Science in the Modern State'. *Encyclopaedia Britannica,* 10th edition, *32* (volume 8 of new volumes), vii-xxxvii.

Pearson, K. (1903a). 'The Law of Ancestral Heredity'. *Biometrika, 2,* 211-29.

Pearson, K. (1903b). [Editorial] 'On the Probable Errors of Frequency Constants'. *Biometrika, 2,* 273-81.

Pearson, K. (1903c). 'On the Inheritance of the Mental and Moral Characters in Man, and its Comparison with the Inheritance of the

Physical Characters. The Huxley Lecture for 1903'. *Journal of the Anthropological Institute of Great Britain and Ireland, 33,* 179-237.

Pearson, K. (1904a). 'Mathematical Contributions to the Theory of Evolution. XII. On a Generalised Theory of Alternative Inheritance, with special reference to Mendel's Laws'. *Phil. Trans.,* A, *203,* 53-86.

Pearson, K. (1904b). 'Mathematical Contributions to the Theory of Evolution. XIII. On the Theory of Contingency and its Relation to Association and Normal Correlation'. *Drapers' Company Research Memoirs. Biometric Series,* I. London: Dulau.

Pearson, K. (1906). 'Walter Frank Raphael Weldon, 1860-1906'. *Biometrika, 5.* Reprinted in E. S. Pearson and M. G. Kendall (eds) (1970, 265-321).

Pearson, K. (1907). 'Reply to certain Criticisms of Mr G. U. Yule'. *Biometrika, 5,* 470-6.

Pearson, K. (1908). 'On a Mathematical Theory of Determinantal Inheritance, from Suggestions and Notes of the late W. F. R. Weldon'. *Biometrika, 6,* 80-93.

Pearson, K. (1909a). 'The Theory of Ancestral Contributions in Heredity'. *Proc. Roy. Soc.,* B, *81,* 219-24.

Pearson, K. (1909b). 'On the Ancestral Gametic Correlations of a Mendelian Population Mating at Random'. *Proc. Roy. Soc.,* B, *81,* 225-9.

Pearson, K. (1909c). 'The Scope and Importance to the State of the Science of National Eugenics'. *Eugenics Laboratory Lecture Series,* I. Second Edition. London: Dulau.

Pearson, K. (1909d). 'The Groundwork of Eugenics'. *Eugenics Laboratory Lecture Series,* II. London: Dulau.

Pearson, K. (1909e). 'The Problem of Practical Eugenics'. *Eugenics Laboratory Lecture Series,* V. London: Dulau.

Pearson, K. (1910a). 'On a new Method of determining Correlation when one Variable is given by Alternative and the other by Multiple Categories'. *Biometrika, 7,* 248-57.

Pearson, K. (1910b). 'Nature and Nurture, the Problem of the Future'. *Eugenics Laboratory Lecture Series,* VI. London: Dulau.

Pearson, K. (1911). 'The Academic Aspect of the Science of National Eugenics'. *Eugenics Laboratory Lecture Series,* VII. London: Dulau.

Pearson, K. (1912a). 'Mathematical Contributions to the Theory of Evolution. XVIII. On a Novel Method of regarding the Association of two Variates classed solely in Alternate Categories'. *Drapers' Company Research Memoirs. Biometric Series,* VII. London: Dulau.

Pearson, K. (1912b). 'Darwinism, Medical Progress and Eugenics'. *Eugenics Laboratory Lecture Series,* IX. London: Dulau.

Pearson, K. (1913a). 'On the Measurement of the Influence of "Broad Categories" on Correlation'. *Biometrika, 9,* 116-39.

Pearson, K. (1913b). 'Note on the Surface of Constant Association'. *Biometrika, 9,* 534-7.

Pearson, K. (ed.) (1914). *Tables for Statisticians and Biometricians.* Cambridge: Cambridge University Press.

Pearson, K. (1914-30). *The Life, Letters and Labours of Francis Galton.* Cambridge: Cambridge University Press.

Pearson, K. (1920a). 'The fundamental Problem of practical Statistics'. *Biometrika, 13,* 1-16.

Pearson, K. (1920b). 'Notes on the History of Correlation'. *Biometrika, 13.* Reprinted in E. S. Pearson and M. G. Kendall (eds) (1970, 185-205).

Pearson, K. (1922). 'On the χ^2 test of Goodness of Fit'. *Biometrika, 14,* 186-91.

Pearson, K. (1924). 'Historical Note on the Origin of the Normal Curve of Errors'. *Biometrika, 16,* 402-4.

Pearson, K. (1931). 'Historical Note on the Distribution of the Standard Deviations of Samples of any Size drawn from an indefinitely large Normal Parent Population'. *Biometrika, 23,* 416-8.

Pearson, K. (1941). 'The Laws of Chance, in Relation to Thought and Conduct'. *Biometrika, 32,* 89-100.

Pearson, K. (1978). *The History of Statistics in the 17th and 18th Centuries against the Changing Background of Intellectual, Scientific and Religious Thought* (ed. E. S. Pearson). London and High Wycombe: Griffin.

Pearson, K. and Filon, L. N. G. (1898). 'Mathematical Contributions to the Theory of Evolution. IV. On the Probable Errors of Frequency Constants and on the Influence of Random Selection on Variation and Correlation'. *Phil. Trans.,* A, *191,* 229-311.

Pearson, K. *et al.* (1901). 'Mathematical Contributions to the Theory of Evolution. IX. On the Principle of Homotyposis and its Relation to Heredity, to the Variability of the Individual, and to that of the Race'. *Phil. Trans.,* A, *197,* 285-379.

Pearson, K. and Heron, D. (1913). 'On Theories of Association'. *Biometrika, 9,* 159-315.

Pearson, K. and Lee, A. (1900). 'Mathematical Contributions to the Theory of Evolution. VII. On the Application of certain Formulae in the Theory of Correlation to the Inheritance of Characters not capable of Quantitative Measurement'. *Proc. Roy. Soc., 66,* 324-7.

Pearson, K., Lee, A. and Bramley-Moore, L. (1899). 'Mathematical Contributions to the Theory of Evolution. VI. Genetic (Reproductive) Selection: Inheritance of Fertility in Man, and of Fecundity in Thoroughbred Racehorses'. *Phil. Trans.,* A, *192,* 257-330.

Pearson, K., Nettleship, E. and Usher, C. H. (1913). 'A Monograph on Albinism in Man. Part II'. *Drapers' Company Research Memoirs. Biometric Series,* VIII. London: Dulau.

Pearson, K. and Pearson, E. S. (1922). 'On Polychoric Coefficients of Correlation'. *Biometrika, 14,* 127-56.

Peile, J. H. F. (1909). 'Eugenics and the Church'. *Eugenics Review, 1,* 163-73.

Perkin, H. (1972). *The Origins of Modern English Society 1780-1880.* London: Routledge and Kegan Paul.

Pickens, D. K. (1968). *Eugenics and the Progressives.* Nashville: Vanderbilt University Press.

Plackett, R. L. (1972). 'The Discovery of the Method of Least Squares'. *Biometrika, 59,* 239-51.

Poulantzas, N. (1975). *Classes in Contemporary Capitalism.* London: New Left Books.

Pratt, J. W. (1976). 'F. Y. Edgeworth and R. A. Fisher on the Efficiency of Maximum Likelihood Estimation'. *Annals of Statistics, 4,* 501-14.

Provine, W. B. (1971). *The Origins of Theoretical Population Genetics.* Chicago: University of Chicago Press.

Provine, W. B. (1978). 'The Role of Mathematical Population Geneticists in the Evolutionary Synthesis of the 1930s and 1940s'. *Studies in the History of Biology, 2,* 167-92.

Punnett, R. C. (1915). *Mimicry in Butterflies.* Cambridge: Cambridge University Press.

Punnett, R. C. (1917). 'Eliminating Feeblemindedness'. *Journal of Heredity, 8,* 464-5.

Punnett, R. C. (1925). 'As a Biologist sees it'. *Nineteenth Century, 97,* 697-707.

Punnett, R. C. (1926). 'William Bateson'. *Edinburgh Review, 244,* 71-86.

Punnett, R. C. (1930). 'Genetics, Mathematics and Natural Selection. Review of R. A. Fisher's *The Genetical Theory of Natural Selection'. Nature, 126,* 595-7.

Quetelet, A. (1849). *Letters on the Theory of Probabilities.* London: Layton.

Ravetz, J. (1973). *Scientific Knowledge and its Social Problems.* Harmondsworth: Penguin.

Reader, W. J. (1970-75). *Imperial Chemical Industries: a History.* London: Oxford University Press.

Richards, J. L. (1979). 'The Reception of a Mathematical Theory: Non-Euclidean Geometry in England, 1868-1883'. In Barnes and Shapin (eds) (1979, 143-66).

Ritchie, D. G. (1889). *Darwinism and Politics.* London: Swan Sonnenschein.

Rose, N. (1979). 'The Psychological Complex: Mental Measurement and Social Administration'. *Ideology and Consciousness,* number 5, 5-68.

Rosenberg, C. E. (1961). 'Charles Benedict Davenport and the beginning of Human Genetics'. *Bulletin of the History of Medicine, 35,* 266-76.

Rosenberg, C. E. (1974). 'The Bitter Fruit: Heredity, Disease, and Social Thought in Nineteenth-Century America'. *Perspectives in American History, 8,* 189-235.

Rothblatt, S. (1968). *The Revolution of the Dons.* London: Faber.

Rowbotham, S. (1973). *Hidden from History.* London: Pluto.

Rowbotham, S. (1977). *A New World for Women: Stella Browne – Socialist Feminist.* London: Pluto.

Royal Statistical Society (1934). *Annals of the Royal Statistical Society, 1834-1934.* London: Royal Statistical Society.

Rubinstein, W. D. (1977). 'Wealth, Elites and the Class Structure of Modern Britain'. *Past and Present,* number 76, 99-126.

Russell, E. J. (1966). *A History of Agricultural Science in Great Britain 1620-1954.* London: Allen and Unwin.

Salisbury, Marquis of (1894). [Presidential Address.] *British Association Report*, 3-15.

Salmon, G. (1859). *Lessons Introductory to the Modern Higher Algebra*. Dublin: Hodges, Smith.

Salvemini, T. (1968). 'Gini, Corrado'. *International Encyclopedia of the Social Sciences, 6*, 187-91.

Särndal, C. (1971). 'The Hypothesis of Elementary Errors and the Scandinavian School in Statistical Theory'. *Biometrika, 58*. Reprinted in M. G. Kendall and R. L. Plackett (eds) (1977, 419-35).

Savage, L. J. (1976). 'On rereading R. A. Fisher'. *Annals of Statistics, 4*, 441-83.

Schenk, F. and Parkes, A. S. (1968). 'The Activities of the Eugenics Society'. *Eugenics Review, 60*, 142-61.

Schols, C. M. (1886). 'Théorie des Erreurs dans le Plan et dans l'Espace'. *Annales de l'Ecole Polytechnique de Delft, 2*, 123-78.

Schumpeter, J. A. (1954). *History of Economic Analysis*. New York: Oxford University Press.

Schuster, E. (n.d.). *Eugenics*. London: Collins.

Seal, H. L. (1967). 'The Historical Development of the Gauss Linear Model'. *Biometrika, 54*. Reprinted in E. S. Pearson and M. G. Kendall (eds) (1970, 207-30).

Searle, G. R. (1971). *The Quest for National Efficiency: A Study in British Politics and Political Thought, 1899-1914*. Oxford: Blackwell.

Searle, G. R. (1976). *Eugenics and Politics in Britain, 1900-1914*. Leyden: Noordhoff.

Searle, G. R. (1978). 'Eugenics and Class'. In *The Roots of Sociobiology* (Past and Present Society/British Society for the History of Science Conference Papers). Oxford: Past and Present Society.

Searle, G. R. (1979). 'Eugenics and Politics in Britain in the 1930s'. *Annals of Science, 36*, 159-69.

Semmel, B. (1958). 'Karl Pearson: Socialist and Darwinist'. *British Journal of Sociology, 9*, 111-25.

Semmel, B. (1960). *Imperialism and Social Reform: English Social-Imperial Thought 1895-1914*. London: Allen and Unwin.

Shapin, S. and Barnes, B. (1979). 'Darwin and Social Darwinism: Purity and History'. In Barnes and Shapin (eds) (1979, 125-42).

Shaw, G. B. (ed.) (1889). *Fabian Essays in Socialism*. London: Fabian Society.

Shaw, G. B. (1972). *Man and Superman*. Harmondsworth: Penguin.

Sheppard, N. F. (1938). 'W. F. Sheppard, F.R.S.E., SC.D., LL.M.: Personal History'. *Annals of Eugenics, 8*, 1-9.

Sheppard, W. F. (1889). 'On some Expressions of a Function of a Single Variable in terms of Bessel's Functions'. *Quarterly Journal of Pure and Applied Mathematics, 23*, 223-60.

Sheppard, W. F. (1897a). *The Stories of 'Der Ring des Nibelungen' and 'Parsifal'*. London: David Nutt.

Sheppard, W. F. (1897b). 'On the Calculation of the Average Square, Cube &c., of a large number of Magnitudes'. *J.R.S.S., 60*, 698-703.

Sheppard, W. F. (1898a). 'On the Relations between Bernoulli's and Euler's Numbers'. *Quarterly Journal of Pure and Applied Mathematics, 30,* 18-46.

Sheppard, W. F. (1898b). 'On the Application of the Theory of Error to Cases of Normal Distribution and Normal Correlation'. *Phil. Trans.,* A, *192,* 101-67.

Sheppard, W. F. (1898c). 'On the Calculation of the most Probable Values of Frequency-Constants, for Data arranged according to Equidistant Divisions of a Scale'. *Proceedings of the London Mathematical Society, 29,* 353-80.

Sheppard, W. F. (1899a). 'On the Statistical Rejection of Extreme Variations, Single or Correlated. (Normal Variation and Normal Correlation.)' *Proceedings of the London Mathematical Society, 31,* 70-99.

Sheppard, W. F. (1899b). 'A Method for Extending the Accuracy of certain Mathematical Tables'. *Proceedings of the London Mathematical Society, 31,* 423-48.

Sheppard, W. F. (1899c). 'Central-Difference Formulae'. *Proceedings of the London Mathematical Society, 31,* 449-88.

Sheppard, W. F. (1900). 'On the Calculation of the Double-Integral expressing Normal Correlation'. *Transactions of the Cambridge Philosophical Society, 19,* 23-68.

Sheppard, W. F. (1903). 'New Tables of the Probability Integral'. *Biometrika, 2,* 174-90.

Sheynin, O. B. (1966). 'Origin of the Theory of Errors'. *Nature, 211,* 1003-4.

Sheynin, O. B. (1970). 'Daniel Bernoulli on the Normal Law'. *Biometrika, 57,* 199-202.

Sheynin, O. B. (1971a). 'On the History of some Statistical Laws of Distribution'. *Biometrika, 58,* 234-6.

Sheynin, O. B. (1971b). 'J. H. Lambert's Work on Probability'. *Archive for History of Exact Sciences, 7,* 244-56.

Sheynin, O. B. (1972a). 'D. Bernoulli's Work on Probability'. *Rete: Strukturgeschichte der Naturwissenschaften, 1,* 273-300.

Sheynin, O. B. (1972b). 'On the Mathematical Treatment of Observations by L. Euler'. *Archive for History of Exact Sciences, 9,* 45-56.

Sheynin, O. B. (1973a). 'Mathematical Treatment of Astronomical Observations (A Historical Essay)'. *Archive for History of Exact Sciences, 11,* 97-126.

Sheynin, O. B. (1973b). 'Finite Random Sums (A Historical Essay)'. *Archive for History of Exact Sciences, 9,* 275-305.

Sheynin, O. B. (1974). 'On the Prehistory of the Theory of Probability'. *Archive for History of Exact Sciences, 12,* 97-141.

Sheynin, O. B. (1976). 'P. S. Laplace's Work on Probability'. *Archive for History of Exact Sciences, 16,* 137-87.

Sheynin, O. B. (1978). 'S. D. Poisson's Work in Probability'. *Archive for History of Exact Sciences, 18,* 245-300.

Sheynin, O. B. (1979). 'C. F. Gauss and the Theory of Errors'. *Archive for History of Exact Sciences, 20,* 21-72.

Bibliography

Simon, B. (1971). *Intelligence, Psychology and Education: a Marxist Critique*. London: Lawrence and Wishart.

Singer, B. (1979). 'Distribution-Free Methods for Non-Parametric Problems: a Classified and Selected Bibliography'. *British Journal of Mathematical and Statistical Psychology, 32*, 1-60.

Snow, E. C. (1912). 'The Application of the Correlation Coefficient to Mendelian Distributions'. *Biometrika, 8*, 420-4.

Soper, H. E. (1913). 'On the Probable Error of the Correlation Coefficient to a Second Approximation'. *Biometrika, 9*, 91-115.

Soper, H. E. *et al.* (1917). 'On the Distribution of the Correlation Coefficient in Small Samples. Appendix ii to the Papers of "Student" and R. A. Fisher. A Cooperative Study'. *Biometrika, 11*, 328-413.

Spencer, H. (1873). *The Study of Sociology*. London: King.

Spottiswoode, W. (1861). 'On typical Mountain Ranges: an Application of the Calculus of Probabilities to Physical Geography'. *Journal of the Royal Geographical Society, 31*, 149-54.

Stehr, N. (1975). 'Factors in the Development of Multi-Paradigm Disciplines: the Case of Sociology'. *Journal for the History of the Behavioral Sciences, 11*, 172-88.

Stephan, F. F. (1948). 'History of the Uses of Modern Sampling Procedures'. *Journal of the American Statistical Association, 43*, 12-39.

Stevens, S. S. (1946). 'On the Theory of Scales of Measurement'. *Science, 103*, 677-80.

Stigler, S. M. (1978). 'Francis Ysidro Edgeworth, Statistician'. *J.R.S.S., A, 141*, 287-313.

Stratton, F. J. M. (1909). 'The Constants of the Moon's Physical Libration'. *Memoirs of the Royal Astronomical Society, 59*, 257-90.

Stratton, F. J. M. and Compton, R. H. (1910). 'On Accident in Heredity with special reference to Right- and Left-Handedness'. *Proceedings of the Cambridge Philosophical Society, 15*, 507-12.

Stuart, A. and Kendall, M. G. (eds) (1971). *Statistical Papers of George Udny Yule*. London: Griffin.

Thiele, J. (1969). 'Karl Pearson, Ernst Mach, John B. Stallo: Briefe aus den Jahren 1897 bis 1904'. *Isis, 60*, 535-42.

Thompson, E. P. (1968). *The Making of the English Working Class*. Harmondsworth: Penguin.

Tilling, L. (1973). *The Interpretation of Observational Errors in the Eighteenth and Early Nineteenth Centuries*. Ph.D. thesis: University of London.

Todhunter, I. (1858). *Algebra*. Cambridge: Macmillan.

Todhunter, I. (1865). *A History of the Mathematical Theory of Probability from the Time of Pascal to that of Laplace*. Cambridge and London: Macmillan.

Turner, F. M. (1974a). *Between Science and Religion: the Reaction to Scientific Naturalism in Late Victorian England*. New Haven, Conn.: Yale University Press.

Turner, F. M. (1974b). 'Rainfall, Plagues, and the Prince of Wales: a Chapter in the Conflict of Religion and Science'. *Journal of British Studies, 13*, 46-65.

297

Turner, F. M. (1978). 'The Victorian Conflict between Science and Religion: a Professional Dimension'. *Isis*, *69*, 356-76.

Van der Daele, W. and Weingart, P. (1976). 'Resistance and Receptivity of Science to External Direction: the Emergence of New Disciplines under the Impact of Science Policy'. In Lemaine *et al.* (eds) (1976, 247-75).

Venn, J. (1866). *The Logic of Chance*. London and Cambridge: Macmillan.

Venn, J. (1889). 'Cambridge Anthropometry'. *Journal of the Anthropological Institute*, *18*, 140-54.

Venn, J. (1891). 'On the Nature and Uses of Averages'. *J.R.S.S.*, *54*, 429-48.

Walker, H. M. (1928). 'The Relation of Plana and Bravais to the Theory of Correlation'. *Isis*, *10*, 466-84.

Walker, H. M. (1929). *Studies in the History of Statistical Method*. Baltimore: Williams and Wilkins.

Wallace, A. R. (1890). 'Human Selection'. *Fortnightly Review*, *48*, 325-37.

Warren, E. (1902). 'Variation and Inheritance in the Parthenogenetic Generations of the Aphis *Hyalopterus trirhodus* (Walker)'. *Biometrika*, *1*, 129-54.

Waterman, L. S. (1975). *The Eugenic Movement in Britain in the Nineteen Thirties*. M.Sc. thesis: University of Sussex.

Watson, H. W. (1876). *A Treatise on the Kinetic Theory of Gases*. Oxford: Clarendon.

Watson, H. W. (1891). 'Observations on the Law of Facility of Errors'. *Proceedings of the Philosophical Society of Birmingham*, *7*, 289-318.

Watson, H. W. and Burbury, S. H. (1879). *A Treatise on the Application of Generalised Coordinates to the Kinetics of a Material System*. Oxford: Clarendon.

Watson, H. W. and Burbury, S. H. (1885-89). *The Mathematical Theory of Electricity and Magnetism*. Oxford: Clarendon.

Watson, H. W. and Galton, F. (1874). 'On the Probability of the Extinction of Families'. *Journal of the Anthropological Institute*, *4*, 138-44.

Webb, S. (1907). *The Decline in the Birth-Rate*. Fabian Tract No. 131. London: Fabian Society.

Webb, S. and B. (1975). *Methods of Social Study*. Cambridge: Cambridge University Press. First published in 1932.

Wedgwood, C. V. (1951). *The Last of the Radicals: Josiah Wedgwood, M.P.* London: Cape.

Wedgwood, J. C. (1912). [Speech in House of Commons.] *The Parliamentary Debates (House of Commons): Official Report*, series 5, *38*, cols. 1467-78.

Weiling, F. (1969). 'Quellen und Impulse in der Entwicklung der Biometrie'. *Sudhoff Archiv*, *53*, 306-25.

Welch, B. L. (1958). '"Student" and Small Sample Theory'. *Journal of the American Statistical Association*, *53*, 777-88.

Welch, B. L. (1970). 'Statistics – a Vocational or a Cultural Study?' *J.R.S.S.*, A, *133*, 531-43.

Weldon, W. F. R. (1890). 'The Variations occuring in Certain Decapod Crustacea – I. *Crangon vulgaris*'. *Proc. Roy. Soc.*, *47*, 445-53.

Weldon, W. F. R. (1892). 'Certain Correlated Variations in *Crangon vulgaris*'. *Proc. Roy. Soc.*, *51*, 2-21.

Weldon, W. F. R. (1893). 'On certain Correlated Variations in *Carcinus moenas*'. *Proc. Roy. Soc.*, *54*, 318-29.

Weldon, W. F. R. (1894). 'The Study of Animal Variation'. *Nature, 50*, 25-6.

Weldon, W. F. R. (1895). 'Report of the Committee for Conducting Statistical Inquiries into the Measurable Characteristics of Plants and Animals'. *Proc. Roy. Soc.*, *57*, 360-82.

Weldon, W. F. R. (1902a). 'Mendel's Laws of Alternative Inheritance in Peas'. *Biometrika, 1*, 228-54.

Weldon, W. F. R. (1902b). 'On the Ambiguity of Mendel's Categories'. *Biometrika, 2*, 44-55.

Weldon, W. R. F. (1905). [Contribution to Discussion.] *Sociological Papers 1904*, 56. London: Macmillan.

Werskey, P. G. (1969). '*Nature* and Politics between the Wars'. *Nature, 224*, 462-72.

Werskey, P. G. (1971). 'Haldane and Huxley: the First Appraisals'. *Journal of the History of Biology, 4*, 171-83.

Werskey, P. G. (1972a). *The Visible College: a Study of Left-Wing Scientists in Britain, 1918-39*. Ph.D. thesis: Harvard University.

Werskey, P. G. (1972b). 'British Scientists and "Outsider" Politics 1931-1945'. In Barnes (ed.), *Sociology of Science*, 231-50. Harmondsworth: Penguin.

Werskey, P. G. (1978). *The Visible College*. London: Allen Lane.

Westergaard, H. L. (1932). *Contributions to the History of Statistics*. London: King.

White, A. (1895). *Problems of a Great City*. Fourth edition. London: Remington.

White, A. (1901). *Efficiency and Empire*. London: Methuen.

White, W. R. (1960). 'Ernest Charles Snow, C.B.E., D.SC., 1886-1959'. *J.R.S.S.*, A, *123*, 355-6.

Whitley, R. (1974). 'Cognitive and Social Institutionalization of Scientific Specialties and Research Areas'. In R. Whitley (ed.), *Social Processes of Scientific Development*, 69-95. London: Routledge and Kegan Paul.

Whitley, R. (1975). 'Components of Scientific Activities, their Characteristics and Institutionalization in Specialties and Research Areas: a Framework for the Comparative Analysis of Scientific Developments'. In Knorr *et al.* (eds) (1975, 37-73).

Williams, R. (1968). *Culture and Society 1780-1850*. Harmondsworth: Penguin.

Willis, J. C. (1922). *Age and Area*. Cambridge: Cambridge University Press.

Wilson, D. B. (1977). 'Concepts of Physical Nature: John Herschel to Karl Pearson'. In U. C. Knoepflmacher and G. B. Tennyson (eds), *Nature and the Victorian Imagination*, 201-15. Berkeley and Los Angeles: University of California Press.

Wittgenstein, L. (1967). *Remarks on the Foundations of Mathematics*. Oxford: Blackwell.

Wood, T. B., and Stratton, F. J. M. (1910). 'The Interpretation of Experimental Results'. *Journal of Agricultural Science, 3,* 417-40.

Worboys, M. (1976). 'The Emergence of Tropical Medicine: a Study in the Establishment of a Scientific Specialty'. In Lemaine *et al.* (eds) (1976, 75-98).

Wright, E. O. (1978). 'Intellectuals and the Working Class'. *Insurgent Sociologist, 8,* 5-18.

Wright, S. (1931). 'Evolution in Mendelian Populations'. *Genetics, 16,* 97-159.

Wright, S. (1964). 'Biology and the Philosophy of Science'. In W. L. Reese and E. Freeman (eds), *Process and Divinity – the Hartshorne Festschrift,* 101-25. La Salle, Ill.: Open Court.

Wrong, D. (1976). 'The Oversocialized Conception of Man in Modern Sociology'. In L. A. Coser and B. Rosenberg (eds), *Sociological Theory,* 104-13. New York: Macmillan.

Wynne, B. E. (1977). *C. G. Barkla and the J Phenomenon: A Case Study in the Sociology of Physics.* M.Phil. thesis: University of Edinburgh.

Wynne, B. E. (1979). 'Physics and Psychics: Science, Symbolic Action, and Social Control in late Victorian England'. In Barnes and Shapin (eds) (1979, 167-86).

Yates, F. (1951). 'The Influence of *Statistical Methods for Research Workers* on the Development of the Science of Statistics'. *Journal of the American Statistical Association, 46,* 19-34.

Yates, F. (1952). 'George Udny Yule, 1871-1951'. *Obituary Notices of Fellows of the Royal Society, 8,* 309-23.

Yates, F. and Mather, K. (1963). 'Ronald Aylmer Fisher 1890-1962'. *Biographical Memoirs of Fellows of the Royal Society, 9,* 91-129.

Yeo, E. (1976). 'The Early Years of Social Science'. Paper read to Sociology Workshop Conference, City University.

Young, G. M. (1960). *Victorian England: Portrait of an Age.* London: Oxford University Press.

Young, R. M. (1969). 'Malthus and the Evolutionists: the Common Context of Biological and Social Theory', *Past and Present,* no. 43, 109-45.

Yule, G. U. (1895-96). 'On the Correlation of Total Pauperism with Proportion of Out-Relief'. *Economic Journal, 5,* 603-11 and *6,* 613-23.

Yule, G. U. (1896). 'Notes on the History of Pauperism in England and Wales from 1850, treated by the Method of Frequency Curves, with an Introduction on the Method'. *J.R.S.S., 59,* 318-49.

Yule, G. U. (1897a). 'On the Significance of Bravais' Formulae for Regression, etc., in the Case of Skew Correlation'. *Proc. Roy. Soc., 60,* 477-89.

Yule, G. U. (1897b). [Contribution to discussion of paper by A. Milnes.] *J.R.S.S., 60,* 608-12.

Yule, G. U. (1899). 'An Investigation into the Course of Pauperism in England, chiefly during the last two Inter-Censal Decades'. *J.R.S.S., 62,* 249-86.

Yule, G. U. (1900). 'On the Association of Attributes in Statistics'. *Phil. Trans.,* A, *194.* Reprinted in A. Stuart and M. G. Kendall (eds) (1971, 7-69).

Yule, G. U. (1902). 'Mendel's Laws and their probable Relations to Intra-Racial Heredity'. *New Phytologist, 1,* 193-207 and 222-38.

Yule, G. U. (1906a). 'On a Property which holds good for all Groupings of a Normal Distribution of Frequency for two Variables'. *Proc. Roy. Soc.,* A, *77,* 324-36.

Yule, G. U. (1906b). 'On the Influence of Bias and of Personal Equation in Statistics of Ill-defined Qualities'. *Journal of the Anthropological Institute, 36,* 325-81.

Yule, G. U. (1910). [Review of Heron (1910).] *J.R.S.S., 73,* 547-51.

Yule, G. U. (1911). *An Introduction to the Theory of Statistics.* London: Griffin.

Yule, G. U. (1912). 'On the Methods of Measuring Association between two Attributes'. *J.R.S.S., 75.* Reprinted in A. Stuart and M. G. Kendall (eds) (1971, 107-70).

Yule, G. U. (1920). 'The Wind bloweth where it listeth'. *Cambridge Review, 41,* 184-6.

Yule, G. U. (1921). 'Critical Notice [of Brown and Thomson, *Essentials of Mental Measurement*]'. *British Journal of Psychology,* General Section, *12,* 100-7.

Yule, G. U. (1924). 'A Mathematical Theory of Evolution based on the Conclusions of Dr. J. C. Willis, F.R.S.'. *Phil. Trans.,* B, *213,* 21-87.

Yule, G. U. (1936). 'Karl Pearson, 1857-1936'. *Obituary Notices of Fellows of the Royal Society of London, 2,* 73-104.

Yule, G. U. (1944). 'Reginald Hawthorn Hooker, M.A.' *J.R.S.S., 107,* 74-7.

Zarkovich, S. S. (1956). 'Note on the History of Sampling Methods in Russia'. *J.R.S.S.,* A, *119.* Reprinted in M. G. Kendall and R. S. Plackett (eds) (1977, 482-4).

Zarkovich, S. S. (1962). 'A Supplement to "Note on the History of Sampling Methods in Russia"'. *J.R.S.S.,* A, *125.* Reprinted in M. G. Kendall and R. S. Plackett (eds) (1977, 486-8).

Index

. . . . .
. . .
.